GLOBAL INDIOS

Narrating Native Histories aims to foster a rethinking of the ethical, methodological, and conceptual frameworks within which we locate our work on Native histories and cultures. We seek to create a space for effective and ongoing conversations between North and South, Natives and non-Natives, academics and activists, throughout the Americas and the Pacific region.

This series encourages analyses that contribute to an understanding of Native peoples' relationships with nation-states, including histories of expropriation and exclusion as well as projects for autonomy and sovereignty. We encourage collaborative work that recognizes Native intellectuals, cultural interpreters, and alternative knowledge producers, as well as projects that question the relationship between orality and literacy.

Global Indios

THE INDIGENOUS STRUGGLE
FOR JUSTICE IN
SIXTEENTH-CENTURY SPAIN

Nancy E. van Deusen

Duke University Press
Durham and London   2015

© 2015 Duke University Press
All rights reserved
Printed in the United States of America
on acid-free paper ∞
Typeset in Minion Pro by Westchester Publishing Services

Library of Congress Cataloging-in-Publication Data
van Deusen, Nancy E.
Global indios : the indigenous struggle for justice in sixteenth-century
Spain / Nancy E. van Deusen.
pages cm—(Narrating Native histories)
Includes bibliographical references and index.
ISBN 978-0-8223-5847-3 (hardcover : alk. paper)
ISBN 978-0-8223-5858-9 (pbk. : alk. paper)
ISBN 978-0-8223-7569-2 (e-book)
1. Indians—Legal status, laws, etc.—History—16th century.
2. Indians, Treatment of—Spain.
3. Indians, Treatment of—Latin America.
4. Spain—Colonies—America—History—16th century.
5. Spain—History—16th century.
6. Indians—Civil rights.
I. Title. II. Series: Narrating Native histories.
F1411.V363 2015
946'.04—dc23   2014039593

Cover art: Juan Cordero, *Christopher Columbus at the Court of Catholic Kings* (detail), 1850, oil on canvas, Museo Nacional de Arte. Photo: Scala / Art Resource, N.Y.

FOR THOSE
WHOSE VOICES
HAVE YET
TO BE HEARD.

CONTENTS

Map of the world with places cited in litigation suits. Designed by Sarah Bell.

Map of Latin America with places cited in litigation suits. Designed by Sarah Bell.

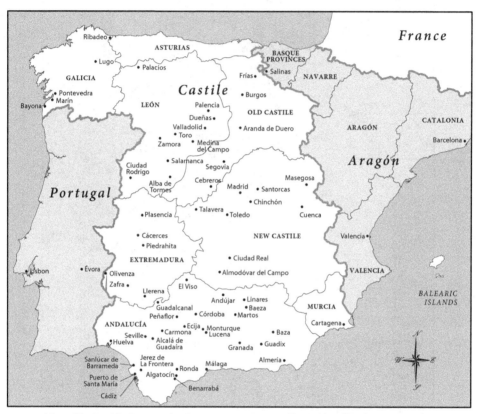

Map of Iberia with places cited in litigation suits. Designed by Sarah Bell and Susanne Seales.

PREFACE

On a day during the cold months of 1549, the slave Catalina de Velasco waited to meet the friar Bartolomé de las Casas, a famous man whom she fervently hoped would testify on her behalf as she petitioned for her freedom in a Spanish court. She stood in an austere and dimly lit room of the monastery furnished with high-backed chairs and a long, polished table. Religious paintings hung on the walls. Catalina was a minor of twenty years, and her legal representative (*curador*) had insisted she be examined in person to see if she was truly an *india*. Only a few days before, she had been granted permission by the Council of the Indies to travel over a two-day period to the Monastery of San Pablo, the temporary residence of several notable friars. These men were experts in all things Mexican; they could examine her physiognomy—the shape of her head and face, her coloration—with great authority. She was certain they would help her win her freedom.

Months before, several judges of the council had scrutinized her while the curador stood by her side. Her mistress, the marquess of Villafranca, Doña Inés de Pimentel, had also demanded to be present at the hearing, if only to intimidate her.[1] The judges had then determined that she was an india, but not a mestiza—the daughter of a Spanish Christian and an india—as Catalina had claimed. She had made this claim because her deceased mother had once told her that her father was a Christian.

The New Laws of 1542 had been passed in Castile, stating that *indios* from Spanish domains were free and could no longer be enslaved. Catalina bore no scar or royal brand on her face that would have marked her as a legally captured slave from the Spanish territories, yet to gain her freedom, she still had to prove that she had come from Mexico, not somewhere in the Portuguese empire as her mistress claimed. As her legal representative explained to her, indio slaves from the Portuguese domains had no legal rights to be free, whereas those from the Spanish kingdoms did, thanks to the efforts of Las Casas and others. Like many indios who had crossed the Atlantic, Catalina had made the journey as a small child and could not remember her place of origin, although Mexico occurred to her later.[2] The problem, however, was that she had traveled by ship from Mexico to Lisbon, and it was there that Doña Inés de Pimentel had purchased her and taken her to Castile to join the retinue of servants and other slaves in the palace, now Catalina's prison. Given these circumstances, what evidence besides her physical person and the remembrance of things past did she have to prove her origins?

It had been so difficult to leave her mistress's palace, with guards hovering about her bedroom door at all hours. What a relief to have been granted permission to appear before such important friars at the monastery. She straightened her back and folded her hands as she heard footsteps approaching. A moment later, Bartolomé de las Casas stepped through the door, his black robes skimming the floor. Catalina had heard stories about this great man, who was slightly stooped with years: how he had freed many indios from slavery, how he had fought in New Spain and in Castile for their freedom from tyranny.

After silently considering her aspect, facial features, and coloration, Las Casas nodded to the scribe, who began writing. Yes, the friar affirmed, the young woman was from somewhere in New Spain, the broad territorial domain that included Mexico. He dictated: "It seems to be so to this witness, because, as it is well known, I resided for many years in New Spain and I have much experience with the indios and indias of that land." He then added, "Although she is not a mestiza, she could easily have been stolen and brought as a child to these kingdoms and [brought to Castile] from Portugal by passengers who come to these kingdoms."[3] In two sentences he thus confirmed that she looked like an india from the Spanish domains. He also made it clear that the illegal traffic in slaves between Spanish America and Portugal and between Portugal and Castile made Catalina's journey into bondage plausible.

That same day, on the heels of Las Casas's testimony at the monastery, came those of Rodrigo Ladrada, the longtime companion of Las Casas, and of Vasco de Quiroga, another virtuous man who had worked diligently to protect the indios of Mexico from mistreatment. Both confirmed what Las Casas had said.

Once the council had deliberated over these testimonies and those of the marquess, Catalina was freed. No doubt that singular day in the brief company of Bartolomé de las Casas remained etched in her mind for the rest of her life. Before his death, in 1566, Las Casas went on to issue other terse statements confirming the places of origin of indios named Esteban, Martín Quintín, and Balthasar, all of whom were also freed.[4]

ACKNOWLEDGMENTS

How to give voice to the voiceless indigenous slaves of early colonial Spanish and Portuguese America has been a preoccupation of mine for nearly a decade. But this critical inquiry would not have come to fruition without the support of several grant agencies and institutions. An International Lecture-Research Award from the Fulbright Commission (2004) and a Library of Congress Fellowship in International Studies (2005) provided research leaves to begin this endeavor. A National Endowment for the Humanities (2008–2009), a Queen's Research Initiation Grant (2007), an Advisory Research Grant (2009), and a sabbatical from Queen's University in 2011–2012 enabled me to collect archival information at the General Archive of the Indies, in Seville, Spain, and to work at the Nettie Lee Benson Latin American Collection, in Austin, Texas.

I would like to thank the directors and staff of the archives I consulted, especially the Archivo General de Indias (AGI) and the Archivo General de la Nación, Perú (AGNP). I am grateful to the History Department at Western Washington University for support in gaining essential library privileges during the summers, since 2007, that I have spent researching and writing in Bellingham.

I am especially grateful to Luis Miguel Glave for his decades-long friendship and for providing excellent transcriptions of several of the Justicia court cases. I also thank María Jóse Fitz and the two *superheroes* for their wonderful hospitality during my stays in Seville. Susanne Seales also deserves special recognition for her tireless work designing the structure of the database and entering data into FileMaker, her revisions of bibliographies, her drawing of maps, and her editorial critiques I have the geographer Sarah Bell to thank for most of the maps and charts. Amelia Almorza Hidalgo found some treasures digging through the notarial records of the Archivo

Municipal de Carmona. Finally, for her editorial assistance and advice on good writing, I extend a very special thanks to Maureen McCallum Garvie. I have learned a great deal from her.

I would also like to thank the dedicated editors and staff at Duke University Press for shepherding the manuscript through to publication. In particular I thank Gisela Fosado for her faith in the project; Joanne Rappaport and Florencia Mallon, two of the editors of the Narrating Native Histories series, for their encouragement; the clarity and expediency with which the editorial assistant Lorien Olive and the assistant managing editor, Danielle Szulczewski Houtz explained complicated procedures and kept me on task; Christine Choi Riggio for her care in making necessary changes to the maps; and Patricia Mickelberry, whose keen editorial eye has helped make this a better book. I also thank Mark Mastromarino for preparing the index.

Along the way I have had the enormous pleasure of benefiting from rich discussions, with friends and colleagues, about slavery, narrative voice, and well-being. In particular, Alan Gallay and Joanne Rappaport gave critical commentary on various portions and versions of the manuscript, and their advice has been invaluable. The critiques of the two anonymous readers for Duke University Press were tremendously helpful for revising the manuscript. Other colleagues and friends whose voices resonate in these pages are Kenneth Andrien, Wendy Brooks, Sherwin Bryant, Kathryn Burns, James Carson, Amitava Chowdhury, Elizabeth and Tom Cohen, David and Sasha Cook, Karoline Cook, the members of Dance Gallery, Cecilia Danysk, Natalie Zemon Davis, Susan Deans-Smith, Alan Durston, Robert, Lesley and Sarina Fong, Peter Gose, Lori Ames Grant, Susan Kellogg, the members of Latin American Research Group in Toronto, Abril Liberatori, James Loucky, George Lovell, Jane Mangan, Kenneth Mills, T.Y. and Eliza Pang, David Parker, Matthew Restall, Ariel Salzmann, Heidi Scott, Rebecca Scott, Margarita Suárez, and Dot Tuer.

As always, my parents, Nancy G. and Edwin H. van Deusen, are there for me in every way. I am so grateful to have shared these decades together. To Preston, my husband, who has read every page of this book several times over, I thank you for tolerating all the time I spend "in the sixteenth century." My journey through life is especially blessed because of you.

Chapter 5 was previously published, in a modified version, as "Seeing *Indios* in Sixteenth Century Castile," *William and Mary Quarterly* 69.2 (April 2012): 205–34.

Introduction

No need to heed your voice when I can talk about you better than you can speak about yourself. No need to hear your voice. Only tell me about your pain. I want to know your story. And then I will tell it back to you in a new way. Tell it back to you in such a way that it has become my own. Re-writing you I rewrite myself anew. I am still author, authority. I am still colonizer, the speaking subject, and you are now at the centre of my tale.

—bell hooks, "Marginalizing a Site of Resistance"

Bartolomé de las Casas (1484–1566) is considered by some to be the first human-rights advocate, a "larger-than-life archetypal hero."[1] Named Legal Advocate and Universal Protector of the Indios (Procurador y Protector Universal de los Indios de las Indias), he helped, through his tireless efforts, to eliminate the most egregious forms of indigenous slavery in Spanish America.[2] Biographies of the influential man abound, some of them hagiographic, others oriented toward his philosophy and political aspirations. One of the most respected Latin Americanists of the twentieth century, Lewis Hanke, dedicated several works to the study of Las Casas. His most seminal work, *The Spanish Struggle for Justice in the Conquest of America* (1949), became essential reading for students and aspiring Latin Americanists in the 1960s, 1970s, and 1980s.[3]

But this volume is not about Bartolomé de las Casas and his remarkable accomplishments. It is about indigenous men and women called *indios* who were interviewed by famous friars like

Las Casas and who, like Catalina in this book's preface, made great efforts to acquire a piece of paper from the Spanish courts saying they were free vassals. It is about the indigenous struggle for justice, a struggle that occurred on a local and global scale. There is no question that Las Casas's advocacy was central to those efforts. By testifying on behalf of several slaves, Las Casas did what he felt compelled to do: help them achieve their freedom before the Spanish tribunals of the Casa de la Contratación (the House of Trade, henceforth referred to as the Casa, established in 1503) or the Council of the Indies (established in 1524). But the indigenous role in that effort, long overshadowed by the larger-than-life presence of Las Casas, has yet to be told.

I began work on this book with two questions. First, what happened to the hundreds of thousands of native peoples who were enslaved and transported to foreign places in the Americas and Europe? Second, would it be possible, given the paucity of historical records, to trace the pathways of several thousand who went to Castile, and the histories of the scores who initiated lawsuits against their masters? As I began to probe these questions, I discovered that in the sixteenth century at least 650,000 indigenous people were enslaved and forced to relocate to foreign lands throughout the inter-American and transatlantic Iberian world.[5] The process began in the 1490s, when several thousand unsuspecting individuals were loaded into the holds of the first caravels returning across the Atlantic with Columbus and merchants eager to develop a lucrative transatlantic indigenous slave trade.[6] An alarmed Queen Isabel responded first by ordering that the indigenous people be freed and returned to their homelands, then by declaring, in 1501, that Indians were instead Castilian free vassals who should be treated well and pay tribute to the Crown.[7] This decree, although important in the sense that it curtailed the massive importation of indigenous slaves to Spain, did little to stop slave-raiding ventures throughout the Americas for decades to come.[8]

As part of this monumental inter-American forced migration, more than two thousand indios made the transatlantic journey to lead humble lives in the Spanish kingdom of Castile.[9] It is these individuals who are the subject of my book. Some arrived with seamen, some with their masters, some with merchants who sold them once they reached Seville. The earliest records of slaves being sold in Seville appear with the labels *muchacho* (boy), *obispo* (perhaps a reference to the slave's master, a bishop), and *una niña* (a young girl), and with the name Cosme.[10] In their travels, many slaves crossed Spanish-Portuguese imperial borders, thus complicating their identities as "transimperial" subjects.[11] Most indigenous servants and slaves lived in Seville, but hundreds eventually settled with their masters in the villages and towns of Almería, Baeza, Cádiz, Ciudad Real, Granada, Madrid, Toledo, and Valladolid (see map).[12] A portion of these slaves later litigated for their freedom, ultimately questioning the bondage of indios and redefining what it meant to be an indio in the early modern Iberian world.

Why, then, were such large numbers of indigenous peoples in Spanish America enslaved? Moreover, why did Spaniards think they had the legal right to enslave indigenous people?

Fifteenth- and early sixteenth-century Castilian theologians, merchants, commoners, and men of the sea had conflicting attitudes toward indigenous slavery. Most scholars, ecclesiastics, and jurists of the time agreed that applying the Aristotelian notion of natural slavery (*servidumbre natural*) to indios had no legal or theological basis. Those who disagreed, including those who stood to profit from a well-developed slave trade, believed that the people labeled as indios lacked humanity; being little more than bestial animals, indios could therefore be enslaved.[13] But as many polemicists, and particularly Bartolomé de las Casas, argued, God did not create natural slaves; all humans were free by their nature (*a natura*) and had the capacity to contemplate God. In other words, indios were humans and fell within the governance of natural law. They were the sons of Adam and should be treated accordingly. This opinion was iterated in Isabel's declaration of 1501, the Laws of Burgos (1512), Paul III's papal bull *Sublimus Deus* of 1537, and the New Laws of 1542.[14]

With a few exceptions, the rationales used to support the continued enslavement of indios did not refer to whether they were rational beings or barbarians; instead the focus was on certain practices of civil slavery. According to the *Siete Partidas*, persons could be taken as slaves because their parents had been slaves, because they had committed a crime, or as a result of poverty or debt. Cannibalism was another reason. Queen Isabel may have qualified indios as free vassals in 1501, but in 1503, at the insistence of the merchants and authorities of Santo Domingo, she issued a further decree stating that *indios caribes* (*caribe* meaning "man-eating") from "the Caribbean islands and Cartagena" could be captured as slaves. The rationale behind the decision was that indios caribes were barbarians (not quite human) and so fell outside of natural law.[15]

Even though Isabel had determined that indios were not infidels—unlike the Muslim people throughout the Mediterranean who had been enslaved for centuries—she decreed that they could be enslaved if they resisted Christianity, as captives of just war (*guerra justa*). This policy had a long tradition. Not only did Christian heritage determine status, position, and the ability to migrate, confessional faith had for centuries been the raison d'être in Christian Iberia for the enslavement of non-Christian enemies dwelling in lands not subject to Christian rule (infidels), who, once captured, were labeled as captives of just war because they had refused to capitulate to the king.[16] As several scholars have shown, identifying the jurisdiction of such captives could be strategic and calculating. In the 1440s slaves who were bartered or purchased in the Portuguese territory designated as "Guinea" were purposefully conflated with so-called infidel Moors to justify their enslavement as captives of just war.[17] We see this same modus operandi with the people of the Canary Islands, and soon thereafter in America, until Queen Isabel determined that the neophyte indios of the king of Spain were rationally capable—they had *ingenio* or *capacidad*—of understanding Christianity and could not be captured as infidels.[18]

Although the indios of America could not automatically be enslaved as infidels, the legal document known as the Spanish Requirement ("El Requerimiento," 1513) validated violent Spanish military action, especially when authorities could demonstrate the unwillingness of indios to succumb to Catholic rule.[19] The established protocol of reading the Spanish Requirement—a declaration of the Spanish right to rule the people and territories of the Indies by divine right, which was employed until 1573—meant that if the members of the male "audience" resisted becoming willing vassals of the (Catholic) Spanish Crown, they, their wives, and their children could be enslaved.[20] Many contemporaries considered it a ludicrous ritual, including the chronicler Gonzalo Fernández de Oviedo, who mockingly suggested plying the targeted indios with food and drink and offering them cloth and "other little trifles from Castile" so they would more easily succumb to the tenets of the document.[21]

In the early colonial period, usage of the term *just war* could be applied to warlike or particularly belligerent ethnicities from the circum-Caribbean area, who could be enslaved because they had initiated armed responses to Spanish military incursions.[22] But embedded in the application of just war was the idea that particular ethnicities were, by their nature, warlike. Thus, over the decades, Spanish authorities designated certain territories (*naturalezas*) as harboring bellicose and barbarous people, and deemed enslaveable particular ethnicities (the Chontal or Chichimeca, for example) because they purportedly lacked the characteristics of humanity.[23] Consequently, the compartmentalization of certain territories and particular indigenous peoples conveniently fit the criteria for enslavement. The rationale also explains why the Crown issued licenses and ordinances granting individual Castilian merchants free rein to capture peoples inhabiting certain territories on a piecemeal basis. Understanding the costs that this carte blanche authority would have for innocent indigenous peoples led Bartolomé de las Casas to argue that *all* Indians had ingenio, or the capacity for rational thinking, no matter what place in the Americas they inhabited.[24]

Equally complex was the legitimizing term *rescate*, or ransom, which had a long history, both in the Mediterranean and in Latin America. In principle, rescate transactions occurred between a local cacique or lord and a Spanish buyer, authority, or *encomendero*, who exchanged indios already held in bondage for goods. The practice expanded on local customs of slavery, but other connotations of the term *rescate* included redemption (from the Latin root *redemptio*), or rescue.[25] In Castile the term was used to refer to the ransoming of Christian vassals held as captives in various Mediterranean sites, or to the purchasing of freedom of West African and Muslim peoples held as captive slaves in Castile. It was also used in the redemptive sense of saving Christians and vulnerable non-Christian children from the "infidels," or non-Christian peoples.[26] Thus *rescate* could signify the exchange of one commodity for another, the rescue from people seen as perilous to the Christian Spaniards, or the purchase of freedom by someone in bondage. In Latin America the practice of rescate was commonly used to exchange indios already enslaved by other native peoples, primarily through an agreement between the cacique or native overlord and the interested Spaniard, but it was also a pretext to enslave thousands of innocent men, women, and children. As the historian William Sherman so aptly put it, "The pre-existence of slavery as a native institution served to reinforce the justification for its continuance under Spanish rule."[27]

Finally, ordinances and decrees passed in Castile by the Crown and rescinded over the decades were contradictory and piecemeal. They excluded slavery only in some areas, temporarily prohibited slavery (1530), later reestablished slavery under conditions of just war and ransom (1534, 1550), and granted exceptions to individual merchants and families making the transatlantic journey to Castile by ignoring laws that prohibited the transportation of slaves away from their provinces of origin. A bird's-eye view of the policies enacted by Kings Ferdinand and Charles V over the decades reveals the monarchs' ambivalence about the status of indios as completely free, rational beings.[28]

No less problematic were indios labeled by Crown authorities as *naborías* (a Taíno term adopted by Castilians who had settled on Hispaniola at the beginning of the sixteenth century).[29] Designated as neither slaves nor free, naborías could not be sold but were to remain lifelong servants under the guardianship of Spaniards. Despite laws that stated that naborías could not be sold, many were branded like slaves and removed from their homelands against their will.[30] These were individuals with a knotty juridical status, much like those designated as *siervos*, or servants, in medieval Castile and elsewhere.[31] Although the term *naboría* was used to distinguish inalienable from alienable property, naborías were often forced to move from one location to another, were sold despite laws to the contrary, and in situations of just war were captured and distributed to interested parties.[32] As several decrees issued for different parts of America emphasized, naborías were free but permanent servants in need of the guidance of Spaniards.[33] It was a construct with multiple contextual applications in Latin America, pertaining to free servants who attached themselves willingly to individual Spaniards, to military allies who gained certain privileges for serving Spanish masters on military excursions, and to captured individuals, mainly children, who were never branded but who remained with masters for life. In short, it was a catch-all term that blurred the legal boundary between freedom and slavery and between servant and slave.

If a close inspection of the term *naboría* exposes the liminal status of many indios in early colonial Spanish America, a historicized analysis of the *encomienda* system illustrates a lack of clarity about whether indios were truly free subjects. From the early period of Spanish settlement in the Greater Antilles, the Crown created a compulsory but multifaceted labor system that utilized able-bodied adult indigenous males. As a reward for military services, Spanish conquerors and settlers called encomenderos were granted a set number of indigenous laborers with a cacique as their lord in encomienda or trust. By the Crown's authority, encomenderos received tribute in labor, goods, or hard currency. Because indigenous people were legally considered free vassals, the utilization of this labor system, which remained in place throughout much of the sixteenth century, was a way for Crown authorities to avoid committing to a complete endorsement of indigenous slavery. Critics of the system, however, wondered whether indigenous males held in encomienda were actually being treated as chattel, rather than as wage-earning laborers. The answer is complex. The archives are replete with accusations against encomenderos: that they were selling indios to pay off debts or to finance upcoming ventures; or that indios were severely overworked, bequeathed as property in testaments, or forcibly relocated and separated from family members and communities. Although the legal distinction between an encomienda laborer and a slave was clear, in practice the encomienda system was thinly disguised slavery. Moreover, the enslavement of indios actually bolstered the system; one practice reinforced the other.

Between 1500 and 1542, the open-ended exceptions of just war and ransom served as ruses to enslave hundreds of thousands of people from the Americas and elsewhere. But the promulgation of the New Laws, issued by Charles V in 1542, was considered a watershed event. These laws included ordinances for the governance of the newly established Audiencias of New Spain, Peru, Guatemala, Nicaragua, and Hispaniola, and twenty-three articles dealing specifically with the status and treatment of the Indians.[34] They iterated Queen Isabel's 1501 proclamation, and the 1537 papal bull *Sublimis Deus*, which stated that Indians were truly human, vassals of the Crown of Castile, and free by their nature. The enslavement of Indians for just war and ransom, and even in cases of rebellion, was now strictly prohibited (although exceptions abounded). Audiencia members or governors were charged with inspecting all titles of slave owners and freeing any indigenous peoples who had been unjustly enslaved, while special legal representatives were assigned to represent indigenous litigants in court.[35] In sum, the New Laws were meant to enhance Crown governance, improve the labor conditions of indigenous people, eliminate slavery and personal free servitude, and limit the term of the encomienda grant to one lifetime.

But the same clause prohibiting the enslavement of indios for just war or ransom also specified that slave owners who had documentation that proved legitimate possession would be allowed to keep their indios as slaves. This loophole is the arena in which the indigenous struggle for justice occurred, since it was now incumbent on indios to initiate lawsuits against those masters who refused to treat them as free persons. Moreover, although the laws provided the legal cornerstone for indio slaves to litigate for their freedom in the Spanish courts, it did not guarantee a successful outcome.[36]

Despite provisions granting all non-enslaved indios free status as wage laborers, it would take several decades after the New Laws were instituted before Castilians would cease to equate the category *indio* with permanent bondage. Moreover, well into the seventeenth century, indios continued to be taken as the slaves of just war in several locations throughout Spanish America. The Crown was complicit in these practices, since the bodies of slaves of just war and rescate were required by royal law to be seared with an official brand fashioned into an *R* for *rescate* and a *G* for *guerra*, and the Crown was to be paid 20 percent of the slave's sale value, called the "royal fifth." Thus, even the logic embedded in royal legislation shaped the meanings and practices of slavery and helped it to endure as long as it did.[37]

As a result of the inconsistent implementation of laws, the continuation of practices of enslavement based on just war and ransom, and persistent doubts about the status of indios as natural slaves, hundreds of thousands of slaves and servants were deracinated from their homelands and shipped to disparate sites. Thousands came from the Lesser Antilles, off the northern coast of Venezuela; hundreds of thousands came from Central America, particularly Guatemala, Honduras, and Nicaragua. Large numbers were shipped from the province of Pánuco, in Mexico, to Santo Domingo, and slaves from northern South America, especially Brazil, were also uprooted. As the trajectories of conquest and invasion proceeded from the Greater Antilles, Brazil, and northern South America, to the mainland of North America, in what is now Mexico, then into Central America, Panama, and then south along the western coast of South America, thousands of indios were captured or bartered and placed in bondage. Hundreds of adult indios served as military auxiliaries on exploratory ventures, as domestic servants, and, in the case of the oft-branded females, as the partners of men who had raped, enslaved, and occasionally married them.[38]

Many were children, the victims of military encounters, shipped as commodities throughout the Iberian colonial world.[39] The application of the term *child* (*niño*) ranged from infants (sometimes called "niños de pecho," or babies still breastfeeding) to early adolescents, depending on their height. The Spanish Requirement of 1513 specified that if a group of indigenous people refused to accept Catholicism and Castilian rule, then Crown representatives had the legal right to make war on them and to enslave their women and children. It was not until 1534 that royal legislation prohibited the enslavement of women and niños under the age of fourteen.[40] In addition, provisos in the 1534 law emphasized that children could be taken as naborías, as neither slave nor free, and placed in the permanent custody of an individual Castilian. This left open a legal loophole which made it difficult for children initially designated as naborías who were sold once they arrived in Castile to prove their legal status as free vassals.

The enslavement or creation of indigenous children as legal dependents was not new. By the sixteenth century Castilians and other Iberians were accustomed to having enslaved children in their midst. Quantitative assessments bear out the assertion that children, while not always the majority of slaves brought to Europe from North and West Africa, still came in significant numbers.[41] Some of these captured children were sold at commercial fairs in Castile or were taken directly by ship to Seville. Throughout the fifteenth century, children were appropriated as a result of the profit-making and military raids on the Canary Islands or on the North African coast. They were also taken as captives by Castilians and Portuguese hoping to ransom Christian captives, or as the victims of ongoing religious wars in areas where Europeans deemed that local inhabitants were resisting Christian rule.

Although children were so often the victims of others' choices, such brutality is rarely mentioned in the documentation. Underlying the enslavement of children was the assumption that they were docile and adaptable, and they could easily be sold in Latin America or Castile to families eager to gain an extra hand as household laborers. These children underwent deep natal and cultural alienation that affected how they identified themselves later in life.[42] Many of them could not remember their places of origin; others could recall only snippets of their mother tongue when questioned years later in the Spanish courts. Children in bondage experienced a distinct kind of cultural disruption in their lives than adults, and once on Castilian soil they worked just as hard as the children of the *pecheros*, or tax-paying commoners. Enslaved children were key colonial subjects who cannot be ignored in our discussions of the making and unmaking of indigenous slavery and of the day-to-day processes of household formation where intimacy and violence were intertwined.[43]

Both children and adult indios who were forced to migrate to Castile lived in proximity to other slaves from disparate parts of the globe. In a single elite household in Seville, for example, one might find *moriscos* (forced converts from Islam to Catholicism), West Africans, and indios from Santo Domingo, Mexico, or Peru doing chores together.[44] Seville—a city known as "the endless globe"—was truly international, filled with diverse northern (Berber) and West African, Flemish, Portuguese, French, German, Basque, and Genoese peoples. It was also an increasingly cosmopolitan entrepôt that attracted thousands of slaves from different parts of the world.[45] There, indios would have learned what it meant to be an Old Christian, as well as who was considered marginal in Castilian society.

Indios living in Seville were well aware that they were not the only nation (*nación*)—an abstract category of groupness based on territorial, cultural, residential, or imperial affinity—of foreigners living in bondage and enduring poverty, prejudice, and cruelty. Second to Lisbon, Seville, "asylum of the poor and refuge for the outcast," had the largest slave population in Europe in the sixteenth century.[46] In addition to the hundreds of slaves from Latin America, captive indios from Brazil, Calicut, and Goa, often described as *loro* (greenish-brown) in coloration, were sold in Seville's markets. By 1565, there were 6,327 slaves in Seville, most of whom came from the sub-Saharan

African territories of Guinea, Mina, Cabo Verde, and Angola, and were imported via Portugal through Extremadura or by other routes. Some of these slaves were destined to cross the Atlantic to Caribbean cities and elsewhere, but by the 1570s, 90 percent of them remained in Seville or its vicinity.[47]

Like Africans and others who came as slaves to Iberia from disparate parts of the globe, indios traveled on vessels with European merchants and masters and then worked in the artisan shops and homes of Iberian people. Unlike African peoples, however, indios were not wedged into vessels that had been altered to fit as many commodified humans as possible.[48] But they were exchanged for goods, pawned, or captured during warfare in locations removed from the European continent. They were also the victims of early exploratory ventures and the establishment of colonial outposts throughout the globe. For a few, their translation skills and geographical and cultural knowledge had once proved useful. As Africans and indios entered Portuguese and Castilian households, they participated actively in the process of creating a more expansive community and enhancing European understandings of philosophy, culture, and difference.[49] They were, as recent scholarship has shown, more than chattel in the slave trade, more than demographic statistics on fertility and mortality rates, and more than the sum of the kinds of labor they performed. Slaves, according to the medieval legal code, the *Siete Partidas*, were both property and persons with the civil right to self-purchase and the ability to sue in a court of law. As baptized Catholics, slaves were protected by canon law. Moreover, like the indigenous men and women studied in this book, Africans in Europe and America brought with them diverse notions of what it meant to be part of a collectivity in a particular locale in Africa, even though they were now inscribed as *African* or as *black*.[50] In Iberia they cultivated networks of social and cultural relations based on their own notions of ethnicity, kinship, and family.[51] The social and cultural ties established in Iberia then influenced how Africans experienced their dispersal to the Western Hemisphere.[52]

Contrary to the documentary lacuna about them, indios in Castile were not marginal figures, but rather, like enslaved Africans and others, integral to the development of understandings of self in relation to other and to the formation of social and cultural governance as European contacts throughout the globe expanded. But unlike the rapid commodification of West Africans that proliferated in the late fifteenth century, indigenous slavery never developed on such a large scale. There was never a contract (*asiento*) system for purchasing and transporting indios from their homelands, nor did indigenous slaves serve as agricultural laborers on sugar plantations on the

Atlantic islands or, later, in Spanish America. Thus indigenous slavery was comparable to other concurrent practices of bondage in some ways, but not in others.

As I argue in this volume, it was difficult to identify who was an indio and who was not because, over the course of the sixteenth century, the use of the descriptor *indio* in Castile referred to people from the East and West Indies, China, the Moluccas, India, Brazil, Hispaniola, Mexico, and Peru. Such conflation was particularly evident at the fairs and in the plazas of the major Castilian towns where captive subjects from around the globe were branded and sold as indios to Castilians without regard to their place of origin. The presence in Castile of indios from both Portuguese and Spanish domains indicated the continual seepage of imperial borders and the overlapping imaginary domains on the ships, in the slave markets, and in the homes of Castilians.[53]

Distinguishing the imperial origins and status of indios in a legal setting was often thorny for one crucial reason. Although Spain never formally determined that the indios of the New World were heretics, the Portuguese kings John III (1502–57) and Sebastian (1557–78) authorized the conquest, subjugation, and enslavement of indigenous peoples specifically as the enemies of Christ—heretics and infidels who were to be converted to Catholicism. They were labeled as *indios* or as *gentios* by Portuguese Jesuits and authorities.[54] By Portuguese law, indios in Brazil and elsewhere could also be captured as slaves of just war or because they practiced cannibalism. They could also be acquired by exchange (ransom). These indios had no legal recourse, no New Laws to support their struggles for justice.[55]

But the process of identifying indios in Castilian legal chambers was also difficult because it was such an all-encompassing term. Early on, Iberians had created a new category, *indios* ("people of the Indies"), to define a new "people" in relationship to themselves.[56] From its inception, *indio* was a homogenizing label that constituted difference based on unequal power relations. Similar to the process of determining that extremely diverse African people should be labeled *black*, categorizing vastly distinct ethnicities as indios was part of colonial governance—understood as the creation of understandings of difference based on a comparative knowledge of slavery, labor extraction, and belonging.[57] Works such as Stephanie Smallwood's *Saltwater Slavery* reminds us of how central identifiers were to the process of creating slaves out of West Africans, including words such as *lusty*, which defined an ideal slave before he boarded a ship, or phrases such as *full complements*, which designated human beings as aggregate cargo.[58] The practice of creating monikers, some based on desire and others on contractual obligations, resonates with my analyses of how, for instance, the legal term "slave of just war" (*esclavo de buena guerra*) could be used in a document to describe a vulnerable indigenous boy who had once been held in encomienda, or how a brand on a face said more than any paper ever could.

But the construction of indioness in Castile and elsewhere also occurred in a relational, temporal, and contextual manner, as constituted by the diverse African, indigenous, and South and East Asian slaves and freemen and women servants who worked side-by-side in the villages, towns, and cities of Castile and who also had experienced serial dislocation and bondage.[59] Such subjectivities point to the fact that slavery was "read" in different ways and that the conditions of bondage were defined by other, concurrent forms of servitude and unequal power relations.[60]

Despite the severe disruptions in their lives and being objectified as laborers by owners, indigenous slaves, like their African counterparts, formed families and kinship alliances in their new households and the local environment. Thus, diasporic experiences of bondage involved the creation and re-creation of new expressions of kinship, along with experiences of alienation, liminality, and integration.[61] Experiences of bondage also involved the exertion of free will, however minimal. Walter Johnson's work on the brutal New Orleans slave market in nineteenth-century America and Vincent Brown's work on cultural notions of death and mortuary practices among diasporic Africans in Jamaica poignantly demonstrate that slaves exercised volition, even in the most unlikely of places.[62]

Given that indigenous slaves labeled as *indios* in the sixteenth century were highly mobile, how do we chart the practices of being indio to show how local practices in Castile resonated with global ones? Here it is useful to evoke Arjun Appadurai's neologism *ethnoscape*, which he used as a framework for discussing highly mobile migratory peoples—immigrants, tourists, or refugees—of the late twentieth century no longer connected to a given place.[63] The term *ethnoscape* has relevance in considering how deterritorialized indios in the sixteenth century—no longer associated with an ethnic lord, an ethnicity, or a single master—were being defined in Castilian legal contexts. In this book I adapt Appadurai's construct to the neologism *indioscape* to argue that indio identities were no longer spatially bound or culturally homogeneous, but rather transimperially present in the imaginations of those slaves and masters whose own "local" experiences—whether in Peru, Goa, Carmona, or Mozambique—were mirrored against the experiences of other slaves and masters. The notion of an indioscape includes a sense of rootedness—in this instance, of belonging to places and cultures other than Castile *and* in Castile—and routedness, or a distinct sense of time and space based on experiences of bondage and deracination.[64] Here, in the power to imagine the lived and fictional "lives" of others, we can see the realisms of the larger-scale temporal and spatial perspectives of Spanish colonialism.[65] In that sense, this volume is more than a history of slavery; it is a study that examines the creation of "indioness" as a process of local and global interactions, connecting East to West and West to East, that deepened over the course of the sixteenth century. It demonstrates how indios were central to early colonial enterprises in Latin America and elsewhere.

By exploring the microcosmic and international dimensions of the fragmented lives of slaves, most of them from Spanish America and Brazil but several from Africa or South and East Asia—their interactions with others, and how others saw them—I strive in this volume to expand our understandings of the multiple and contextual definitions of indioness in the heart of the Spanish empire. I place in perspective the prevailing notions of indios as tribute-paying subjects of indigenous lords in Latin America and enhance our comprehension of the multivalent usage of the term *indio*, which encompassed the global experiences and perspectives of those individuals who self-identified or were labeled by others as indios. Just as the presence of displaced Moroccan captives and West African people in Latin America deepens our understandings of the types of Atlantic exchanges that were occurring there, so, too, did the presence of indios in Castile complicate notions of indioness in Spanish America and elsewhere.[66] In this volume I show how notions of belonging and identity were not simply defined by place of origin—although that was important—but were constituted in local and global contexts where mobility and perception were a part of a continual reformulation of self in relation to other.

Employing an ethnographic focus, I hope to give the men and women who litigated in the Castilian courtrooms a spatial and temporal history and their rightful place in the historiographies of Latin America, Iberia, the Atlantic world, and global history. To show how individual slaves were engaged in knowledge making about the world in a European context, I employ both a cis-Atlantic methodology (examining larger Atlantic processes through local particularities) and a circum-Atlantic one (examining broader circulations around the four continents). The litigation suits refer as well to local practices of slavery in disparate locations of Latin America which also informed global processes of imperial sense making and defined the boundaries of identity, sovereignty, and territoriality. I argue that the slavery of indigenous people in Spanish and Portuguese America was also informed by past and concurrent slaveries of the sub-Saharan, North African, and South and Southeast Asian regions. It was influenced by movements of people and goods from the sub-Saharan region (known to Europeans as Guinea) through the western Maghreb, along the western coast of Africa; of the human traffic from and to the Atlantic islands of Madeira and the Canaries; and concurrently, of the slaveries of people from East Asia, along what is now the Chinese coast and Malaysia east to Mughal India.[67] Merchants in different ports of call enhanced the rapid globalization of people and fundamentally changed the domestic and artisanal landscape of Iberia in the fifteenth and sixteenth centuries.[68] The voluntary and involuntary movements of children and adults from locations throughout the globe had a profound impact on how indios were tolerated and how they saw themselves in Castile and elsewhere.

Finally, this book is not only about enslaved native men and women in Castile, but about the Castilians and other Europeans who attempted to make sense of the world of that time. Many Castilian men and women had read about, heard talk of, or had traveled extensively throughout the globe. Those who traveled returned not only with goods but with enslaved children and adults, and the travelers' conceptualizations of the world changed local practices in their respective villages and towns. The attempts of Castilians to control the lives of others inevitably informed the governance of slavery at the household, legal, and imperial levels. But more broadly, slavery reconfigured how Europeans and others imagined the world.

Catalina's Tale

Drawing on methods used in microhistorical analyses developed by Carlo Ginzburg and others, I compare evidence from over one hundred litigation suits with other records to access the global and local dimensions of slavery in individual lives.[69] I reconstitute fragmented tales about loss and cultural relocation to show how enslaved individuals made sense of bondage. Although the tales of mobility and migration of those indigenous slaves who litigated for their freedom vary considerably, certain experiential patterns emerge when the trajectories of the Spanish conquest and economic trade are weighed. The story told to a Spanish lawyer in 1552 of the abduction of Catalina, a Pipil, illustrates the severe disruption that she and many other indigenous people experienced and how her forced mobility and ultimate freedom is illustrative of early colonial governance. As a child in the 1520s,

Catalina was known as Xagua and lived with her family in the village of Nonoalco (in the province of Nequepío, the older name for modern-day El Salvador's Cuzcatlán). In 1527 the soon-to-be famous conqueror Sebastián de Benalcázar passed through her village and appropriated (*cupo*) Xagua, baptizing her and renaming her Catalina. She had just lost her baby teeth (*que mudó los dientes*) when she entered Benalcázar's household.[70] She then spent nearly five years as part of his domestic entourage in Jolota, Honduras, witnessing large numbers of captured indigenous "rebels" arriving at the town square in chains following Benalcázar's "just war" forays into the countryside.[71] She saw groups of men and women being lined up, branded, and sold into slavery. When Catalina's parents became aware of her whereabouts and attempted to remove her from Benalcázar's custody, her master decided to brand her face and pay the royal fifth to the appropriate authority. This sealed Catalina's fate as a common slave and made it impossible for her parents to claim her.

After this devastating event, in 1532, Catalina boarded a ship with her master in Realejo, Nicaragua, and journeyed to South America. Along with dozens of other Central American slaves, she landed in the large village of Coaque (in the modern-day province of Manabí, Ecuador), where Benalcázar reconnoitered with Francisco Pizarro.[72] From there, the combined armies, which included indigenous slaves, linguists, and military auxiliaries, made their way by land to Cajamarca. After the brutal slaughter of Atahualpa's people, in November 1532, Catalina remained in Cajamarca for nine more months, until Juan Pantiel de Salinas (also referred to as Juan de Salinas Farfán) drew up a debt contract with Benalcázar and purchased her for 350 pesos. Catalina later recalled seeing an exchange of "silver jars and bars of gold"—perhaps Inca treasure—taking place between the two men.[73] From Cajamarca, she accompanied Salinas to the newly renamed Spanish city of Cuzco (1533) and was present there during the siege by Manco Inca (1536–37). She then made the trek to Lima, where she boarded a ship bound for Spain.[74] More than a decade later, she testified before the Council of the Indies, expressing her desire to return home as a free woman. She gained her freedom, but whether she returned home to Cuzcatlán was never confirmed.

Like the dozens of other testimonies of slaves analyzed in this book, Catalina's deposition reveals a slave's perspective on conquest, upheaval and mobility, and survival in the early colonial period. Her tale exposes the centrality of slavery and slave trading in the economic and social formation of the early Iberian colonial world and its impact on the lives of individuals throughout Latin America and the broader Atlantic world. It reveals the

TABLE I.1 Number of Litigants by Decade

	Male	Female	Unknown	Total No. of Individuals
1530s	4	0	0	4
1540s	45	33	0	78
				1543 (48)
				1549 (27)
1550s	22	25	0	47
				1549 (11)
1560s	10	11	0	21
1570s	18	15	0	33
				1543 (1)
1580s	0	1	0	1
TOTAL	99	85	0	184

Note: Numbers in parentheses indicate lawsuits resulting from the Inspections of 1543 or 1549

power of mobility and how the control of masters over slaves transcended geographic and oceanic spaces. Through the deracination and mobility of indio slaves, different parts of the world became connected. And yet we know so little about these slaves. A growing body of scholarship on the Atlantic world details the migrations and "globetrotting" tales of European and African peoples, but few studies show the effects that forced mobility had on native people.[75]

We learn about the Pipil Catalina and others because a total of 184 slaves initiated 127 lawsuits or appeals, or were the defendants in the courts of the Casa (in Seville) or of the Council of the Indies between 1530 and 1585 (see Table I.1).[76] The Chancellery of Valladolid (Chancillería de Valladolid) and the Audiencia de las Gradas in Seville also considered a few cases before 1545; one or two litigants appeared at these courts and at the Casa in the 1530s.[77] Over the course of the 1530s and 1540s, Crown officials also ordered inspections of free and enslaved indios living in Seville. But what led to an increase in litigation and a spike in legal appeals initiated by slave owners were the New Laws of 1542, which abolished indigenous slavery in most instances, and the freeing of over one hundred indio slaves in Seville following an inspection, in 1543, by Gregorio López, a member of the Council of the Indies. A subsequent inspection, in 1549, by Hernán Pérez de la

Fuente caused another increase in appeals by spurned masters. Although the Council of Indies generally served as an appellate court for the Casa, by the 1550s the superior judicial body had begun to hear some of these suits directly.

The profiles of these 184 indio litigants varied considerably. Some were mothers seeking to protect their children from the lifelong fate they themselves had suffered; others were single men and women, still fairly young because they had been abducted as infants or young children. Some adult slaves had been in Castile since childhood, for twenty or thirty years; others were freed soon after disembarking in Seville. Many stated that they were under the age of fourteen when they were abducted, contrary to the 1534 law. Several elites litigated because they were eager to regain a vestige of their former status as esteemed servants of important men. Married couples sued and won their freedom, and a few elderly plaintiffs expressed a wish to die as free men. They came from a broad swath of the Spanish colonies, including Nueva Galizia, Pánuco, and Zacatecas in the north; Cuzcatlán, Guatemala, and Nicaragua in Central America; and Santa Marta, Río de la Plata, and even Peru in the south.[78] Many had passed through Santo Domingo, but only a few were culturally Taíno, perhaps because by the time most of the cases were initiated, the first generation of slaves from Hispaniola or the Bahamas had already died.[79] Some of the young children of female litigants were born in Castile.

To add breadth, depth, and complexity to the stories of the indigenous subjects I consider in this book, I have combined information found in the litigation suits with other records amassed in local and imperial archives in Spain and Latin America. These include notarial records of slave sales, inventories, dowries and wills, ship registries, travel certificates, official correspondence, royal decrees, legislation, contemporary political treatises, and Portuguese and Spanish chronicles that have much to say about the contested imperial domains of Latin America, Africa, and South and East Asia. Such sources contain narratives or narrative fragments that help us understand the power of perception and naming, the sense-making processes and rationales involved in turning children and adults into slaves, and the knowledge that created and upheld believable epistemologies about slavery.

My own conceptualizations about indigenous bondage are deeply informed by the work of other scholars who have studied indigenous slavery.[80] A recent, important monograph by Esteban Mira Caballos (*Indios y mestizos americanos en la España del siglo XVI*), provides an overview of the juridical and social aspects of indigenous slavery in Castile that is based on some of the litigation suits I analyze in this book. Other works emphasize the miniscule presence in Spain of indio slaves compared to those from sub-Saharan and North Africa.[81] For slavery in Latin America, we can rely on the meticulous work of historical demographers and ethnohistorians who have pored over royal decrees and ordinances to detail the severe and unprecedented loss of life and the enslavement of hundreds of thousands of individuals lost to history in specific regions of Latin America.[82] By detecting migration patterns, we can see how much the movement of enslaved peoples reflected the Spanish-directed (forced) and indigenous-initiated (voluntary and strategic) movements of peoples, most of which did not occur without havoc and loss. We need only to leaf through the letters of friar Domingo de Santo Tomás or the treatises of Bartolomé de las Casas to reawaken and resensitize ourselves to the monstrous episodes of human violence that occurred recklessly and continuously. Still, the tales of the people who experienced that horror remain fixed and absolute, as part of an *ilud tempus* forever embedded in debates over the legal and theological viability of the slave system itself.

Considerations of nonelite indios in the conquest period tend to focus on their extermination or on their broken bodies exploited excessively as encomienda laborers. They are studied as part of a slave trade that rendered them expendable, and those who survived, we are told, were acculturated: they adapted to the ways of the dominant Spaniards. The master narrative of the invasion period still tends to articulate either the demographic and social disintegration of a largely helpless population or their resistance to the invaders. They remain voiceless, in a sense, because most often they are recorded as commodities, cargo, and branded bodies, all "things that don't lend themselves to representation, at least not easily."[83] We know more about the slaves who died aboard vessels in the middle of the vast sea than we do about the survivors who tried to make sense of their lives in a foreign location.

Of course, the tales of heroic free individuals—like Hatuey, the Taíno lord from the island of Hispaniola, or Enriquillo, another Taíno rebel, or Manco Inca Yupanqui, the Sapa Inca whose large army laid siege to Cuzco and Lima—are crucial to our understanding of history, as are accounts of others who rejected the incursions of the Spaniards on their bodies and landscapes. But of interest here are the several thousand indio slaves living in Castile who were not heroes in any large sense. I seek to show how indigenous servants and slaves, as severely disrupted individuals, made sense of themselves as they endured bondage, experienced intimacy, and litigated for their freedom in sixteenth-century Castile. Although I focus on the circumscribed tales told by litigants, I aspire to offer something more than a collective biography or a compilation of interesting stories. Simply put, what I have written about is the local, transatlantic, and global dimensions of indigenous slavery.[84]

Entering the Courtroom

Before 1542, indios living in Castile who hoped to gain their freedom relied on special legal representatives (*procuradores*) to defray their legal costs because they fell under the legal category of poor and miserable persons protected by the Castilian Crown and assigned special privileges.[85] Like the enslaved moriscos, West Africans, and Canary Islanders in their midst, indios had to rely on the practice of rescate, whereby an interested party paid money to buy their freedom, or on the paternalistic benevolence of masters who liberated them on their deathbeds.[86]

It took thirty-six years for Pope Paul III to declare in a papal bull in 1537, that indios of the Spanish domains were, indeed, men with souls who could be saved; this was followed by the New Laws of 1542, which declared indios to be free vassals of the Spanish Crown. Given the time lapse and lack of clarity, it would have been difficult for Crown authorities to alter patterns of slavery that had been in place for fifty years. When it became clear to Charles V that resistance to the New Laws would be formidable in Spanish America, since many Spaniards had come to depend on slavery and the slave trade for profit and a steady labor supply, he decided to begin at home, in Castile. The inspections of slaves the king ordered in Seville in 1543 and 1549 mandated that indios be freed immediately if they were being held without documents proving their legal acquisition. As a result, more than one hundred indigenous slaves in Seville were freed. As is evident from the plethora of lawsuits that ensued (generally initiated by disgruntled slave owners) and handled quickly as summary justice (defined as relying on oral rather than written depositions, and not using a panel of judges), indio witnesses and litigants found this period to be transformative.

Indios justifiably feared the repercussions of stepping forward to petition for their freedom. Even so, many did, and the word spread quickly among indios in Castile that they *could* litigate for their freedom and that they were exempt from court costs. The process, however, was rarely easy or straightforward. Litigants were beaten, branded, sold, or intimidated into telling lies by prosecuting attorneys in the corridors outside the chamber where the judges convened.[87] Only rarely are we privy to the extralegal mechanisms—support from a friar or a recently freed indio—that aided or dissuaded an indio from pressing forward with a lawsuit. Even in the depositions presented to the judges indios and masters purposefully manipulated the meanings of the brands on bodies, tried to determine the places of origin of slaves, and described physiognomic characteristics, with the intention either of fixing indios as perpetual slaves or of liberating them from decades of bondage. Determining the status as a free or enslaved subject was rarely clear-cut, and as the lawsuits demonstrate, it took years for protective legislation to be systematically implemented in Castile.

Faced with increasing legal restrictions, petitioning slave owners who appeared before judges in Castile developed two strategies that aided in identifying their indios as legitimate slaves. The first was to argue that their indio slaves did not originate from a domain under the control of the Indies of the Ocean Sea of the King of Spain; rather, they were said to be Portuguese vassals, who were by law still considered slaves even after the political unification of the Iberian peninsula in 1580.[88] The second line of attack was to emphasize the lineage of a slave over his or her place of birth. In this context, naturaleza, or nativeness, was defined as a particular community or cultural habitat.[89] This meant that in some cases indio litigants were being asked to prove that their mothers were not of Islamic or North or West African heritage. Because slave owners generally did not have documents to prove that slaves had been captured in just war (required after 1536), and indios had difficulty proving their places of origin or who their mothers were, both litigants and defendants relied on expert witnesses—including other free and enslaved indios—to identify the imperial status or lineage of each indio litigant. Determining who was indio and who was not depended heavily on the experience of witnesses, whether indigenous or Castilian, male or female, elite or nonelite. Witnesses were called on to use their "skilled vision" to attest to the qualities of the individual litigants.[90] Some of those who testified had followed the compass and had actively engaged in the slave trade, while others remained in the global entrepôt of Seville, surrounded by "foreign" slaves from the Portuguese domains—including Brazil, West Africa, and South and East Asia—in addition to moros (a Castilian term used in the sixteenth century to refer to people of the Islamic faith, especially those of Arab or Berber descent living in North Africa) and moriscos from Málaga, Berbería, and elsewhere.[91] To strengthen the case for continued bondage or freedom, they also relied on bills of sale and travel documents that included geographic and physiognomic descriptors. Litigants, on the other hand, even if they did not originate from Spanish-controlled territories, adopted the term *indio* as a strategy to prove that they were free vassals.

Because slaves were property and by law not permitted to represent themselves in court, *procuradores* (legal advocates), *solicitadores* (solicitors), or *abogados* (lawyers) represented them. After 1549, a special *procurador de los indios* advised and guided litigants through the legal labyrinth.[92] Minors under twenty-five had a legal representative (curador) assigned to represent them.[93] At the Council of the Indies, the *fiscal* (prosecutor) represented the interests of the king (as the protector of the Indians) in the name of the indigenous litigant and worked in tandem with the procurador who drew up the petition on the indigenous slave's behalf.[94] The caliber and training of lawyers and legal advocates varied considerably. Some were more adept and successful than others at effectively using both law and procedure to free their clients. Many of these representatives had no legal or university training.[95] To make their arguments, legal representatives were able over time to draw on previous or concurrent cases as precedents.[96]

In the process of litigating, indigenous deponents relied on legal discourse, documentation, and the cluster of legal advocates and their staff to launch a successful lawsuit. But they also depended on networks through which claimants and deponents and legal knowledge circulated and the social relationships, institutions, and practices that sustained such networks.[97] Communication circuits among slaves and freedmen proved to be a powerful dimension of litigation, before, during, and after the process. In the heart of the empire—Castile—slaves and freedmen actively engaged with colonial discourse about what it meant to be identified as indio. Indigenous litigants and witnesses communicated, especially in tightly knit locales such as the Spanish court or Seville where it was easy to transmit information verbally. Given the legal contingencies they faced and the need to disprove bondage, they also formed what James Sweet has called a "therapeutic community," whereby indios helped others heal from the ravages of bondage in the best way they knew how: by testifying in court.[98] Witnesses who deposed before notaries were legally savvy men and women who gleaned useful information from conversations with secular and ecclesiastical authorities and other indigenous slaves, then focused their efforts on procuring the freedom of other indios.[99] Although they numbered only in the dozens, these individuals were actively shaping, from the ground up, how indios could gain access to due process in Castile.[100] Nearly invisible in the historical record, these humble men and women were at the core of the indigenous struggle for justice.

The actual litigation process would begin when a slave litigant issued a *relación,* a statement that specified how and why the litigant had been mistreated and why he or she should be freed. The initial statement was recorded by a notary before an appropriate legal authority, which could be the portero of the Casa or the fiscal of the Council of the Indies. The solicitor chosen to represent the indio then framed the information with specific legal objections into a formal complaint, which was then recorded by a notary and filed before the court—which was, in reality, simply a room or series of rooms inside the Casa or Council of the Indies. In the Casa, a panel of three authorities reviewed the petition. At the Council of the Indies, a team of solicitors, judges, and attorneys reviewed the initial complaint to make certain there was just cause for the case to proceed. At that point, the plaintiff's lawyer ensured that the defendant was served with a summons stating that a lawsuit had been filed against him or her and was provided with a copy of the complaint. The complete court record consisted of the complaint, the rebuttal, the witness statements, the cross-complaints, and the final judgment. Witness statements and other materials could be collected without representatives of one side coming face to face with those of the other.

Once the plaintiff had presented a series of legal claims, the defendant (usually the slave owner) answered the charges, generally by denying each allegation. Next came the identification of the plaintiff to prove in instances of doubt that there was sufficient reason to believe that the litigant was an indio from the kingdoms of Spain. The plaintiff then produced witnesses and established the questions (which contained the answers) that would be asked in the interrogatories. Witnesses were to address each question in order. The defense could set up its own interrogatories with witnesses to counter what previous witnesses had said or to support the defendant's claim. Occasionally a *tacha,* or defamation of witnesses, occurred. Interspersed in this stage of the lawsuit were royal summons, called *emplazamientos,* issued to defendants or complainants, stating that they needed to appear (*comparecer*) before the judge of the Casa or of Council of the Indies courts within the prescribed time. The summons could also ask defendants to respond to the complaint or to present evidence if they had not initially done so within the *plaza,* or allotted time. Litigants and defendants also petitioned for additional time to gather witness testimonies from abroad (most often from Portugal, but occasionally from America) or to protest certain legal procedures. If mistreatment or abuse had occurred in cases where the owner prohibited the litigant from pursuing justice, the solicitor might ask the court for the litigant to be held in *depósito* (the legal placement of the litigant in the home of a trustworthy individual for protection) while the case was in motion.[101] This practice was most often deployed in instances where lashings and other threats had led to a forced confession that favored the slave owner.[102] Slave owners were required to pay the costs of the legal suit, unless the court ordered otherwise. They were also responsible for paying the depósito of the indio litigant while the case was pending. Verdicts would specify whether slave litigants were free, whether slave owners had to pay back salary and what amount, and whether owners would be absolved of court costs or fined for illegal branding. Generally, the judge absolved the court costs for slave owners who initiated appeals, unless flagrant abuse or misconduct toward the indigenous litigant had occurred.[103]

A slave owner or indio who lost the initial litigation suit could and did appeal the decision. A slave owner could also appeal the decision to render a salary to a former slave. Numerous cases ended abruptly, without witnesses ever being called.[104] Some cases were straightforward and quickly resolved; others dragged on for years, even decades. Still others remained inconclusive. Some lawsuits ended because of legal technicalities: the allotted time for a witness to appear might have expired, or crucial paperwork might have been lost or incomplete. In several instances where the evidence clearly favored the indigenous litigant, sentences of *not free* seemed to be based on immediate political contingencies rather than on faithful application of the law. There were also occasions where a case languished even after witnesses had been called; we can only speculate in those instances that the slave owners and indio litigants had reached some sort of agreement.

Ninety-five percent of indigenous litigants whose cases reached completion were freed. Such a fact is impressive, but is this statistic a false positive, forever effacing the dozens, if not hundreds of indios who never initiated a lawsuit? We will never know. But what we do know is that such a monumental change in status for litigants meant freedom of movement, protection of their children from a similar fate, and the independent ability to draw up legal documents such as wills or dowries. The majority of freed slaves remained in Castile with their families and friends, some of whom they called *primos*, or cousins, even if they were not related by blood. Freed indios testified on behalf of other indios whose stories of deracination might be different from theirs but whose experiences of humiliating bondage struck a resonant chord. Some remained in the homes of former masters, but with a change in status. One india proudly proclaimed that she now ate her bread like any free woman in the home of her mistress.[105] Others assiduously avoided revenge-seeking former masters. A few insisted on returning to their home-lands in Guatemala or Peru or Mexico.

Generally we have access to the circumscribed opening statement made by the indio complainant, but occasionally the judges called the plaintiff in for additional questioning. The opening statement generally shifted be-tween the first- and third-person voices of the plaintiff and lawyer. Catalina Nicolasa, for instance, began her swearing in by saying, "God help my body in this world and my soul in the next."[106] Much of the information recorded in that instance was formulaic and couched in legal tropes. The tales liti-gants relayed encapsulated their abduction from their places of origin and their subsequent migratory paths to Spain. Indigenous litigants speaking in Spanish began by recounting the initial deracination. Deponents then ex-plained their movements from one location to another with different own-ers or merchants, and ended their testimonials by detailing how they had come to serve their current masters.

In a seminal essay written in the 1980s, the anthropologist Clifford Geertz argued that it would be useful to see "laws" as a "complex of characteriza-tions" and a "distinctive manner of imagining the real."[107] In local contexts, complainants, defendants, and witnesses utilized the law to render the past into a palatable present. The testimonials established a spatial and temporal sense of the historical context of bondage, detailing movements away *from* places of origin after displacement had occurred. They relayed journeys through other landscapes, across seas and oceans, and eventually to Castile. They retraced movements through time and space, following the path-ways they had taken with masters to other loci in America before reach-ing Spain. Implied was an assumption that in the course of their journeys, litigants also moved along a continuum from free to enslaved. Having once been free persons in a given habitat (naturaleza), they had traveled down the slippery slope of identity loss and now hoped to regain their individuality through particular narrative strategies. The past became an essential part of the present, not a "weight" holding them back from progress toward lib-eration. It served as proof that they had been and still were *other* than how they had come to be seen: that they were free, by birth, by their naturaleza, by virtue of having been abducted illegally before the age of fourteen, or by being female (a law issued in 1534 prohibited the enslavement of women).

For these litigants, the past was a tool of self-affirmation.[108] The com-mon phrase "while being in my naturaleza" (*estando en mi naturaleza*) repre-sented for them a place of uninterrupted life that identified them according to a particular "*ness*." That identification, although it remained internalized, was no longer visible once the litigants had been uprooted. Thus, their goal was to restore their original status and to experience (return to) a vestige of what had at one time been their reality. The identification and intersection of immobility (before) and mobility (after) were key to the litigant's success in recuperating these "origins."

The magnitude of these cases and the impact they had on scores of indigenous lives in Castile and throughout America cannot be overestimated. Yet the depositions were textual and theatrical productions. Frequently, the suits were filled with invention, strategizing, deceit, and intrigue. The testimonies of litigants, slave owners, and their respective witnesses were informed and circumscribed by the advice of poorly paid solicitors, interpreters, self-interested lawyers, attentive friars, and corrupt or law-abiding magistrates. Notaries recorded the depositions with their own biases, and the procedure followed a particular and logical sequence.

Before, during, and after legal suits had begun, the litigants faced serious threats. Some were severely beaten, brutally branded, chained by the neck, or sexually violated. Several cases ended abruptly when the slaves vanished. We will never know what happened to them, or to the many slaves—perhaps even hundreds of them—who were furtively sold to evade the scrutiny of the authorities. They remain silenced because they never entered the historical record. By the 1540s, however, as the scales of justice began to tip in their favor, dozens of indigenous slaves, an ocean away from home and now serving cruel and demanding masters, were willing to take the risk. They entered the courtroom to question what for decades had been the natural order of things. Many could not have realized the geographic scope and scale of slaving practices until they were crammed body-to-body into ships or until they stepped onto the sandy shore of the Guadalquivir. Most, however, would realize at some point that large-scale human bondage was not confined to their village, region, or larger polity, but that it involved a vast expanse of the Indies. For some, Seville became a code word for "freedom" as they talked among themselves, and word spread from town to village that the courtroom was a place where they could speak.

It is just as important to pay attention to the contradictions, strategies, and meanings of slavery deliberated by slave owners and slaves, as Brian Owensby has argued in his work on colonial Mexico. As complainants and defendants relayed their perspectives on bondage, they used geographic and legal knowledge to invent, re-create, or purposefully recalibrate the histories of forced migration—sometimes decades after the deracination occurred. In mediated courtroom contexts, litigants traced circuitous pathways leading to

Spain from Santo Domingo, Nicaragua, Mexico, Peru, and elsewhere. Indio litigants strategically altered or emphasized geographic and cultural origins as they took part in the production of testimonials that were recorded and later read and commented on by magistrates, and they assisted in the production of documents, including evidence of sales, travel permits, copies of laws, and the recorded witnesses' testimonies.

The indigenous struggles for justice evolved and responded to contingencies and constraints, as different in the 1530s as they were in the 1540s and 1550s.[109] The historicity of the changing legal culture in Castile had a direct impact on how arguments about one's indio identity were calibrated. The legislative changes of the 1540s—particularly the New Laws, which were so hotly contested throughout Latin America—gave the larger philosophical discussions in the courts added weight. Courtroom debates revolved around the use or dismissal of legal terms such as *rescate* (ransom), *buena guerra* (just war), or *naturaleza* (emphasis on place of origin), and, after the 1550s, around whether indigenous litigants were Spanish or Portuguese imperial subjects. The "courtroom" was a locus of historical process, where the meanings of what it meant to *be* indio in sixteenth-century Castile were contested and discordant.[110] Even the manner by which laws were implemented was a product of social relations between slaves, slave owners, legal advocates, and judges over the decades encompassed by this study.

It would be hazardous to assume that these tales involved unscripted agency on the part of indio litigants. The narratives presented by litigants and defendants and their witnesses in a "legally comprehensible medium" were crucial to a favorable outcome for one side or the other.[111] The stories repeated to varying degrees by supportive witnesses had to have internal coherence, and the storytelling frame did not necessarily make sense outside the courtroom locus. A coherent plot might require certain outcomes due to unjust or illegal bondage or the misrepresentation of a place of origin, and some details were more important than others.[112] To quote Laura Gowing, "The story of the production of these texts is, at one level, the history of the struggle between 'answer,' in a legal sense that relies upon question and response quite different from ordinary speech, and 'story,' the model through which witnesses presented their testimonies."[113] But the stories of slavery were just as evident in formulaic bills of sale or the brands on some litigants' faces—each recalling historic moments of inscription that exhibited certain kinds of legal truths. The courtroom narratives of complainants and defendants constituted only one aspect of a larger legal web of constructed knowledge about what it meant to be an indio in sixteenth-century Castile.

On an even wider scale, these courtroom narratives illustrate how much the past was in the present: how America was present in Castile and Castile in America, or how the global economy was present in an encounter on the street or in a tavern. The narratives encapsulated other moments in space and time. Slave owners and indigenous litigants and their witnesses recalled the past and reformulated and recontextualized it in the present, bringing to bear a moment of deracination, the crossing of the sea, or a snippet of a conversation held long ago. Although this book focuses on indios who lived in Castile, it is just as much about indigenous peoples in Latin America. The litigation suits show how the historical production of the reconstituted past of indio slaves collapsed time and space before, during, and after the suits occurred. Indios in Castile were still deeply connected—metaphorically, legally, and culturally—to the plethora of ethnicities in Latin America. Although arguments were being made in a post-1542 legal context, and indios were reducing their pasts to a coherent narrative, it was nevertheless a knowable past that informed how the present (the litigation suit) would unfold. The cases reveal the juxtaposition of temporal-spatial narratives that tell us as much about slavery in Latin America as in Castile.

Who Is an Indio?

Much of what we know about how indios were perceived and how the category *indio* was constructed comes from studies of legal and labor systems, philosophical debates over their status as vassals, or considerations of political elites in Latin America.[114] If *indio* originally distinguished people of the Indies from Castilians, the term soon became a political and legal identifier reflecting the Crown's efforts to standardize contradictory laws that applied to the status of the indigenous peoples of the Americas. Instead of identifying a race, the historian Jovita Baber has argued, "the qualifier *indio* was used by the Castilian Crown to identify one of the *naciones* under its authority and to define the rights, protections and obligations possessed by that population."[115] Indios were equated with legal minors in need of protection, and as Brian Owensby argues, they "could be made to work—to ensure they were not idle and for the common good—but they could not be abused."[116] Indigenous peoples, whether elite or commoner, had their own usages of the term inside and outside the courts of Latin America.[117] The term could be qualified by indigenous people and Castillans with adjectives related to status (*calidad*)—such as in *indio noble* (noble Indian) or *indio bárbaro* (barbaric Indian)—as well as to ethnicity, such as in *indio chontal* (an ethnic group in Nicaragua). The historian José Carlos de la Puente and others have shown that native elites preferred not to be called indios, even if Spaniards identified them as such. For native lords who did not pay tribute and maintained indigenous subjects under their authority, _indio distinguished tributary subjects from themselves_.[118] But the elite indigenous leaders' lack of identification with the term has other roots. Even in the court cases taking place in Castile, some indio complainants preferred to identify with their places of origin, be it village, city, or broad territorial and political domain—just as men and women from Castile only rarely employed the self-identifying descriptor "Spaniard" in wills and other notarized documents.[119] In its deployment by indigenous people in the sixteenth century, the term _indio_ was not yet a referent that subsumed other forms of cultural and ethnic identity.

Equally important to a consideration of the multivalent meanings of _indio_ is that, before 1550, hundreds of thousands of indios in Latin America lived their lives in bondage. For many Castilians, indios were natural slaves. That status was still a matter not fully resolved by the Spanish Crown, despite laws that stated the contrary. Pre-1550 notarial records in Mexico City or Lima often distinguished an indio either as a slave (esclavo), as free (_libre_), as a perpetual free servant (naboría, _yanacona_), or as pertaining to an encomendero or a cacique (indigenous lord). Here we see a continuum of meanings related to the kind of labor indios provided as free or attached subjects. These distinguishing legal terms continued to be used well into the seventeenth century in areas of Latin America—Chile and Northern Mexico, for example—where the slavery of indios based on just war continued unabated.

Given the multiple ways in which the term _indio_ was used, I make an effort to argue against the sameness of those individuals called indios. To the contrary, by representing the complexities and panoramas of their lives, the construct _indio_ reveals the dimensionality of slavery itself as well as what being an indio could mean to Castilians and to indios and other slaves. I consider the complications of lives that were conditioned by but not reduced to the status of being slaves.[120] I also try to avoid a bifurcated paradigm of slaves versus masters, the latter of whom are depicted as cruel and power hungry. Instead, I seek to understand and contextualize the motivations and considerations of masters who would go to great lengths to maintain their property. Indio slaves in Castile were severely compromised individuals who had lost families and homes and cultures and who had to remake themselves in the households and shops where they labored and in the courts where they told their stories. They faced the dilemma of not only having to tell their stories, but also, as the epigraph by bell hooks suggests, having to listen to others talk about them better than they could talk about themselves. In the judicial chambers of the Casa or the Council of the Indies, they told their stories and heard others tell it back to them in new ways, framed by discourses that suited the various purposes of the slaves, witnesses, slave owners, and legal experts. These life-narratives fit within a legal template, but they also helped to shape that legal template.[121]

The legal and cultural production of indioness that took place in the judicial chambers of the Casa and Council of the Indies directly related to the social and political contexts of the broader sixteenth-century Castilian, Atlantic, and Pacific worlds and to the individual subjective experiences of Castilians and others who wished to objectify the indios of the Indies. That did not mean, however, that indio slave litigants were continually forced to refashion themselves, given the heavy constraints they faced in how others saw or wanted to see them. They were not "protean cultural artifacts."[122] They certainly articulated themselves as indios in Castile in different ways than they would have in America, but they still drew on those contextual experiences and reconstituted memories. As individuals and as a corporate group or nation, indios in Castile positioned and defined themselves as such based on repertoires of meaning and distinct patterns of struggle and engagement that changed radically between 1530 and 1585. Their articulation as indios was historically and legally situated.[123] Their efforts to seek justice helped to eradicate long-standing empire-wide practices of illegal enslavement.[124] Although in the litigation suits their talking-back voices—which "moved from silence into speech"—were filtered through others' pronouncements, they were still voices with important historical density. Theirs are not empty words.[125]

The Book's Architecture

In chapter 1, a case study of the village of Carmona, twenty miles northeast of Seville, I highlight this volume's many themes related to slavery and migration, the vicissitudes of legal culture, the politics of identification, the relevance of witnesses and kinship alliances, the construction of cultural geographies, and the entanglement of empires. Two litigation suits spanning fifteen years, from 1557 to 1572, and encompassing three generations (two women, their daughters, and their grandchildren) pitted the inhabitants of the village against each other, many of them slaves from India, Africa, and disparate parts of Latin America. Contrary to statistics that show that most slaves were freed, one of the slave litigants in Carmona lost her appeal. This is unusual, but the lengthy testimony given in both the original litigation suit and in the appeal provides a wealth of information about the intricacies of bondage and the power of perception as local and global interests interacted. These are relatively late cases, since most lawsuits took place in the 1530s and 1540s, but I consciously chose to place them at the beginning of the book for several reasons. At play are the relationships of power and class distinctions among the factionalized local elite and the polarized pecheros, or Spanish laborers, who worked side by side with the slaves. This microhistorical exploration of village and imperial politics is carried out against the backdrop of the shifting assessments of human bondage in an increasingly globalized economy. In chapter 1 I emphasize how some of the most peripheral individuals of empire—people in bondage—actively forged large-scale changes on a local level. I also argue that the label *indio* was given meaning in a relational, contextual manner, whether on the streets of the village, in the court, or in imperial legislation.

Following the broad overview of chapter 1, I move the reader to Latin America, in chapter 2, to detail the Atlantic crossing of indio slaves to Castile. Mobility and serial displacement were integral to the bondage of native people and directly correlated with Spanish military incursions into new territories. If the history of indios who crossed the ocean was one of stealth, promises, and forced mobility, it was also a bureaucratic one, involving papers, brands, and increasing scrutiny by Crown authorities. The vast ocean, hemmed by different continents, was a space that sectioned the lives of indio slaves into before-and-after segments related to freedom, capture, bondage—and freedom again. This oceanic mobility and the logic of documentation that accompanied this forced migration helped to disseminate the bureaucratic ideal of the indio slave.

Following this dramatic rupture in the fabric of their lives, indio slaves generally entered households. In the second part of chapter 2 I take the reader into the microcosm of the household, the slave's world once he or she arrived in Castile. I consider the labor expectations of masters, the relationships of indios with the extended families of their masters, and the fine line between intimacy and violence, and personhood and commodity. In chapter 2 I argue that the label *indio* acquired meaning in relation to masters with their own sets of expectations and vis-à-vis other members of the household—slaves and freedmen and women—and Castilian communities at large. In the dismantling of these fragile patriarchal ties we can begin to understand the circumstances that led indigenous slaves to formalize pent-up grievances against their masters.

In chapter 3 I follow indios as they moved from the household setting into the judicial chambers to petition for their freedom. I take the reader into the courtroom to detail the formation and implementation of a colonial bureaucracy and legal apparatus to deal with indigenous slavery in Castile. I explain the repercussions of two inspections that took place in Seville as the Crown sought to establish a legal apparatus for dismantling a well-entrenched system of indigenous slavery. A number of lawsuits attempted to challenge that system, undermining decades of assumptions that indios were natural slaves. In chapter 4 I consider the bureaucratic and legal culture of the "courtroom," including procedure, what constituted evidence (including branding), the authority of documents, and the power of expert witnesses, including indios, all of which resulted in the creation and maintenance of legal indios. Documents were active sites of power upheld by the law and governance of slavery. But these truth-objects were also given relational value by the ways in which slave owners and litigants interacted with or interpreted them. Slaves and masters objectified such documents as truth-telling evidence by registering them with their own grains of truth. Thus, documents were integral to a broader epistemology of bondage. In chapter 5 I analyze the legal vocabulary used to justify the continuation of indigenous slavery: the meaning of "natural" slavery, the practices of just war, ransom (rescate), and cannibalism. Slave owners in the courtroom read the past from the vantage point of five, ten, or even twenty years after the moment of capture. As producers of their own knowledge, indio slaves responded to charges made by their masters by expressing their understandings of these legal categories in relation to their own versions of the past.

The scope of the book then broadens out to consider imperial politics and how indios became transimperial subjects and border crossers. In chapter 6 I examine how an indio was discerned according to abstract physiognomic and imperial conventions of the time. In the quest to identify imperial (Spanish versus Portuguese) and geographical indio origins, witnesses and litigants navigated physiognomic identity markers and other criteria, including language, which ultimately helped determine whether indigenous litigants would become free vassals of the Spanish Crown. Identification was a subjective art that depended heavily on the cultural experiences and motives of witnesses, as well as on the presence in Castilian towns and villages of other slaves, including Brazilians, West Africans, and South and East Asians.

Throughout the sixteenth century, European incursions into new areas of the globe occurred at a rapid pace and the boundaries of territorial sovereignty were highly contested. For indio slaves affected by these invasions, mobility and dislocation often involved crossing from one imperial "realm" to another. In chapter 7 I analyze the entangled nature of slavery in three areas of conflict—the Moluccas, the confines of the Rio de la Plata–Brazil area, and Burma—where indios and Flemish, Norman, Portuguese, Castilian merchants were caught up in imperial disputes over the meanings of sovereignty. At the heart of these dilemmas were notions of cultural geography—the imagined meanings of land, boundaries, and space—that helped to determine the imperial status of indios in the courtroom and exposed the tenuous nature of colonialism more broadly. Above all, these debates reveal the expanding indioscape of the sixteenth century and just how broad conceptualizations of the term *indio* had become.

I have structured this volume according to both a chronological and thematic arc. Following chapter 1, the book's overture, I trace the pathways of slaves, from the ocean crossing into Castilian households and then into the locus of the Castilian courtroom. I consider slavery from their perspective, as much as is ever possible. In the judicial setting I analyze the logic and rationality of laws, the structure of lawsuits, and the weight given to documentation and terminology that influenced the making and unmaking of indio slaves. I then expand my focus outward to consider how the slave trades of the Mediterranean, Atlantic, and East Asia created indios via their physical identification and through imaginary notions of imperial identities. From there, I examine different imperial sites contested by the Portuguese and Spanish Crowns, sites where the empire to which particular slaves pertained was unclear. I conclude by showing how, by the end of the sixteenth century, the term *indio* had come to embody the cultural imaginary of the entire globe.

In *Global Indios* I address slavery, but I also examine what it meant to be indio in sixteenth-century Castile and beyond. A composite of dozens of individual stories provides a complex portrait of indios, indigenous slavery, and the connections the histories of indigenous peoples of Latin America had with the histories of indios from other parts of the globe.[126] The stories of the indios illuminate the inner workings of households, the differences between servant and slave in a particular context, why the slaving practices of "just war" were unjust, and what it meant to live in a village that was becoming increasingly globalized. While the act of enslavement and possession of another human being occurred in situ—in a remote port of Nicaragua, in a mountain town in the Andes—(such actions were connected to and had repercussions for slavery occurring simultaneously in other parts of the world.) The governance of bondage, its regulation, and the making of indio subjects in evidence in the courtrooms of Castile also influenced what would occur elsewhere and vice versa. The production of indigenous slavery and indios was both local and global in scale and scope. And it was just as much about others who had also experienced the traumas of bondage, deracination, and colonial rule as it was about those Castilians and other Europeans who hoped to prolong or eradicate such practices as they made sense of the changing world.

ONE

All the World in a Village
Carmona

+>——=+

I [Beatríz] am from Mexico City in New Spain and for more than twenty
years Juan Cansino, magistrate of the village of Carmona has held me
and my six children captive; he [even] sold one of them. Because he is
the magistrate and favored in the village of Carmona I have not been
able to attain justice, as I and my children are free in conformity with
the royal provision of His Majesty.

—"Demanda de Beatríz, india," 17/V/1558,

AGI, Justicia 908, n. 1, pieça 2, 3r

A sketch of Carmona from 1567 shows a fortified Castilian
town situated atop a lofty plateau, viewed at a distance from
the west. The work is by Anton van den Wyngaerde, then Europe's leading topographical artist. Above the walls at the town's
summit can be seen the Alcazar del Rey Don Pedro, which,
until the end of the fifteenth century, had served as a military
outpost, commanding a panoramic view in all directions. In
the valley below, fertile alluvial soil from the Guadalquivir and
Guadaira Rivers produced a rich agricultural and pastoral environment for wheat, olives, and livestock. Another river, the
Corbones (then called the Guadajoz), afforded an ample, clean
water supply for crops, animals, and humans. To the west lay
Seville, a half-day ride by cart (twenty miles); to the northeast
was Córdoba, famed for its leatherwork, pottery, textiles, and

an array of fruits and vegetables introduced by the Muslim rulers centuries before.[1]

A modestly populated town that inhabitants still referred to as a village, Carmona at that time was deeply affected by changing reconceptualizations of the broader world. From the late fifteenth century, with each passing decade, the mental lives of its inhabitants expanded to encompass the vast transformations of the times. Generally what comes to mind when considering the repercussions of global changes on village life are the push-pull factors of migration and their effects on family ties or gender relations, or the impacts on Spanish families and local economies of wealth amassed in America.[2] The meticulous work of Ida Altman has traced the deep-seated connections, the movements of goods and peoples, and the intergenerational transculturation of specific practices between villages and towns in Spain and America.[3] The historian Javier Pescador has asked how the enterprise of empire building changed the lives of the inhabitants of specific villages. Castilian communities, Pescador argues, were both "indispensible components of the colonial world" and sites of microhistories of Atlantic exchanges.[4]

While many studies focus on the globalized city of Seville, I draw on notarial sources and the litigation suits of two indigenous women, Beatríz and Felipa, and their respective daughters, Catalina and Barbola, to explore how the four parts of the world could inhabit Carmona.[5] The New Laws of 1542, which abolished indigenous slavery in most instances, and two inspections in 1543 and 1549, which freed over one hundred indio slaves in Seville, meant that slaves and the children of slaves would enter the courts to ensure freedom for themselves. But the lawsuits I discuss here, initiated in the late 1550s, are not straightforward cases related to legal freedom. Integral to both is how the histories of individual indigenous slaves could relate to the larger global palette of the times; both also illustrate how the contact that Spanish masters made with other land masses and peoples came to be reflected in the intimate relations that developed in the village of Carmona.[6] In this setting, assertions about the transimperial identities of the two litigants crossed imaginary and real geographic and cultural Spanish and Portuguese borders, revealing broader notions of an indioscape in the sixteenth century. In short, these cases illuminate how reckoning with global changes resonated with local responses.[7]

There is no need to look to America, Asia, or Africa to trace the interconnectivities of the Atlantic or global world; one can see these changes within Castile itself.[8] One can traverse the roads and fields and observe the world in the languages and physical features of local inhabitants, in the stories told in taverns, or in the goods travelers have brought back from distant lands. While much is known about Spanish emigrants and the ways in which their experiences, wealth, and knowledge transformed Iberia, next to nothing is known about how the slaves and servants who were brought to Spain transformed Castilian notions of the broader world. People held in bondage trickled into Castile decade after decade, reflecting the timeline of Iberian incursions into the Berber lands, the Malabar Coast, Brazil, West Africa, and Mexico. Although they are nearly absent in the historical record of Carmona, those who worked day by day in the fields and shops and stables, and those who passed the elite with heads bowed on the cobbled streets, transformed the real and imagined notions of other habitats and cultures. They entered the homes of the elite, becoming part of those households, as segregated but vital family members. Through their conspicuous presence and interactions with others, they globalized Carmona.

Some of these men and women were labeled *indios*. In Castile this signifier could refer to someone from the Portuguese domains of East or South Asia, or to the naturalezas (environments) of Spanish America. The term was also often associated with geographical fixity, since it was employed in the courtroom (often unsuccessfully) to indicate a type of nation of peoples. We usually think of the contested territories of empire—whether in Brazil, East Asia, or even in the borderlands between Extremadura (Spain) and the Algarve (Portugal)—as arenas of conflict far from the stable centers of empire. Yet a Castilian village might experience those same dynamics, as we can see in the court suits of Felipa and Beatríz. In the details and the twists and turns of these case studies, we can see how in the sixteenth century *indio* was a floating construct, as the term moved in its usage from the Americas or India to Spain, or from North Africa to the village of Carmona and back again.[9] We can see how the construct marked individuals with specific qualities, depending on the experiences, political alliances, and cultural imaginations of the litigants and witnesses doing the categorizing.

In Carmona a multitude of ideas about human distinctions resulting from the presence of indios and other slaves converged and were reconfigured. As local inhabitants, indios responded to daily contingencies such as droughts, the formation of new family alliances, and military incursions occurring elsewhere in Spain and Northern Africa. Moreover, as the original inhabitants of other locations now living as permanent, long-term residents in the village, they constituted themselves and were constituted in complex and sometimes contradictory ways. Their presence, rather than fostering more openness and a productive sense of belonging, cemented distinctions between the haves and the have-nots, and between Christian and non-Christian. Determining the kind of indio one was—and especially imperial status—was based on physical and other personal attributes and on the individuals with whom one associated.[10]

The World of Carmona

What was the social and cultural milieu of sixteenth-century Carmona? The village was considered a *realengo*, a territory directly subject to the king and queen of Castile, yet during the sixteenth century the Crown's holdings had been reduced as its lands were sold off to finance various military endeavors.[11] Much of its fertile soil pertained to absentee landowners, which included key ecclesiastical institutions in Seville. Carmona fell within the jurisdiction of the diocese and archbishopric of Seville.[12]

Throughout the sixteenth century, the village population grew slowly.[13] Out of a population of more than nine thousand inhabitants in 1587, a handful of families dominated the political and economic landscape. Renowned families such as the Baezas, Céspedes, Cansinos, de la Millas, Góngoras, Melgarejos, Ruedas, and Sotomayors owned large tracts of land in the vicinity, kept significant herds of cattle and sheep, and cultivated sizeable vineyards, orchards, and olive groves. Generation after generation, they monopolized the village administration, handing down the most important municipal offices of *jurado* (parish representative) and *regidor* (town council member) from father to son.[14]

While the town boasted a small but powerful aristocracy, the majority of its inhabitants were pecheros, workers who paid taxes to the Crown.[15] Some tilled a slender parcel of their own land for subsistence purposes or cultivated olives or grapes for local use. Despite the sometimes testy political relationship between Seville and Carmona, temporary salaried laborers (*jornaleros*) came and went between the two centers, except during times of famine or plague.[16] Following the rhythms of the agricultural seasons, from sunup to sundown jornaleros picked grapes, harvested wheat and other grains for local consumption, and assisted in the production of foodstuffs. They also raised silkworms and sold silk to merchants from nearby Córdoba, who, after negotiating a price for the valuable product, carried it away on mules.[17] The laborers slept in simple shacks in the fields, accumulating few possessions by the end of their lives.[18] Impoverished widows relied on their looms to make ends meet.[19]

Some of the humbler adolescent boys and girls of the village worked by contract (*soldadas*) as life-cycle servants called *mozos or mozas*. In exchange for room and board, a meager salary in cash or kind, and a change of clothes for each year of service, they performed sundry tasks until reaching adulthood. Occasional foreigners (*forasteros*), including some Portuguese, came to the village to seek apprenticeships, perhaps with a hatmaker, or to help tend olive trees.[20] Seville siphoned medium-term laborers from the village, who would then send their earnings back to their families.[21] Among the free population of Carmona, the poorest were called *los pobres de solemnidad* (literally, the poor of solemnity), who begged in church vestibules and during religious festivities. Following crop failures and other natural disasters, their numbers soared.[22]

Laborers came and went, creating in the village a sense of porous connectedness to other towns and cities scattered throughout Iberia. But Carmona also had its share of slaves who had been brought by force from their places of birth. Some were sold in Seville, others at the fair at Zafra, near the Portuguese border. Agents from Carmona would negotiate there with Portuguese middlemen who were selling men and women from such far-flung places as Cabo Verde, Senegambia, the interior of the slavery-designated territory called Guinea, Brazil, Mexico, Venezuela, Calicut, or Goa. Evidence suggests that Portuguese merchants also brought human merchandise directly to Carmona to sell.

Mobility was thus a fixture of village life, whether it involved young laborers searching for a trade or slaves imported from distant locations to tend to the horses and polish the cutlery of Carmona's elite. Castilians traveled regularly throughout Andalucía and Iberia, plying their wares, evading the law, or looking for work. For military, economic, and cultural reasons, they were also drawn toward the northern coast of Africa and to other shores of the Mediterranean. Men from families with a long tradition of military service to the kings and queens of Castile risked their lives to occupy key cities, like Oran, in Algeria, or conducted trade to counteract what they perceived to be the growing influence of the Ottoman empire in the region. As many knew well, the equilibrium in the Mediterranean area was fragile; military outposts were always tentative, unstable, and subject to attack or capitulation. Interviews with soldiers posted in Oran at that time revealed their trepidation of the "Turks."[23] The coastal cities of North Africa were also ports of entry for the *cabalgadas* (raids on horseback) that some Carmonenses conducted into the interior, to capture "Berber" slaves for sale in Castile or in their own village.[24] In 1549 Captain Sancho Caro, from one of the oldest, most prestigious families of Carmona, commanded three hundred archers and harquebusiers from the province of Seville, leading them on a mission to capture slaves near Oran. He enlisted a number of men from Carmona, including Juan de la Milla, an owner of indio slaves.[25] For his military services, Caro was named a councilor of Carmona, in 1549. Another Carmonense, closely related to Caro, was Captain Luis de Rueda (a street in Carmona still bears his name), who spent several years in Oran. His 1555 will gave to his son, Rodrigo de Rueda, land he had received from the prince of Oran as a grant (*merced*) in Mers-el-Kabir.[26] The physical presence of Carmonenses in northern Africa and their sense of knowledge and entitlement in controlling some of these areas contributed to notions circulating in Carmona about empire, belonging, and possession.

If connections to places throughout Iberia and Northern Africa were strong, Carmona's residents also felt the lure of America.[27] The bricklayer Alfonso Rodríguez, who accompanied Columbus on his third voyage, in 1498, was the town's first recorded emigrant to what was then called the Indies. Catalina Sánchez was the first woman to leave Carmona for America, in 1512. Nine members of the village, including an entire family, left in 1514, some bound for Cuba, others for Santo Domingo. Year after year, the outward trickle continued, and many emigrants never returned.[28] In 1529 Pedro Martín de Villareal left for "Peru," returning to Carmona several years later, but he then returned, this time to Chile. Luis de Céspedes—whose father, Alonso de Céspedes, was the alcalde of the fortresses of Carmona—sold his wife's dowry, his home, a mill for making olive oil, two slaves, and other possessions before departing, leaving his wife destitute.[29] In 1534 Andrés Bernal traveled with "the Germans" (the Federmans and Welsers) to Venezuela. The following year Cristóbal de Quesada, a painter, and his wife, Mariana de Robles, accompanied the viceroy of Mexico to his new post; in 1539 Quesada received the approval of the viceroy to go to Cíbola to "paint the things of the land."[30] In 1536 Diego de Torres left for the New Kingdom of Granada, and two years later participated in the conquest of Tunja, where he became an encomendero. He later returned to Carmona a widower, fetched his three children, and returned to Tunja. Pedro Maestre, a surgeon, left for Cuba in 1537. Alonso de Carmona went to the newly founded city of Arequipa in 1539, and Alonso de Vilches traveled to the Rio de la Plata in 1540. María de la Cueva went to Santo Domingo in 1558 as a *criada* in service to Licenciate Echagoya. In 1559 Juan de Marchena went to Tierra Firme to work as a business agent for Francisco Núñez. We can also trace transatlantic links in the ransoming of captives, in the donations for chaplaincies and masses, and even in the financing of an embroidered cape for the Virgin de Gracía.[31]

Because of these outward migrations, bits of information about new people and places trickled into the homes of the wealthy. Some sent news or the rare and precious letter with returnees.[32] If we imagine the dinner conversation of an elite Carmona family with a son or daughter just returned from another part of the world, it might range from the local weather to productive harvests to goings on in Seville, then drift farther afield to news of goods acquired at the fair of Zafra or to the east in Granada. It might dwell on military activities in Oran, then cross the Atlantic to the islands and continents of America. Such a conversation—where the mind's eye could scan the globe—would have much to say about how elite Carmonenses saw the world in the sixteenth century. There were new ways of linking heretofore unforeseen islands and continents. The surrounding décor, too, the blue-and-white porcelain from China that graced the cupboards and tables, the garments made from Rouen cloth using Brazilian dyes or silk from Carmona and India, the exotic seasonings in the food they ate—such objects would have also influenced their perceptions. The Rueda family most certainly would have talked about the land they held in Oran, and the parents of Alonso de Vilches would have wondered what life was like in Rio de la Plata for their emigrant son.

In the shadows of these exchanges would stand the servants, waiting to fetch a plate or serve the soup. Some would have known in their bones about the places being discussed.

Within the context of intimate congress and the sharing of knowledge about an expanding globe, life radically changed for indio slaves living in Carmona. They, too, experienced the contours of empire in new ways. Following the passage of the New Laws in 1542, some indios were automatically freed, although a few had to initiate lawsuits against their masters to gain their freedom. Anyone labeled as an indio from the Portuguese domains was not freed, however, since indigenous slavery continued unabated in those imperial territories. Until that historic moment, indios of the village might have been known as "la Mexicana" or as the slave of so-and-so. But when they entered the courtroom as litigants or witnesses, their identities as indios from the Spanish-dominated naturalezas became essential to their freedom or to the freedom of others. Male and female litigants who were labeled *indios* wanted to be seen as having a fixed identity as Spanish imperial subjects and as having originated from a place where slavery was not a given. They did not want to be seen as transimperial subjects moving from one imperial domain to another—although many in fact were.

Beatríz and Felipa did not join the first flurry of litigants, who rushed to the courts following the implementation of the New Laws. Both women (or their daughters) waited until 1558 and 1559 to gather the necessary paperwork and witness testimony. By then, they were seen as local inhabitants of Carmona, having lived there for decades. But they were still mentally engaged with other parts of the world that could prove that they were who they claimed to be: indias from the Spanish domains. Their masters and witnesses for the defense engaged with their own experiences and understandings of other parts of the world to prove otherwise.

Beatríz and Catalina

Two separate lawsuits and appeals spanning sixteen years (1558 to 1574) illustrate how the world could be in a village. The first suit, initiated in May 1558, pitted the india Beatríz (b. 1496?-d. 1571), her daughter Catalina, and one grandchild against their master, Juan Cansino, the current magistrate (regidor) of the village. Although the Cansinos had roots in Aragón, they claimed to have ties to Carmona dating to the *reconquista* of the village, in 1247. Juan's marriage to María Gómez de Castroverde further strengthened his economic and social ties to Carmona's oligarchy.[33] In fact, Cansino's position of political and cultural authority in the village may help to explain why Beatríz waited until 1558—sixteen years after the passage of the New Laws—to initiate a demand for her freedom before the Casa. Now in her fifties, she argued before the tribunal of Seville that she was from Mexico City and that for over twenty years—since 1538—Juan Cansino had held her against her will.[34]

Like a number of other indigenous slaves, Beatríz had been transported illegally to Lisbon around 1530 by a Portuguese ship captain named Antonio Correa, who sold her there. She lived in that city for many years, learning to speak Portuguese and giving birth to a son by an unidentified father. It was said that the "son of a 'Moor' "had had his way with her" when she went to fetch water from the public fountain.[35] Beatríz claimed that at some point she was purchased by a Spanish merchant visiting Lisbon. She then traveled by cart across southern Portugal, through Extremadura, and eventually joined the Cansino household. For two decades, she lived and labored in Carmona, but she also spent some time in Triana, a neighborhood of Seville, where she established a relationship with an indigenous man and developed friendships with other indias. She had five more children in Carmona, although the father (or fathers) was never mentioned in the court documents.[36] Beatríz's legal representative requested the stiffest penalties and justice for her and her children on the grounds that Cansino had branded Catalina, then eighteen years old, had sold Beatríz's son Simón, and had treated her like a captive for too long.

Cansino countered by stating emphatically that Beatríz was the daughter of an Arab Moor (*arabe, hija de moro*) and had been raised in Portugal until a merchant delivered her to his father-in-law in Carmona, in 1530.[37] Cansino's wife had received Beatríz as a part of her dowry and when she died, Cansino inherited Beatríz. According to the defendant, Beatríz talked consistently about being Portuguese; she was familiar with Portuguese foods and spices. Only recently, after receiving bad advice from other indios in the village, had she changed her story.[38] Cansino relied on the arguments used by other slave-master plaintiffs: he had owned her for so long that she could not possibly be freed, and even if she were from Mexico, his possession of her preceded the passage of royal decrees freeing indios from that domain. To the question of why he had branded Catalina, Beatríz's daughter, he replied that she had run away from him many times and had stolen a bag of money, a chain bathed in silver, other jewels, wheat, cheese, wine, and wool.[39] He said he had sold Simón because he stole a lot and was mischievous.[40]

In July 1559 the Casa determined that Beatríz and, by extension, Catalina would remain slaves. No one questioned Cansino's illegal branding. No authority ordered a search for Simón. No one mentioned Catalina's other siblings, who also lived in the village. Some said that the verdict broke Beatríz's spirit. She turned to drink, but still survived to the age of seventy-five. Catalina waited until after Beatríz had died, in 1571, to appeal the case before the Casa. She hoped to prove that her mother was a simpleton who had been coerced into saying things she did not mean. But once again, in November 1572, the Casa ruled against her. However, two years later, the Council of the Indies reviewed the evidence and reversed the decision, freeing Beatríz posthumously and allowing Catalina, her brothers, and her children to live lives free from bondage.

Felipa and Barbola

The second case also involved three generations: Felipa, her daughter Barbola, and Barbola's children. In 1559, following her mother's death, Barbola petitioned for her freedom against Silvestre de Monsalve, who had also owned Felipa. In this case, it was the daughter who would tell her mother's story. By most accounts, Felipa had arrived in Carmona thirty years before, in 1529, after Monsalve purchased her for 10,000 maravedís at the fair in Zafra.[41] Ten years later, Barbola was born, and within two years of her birth, Monsalve sold Felipa to one of his relatives, Pedro de Rueda, a village friar. But Barbola remained in Monsalve's possession, separated from her mother, and in time had two children of her own. One villager claimed that Catalina de Marmolejo, Monsalve's wife, had offered Barbola her freedom in exchange for leaving one of her children with her, presumably as a slave.[42] Both plaintiff and defendant agreed that Felipa was an india; however, Barbola claimed that her deceased mother was from Mexico, while Monsalve argued that she was from Calicut (now Kozhikode, located on what is today called the Malabar Coast of India). Once the depositions had been recorded, in March 1561, Monsalve issued a series of tachas, or defamations, against Barbola's witnesses, most of them slaves, servants, or humble artisans or laborers. A decision was rendered against Barbola on 23 February 1562, and she immediately appealed the decision before the Council of the Indies. Despite the strong evidence in her favor, the council ruled, in May 1564, that she and her two daughters were to remain enslaved.[43]

The Social Milieu of Felipa and Beatríz

It is likely that Felipa and Beatríz ran in the same social circles in the village, a world divided into the haves and the have-nots.[44] Presumably they knew one another, since by some accounts they arrived in the village within a year of each other. They may have conversed in Portuguese, a language both had learned to survive in Lisbon, or in Nahuatl, if they actually were from Mexico, as they claimed. Yet, although Beatríz initiated her lawsuit in 1558 and Felipa's daughter Barbola did so in 1559, neither party mentioned the other. Nor did any of their indigenous, African, or morisco witnesses overlap. Both litigants relied mainly on the laborers and slaves of the village and, in Beatríz's case, from nearby Seville for support.[45] Only rarely did a priest or someone of social standing in the village pledge to speak on their behalf.

That so many witnesses were willing to face repercussions from the Monsalve and Cansino families, who could bring ruin on the powerless with a single order, is somewhat astonishing. It was said that both Silvestre de Monsalve and Juan Cansino kept lists of the witnesses and used intimidation tactics to dissuade them. That may explain why Beatríz relied on the small indio networks in Seville, where several of her indigenous friends, freed in Carmona after the 1543 inspection, had moved to seek work; there, they would have been better able to avoid the long reach of Cansino's power. On the other hand, Barbola, Felipa's daughter, relied on a support network of slaves or former slaves in the village, who bore the surnames of their powerful masters: Céspedes, de la Milla, Quintanilla, Sanabria, and so on. Some of these individuals, although now free, still relied on the patronage of their former masters to help them gain additional status, security, and even freedom in the village. Although the repercussions these people may have faced were never directly mentioned in the lawsuit, they may have risked a loss of employment or faced other sobering repercussions for speaking on Barbola's behalf.

In the summer of 1530, the year of Felipa's arrival in the village, there was a drought, and the cattle were led to the mountains, where it was cooler, to avoid dying of thirst.[46] Plans were under way to establish a *pósito* (storage deposit) of wheat, whereby the largest landowners would set aside a portion of the cereal crops to prevent starvation in times of scarcity and need.[47] Felipa and Beatríz did not mention these circumstances in the lawsuit; their primary concern was to assimilate and insinuate themselves into daily life without attracting undue attention. By then, over two dozen indios were living in Carmona, including some from Mexico who served the prominent de la Milla family.[48] As the village became increasingly globalized, Felipa and Beatríz would have developed friendships with poor Castilians—butchers, jewelers, and bricklayers—and with the slaves and servants from South Asia, North Africa, and sundry places in Spanish and Portuguese America whom they met on daily rounds to fetch food, supplies, and news for their households. Spatial proximity in the walled town and on the winding streets led to frequent exchanges with men and women of African heritage, with Castilians (called moriscos), and with people described variously in bills of sale, dowries, and wills as of the colors white, black, *loro*, and *mulato*.[49] Felipa and Beatríz knew who worked for whom and that four or five slaves in an elite household had formed their own inner circle.[50] Felipa and Beatríz also knew other slaves who, like themselves, had remained with a family for decades, passed from father to daughter in wills or dowries.[51] The two women had felt the sadness of losing a child to a new owner, though they continued to have access to some of their children and grandchildren. They understood the historical configurations of slavery in the village, evident in the earlier generations of morisco slaves who had come from Málaga after its capitulation to the Christian forces of Ferdinand and Isabel in 1487.[52] In the 1520s there were those could still remember when Hamet el Zegri, the chief justice of Málaga and a member of the Granadan Muslim nobility, arrived in chains in Carmona, where he spent the rest of his life imprisoned. Whether any of the thousands of slaves from the Canary Islands came to Carmona in the late fifteenth century is not known, but the number of slaves from West Africa increased in the village over the decades, as it did in other Andalusian villages and towns.

An important aspect of local governance was to demarcate and differentiate who was whom based on both older and emerging criteria. As more indios arrived in Carmona, some of the more powerful villagers gained a comparative and intimate knowledge of distinct peoples whom they could categorize or name and thus control. Just as the catch-all term *morisco* could mask generational or cultural differences, or efface distinct places of origin, whether Málaga, Oran, or Granada, the construct *indio* used to identify Beatríz and Felipa also collapsed and homogenized ethnic, generational, and geographic differences. Such an overarching rubric might then require, under certain circumstances, the use of other forms of perception to distinguish among the different indios. Perceiving who was an indio and who was not was based on the particular demographic configuration of Carmona, where everyone would have had ample opportunity to observe and distinguish among indigenous men and women from both the Spanish and the Portuguese domains, then derive conclusions, such as that of the *moreno* (brown) villager Melchior, who determined that because Felipa was whiter and better formed, she must come from Mexico.[53] Such comparisons were based on notions of physiognomy or physical characteristics that supposedly distinguished a person native to one habitat (naturaleza) from a person native to another.

Just as the perception of physical qualities might distinguish an indio from a morisco, other criteria also helped to demarcate identities. Language was among them, but it could also complicate the process. Having lived in Lisbon for several years, for example, Beatríz could speak in Portuguese to the other indios from Calicut who were also present in Carmona. But speaking Portuguese was not unique to slaves in the village: other Carmonenses, like the tailor Juan Muñoz, had picked up the language from having traveled to Lisbon and Evora and throughout Castile, and from having met many indios from the Portuguese domains and Mexico.[54] Prior to the 1540s, Carmonenses had had no need to draw sharp contrasts between imperial domains, because it had not been unusual for the Portuguese and Spanish languages or inter-imperial experiences in other locations to intermingle in village life. Such was the nature of local life in Castile.

But ways of perceiving and differentiating among indios in Carmona shifted after the passage of the New Laws in 1542 and the inspection conducted by

Gregorio López in 1543, which freed over one hundred indio slaves. In Carmona this meant freedom for several indias, a few of whom moved to Seville to find work. It also meant creating new ways of differentiating among those who were free by their nature and those who were not, and among who was Portuguese and who was Spanish.

The implementation of the New Laws affected Felipa and Beatríz, but not in the way one might expect. Because their two lawsuits were initiated sixteen and seventeen years after the New Laws came into effect, witnesses were at pains to answer why neither woman had presented herself for inspection before López in Seville in 1543. In the appeal on behalf of Beatríz, in 1572, her daughter Catalina's lawyer formulated a question for witnesses, asking "whether many people blamed [the free] Beatríz, india, from New Spain and her children because she did not go to the House of Trade in Seville to petition for her freedom," pointing out that "Beatríz had said she did not want to [go there] because she was content and did not want to ask for her freedom, so her master would not mistreat and punish her."[55] Depositions on behalf of the complainants in both lawsuits pointed to their fear of retribution and to the fact that they had thought they were already free.[56] Leonor Gómez, a sixty-year-old freed black, claimed that on many occasions Felipa had confided to her, "Here where you see me I am free because I am from the land of Mexico, and in time you will see that I and my daughters will be free."[57]

The question of why the women had taken so long to petition for their freedom was an important one, which neither Barbola nor Catalina nor their witnesses could definitively answer. No doubt the threat of punitive actions deterred slaves from pressing for their freedom. Yet fear was only one factor. Felipa's and Beatríz's statements, reconstituted by witnesses, expressed a mix of contentment with their condition of servitude, fear of their masters, and pride in their free status. It raises questions as to whether the 95 percent success rate for indio litigants whose cases reached completion might amount to a "false positive," given the dozens, if not hundreds, of slaves who, for one reason or another, never initiated lawsuits. Moreover, many slaves assumed they were free, until a master tried to sell them or their children. This was particularly true for women. The tipping point for Beatríz may have come when Cansino tried to sell her son Simón and branded her daughter Catalina. Felipa, on the other hand, died without ever having petitioned for her freedom, so it is hard to determine why she remained so passive—unless, of course, she really was from Portuguese territories. We cannot know the true motivations behind the women's reticence, but only how they were labeled by others in the post-1542 context. They were indios, but now free or enslaved ones from either the Spanish or Portuguese imperial domain.

Because imperial status now determined whether indios were slaves or free by their nature the indios of Carmona and elsewhere in Castile were being defined in a newly bifurcated manner. They were now identified according to imperial standards; their histories of bondage and displacement from "Portuguese" or "Spanish" geographic sites became central to the arguments made about them in the courtroom. Anyone proximate to Seville who had not been presented by slave owners for inspection before López was thus assumed to be a Portuguese slave—or someone who had been captured and enslaved in Portuguese imperial domains. This reformulation of identity had deep impacts on village life, which is why it seemed obvious to Cansino and Silvestre that neither woman had any reason to seek justice.

Felipa's Trial(s)

Calibrating a slave's identity in a legal context involved bringing to bear perceptions based on historical and local knowledge, experience, or even fantasy. Because imperial status and place of origin were determinants of free or enslaved status, and because Felipa was being accused by her master, Monsalve, of being from the Portuguese domains some thirty years after she had arrived in Carmona, it was incumbent on Felipa's daughter, Barbola, to prove otherwise. To counter the argument that Felipa was a Portuguese india from Calicut, Barbola called on several witnesses whom she thought could help. The Mexican india Leonor de la Milla, who considered herself a *vecina* (permanent resident, citizen) of Carmona, had arrived in the village from Mexico in 1526, the same year that King Charles V and his bride, Isabel of Portugal, lodged briefly in the village, following their marriage ceremony at the Alcázar of Seville.[58] Although Leonor and her children had been freed after the inspection of indios in Seville by Gregorio López in 1543, she had once been the slave of Cristóbal de la Milla, a member of the prestigious Carmona family, with extensive sheep and cattle and land holdings.[59] But Leonor either had a good memory or was a good liar. She recalled that when she arrived in the village, she and Felipa exchanged questions that slaves often asked each other when they first met, including "Where are you from?" Felipa had answered, "Mexico City." The friendship between the two women had endured for many years; during Barbola's birth, Leonor had been at Felipa's side, but they had lost track of one another when Felipa went to work for the cleric Rueda. Years later Leonor had learned second-hand that

Felipa had died.[60] According to one slave's testimony, Felipa had also been friends with an india named Inés, whom she had called cousin (prima), and who had also served Cristóbal de la Milla.[61]

Since judges relied on evidence from depositions to prove intimate (and reliable) interactions based on imperial affiliations, it was crucial for Barbola to demonstrate a clear friendship with the Mexican Leonor as evidence of camaraderie with "like" indios. It was sometimes the only evidence judges had to rely on to prove the place of origin of a slave litigant. Carmonenses who deposed would have had snapshot memories of incidental exchanges among indios—from a glance over the shoulder while buying a piece of mutton for soup, from overhearing snippets of a conversation while sweeping the dust away from the entryway—which would now fit into a broader logic about being from Mexico, or not. The association of indios fraternizing with other indios from the same imperial domain was certainly emphasized in the interrogatory on Barbola's behalf.[62] Catalina de Vilches, identified as being the color lora, born in Carmona, and currently the slave of the local jeweler María Hernández, was only twenty-two, too young to know much about Felipa. But her deceased mother, Gracia, whom Catalina claimed was an india from Mexico (although others countered by saying that anyone could tell she was a black morisca from the land of the Berbers), knew a great deal about Felipa.[63] Catalina remembered the two speaking together "the language of indios," and she had learned from her mother that Felipa had given birth to Barbola.[64] The friendship continued into the next generation; Catalina had been at Barbola's side both times Barbola had delivered a child.[65] But the court suspected that Catalina had transformed her own mother from a morisca slave into an india to help her friend's cause, which resulted in the elimination of her testimony as biased and unreliable. In light of the New Laws and accusations that Felipa was, specifically, a Portuguese india, Catalina de Vilches understood the ramifications of being a Mexican india and had risked adjusting her mother's identity accordingly.

Other witnesses from the village, many with histories of bondage and perhaps a rooted knowledge of other parts of the globe, recalled interactions among villagers that had occurred some twenty to thirty years earlier.[66] Some stressed that Felipa and Leonor were good friends, maybe even cousins; others emphasized that Felipa was commonly referred to as "la Mexicana," that she looked india, and that she spoke in indio with others. Such detailed observations about "la Mexicana" and her deep ties with the freed woman Leonor de la Milla certainly would have helped convince the judges of Felipa's imperial affinity were it not for additional evidence that surfaced for the defendant. Witnesses on behalf of Silvestre de Monsalve (and his son Luis, who was also involved in the lawsuit before and after his father died, in 1562) stressed the imperial ties of camaraderie between Felipa and a small group of slaves, who were named Juan, Lisuarte, Antonio, and Andrés, all originally from Calicut. In his deposition, Juan identified himself as a forty-five-year-old indio slave of Leonis Méndez de Sotomayor, the current judge of the village, and the nephew of Catalina Marmolejo, Monsalve's wife. Juan's association since adolescence with such a prestigious family—decorated by Isabel and Ferdinand for previous military contributions—would have certainly enhanced his status vis-à-vis the other slaves and servants of the village.[67] Even more vital for the case was his assertion that he had had a close association with Felipa for thirty years. Born in 1516, Juan had survived the sea journey from Calicut, an entrepôt where Portuguese merchants, far from the dominant presence there, haggled with local brokers who sold them goods from afar, including slaves.[68]

Juan mentioned none of this. Instead, to demonstrate a clear, intimate connection with Felipa, he said that he considered himself to be Felipa's relative (*pariente*) because "they were from one land [with] one language, and [when] they spoke they talked about the things of their land in their language of the same land."[69] Here was a strong antidote to the thesis that Felipa was called "Mexicana," spoke in the same language with her Mexican friend Leonor de la Milla, and had communed with other indios from her land in New Spain. Another distinctly shaped global knowledge, this time from Calicut, was being used to calculate Felipa's true identity.

Camaraderie could also extend to knowledge of that person in their shared place of origin. The second witness, Lisuarte, another indio from Calicut, was older than Juan. Born in 1506, he would have been aware of the range of multifaith inhabitants who plied their trades in Calicut. He would have also known that the Portuguese conqueror Alfonso de Albuquerque had increased Portuguese contacts with the Hindu Chettis and Muslim foreigners once he decided to promote Calicut as a spice trade center. Even more interesting than the testimony of the first witness was Lisuarte's brief statement that he had known Felipa in Calicut. He offered no specifics, nor did he explain how or why he had been enslaved.[70] Nor did he mention whether he had spent time in Lisbon or how he had reached Carmona. Like Juan, Lisuarte served another member of the local oligarchy, Juan Jiménez de Góngora Céspedes, also the nephew of Catalina Marmolejo.

All in all, this small cohort of male slaves from Calicut claimed that they had seen Felipa in Calicut, that they and she were from the same land or nation (nación), and that in the village they had regularly fraternized and conversed in their native language with her. They referred to Felipa as prima.[71] Others, including prominent Spaniards, the slave of a mistress related to the Monsalve family, and Felipa's former master, the cleric Pedro de Rueda, corroborated what the slaves from Calicut had said.[72] Such evidence would have made it difficult for Barbola to contest the accusation that her mother was a "Portuguese" india. An individual's connections to another foreign culture (Mexico versus Calicut) were being read in new ways in the intimate exchanges that took place in Carmona. In the entangled arena where the global met the local, a broader indioscape was being imagined, and witnesses re-created Felipa's identity in believable ways.

All these assertions were deeply problematic for Barbola. Undoubtedly, Felipa had interacted with the men, and they may have conversed in rudimentary Portuguese. Such cross-cultural interactions among slaves from different diasporic sites were common and perhaps even strategic, but that did not make Felipa a "Portuguese" slave. Under "normal" circumstances, being seen with someone from a different part of the world was neither problematic nor extraordinary. It was only in the context of the changing laws related to indigenous slavery and the nature of the accusations in the courtroom context that such innocent quotidian interactions took on a different cast.

It is impossible, however, to separate imperial politics from local ones. Behind the imperial associations were close family ties and the influence of a wealthy man—Monsalve—on the humbler and perhaps more vulnerable members of the community. The slaves from Calicut who called Felipa prima and swore that she spoke their language were slaves of Monsalve's relatives or of his wife.[73] As it turned out, *all* of Monsalve's witnesses either were relatives, "interested parties," neighbors, or intimate friends, or they rented property from, owed money to, worked as servants for, or lived in the home of Monsalve. Given his power and connections, it was not difficult for Monsalve to construct the story that Felipa was from Calicut, not from Mexico. In the end, despite the contradictory testimonies showing that Felipa had had contact with both indias from Mexico and indios from Calicut, and the fact that those who deposed on behalf of Monsalve were biased, Barbola's appeal was denied in 1564. Barbola and her children were condemned by the court to perpetual bondage with no further legal recourse.

Underlying this legal theater was a heavy-handed assumption: that "like" indios would fraternize with "like" indios. In the courtroom context, cultural boundaries denoting who was Portuguese and who was Spanish were clearly demarcated, at least in the abstract. It was assumed that individuals like Felipa would naturally gravitate toward "their own," since they were "one people." Indeed, over the decades, a common language and shared memories of a landscape growing increasingly dim would likely have created bonds among men and women of the same geographic origin, many of whom had come to Carmona as children or early adolescents. Yet bonds based on naturaleza, however fragile or illusory, did not preclude indios of Mexico from associating with indios from Calicut. As the historian David Vassberg has remarked, cohesiveness, solidarity, and ties developed in a pueblo (village) by the *pueblo* (people, inhabitants) could easily have transcended kinship ties. Everyone knew everyone else and shared in their misfortunes and pleasures.[74] It was only in the premeditated warp and weft of the courtroom depositions that rigid demarcations were highlighted or exaggerated.

When separated from the legal dramas and framed responses, the testimonies reveal layered quotidian encounters between men and women from West and North Africa, South Asia, and disparate parts of Spanish America and Castile itself. They reveal what the historian Emma Rothschild has called the "inner life of empires." Carmona was a nucleus where a cacophony of voices with distinct imperial histories and experiences of early colonialism could speak on behalf of or against a beleaguered woman who had spent thirty years walking the same streets. The village walls contained individuals with ties to bondage, including mothers and grandmothers who had left their homes in chains. It was a village where power and authority was vested in military performance in Granada or North Africa or America, and where those families who held political office and carried the history of the reconquista of Carmona in their veins could influence the fate of the slaves and servants who worked for them.

In Carmona the label *indio* took on a particular cast because of social interactions but also because of different perceptions about places of origin and culture. When the moment came to inscribe testimonies into the archival record, these constructs of indio became a site of contestation. This is evident when the deponent Leonor de la Milla, who was crucial to Felipa's identification, did not identify herself as an india but instead used the term *vecina*, indicating her rootedness in village life. Many other witnesses, however, were willing to identify Leonor as a Mexican india. At issue here is not who was whom, but that the label *indio* had such a powerful resonance in the context of Carmona, because people from vastly different domains fit the criteria, depending on how those with vested interests wanted to characterize them. As was evident in Catalina's appeal on behalf of her now deceased mother, relations of class, status, and lineage, in addition to geopolitics, could also play a large part in the process of determining what *kind* of india one's mother was.

Catalina's Appeal

Beatríz's daughter Catalina must have shuddered when she heard that the Council of the Indies had denied Barbola's lawsuit on behalf of her mother. Like Felipa, Beatríz had suffered a resounding defeat against the powerful oligarchy when she lost her initial lawsuit before the Casa, in 1559. As Catalina well knew, slaves generally had to rely on the good graces of their masters, who on their deathbeds could free them, and even then there were sometimes caveats. After Juan Cansino branded her, Catalina stood little chance of receiving sympathy from him or, when he died, from his son, who would become her new master.

Knowing how slaves often fared in the village, Catalina must have thought it would be best to endure her bondage silently. To run away with two small children in tow would be impossible. A slave named Diego, nineteen years old and white (a color often used to describe Castilian morisco slaves or those imported from northern Africa), had recently traveled from Cáceres to Carmona, a distance of nearly two hundred miles, but the name of his master on his cheek gave him away.[75] The unsightly brand on Catalina's cheek would immediately be read as a sign of her unfree status. So she waited, biding her time until conditions were more favorable.

Sometime in 1571, Beatríz died. At the same time as Catalina was considering appealing the court decision before the House of Trade, hundreds of morisco slaves began filtering into the village, the latest influx of slaves to populate the village with distinct histories and cultures. How would Catalina, now grieving both the loss of her mother and her own disfigured face, have reacted to the arrival of the morisca, Beatríz Pérez and her five children in the Cansino household?[76] According to some in the village, Catalina was herself a morisca, whose grandfather was an Arab Moor. They scoffed at her insistence that she was the daughter of an india. Since she was a slave who had been horribly mistreated, Catalina would have known that this was not a pleasant time for anyone of morisco heritage in the village. What historians call the Morisco Revolt or the War of the Alpujarras, between 1568 and 1571, pitted angry moriscos in towns scattered throughout the kingdom of Granada against the Crown of Castile. By 1569, captured moriscos—men, women, and children—presumably guilty of conspiring against the Crown, were enslaved and distributed throughout Andalucía. They began arriving in Carmona in chains during the summer of 1569, in time to till the fields.[77] By 1571, the numbers of moriscos in Carmona had swelled to 1,080, living in 306 houses.[78] Authorities settled most of them in the outlying area of Carmona, where they were employed in agriculture and tended the livestock on the haciendas. A few found gainful employment within the town walls, as bakers, blacksmiths, street cleaners, or weavers. Young and able-bodied women like Beatríz Pérez were taken into the homes of the oligarchy as domestics.[79] Slowly, the moriscos insinuated themselves into village life as artisans and humble laborers, doing the hard work that indios had done before they were freed.[80]

But while many indios in the village now were free, Catalina was not. In 1572 she decided to risk an appeal on behalf of her mother and to release herself from the stigma of being perceived as the daughter of a Moor. Once again she would have to fight against the historicity of the moment (the timing of the Alpujarras uprising) and the weight that the label *morisco* carried in Castile. She had gathered new witnesses and planned new strategies. To undermine the misstatements her mother had made during her own suit, in 1558–1559, Catalina decided to portray her mother as dimwitted and prone to drinking (one witness said the children of the village used to tease Beatriz whenever she stumbled and fell down drunk).[81] At that time, the judges, unable to reach a decision, had called Beatríz in for additional questioning. She had failed to answer questions "in the Mexican language," which was not decisive, since it was not uncommon for those who had been abducted at a young age to have forgotten their language of origin. When asked if elephants, tigers, lions, or camels were found in her native land (naturaleza), Beatríz had replied no. In answer to the next question, however, she declared that pepper, cinnamon, nutmeg, and ginger did grow in her native land, a claim that served as indisputable proof to the judges that she was from a Portuguese domain.[82] On 11 July 1559, the tribunal of the House of Trade determined that Beatríz had not proven her case.

It is possible that Beatríz lost the initial lawsuit not because of a revelatory misstatement or contradictory witness accounts, but because Cansino, a powerful politician, had excellent connections in the village and with key members of the House of Trade. Whether her court loss was due to a reference to a nonnative spice or to behind-the-scenes negotiations between an anxious slave owner and court officials, Beatríz died a shattered, unfree woman. Because of her drinking, Cansino no longer wanted her in his house, and she was moved to a shed on one of his outlying properties in the valley lands, where eventually she died.[83]

Catalina wanted to ensure that such disastrous blunders did not occur again. By now it was 1572, and she faced formidable enemies. Cansino's son Hernando, a village councilor, acted on behalf of his aging father. As determined as his father to keep his slaves, Hernando launched a calculated attack, or tacha, against several of Catalina's deponents in her appeal before the Casa. The most obvious way to eliminate witnesses was to show that they were biased against the defendant in some way. Tachas were sites of inscription where one could openly malign an adversary testifying for the other side. Although they were circumscribed, like other forms of legal evidence they provided insights into cultural interactions going on behind the scenes, interactions that revealed discrimination and the re-creation of local distinctions.

A close reading of the tacha's contents reveals shrewd politics on the part of Cansino's deponents, as well as local assumptions about status and class, discriminatory attitudes based on notions of *raza* (lineage), and condescension toward slaves. Cansino's witnesses openly expressed disdain for Catalina's witnesses, most of whom were laborers, former slaves from foreign locations, and individuals whose genealogies might include Moorish blood.

That witnesses could be discounted in a court of law for not having Old Christian status on both sides of their lineage was not a new practice. Unquestionably, the presence of the Inquisition in nearby Seville since 1481 had affected residents of Carmona.[84] The memory of villagers being condemned as heretics would have carried through to the next generations. Members of the aristocracy began drawing up purity-of-blood certificates to confirm that neither their parents nor grandparents were "of the *casta* of Moors or Jews or of the recently converted."[85]

It is no surprise, then, that Cansino's witnesses would have targeted Catalina's witnesses who might be tainted with heretical blood to ensure that their testimonies would be discounted. Cansino's witnesses relied on a long-standing taxonomy of difference to remove Catalina's connection with indioness and its association with freedom. Juana Ponce, who had once been a slave of Don Lope Ponce, the vicar of Carmona, was of the "*casta* of moros," deponents argued, and her testimony on Catalina's behalf should not be taken seriously. Not only was Juana contaminated with unpure blood, but her mother had been brought before the Inquisition for an undisclosed crime and was made to wear the San Benito yellow habit as a penitent.[86] In the eyes of some villagers, Juana carried the triple stigma of being a former slave, a morisca, and the daughter of a woman punished by the Inquisition.

The question is whether hardening ideas about purity of blood and racism targeted at those of Jewish or Muslim heritage, as David Nirenberg has ably argued, carried over into feelings about non-Castilian foreigners, and especially slaves.[87] Village Spaniards, particularly the elite, had almost certainly become accustomed to, indeed, dependent on, the successive waves of slaves from different locations working in their fields, homes, shops, and stables, yet they still disparaged them. Being an indio in the village could, however, carry a special weight of bias. Some deponents claimed that indios were liars and untrustworthy; others said they lacked mental capacity.[88] And while it was generally assumed that indios would always speak on behalf of other indios, this was clearly not true in either Beatríz's or Felipa's case.[89]

The stain of slavery also mattered. To some, slaves were by their nature unreliable and untrustworthy witnesses. As with those who bore the stigma attached to religious heritage, former slaves bore the invisible brand of the past. Color, too, was significant in the eyes of some. Take, for instance, the witness Ana, who was described as the color black: according to the interrogatory, although now free, she had once been a captive slave, "who wished that all slaves could be free, and that besides being a liar and black, she would say what was contrary to the truth."[90]

But discrimination was extended not only to slaves, foreigners, or people presumed to be blemished because of a different religious faith. Palpable in the testimonies of the village aristocrats were their biases against those who worked with their hands, against those who lived in proximity to animals, and against those who earned their living doing temporary jobs (jornaleros).[91] The judges, they argued, should place little confidence (*poca confianza*) in such people's word. They were merely *hombres paleros*, big-headed shovel makers.[92]

By contrast, Hernando de Cansino said, all of his witnesses—he proceeded to rattle off a long list of names—were honorable, God-fearing Christians and willing to tell the truth.[93] Catalina countered not only that her witnesses were good, upstanding Christians, but that Juan Cansino and his son were "rich and powerful people who [had] many friends and relatives in the village."[94] Among Cansino's witnesses were his relatives, his servants, *compadres* (godparents), *paniaguados* (on his payroll, eating at his table, or rooming at his hacienda), or in some way indebted to father or son. For such a powerful family, finding supportive witnesses had been easy. Cansino had assembled them in his home, agreeing to pay each a bag of wheat, then coached them to say things that would favor him—including that Beatríz and, by extension, her daughter Catalina were Portuguese moriscas. He confronted and intimidated Catalina's witnesses, and made his presence known when each person deposed before the local notary, also a Cansino family friend.[95] Notaries, as Kathryn Burns has argued in *Into the Archive*, could actively influence the creation of trial-ready, "clean" depositions, and Catalina's case was no exception.[96]

Malacata

The defense's browbeating tactics, maligning of witnesses, and open discrimination were only partially effective. Unlike the case initiated by Barbola on behalf of Felipa, Catalina had witnesses who could help prove her deceased mother's place of origin. Furthermore, unlike in Felipa and Barbola's case, which sought to prove that Felipa was either Portuguese or Spanish based on the degree of her intimate associations with other indios and inhabitants of the village, witnesses on behalf of Beatríz and Catalina went to great lengths to explain why Beatríz was from a location called Malacata (or Malagueta; the spelling varied in the depositions). Beyond the name-calling and attempts to claim imperial affinities based on village associations, geography and geographical politics were central features of the litigation suit and appeal. Beatríz became emblematic of how others saw her, as they transferred onto her their own experiences and fantasies about different physical landscapes, mobility, and the global indioscape. Unlike Felipa, who was identified based on her interactions with people in the village who originated from other contexts, Beatríz was identified by her numerous places of origin (see map 1.1). In a mediated legal context, witnesses used geographic and legal knowledge to invent, re-create, or purposefully recalibrate Beatríz's history of forced migration. Beatríz, as various depositions revealed, was from a Malacata that had multiple locations. This may be explained by the fact that, by the 1550s, the possibilities of being from disparate "Malacatas" and eventually arriving in Carmona had become almost limitless, for "Malacata" had become a projection of the "worlds" the inhabitants of the village carried within their imaginations and their memories.

Those witnesses who claimed to know the location of Malacata—and by extension, Beatríz's india identity—included a few indigenous men and women who had been freed in one of two royal inspections of slaves, in 1543 and 1549. Several deponents were from Carmona but now resided in Seville, where at one point Beatríz had also lived and worked. During the initial litigation suit of 1558, two indio vecinos of Seville, Juan Vázquez (who was blind) and his wife (also called Beatríz), both intimate friends of Beatríz, claimed New Spain as their place of origin. Juan explained to the court that the people like the litigant Beatríz from Malacata spoke a language distinct

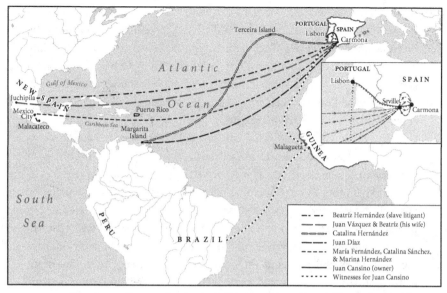

MAP 1.1 Migratory pathways taken by the indigenous litigant Beatríz Hernández, according to witness depositions. Designed by Sarah Bell and Susanne Seales.

from Nahuatl. His wife confirmed that Malacata was close to Juchipila (near Aguascalientes) in Mexico, in Spanish territories where indios were free.

Another key witness, Catalina Hernández, had a different story. She identified herself as from the Rio de la Plata region, but added that she had been raised on the islands of Puerto Rico and Margarita before coming to Spain, and that recently she had been freed by the Casa. Beatríz was her cousin, she claimed, the daughter of her mother's sister, who was from Puerto Rico. Catalina explained that Beatríz's father (named Santiago) had been taken from his place of origin, the island of Margarita (hence the confusion with Malacata), to Puerto Rico, where he met Beatríz's mother, Juana. The couple then returned to Margarita with Catalina. Beatríz was born and raised there with her cousin until she was fourteen. When questioned about the location of Margarita, Catalina answered that it was "near Lima, Peru."[97] A couple then purchased Beatríz and Catalina and put them on a ship, which docked on Terceira Island, in the Azores. The two girls then spent three years there with forty other indias.[98] One night, just before Beatríz and Catalina were to be shipped to Castile, someone came aboard and took away Catalina's brother and Beatríz. Catalina was extremely frightened because she did not know what had happened to them, and was severely beaten when she would not stop crying. When asked why Beatríz had insisted that she was from "Malacata" and not "Margarita," Catalina answered that Beatríz didn't know what she was talking about and that she consistently confused the pronunciation of the two place names. Two other depositions—including one from the indio tailor Juan Díaz, originally from Cubagua, the island proximate to Margarita—confirmed what Catalina Fernández had claimed: that Beatríz had merely been confused in her terminology and that she was actually from the island of Margarita.[99]

Why all the contradictions? Juan Vázquez and his wife, Beatríz, Catalina Hernández, Juan Díaz, and Martín Sánchez obviously did not meet in a tavern to scheme and get their "story straight." But they served as witnesses to get other indios out of litigious scrapes, worked in shops together, and called each other "compadre" or "cousin," having created new kinship bonds. For them, the road between Carmona and Seville was well traveled, so they would have been familiar with Beatríz's dilemma. In addition, having themselves had firsthand experience of how imperial laws played out in the courtroom, they would have been aware that it would be best for slaves to argue that they were originally from New Spain or Peru, as clearly distinguished from the more nebulous domain of Rio de la Plata, which bordered Portuguese territory. Slaves who had passed through or had spent any length of time in Portugal (as Beatríz had) were on dangerous legal ground because it was much easier to argue they were subjects of the Portuguese Crown, and therefore culturally Portuguese. If, as Juan Cansino asserted, Beatríz was the daughter of a Moor, she faced an additional stigma.

While the witnesses for Beatríz would certainly have taken these circumstances into account when they gave their detailed portrayals of "Malacata" in Spanish territory, the geographical discrepancies might have damaged the case. Not only were the contradictions about the location of Malacata obvious, but the various testimonies confused Beatríz's chronology of when and how she had reached Carmona. Some, like Catalina, may simply have been skilled at weaving a good yarn. Another plausible explanation for the inconsistencies is that each witness told the story they were most familiar with: his or her own, or that of a close relative. Juan Vázquez and his wife, Beatríz, talked about the territory near Aguascalientes and displayed a familiarity with the distinct sonorous tones of the region. Then again, "Malacata" did sound a little like "Margarita," and it would have been possible to conflate the two. The vicissitudes and drama of Catalina Hernández's diasporic tale involved the stories of her own parents: her father's displacement from the island of Margarita, off the coast of Venezuela, to Puerto Rico, where he met Catalina's mother. It was a believable story given the dislocation of thousands of indigenous peoples from northern South America during the first half of the sixteenth century. If the ship on which Beatríz had originally sailed included an illegal shipment of slaves, it would have made sense for the ship to stop first in the Azores (a site of much illegal commerce), but why Beatríz would have remained there for three years is unclear. While Catalina Hernández's story did not contradict those of Juan Díaz (from the nearby island of Cubagua) and others, it was most likely her own tale of bondage, not that of Beatríz.

According to the law, Juan Cansino could access witness depositions on behalf of Beatríz, in order to help formulate his own response. To bolster his argument that Beatríz had descended from Moors and that she had come from a very different "Malacata," he called on ship captains and sailors living in Seville to testify on his behalf. These witnesses, however, contradicted Cansino (a discrepancy that was never questioned) and failed to mention that Beatríz was of Arab descent or that she was the daughter of a non-Christian father. Instead, they relied on their own experiences of the West African slave trade and their nautical knowledge to explain that if one sailed from Lisbon to the southeast of Cabo Verde and along the Guinea coast, one would encounter the territory of the Portuguese Crown where *malagueta*, a particular kind of pepper, was commonly found.[100] Never mind that they said only black Africans inhabited this area: one sailor even argued that Malagueta, in Portuguese territory, began near Sao Tomé and stretched along the coast "until you reached Brasil," where "blacks and Indians mixed with one another"—by which he insinuated that Beatríz was the child of a transatlantic union.[101] His experience with the Atlantic slave trade and with the imperial trade connections between Guinea and Brazil united the two territories in the sailor's mind. When Juan Cansino submitted his depositions to the court, in December 1558, he concluded that Beatríz was from Malacata, as the sailors had said, and that Malacata was nowhere near New Spain.[102]

Apparently, the discrepancies in the "Malacata" stories were clarified when the perplexed Casa judges interviewed Beatríz, for the original lawsuit initiated by Beatríz, in 1558, failed when she mistakenly said that the spices cinnamon, ginger, and nutmeg grew in her native land. By 1572, the year Catalina appealed the ruling, the geopolitical drama of "Malacata" continued to unfold, with new india witnesses addressing the continuing mystery. Although significantly younger than Beatríz, the deponents Marina Hernández and Catalina Sánchez claimed to have seen her when they were young girls in Mexico City.[103] Sánchez even went so far as to say that she and Beatríz were on the same ship bound for Spain.[104] Another witness, María Fernández connected the dots between Mexico City and "Malacata," declaring that she had heard from her deceased husband and other indios that Beatríz had been born in a place called Malacateca, between Tehuantepeque and Oaxaca.[105] Marina added,

> Beatríz had told this witness that she came from another land called Malacateca which is in front of Mexico and that after this deponent saw Beatríz in Mexico City a man named Juan Infante brought this witness to these kingdoms. [This deponent] came [in 1539] when there was an eclipse of the sun, and they said that the empress, our lady [Isabel] had [just] died. Around the time they announced in Seville that they were freeing the indios, this witness saw Beatríz in this city [of Seville] and she spoke to this witness in the House of Trade and [Beatríz] mentioned to this witness that she had seen me in Mexico when I was a small girl and even though this witness did not know [who Beatríz was] this witness had remembered the house where [Beatríz] had spoken to me.[106]

Once again, witnesses invented, contradicted, conflated, and conspired to free or detain Catalina and her daughter Ana. At this point, however, no witnesses came forward to support Juan Cansino's claim that Beatríz came from Malagueta in Africa. Instead, to undermine Catalina's case, Cansino focused his efforts on the tacha. Although Catalina's testimonies during the 1572 appeal exposed the contradictions in Cansino's testimonies (and added a few of their own), and although they revealed the flagrant ethical violations in relying on relatives to depose, they were not enough to dissuade the judges of the Casa, who once again ruled in favor of Cansino and against Beatríz, in November 1572. Within two years, however, the Council of the Indies decided to review the case and overturned the Casa's ruling by declaring Catalina, her brothers, and her daughter to be free from bondage.[107]

Conclusions

The disquieting Atlantic journey and ominous full eclipse of the sun certainly made a lasting impression on the deponent, María Fernández. It is unlikely, however, that she or the other two india deponents had seen Beatríz in Mexico City or crossed the ocean together, though there was no way to prove that they were lying. It is unlikely that Beatríz spoke "like an india from New Spain," even though nearly half a dozen indio witnesses testified that she did. Rather, she most likely spoke "ladino, as we all speak," as the witness Pedro Gutiérrez Ferrer claimed.[108] Even more difficult to assess from this distance is who, of all the deponents for either side, had the most viable story. Altogether, Malacata, Malagueta, Margarita, and Malacateca were described as locations in Guinea (and, by extension, Brazil), in the Oaxaca region of Mexico, or near Juchipila, Mexico, or as an island next to Cubagua. The Portuguese sailors placed Beatríz's pathway within their own experiential framework, just as the former slave deponents may have referenced landscapes and experiences of displacement familiar to them. Their stories were reminiscent of the larger diasporas that had uprooted hundreds of thousands of children and adults throughout Latin America.

Then there were the morisco slaves and freedmen of the village, some from Granada or Málaga or the Berber lands, who had also been uprooted from their homelands. Each of these witnesses knew Beatríz and Catalina, or Felipa and Barbola, and each brought his or her particular experiences in a different homeland to bear on those with whom they had regular exchanges. The spatial and cultural knowledge of the Spanish Carmonenses was equally broad. Juan Cansino and Silvestre de Monsalve would have been apprised of the conflicts in Granada within their own Iberian borders; they knew how easy it was to cross into Portugal or to bring Portuguese merchants with knowledge of East and South Asia into their village. They knew men who had fought and lived in Oran. Slaves from these lands walked the corridors of their homes. Their neighbors gave orders to slaves who shared their knowledge of the other worlds they had seen on their seafaring journeys with other servants and slaves in the village. Juan, Lisuarte, and the other slaves from Calicut emphasized a homeland link with Felipa, knowing that it would be difficult to disprove and would please masters and mistresses who carried Monsalve or Marmolejo blood in their veins.

Under normal circumstances, the ruptures and discontinuities caused by the execution of status and power by masters over slaves could be contained. The disregard, contempt, and resentment were always there, beneath the surface, except when an outburst, brawl, severe beating, or sexual violation revealed more insidious truths. What becomes apparent from a close reading of the two trials is that the quotidian expressions of kinship and camaraderie and shared experiences of foreign lands took on an ugly cast in the heightened tensions of the courtroom. The trials fractured Carmonenses along the discriminatory lines of the haves and the have-nots, of those considered to be honorable or tainted. In the midst of all this, defining who was an indio took center stage.

The world was in a village. Despite its image as a fortified town situated atop a hill, Carmona fully inhabited the globe in multiple ways. Disparate peoples from the slave-trading territories of Guinea and Senegambia, who were the victims of the men on horseback near Oran or Tlemcen, or of the slaves taken during the conquests of Hernán Cortés, or of the business ventures of merchants, entered the fortress doors of Carmona, one by one or in small clusters. In their different ways, all were victims of forced incursions into diverse areas—the Mahgreb, West Africa, the Malabar Coast of India, Mexico, the Caribbean, Cubagua, and Margarita. They had their own diasporic tales of journeys at sea, encounters with different masters, and horrific losses of families and names and histories. They formed new alliances and kinship with other diasporic peoples, some unlike themselves. Over the years, as Carmona became a setting both local and familiar, they continued to recall scenarios of life before and after bondage, in locations also distantly familiar. Once they entered the courtroom as deponents, their portrayals became circumscribed refractions of their "multi-resolution"—and sometimes transimperial—experiences with diasporic and local peoples.[109] Each witness, whether slave or free, transmogrified scenes of subjection, of possession, of being possessed, and of no longer being possessed into an intentional argument about what it meant to be an imperial subject in a local setting. The boundaries of the global and local, of that which was intimate or foreign, blurred in their interactions and in their portrayals of one another, contributing to the process of being an indio in an increasingly globalized indioscape.

The case study of Carmona serves as a template for many of the issues I explore throughout this volume. In each chapter I use the lens of slavery to explore how the floating signifier *indio* was expressed in sixteenth-century Castile. I show how the swell of the ocean carried them away from their homelands and toward new Iberian-situated identities; I show how indigenous peoples were portrayed and how they portrayed themselves as diasporic and transimperial. As men and women in bondage, labeled as indios in a Castilian context, they established relations with villagers and townspeople, and defined themselves and were defined by others in terms of the household to which they belonged and the social and economic relations that structured their everyday lives.

These relations were vulnerable and easily subject to ruptures and discontinuities. Key historic moments, including the passage of the New Laws and the inspections of Gregorio López in 1543 and of Hernán Pérez in 1549, resonated deeply in their lives, as they sought to avoid violent retributions from humiliated masters and strategized about how to rid themselves of the physical and psychological shackles of slavery. Some literally redefined themselves as vecinos and neighbors and kin. Those who entered the courtroom to petition for their freedom found themselves reconstructing their stories and identities according to specific legal conventions related to imperial status, the context of war, geography, physiognomy, language, and social relations. Of course, the possibilities of creating fictions or partial truths, of falsifying documents, of taking on someone else's identity to secure freedom, were built into the subjective process of identification and the politics of witness testimony, as the cases of Felipa and Beatríz in Carmona have shown.

TWO

Crossing the Atlantic and Entering Households

+⊱═══⊰+

I [the india Isabel] am from a village called El Charco [in New Spain]
and was brought to Spain by way of Veracruz and Havana when I was
about fifteen years old, still a child, a young girl . . . and the boatswain
sold me to another boatswain and then to a ship captain who was Portuguese and we docked in Lisbon. There I was sold to a Portuguese slave
merchant who brought me to Cádiz, where [my current master] Alonso
de Vera bought me. That was fifteen years ago and all this time I have
been alone without anyone to assist me [legally].

—"Opening Statement, Isabel," 29/I/1554,

AGI, Justicia 1164, n. 6, r. 1, im. 113

We know much more about indigenous litigants like Beatríz
and Felipa in Carmona than we do about the several thousands of slaves who crossed the Atlantic to Castile between 1493
and 1580. We lack complete passenger lists for the many who,
year after year, boarded dozens of vessels that made the five- or
six-week journey. The extant number of licenses granted to each
family and the presence of indios in notarial and baptismal registers in Seville is slim. Even the lack of complete documentary series makes it difficult to trace the changing rationales and bureaucratic sensibilities of those registering and compiling them.[1] Part
of the problem in tracing the historical processes by which indios
were constructed and how they made sense of the radical transformations of the sixteenth century comes from the extremely
disjointed nature of the documentary corpus. Where we do find

the names of slaves—in travel certificates, licenses from the king, and passenger lists—they appear as fragments and factual smatterings. What remain are "small dramas" that do not lend themselves to good, narrative history.[2] From these microscopic traces—the "residuum of a dismembered past"—readers have to imagine the magnitude of deracination and forced migration.[3] We have to imagine a context and a narrative framework even though their experiences of pain, sorrow, and loss exist beyond the pale of language.

In most instances, litigants like the india Isabel did not provide details of the harrowing Atlantic crossings. Therefore, to offer a sense of the historicity of this significant oceanic migration, I connect the unstoried lives of individuals dehumanized by the archives to those of litigants like the Carmona slaves Beatríz and Felipa, whose court records are more complete. The oceanic crossing was not only a means of traveling from one continent to another. By focusing on the Atlantic as a diasporic space, I show the linkages between physical dislocation and relocation, the temporal and spatial incongruities experienced by indigenous slaves, the importance of connections to other worlds, and the power a vast ocean had in reconfiguring indio identities. Like the young healer Domingos Álvares, who was enslaved in the Dahomey kingdom in the early eighteenth century and uprooted several times in Brazil and Portugal, the indigenous subjects I study defy understandings of history "as chronologically ordered and geographically bound."[4] I follow the course of indios' lives in bondage: from their abduction and placement onto ships, to their arrival in Seville, then to their incorporation into a household, with its peculiar sets of demands and expectations. I examine the temporal and spatial ruptures experienced by indigenous slaves in distinct contexts. I argue that bondage was a historical process, continually unfolding and becoming, whether on the Atlantic Ocean, where indios were stripped of spatial and temporal referents, or in the casa (household), where they formed new social bonds, albeit fragile ones.

The most common reason for indios to cross the Atlantic was because they had already been serving for years as laborers in homes, shops, and armies scattered throughout Spanish America. Like the thousands of African peoples who labored in Castile and Portugal before setting forth with their masters for the Caribbean islands or Mexico, indigenous slaves had already experienced the complexities of violent rupture and cultural placement in a new setting with new relations and new kinship possibilities.[5] Many were like the Pipil Catalina: they had entered households in Spanish America as children, which ensured "an erasure of the past" and a kind of docility. *Household* is the key word here, because families transcended nuclear affiliations to include children born out of wedlock, as well as servants and slaves. In the pre-1550 period, families were extremely mobile. This helps explain why, in 1533, Juan Martín Pinzón obtained a license from Queen Isabel to bring home to Spain his mestizo son, whom he had left in the hands of a trusted partner, as well as three male indio slaves.[7] His son and his slaves were part of his household, which he hoped to maintain intact on both sides of the Atlantic. The ocean connected families between continents, and slaves were integral to those transatlantic ties.[8]

Mobility, disruption, and reconfiguration were all essential aspects of early colonialism. This was especially true for slaves. Once indigenous slaves set foot on the sandy soil of the Guadalquivir (or elsewhere, as was Isabel's case), they would soon realize that they remained in their master's possession, no matter on which shore they stood. In that sense, what is more difficult to determine are the kinds of attachments masters formed with their indigenous slaves on either side of the Atlantic. As fragmentary as the passenger licenses are, when read carefully (and pieced together as a "series") they hint at bonds of far greater complexity than terms such as *esclavo*, *naboría*, and *criado* can convey. Some masters brought one or two slaves on the transatlantic journey, hoping the training the slaves had received in America would bring in extra income as owners hired them out to defray travel costs or help the master reestablish himself at home. Other slaves were sold on arrival in Seville.[9] We can only speculate what motivated Alonso Pérez de Valer, a supplier of castings for Nicaragua, to return to Spain with two branded slaves.[10] Or we might wonder why, in 1527, an unnamed man (in some of the earlier documents Indians are not even named) accompanied the wealthy landowner Juan Michel of San Germán, Puerto Rico; the slave may have been intended as a gift to another family member, or Michel may have recognized talents or abilities that made the slave seem too valuable to leave behind.[11] Attachments of masters to slaves could also be motivated by present economic need or future possibilities of wealth or kinship ties.[12] Such bonds were integral to the governance of vassal over subject.

Because slaves were considered movable goods, some indigenous slave children crossed the ocean as a part of a testamentary bequest, since families in Castile made concerted efforts to retrieve material goods of fathers, sisters, and husbands who had died in the Indies.[13] There were also "mail order" slaves, brought by merchants to fill requests made by families in Castile.[14] Some slaves were entrusted to a slave owner's business partner, who at some point would receive an order to send the slaves under his control to

Seville. Occasionally, slave owners in Castile requested that slaves who had been absconded illegally in America be retrieved and sent to them. Diego de Platas, and others like him, hoped that when he returned to Spain, no one would steal and sell the slaves and servants he had left behind.[15]

Merchant activity was one of the main reasons for the displacement and sale of indigenous peoples, but deaths from warfare, disease, displacement, captivity, or over-exacting labor regimes created thousands of orphaned children who then lived their lives as slaves or naborías.[16] Warfare or the selling of villagers by caciques were other explanations for why so many indigenous people were enslaved. Other slaves were attached to the conquerors. Some of the famous leaders of the cavalcades and expeditions—Sebastian de Benalcázar, Gonzalo de Salazar, Hernán Cortés, Nuño de Gúzman—returned to Seville with a retinue of servants and slaves.[17] With their newfound wealth, such conquerors established elaborate households staffed with indio men and women who had crossed the ocean to work in their masters' stables, kitchens, and orchards in Spain.[18] Even the lesser-known conquerors such as Pedro de Valencia, who had been present at Cajamarca, expressed a sense of entitlement that included the right to bring one or two indios back to Spain.[19] The colonial households in Castile reproduced the power inherent in this new kind of imperial mobility, with the conquerors determining who would constitute the household, itself a microcosm of the broader world.

In a society as bureaucratically conscious as Castile, it was necessary to create documents that traced the oceanic movements of slaves from west to east. Travel licenses nearly always named the masters, following both bureaucratic norms and normalizing practices which constituted the slaves' history of bondage vis-à-vis a master or masters. Other "pasts"—including slaves' connections to place, ethnicity, and birth families—were effaced in this kind of documentation. More often than not, notarial and travel certificate documents referencing slaves fail to link their violent pasts to the violent presents taking place in distinct locations. We might learn about a slave's a priori existence as a free-person-turned-captive by reading a witness deposition or other document recounting another, disjointed episode in his or her life. While he was still a boy, Juan was declared a slave "of just war" during the "war in Higuey," one of two brutal clashes between the Taíno people and Spaniards in the eastern most *cacicazgo* (political, territorial, and ethnic jurisdiction of a native lord called a cacique) of the island of Hispaniola, which took place in 1502 and 1504. Or, at least that is how his master, Francisco Velásquez described Juan in a complaint he issued in 1525 in Seville, after Juan had fled his household.[20] The document produced as a result of Velásquez's legal action reveals a transitional moment in Juan's earlier life that was linked to noncompliant behavior more than twenty years later. Why did Velásquez choose to emphasize the connection between past and present two decades later? Was he implying that Juan was just as rebellious in 1525 as his people had been two decades earlier? Was Velásquez a relative of Diego de Velásquez, the conqueror of Cuba, who assisted Nicolás de Ovando in the "pacification" of Hispaniola, and from whom he might have heard many stories? We know from other accounts that the burning alive of a respected Taíno cacique (indigenous ruler) by Spaniards led to one rebellion and then another, which then led the Spaniards to enact a brutal retribution—called a "pogrom" by one scholar—against the women and children who witnessed the atrocities.[21] A historian can see, as if witnessing a ripple flow out into a pool of water, how the initial acts of aggression rationalized as just war resulted in the enslavement of a boy, who crossed the ocean soon after, then, twenty years later, ran away from a brutal master. Although Juan experienced the effects of violence he had witnessed and endured in different ways throughout his life, his attenuated (and mediated) presence in the documents as a fugitive (the effect of the ripple, rather than its original cause) is all that remains for the historian to see.

Juan's configurations as a rebellious indio on both sides of the Atlantic are also the result of the legal documents issued by late fifteenth- and early sixteenth-century Crown authorities who were grappling with the significations of the neologism *indio* as they tried to respond favorably to Spaniards' demands in Hispaniola and Cuba for more slaves. Although Queen Isabel had declared in 1501 that indios from the Spanish Indies could not be placed in bondage, certain indigenous peoples in certain habitats and under certain conditions could be enslaved. Reasons for enslavement included resistance to Spanish military incursions, labeled as "just war" causes, but there were other reasons to enslave indigenous peoples of the Caribbean. As early as 1508, as the geographer Carl Sauer has so aptly illustrated, Spanish residents of the island of Hispaniola urged King Ferdinand to label the Bahamas as "useless islands" and the Lucayan people as potential slaves.[22] Children were particularly vulnerable to enslavement. A travel license I found reveals that Clara Martín de la Peña received a very young "*india yucaya*" as a gift from a former student, Elvira Mazarro, the daughter of the mayor of Santiago in Hispaniola.[23] In 1521 Clara requested a royal license to bring to Castile "an india yucaya slave whom she had raised" and indoctrinated in the Christian faith. The slave who accompanied doña Clara to Castile is the only slave from the Lucayas I have found mentioned in sundry documents, although there were certainly others. She was one of fourteen thousand Lucayans enslaved between 1508 and 1514 and taken to Hispaniola to work in the homes, fields, and gold mines owned by the Crown and individual Spaniards. The capture of these people was legally sanctioned in 1509, after King Ferdinand consulted with his advisors and authorized Governor Ovando to bring Lucaya slaves to Hispaniola "without any sense of remorse."[24] Years later, when the king granted the Lucaya woman permission to travel to Castile with doña Clara, he followed legal protocol by insisting that the woman come of her own free will.[25]

In this travel license, and in other licenses granted throughout the 1520s, 1530s, and 1540s, we see language that embodies the mask of volition, language that blots out an unnamed woman's previous history and current condition of captivity, forced migration, and commodification, and language that creates an illusory facade of protection and choice.[26] Embedded in the mobility of indigenous servants and slaves who crossed the ocean was the fool's gold glimmer of freedom. Paternalistic phrasing—such as claiming to "raise" a child slave or stating that a servant was like a son or daughter to a master—also masked the lack of agency or "choicelessness" of these individuals.[27] The promise to indoctrinate a slave into the Catholic faith also had a false ring to it.[28] The chimerical language of guiding, caring, and comforting shrouds the lack of agency experienced by the slaves; after all, it was the master (or a royal official) who determined when and where a servant or slave could move through time and space.

The flow of human cargo from west to east also depended on the sound governance of laws and regulations. Once decrees were issued in the 1530s prohibiting indio slaves from entering Castile without following proper legal protocol, the traffic in indigenous slaves to Castile diminished; they now arrived by the dozens rather than by the hundreds. After the initial surge of merchant activity (1493–1510), only 421 registered slaves came to Spain between 1511 and 1550.[29] Each Spanish head of household was expected to show the appropriate papers verifying legal ownership of the slaves and to prove that their property had been inspected when they left an American port.[30] The entry point for all passengers leaving and entering Castile was the Casa in Seville. Casa authorities were charged with inspecting the cargo and passengers on ships that docked in Seville. (Originally located in a warehouse near the Guadalquivir docks, the Casa was soon transferred, for safety reasons, to the Alcázar fortress, where its main offices were expanded to accommodate the regular flow of traffic.)[31]

However, it should come as no surprise to those familiar with the vigorous illegal commerce of the era that the numbers of slaves registered at the Casa does not include the hundreds who slipped into Castile through other channels. Some passed through the House of Trade because a ship captain or merchant was on good terms with the inspector; others crossed the scrubby terrain of southern Portugal to be sold at the fairs of Zafra (in Badajoz) or Medina del Campo. As in the cases of Beatríz and Felipa, Castilians regularly traveled to Lisbon to buy slaves in small quantities. Given that Seville was eighty kilometers from the Atlantic Ocean and ships had to navigate the sandbars found at the entry point to the Guadalquivir River at Sanlucár de Barrameda, some slaves disembarked there. The opening of Cadíz to trade, in 1535, also attracted foreign merchants laden with goods and slaves. A few indios entered Spain through the northern ports.[32] Over the decades, Portuguese and Genoese merchant networks (complete with their own ships) regularly brought indigenous slaves into Seville, either directly from Portuguese territory, or from Lisbon.[33]

The traffic in slaves also went from east to west. Before 1536, small numbers of indigenous slaves traveled with little scrutiny from Castile to America and back with families, high-ranking officials, or sea captains. The license needed to travel to America was more difficult to falsify, but shipmasters and captains on both sides of the Atlantic were willing to pocket extra funds to stow away a slave who might later be sold on the cathedral steps of Seville to pay off a debt. To avoid inspections, private vessels avoided the Guadalquivir River and embarked from several Atlantic ports where controls were less stringent. Emigrants transporting slaves illegally to America sometimes boarded in Lisbon, then docked for a brief period in the Canary Islands, where they could procure a license more easily.[34] Some indigenous slaves came through the Azores.

Porous laws, permeable ports, and fragile imperial borders all contributed to the sustained transatlantic traffic in indigenous slaves from America to Castile despite ordinances to the contrary. But royal licenses also played a part. As Casa authorities began to inspect incoming ships and the paperwork of passengers more closely in the 1530s—ensuring, for example, that Crown authorities in America had asked indios if they were traveling of their own volition—the Crown also began to limit to one or two the number of servants or slaves that individual Castilian men or women could bring with them.[35] But there were always exceptions, and some depended on the good graces of the king. After reviewing each petition, Charles V would sometimes grant licenses for larger groups of slaves to cross the ocean.[36]

Just as common were the illegal stowaways coming from America who were never registered in the House of Trade. They were lured with guarantees of wages, food, or better lives. Around 1547, an indigenous servant boy named Machín was small enough to hide in the belly of a ship for three days before it set sail from Panama. He did so because he had been promised a daily wage and was told by his master that he would be taught to read and write.[37] In another tale of deception, Francisco, who came from the province of Tlaxcala, explained in his deposition before the Casa that sailors had lured him and other boys onto a ship anchored in Veracruz around 1530 with the promise of taking them to the "good land" of Castile. Weeks later, as the ship slowly navigated the Guadalquivir River in the dark of night, Francisco's owner smuggled him off the boat before it reached the sandy shore of Seville.[38]

If the history of indios who crossed the ocean to Castile is one of stealth, promises, and forced mobility, it is also a legalistic one, involving paper trails and scrutiny. All stories of bondage have a beginning, but the travel documentation for indios crossing the Atlantic discloses little about indigenous experiences of displacement and the moment when they were legally inscribed as *esclavos indios*. Fortunately, the testimonies of slaves or witnesses in the litigation suits reveal fuller truths about what events ultimately led to the transatlantic journeys. In the opening statement, crafted with a legal assistant, an indigenous plaintiff would state in a formulaic manner that he or she had been brought to Castile "by deceit" perpetrated by "a Spaniard" or "a Portuguese" man. Although this language was framed in a circumscribed way due to legal requisites, the anonymous intermediary—the unnamed Spaniard or Portuguese—speaks to a blank pause in the individual slave's life. The language employed in the opening statement also reveals a possession that was transitory in nature, and an involuntary crossing of the sea that had led to the slave's current objectification as a material object.

At times litigants recounted the transition from self to object having taken place in their naturaleza—their homeland or habitat. In the various depositions, wherein the slaves' compromised voices had a greater range of expression than in the travel licenses, we learn about the effects that military expansion had on their lives. We learn more detail about how the past was connected to the present, as contrived as it might have been. The testimonies of witnesses dimly show the patterns of military expeditions into areas where military clashes—often exaggerated by Spaniards to justify slavery—occurred. We can trace the trajectories of conquest in, for example, the migration pattern of the Pipil Catalina, who traveled from Nonoalco to Honduras to Realejo to Peru, and finally to Spain. As exploratory missions traversed the littoral of the Gulf of Paría down into Brazil, circumnavigated the various islands of the Caribbean, or plunged into the interiors of Panama and Tierra Firme (a broad geographic term that encompassed mainland South America, depending on the state of Castilian geographic knowledge), slaves from these areas trickled into Spain.[39]

The testimonies give a sense of pathways followed by merchants and conquerors and the slaves themselves. They help to connect those events that transformed identities from free individuals with specific ethnic affiliations to slaves labeled generically as indios. But the temporal interval between when they told the tales of their capture and their journeys and when the events had actually occurred might lag by one, two, or even three decades.[40] It is the historian who then must piece the temporal and spatial jigsaw puzzle into a coherent whole, to understand, for example, the brief history of Ana. She was originally from Pánuco, and in 1543, when she was freed in the inspection of Gregorio López, she was thirty years old. Her master, the ship captain and merchant Ginés de Carrión, had purchased her some eighteen years earlier in Havana, around 1525. This fixes her date of capture at around 1523 or 1524, when the initial military forays authorized by Hernán Cortés into her region took place. She would thus have been about ten years old when she was transformed from a free girl into a commodity and then was shipped across the Atlantic.[41]

For many slaves, the transatlantic journey was not their first voyage by sea. By the time they crossed the Atlantic, they were already victims of "serial dislocation."[42] But the telling of this prior dislocation is rarely revealed in the documents. Because it was not crucial to the legal narrative, slaves who testified in the Spanish courts rarely gave details about how many involuntary seafaring journeys they had made before they crossed the Atlantic—a benchmark episode. Tracing the details of those trips would not have added weight to an appeal for freedom unless the jurists were interested in probing more deeply into a slave's place of origin. But in small increments, thousands of slaves were loaded onto vessels harbored at the deep-water ports along the Pacific coast, which then navigated the coast from north to south and back again. A list (registered in León) of passengers who in 1543 boarded the merchant carrack *Santiago*, bound for Peru from Realejo (Nicaragua), provides a snapshot of a handful of itinerant slaves who traveled southward with a ship crew of thirteen, including five black cabin hands.

PASSENGERS
Alonso de Pisa
Damian Sanches, with eight indios and two indias, financed by Pedro de la Palma

Alonso Dávila
Alonso Coronas
Francisco de Tapia
Ruy Dias
An india slave from Guatemala to work on the ship

The pieces (*piezas*) of slaves and free indios who travel on the ship are as follows:

Of the ship captain, an india slave and five free indios from Peru whom he brought to this province [of Nicaragua].

Of Damian Sanches, a free indio from Peru, two black male slaves and one black female slave, an indio slave from Guatemala and an india slave.

Of Miguel Griego, a free india whom he brought to this province.[43]

Hundreds of merchant vessels like the *Santiago* carried thousands of enslaved and free indios from one Pacific port to another.[44] By the time these unnamed slaves had boarded the *Santiago*, they were being registered with generic geographic references like "Guatemala" and "Peru," thus effacing their ethnicities—and any connection to a specific valley, kin group, or ethnic lord—from the historical record. Just as the invention of "Guinea" and other ethnic and geocultural demarcations made by Europeans had little to do with the realities of kinship and other affiliations of the coastal and interior polities on the African continent, terms like "Guatemala" had little to do with how indios defined themselves.[45] As one of the more insidious aspects of turning human beings into commodities, this powerful gesture of naming, whether conscious or not, created new ways of spatially organizing enslaved indios. Not only had they already experienced rupture and cultural dislocation, but they were now being forced to move again. For the time being, some had masters, but it is likely that the ten indios under the authority of Damian Sanchez would have been sold as soon as the vessel docked in Peru. Perhaps one of the unnamed indios aboard the ship eventually crossed the Atlantic to Seville or watched others leave for a place they had heard about in conversation, but the records do not connect these time-space intervals.[46]

Young captives living near the shores of the Caribbean or on the Pacific side of the continent might have had some idea that they were going to Santo Domingo, a major diasporic site for foreign slaves and a port where the Spanish fleet stopped each year. But crossing the Atlantic, at least in the initial years, was probably beyond the "cognitive map" of the captives.[47] They were likely more familiar with the smaller boats and ships that patrolled the coasts and navigated the interior river systems in search of slaves. The passage on the open Atlantic sea was beyond anything they had ever known.[48] Those who had spent time in Santo Domingo would have had a much better idea that the *Carrera de Indias* would push off for Castile after all the goods had been sold or bartered and the new commodities, including slaves, and passengers had been loaded aboard. They would have known this because many indigenous slaves from Peru, Nicaragua, and Cubagua worked cheek-to-jowl on the docks and in the markets and likely found a common language to speak, perhaps a patois now lost to view. They would have known because they would have heard stories of fugitive slaves who timed their escape with the pulling up of the anchor, the hold of the ship to serve as a safe haven for the next six weeks. By the time they arrived in Castile, they had already been uprooted once, if not twice or even three times. They had traversed parched and lush terrain, rivers, mountains, seas, and finally an ocean.

How poignantly historians like Stephanie Smallwood remind us of the horrors of the transatlantic voyage for those in bondage, whether African or indigenous.[49] Although indios were not stacked body to body the way captives from Africa were, crossing the Atlantic was nevertheless for most indigenous slaves a horrendous experience physically and psychically. Death was always dangerously present, and life could slip away from the person next to you. Children were particularly vulnerable. In 1542 the india María and her two daughters boarded a small vessel in Cuba, then stopped in Santo Domingo, where they transferred to a larger ship. While crossing the ocean, Maria watched both of her children sicken. The two died while the ship sat in the Guadalquivir River, before they had a chance to disembark in Seville. Wanting to ensure that the proper number of slaves was being registered, Casa authorities interviewed the passengers, including the india Beatríz, who confirmed the children's deaths.[50]

An examination of travel documents reveals what bureaucracies want them to reveal: the place and date of a child's death, or the names of masters who paid the passage of indigenous slaves. When these records are juxtaposed with laws and ordinances, we see how deliberations taking place in the king's chambers determined when and which indios could travel to Spain and under what conditions. But these synchronic documents do not expose the ruptures, the displacements, or, more broadly, the relationship of slavery to "time." As the decades passed, slaves who crossed the Atlantic also carried within them the anguish of several generations. They psychically embodied the slave raiding practices that had affected their parents or grandparents. They embodied the calculations made by caciques who waged war on enemies to collect slaves for sale to or barter with Spaniards. Pronouncements made by Crown officials in 1504 and 1511 continued to resonate decades later in the lives of slaves such as Catalina, Pedro, Isabel, Francisco, and Juan. Catalina, seven or eight years old when she was sold in Seville in 1537 to Bartolomé Ortíz, the future mayor of that city, was one of the early victims of the conqueror Pedro de Heredia's forays into the interior of what is now Colombia in the 1530s, when hundreds, if not thousands of indigenous people were enslaved.[51] But Heredia's claim to wage war on the people of "Santa Marta" was based on a precedent established several decades before. In what is now known as Colombia, the designation of the coastal inhabitants as *caribes* (cannibals) began in 1504 as a result of pressure that merchants exerted on Crown authorities. The consequences of this new designation reverberated throughout the littoral, exacerbating long-standing interethnic factions and creating new rivalries (and alliances) as groups participated actively in the plunder economy by exchanging enemy peoples for goods and weapons.[52] Beginning in 1511, the Crown awarded open-ended contracts to merchants, which only intensified the capture and marketing of slaves to Hispaniola and elsewhere.[53] Captured indigenous people were labeled as slaves of "Santa Marta"—a geographic conflation— even if they came from rival ethnic groups. By the time Rodrigo de Bastidas founded the Spanish settlement of Santa Marta (Colombia), in 1525, intending it to be a launching point for "exploratory" ventures into the interior, the indigenous groups proximate to that area (from Cabo de la Vela to the mouth of the Magdalena River) had been negotiating with, fighting with, or fleeing from slave raiders for decades.[54] The prevailing logic was that "if the Spaniards did not take the indios away from the province of Santa Marta and provide them with justice, the entire area would rise up, and the indios would kill all the Christians."[55] Heredia merely capitalized on nearly three decades of slaving practices.

By the 1530s, however, few indios from the interior of the New Kingdom of Granada were considered cannibals.[56] Instead, just war served as the means to categorize and collapse the ethnically diverse population as enslavable commodities. Pedro and Isabel were two of "many" indios captured around 1539, then purchased by the merchant Pedro Álvarez, who said he bought them in a public sale from "the soldiers of war in a conquest that took place there," in Santa Marta. After branding them and paying the royal fifth, he obtained a license to bring them to Seville.[57] Three years later, around 1542, the twelve-year-old Juan was captured and sold in Santa Marta by the lieutenant governor, Luís de Manjarres, to a man who was preparing to travel to Castile.[58] Francisco and Isabel arrived in Spain via a more circuitous but popular commercial route.[59] After Francisco and Isabel were captured in Santa Marta, in the early 1540s, merchants took them to the island of Cubagua to be sold. Like hundreds of other slaves, they were then transported to Santo Domingo, where they eventually boarded a ship destined for Castile.[60] When taken together, these episodic fragments reveal the power that naming the region as bellicose had over the region's children, who were captured, deterritorialized, given Christian names, and transported beyond the worlds they had known. Children bore the scars of decades of legal mislabeling—as cannibals, as being from Santa Marta, as inhabitants of a war zone.

But slave owners and merchants who crossed the ocean with their human merchandise also carried with them past experiences that would enter into direct confrontation with the different realities of the present once they were in Seville. Whereas in Santa Marta merchants could await the arrival of a conqueror laden with his "goods," then carry them from place to place before dispatching them to Spain, such common practices were viewed differently in Seville. Witnesses on behalf of one slave owner were astonished to learn that Juan had been freed, since, as the question for the interrogatory stated, "Everyone bought and sold indios there [in Santa Marta]," and Juan's face bore the royal brand.[61] There, in Santa Marta, the enslavement of boys and girls was unfettered, openly sanctioned, even applauded. It had longstanding historical precedents in the broader region of Tierra Firme.[62] In Seville, where indigenous slavery was still legal (until 1542) but increasingly restrained and hampered by titles, laws, and evidence, Catalina, Pedro, Isabel, and Juan became "evidence" of the juxtaposition of two vastly different expectations divided by an ocean. The Atlantic connected two different realities, in ways that were sometimes unexpected.

Crossing the Atlantic could make a difference for slaves in other ways. On one shore, a naboría, deemed to be a permanent indigenous servant who could not be sold, might serve an indigenous lord; on another, a Spanish master. Because the category naboría was so vague, it evolved and took on a specific meaning in different demographic and social contexts. Labels are often the provenance of a particular bureaucratic locus. If in passenger licenses the terms naboría and yanacona (a pre-Hispanic Andean term adapted by the Spaniards to designate free servants) were used, none of the indio litigants who crossed the ocean chose to self-identify as such. Instead they called themselves pages (*pajes*) or servants (criados), specified their occupation, or emphasized that they had "entered the service" (*entró a servir*) of their own free will. Still, many indigenous naborías and others considered "free" in Guatemala, Mexico City, or Santa Fé were transformed into slaves by the time they arrived in Spain. Unless they initiated a lawsuit, it was their word against that of their masters. How could they prove otherwise?

Crossing and re-crossing the ocean was not just a means to an end—getting from a place of departure to a destination—but a transformative experience for indio slaves and servants. The journeys across the vast watery expanse occurred for a variety of reasons. The laws dictated when and how many could come, merchants decided when and where to plunder, and slave owners had their own motivations. By the time they arrived in Castile, many indios had already been on multiple seafaring excursions, with various masters, accompanied by other indios who spoke languages they could not understand. The Atlantic moved young and vulnerable children over land and sea space and further into the unknown.[63] The vastness of the ocean diminished any direct sensorial and cognitive connections to their naturalezas. Over time, their memories of the past, modestly reconstructed in a courtroom setting, would take on a different cast. Crossing the Atlantic could mean conjuring up distantly remembered scenes or ways of doing things that no longer had any cultural referents. It would mean experiencing another passage to another destiny ordered and approved by someone else. It could mean that on a distant shore others might not see them in the same way. A young girl or boy who worked as a servant, page, or artisan in Nicaragua or Venezuela might not have the same status in Seville. Conversely, slaves who had been brutally captured and branded might receive their freedom in Spain and live out the rest of their lives as criados. As slaves learned that they could gain their freedom, and subsequently told their tales of diaspora to court scribes, they looked back at their lives, to the time before they crossed the ocean, to verify who they had once been. The ocean divided their lives into before-and-after segments related to freedom, capture, bondage—and then freedom again. Each story of transatlantic migration had its own contextual grain of truth, which would also depend on the family, the networks, and the political context of the village, town, or city in Castile where they spent their days laboring and, later, litigating. It is to these microhistories or small household dramas that we now turn.[64]

Into the Household

Lives are lived in a temporal thickness. In the courtroom setting, indigenous slaves created a carefully crafted narrative of their lived experiences, mentally snipping into segments the time before they entered the current household and the present. While all stories have beginnings, litigants chose different points in time to commence their histories of bondage in Castile. While one might have expected them to open with what it was like to witness Seville for the first time, their feelings as they glimpsed the animated throngs of *sevillanos* gathered to meet the fleet called the "carrera de Indias" as it came to a standstill on the sandy shore, but their stories never began there. Although slaves might have still sensed the swell of the ocean within them as they disembarked, other realities would have required their full attention. Usually their stories of how they became indio slaves started with a sale. Marina recalled that some twenty-eight years earlier she had been sold on the "bridge of the Archbishop" and carted off by her new master to Talavera.[65] Memories of that moment of trade were seared into her mind, but for Marina the sale was "more than just a financial exchange bounded in space and time."[66] It was a moment of rupture, the moment when she entered a household with its own internal logic of social and hierarchical relations. It was the beginning of her lineage of bondage: tracing her history and self-identification through the name of and her relationship to a new master. It was the beginning of a series of misunderstandings about what her labor meant, then and later in the courtroom, as she sought to redefine her working self in a new way. It was the beginning of a series of intimate encounters.

After the harrowing journey across the Atlantic, most indio slaves settled into a daily routine with their new masters. It is in the microcosm of the household where they were defined as indios, in relationship to a master, a household, and a family, in relationship to their labor and productive skills, and in relationship to other slaves. For, according to the medieval law code, the *Siete Partidas*, slaves were both property and people with certain rights.[67] Although some indios would eventually litigate for their freedom and complain before lawyers about enduring mistreatment and harsh circumstances, the continuities of their identities as slaves began with the first sale in Castile and their entry into a new household. Their status as indios now gained dimensionality in a relational manner to others in the household, some of whom were more powerful than they.

In sixteenth-century Castile, a household, or casa, was the sum of its parts. It consisted of kin and non-kin family members—called *familia*—

who provided the physical labor for producing hemp baskets, slaughtering rams or pigs, or transporting goods to market or a dock.[68] A household garnered profit because its constituents conducted legal transactions, borrowed or loaned money, or bartered or exchanged goods for the services of slaves and servants.[69] Not only did the casa remain viable and vital because it accumulated and utilized capital and labor, it also cultivated cohesive networks and kinship alliances across time and space. Under ideal circumstances, the casa had at its head a male with legal, psychological, and even physical dominion (*poder*) over a wife and children, as well as over distant kin or non-kin members of that household. But women, especially widows, were also the heads of households in Castile, and they exercised similar authority.

Indigenous slaves from Spanish and Portuguese America were an integral aspect of household formation and maintenance in Castile in this period. Far from their homelands and having experienced serial dislocation, they had no other choice than to form alliances, foster new kinship bonds, and rely on their masters for protection, sustenance, and some sort of stability.[70] Despite their circumstances, many were able to establish biological and economic relations with other slaves and free persons, accruing goods and creating ties with relatives "whose exact blood relationship was uncertain."[71] As members of a household, indigenous slaves also established a "lineage of bondage" with their masters. That particular identity—of self in relation to master—was reinforced by how others living in the community saw them and how they were portrayed by scribes and lawyers in legal documents. In such documents, indigenous slaves would refer to themselves (or others referred to them) "as the slave of so-and-so"—that is, as a part of a relational and dependent bond not unlike that of parent and child. As we know from the literature on African American slaves, the psychological and social boundaries of that bond were often unclear, and it was not always apparent where the property/person ended and the master began.[72] Beyond their relationships to their masters, indigenous slaves also formed a part of a larger collective social field—the master's household. Within that broader circle, they established kinship and affinitive relations with the blood relatives of the master as well as with other servants and slaves. These affective and economic ties also exceeded the physical space of the casa, brimming over into the village, town, or city.[73] Although we sometimes perceive of the casa as a world unto itself, in the sixteenth century the interior spaces of the house and the exterior community of social and economic relations were not considered separate, and servants and slaves were often the liaison between what occurred in the kitchen, in the fields, and in the town market.

Once indios had crossed the Atlantic and were completely severed from physical ties to their homelands, the routines and lived experiences of slavery and the making and unmaking of indio slaves occurred in a relational manner at the household or family level. In other words, these intimate and violent exchanges between slave and master continually re-created particular ways of understanding bondage. By the time an indio decided to press for his or her freedom, these insidious household practices had become deeply ingrained. Yet slaves knew the boundaries of what they could or would not tolerate. They knew on a visceral level the differences between the terms *slave* and *servant*. Indigenous litigants generally considered themselves to be free vassals, while masters viewed the litigants as slaves before, during, and, in some cases, after the verdicts that freed them had been rendered.

The litigation suits used to reconstruct family life provide a different perspective than do the notarial records on which scholars often rely.[74] Generally, wills, donations, and letters of freedom—documents that fill the bulky, vellum-covered ledgers kept by notaries—either show masters bestowing gifts and donations for nearly a lifetime of labor or, conversely, reveal how years of a servant's or slave's backbreaking work might be acknowledged by a meager deathbed gesture.[75] Unlike labor contracts, these litigation suits do not show the monotonous continuities in work regimens or the daily manifestations of affective ties and intimacies. They do not reveal the sinking resignation some slaves must have felt as they realized they would remain with the same intransigent master for the duration of their lives.[76] Instead, they expose the ruptures, the micro-tears in the fabric of household relations, the insidious side of power relations. Litigation suits emphasize discord, fissures, violence, and dispossession. More than anything, the lawsuits reveal that the relationships between masters and slaves "held within [them] the threat of [their] own dissolution."[77]

Wills and other notarized documents might hint at the tensions inherent in the unequal power-laden household and family dynamics, but the litigation suits disclose some of the more palpable aspects of the intimacies between masters and slaves in a given household context. These intimacies involved sexual and physical contact, as well as a visceral knowledge of the mangled and shackled body. They were enhanced or exacerbated because of the proximity of master and slave in space and time, or even because of the master's internalized sense of having total dominion over another human being. The relationship included the blurring of clear boundaries of "not-you-but-me," since the master assumed that a slave (or a female indigenous partner who was presumably free) formed a part of his broader patriarchal custody (and sense of self), much like an unemancipated minor.[78] More broadly, the household—as a set of economic and affective relations—could easily encapsulate both compassionate intimacies and the bottomless pit of inhumanity. Given the complexities of household relations, it was not unusual for slaves and servants to harbor sentiments of affection for, as well as frustration at or rage toward, masters and mistresses.[79] Such feelings were not mutually exclusive or even contradictory.

For a few, stories about life in bondage acquired thickness by detailing the period between landing at a dock or standing next to foreign slaves at a fair and gradually becoming familiar with the master's world.[80] On the pier in Seville, there might be managers or agents waiting to retrieve the newly arrived captives or to prod their flesh before deciding to purchase them. Those slaves whose masters lived in cities such as Valladolid, Madrid, Ciudad Real, or Toledo had longer distances to cover, and had to make their way by cart or on foot.[81]

Once the weary indigenous boy or girl (for most of them were still very young) had settled into the new household, they would begin sizing up their new masters: gauging whether they would be intolerant or quick to use the lash, or whether they would allow time for them to meet up with other servants and slaves who shared a similar fate. Young, vulnerable females quickly learned to avoid places where their masters or other workers might grope them, or worse.[82]

Within the physical domain of the *casa*, it was clear who dominated whom by the arrangement of space. Slaves and servants slept in corners, a cramped room, or even at the foot of the master's bed. In Seville, slaves lived near other slaves in the smallest quarters of the larger two- or three-storied rooming houses with their main doors facing a central patio. There the clustered residents shared a water fountain, kitchen, and lavatory, all public spaces where indigents and vagabonds could also find a temporary haven.[83] Home for some slaves might also extend to the corner of an artisan shop, a small shack in the countryside, or a corner of a friar's cell in a monastery: spaces where the master still felt a sense of possession despite the lack of immediate proximity.[84]

What kinds of food did these indio slaves and servants eat? Was it nutritious and plentiful? Or did frugal masters take precautions to make sure no rations were stolen by spitting into the pot of stew or by meting out provisions? Were some owners more generous with hot portions or sizable table scraps? On holidays in Seville, did slaves ever savor a cut of the highly prized castrated ram meat?[85] There are, of course, stories of slaves who pocketed victuals from the pantry or storage bins. Cristóbal, a master chef in a wealthy household, occasionally availed himself of the goods stored in the larder to pay for evenings out with one lady friend or another.[86] Although a master might exaggerate a claim of thievery, slaves did sometimes collaborate to steal valuable items, then pawn them for profit.[87] The motivation to do so was certainly high, since slaves were paid a pittance for the extra work they performed as day laborers. Aside from food, the other basic necessities that masters provided varied tremendously. Some slaves complained that they walked about practically naked and barefoot; others coveted the ornate dresses, velvet jackets, and capes in the slaves' possession. Any servant or slave with more than a single shirt or blouse was considered fortunate, since for most sevillanos, the one outfit they owned would eventually become like a "second skin" (*segunda piel*).[88]

When pressed, slave owners would argue for preferential treatment, qualified by statements about teaching their property the rudiments of Christianity. They boasted that their slaves had never gone without food, shelter, or shoes, or that their female domestic servants were never forced to work as day laborers to produce additional household income. They might say that girls who had blossomed into women under their watch were more like criadas who could come and go as freely "as any free woman could do in her own home."[89] Protection from illness and disease was another matter. The litigation records indicate a fair number of slaves who died from unnamed causes soon after they arrived in Castile. Already weakened from the transatlantic journey, they were more susceptible to the "pestilential" diseases that regularly descended upon Seville and nearby towns.[90] Slave owners complained that "indios tend to get sick a lot," especially because the medical treatment—bleedings, herbal remedies, and even surgeries to remove tumors or lance carbuncles—cost them money they had not counted on spending.[91]

Within the master's home, slaves always had to be vigilant. Even if they resided in more munificent houses and were conspicuously absent from the sightline of the masters, they were conspicuously present because of their labor potential.[92] Year after year, they sat or stood in the next room, nearby, within earshot, hovering and waiting for orders. Servants and slaves were expected to be available at all times. Though they shared the same spaces with their masters, albeit in unequal ways, they had different tactile familiarities with the objects—the tasseled furniture, the thick draperies, the blackened pots and pans—that configured the household. Slaves fingered the same cutlery, walked across the same polished floors, or grasped and nudged work tools worn from daily use.[93] But unlike their masters, they scrubbed, dusted, or put away those same objects with their own knotted hands.[94] They would never have eaten with the same forks or on the same plates. Their physical engagement with those objects varied dramatically from that of their masters.

Servants also developed intimate familiarity with their masters' bodies, each with its own contours. Day after grueling day, slaves gained a sense of the masters' flesh and viscera, their bodily functions, their trysts and gestures of affection. Whether welcomed or unwanted, attachments based on bodily knowledge formed, because slaves cared for the aged or for the master's children, cleaning up their messes or scouring stained garments.[95] They knew, or were forced to know, which spices the mistress favored, which scents she preferred.

Indio servants and slaves in Spain also knew the intimate habits and the comings and goings of the men and women they worked alongside on a daily basis. Beatríz knew that Juan de Olivares crept out at night to spend time with his wife. Leonor remembered seeing Felipa nurse her young son, Ambrosio.[96] Francisco begged the court to let the servants of Bernaldino de Mendoça testify that they had seen him receive a severe beating, since they all resided in the same household.[97] In her master's home, Inés communicated frequently with Marcos, a servant from the Philippines, and learned to say a few words of his native tongue.[98] The indio Juan García was Juan de Olivares's friend and visited him in jail after he was accused of stealing. Juan García also recalled the day the Church of Santa Ana in Triana published the banns for Olivares's marriage. When his own wife died, the grieving García was welcomed into his friend's modest quarters.[99]

Enslaved men and women formed broader kinship networks based on what the historian Ehud Toledano calls the "cohesive undergirding" of social relations, which in turn is based on vertical (within a household) and horizontal (economic and social networks among households) alliances.[100] Unfortunately, only rarely do the litigation suits provide more than shallow glimpses of how indigenous slaves worked together, the kinds of intimate conversations they had, or the material goods they loaned or shared. Each life took its own course, and it is difficult to explain how alliances were formed. For one, relations among slaves in the same household were not always peaceful; they were sometimes fraught with tension and violence.[101] The uncertainties of the future might either unite or separate slaves who had worked together for years.[102] In wealthier households, the handful of servants and slaves in the masters' employ could more easily commiserate, plan, or enjoy free moments together. Lone and isolated servants might be more vulnerable to a master's whims, unless they could form close relations with servants and slaves living nearby. In the more densely populated neighborhoods of cities such as Toledo, Ciudad Real, Valladolid, or Seville, slaves and servants greeted one another at the public fountain, in artisan shops, at markets, at the numerous gates, or on the roads into and out of town. They could share their tales of woe and joy, crucial information about a pending lawsuit, or even gossip. In the larger towns and cities, they were more likely to chance upon another indio or develop friendships with the moriscos who had been captured earlier in the century or enslaved and forcibly relocated after the Alpujarras Rebellion (1568–71) in Granada. They could also meet the increasing numbers of African peoples, labeled by authorities and slave traders as "blacks from Guinea," in cities like Madrid, Seville, Cádiz, or Toledo.[103] Similar to the experiences of Africans in North and South America, indio slaves formed fictive kinship ties with the African and morisco slaves they interacted with on a daily or weekly basis.[104] Some of these Africans and moriscos later testified on behalf of the indios once a lawsuit had been initiated.

In households where indio slaves maintained an active presence, affective ties could also develop.[105] Two indigenous girls named Inés and Isabel, both from Tabasco, may have met when they were sold together in the public plaza of Vera Cruz, Mexico, communicating in a Chontal dialect that each could understand. They crossed the Atlantic together in 1537, were baptized in the Church of Santa Ana in Triana, and lived with the shipmaster Juan Manuel and his wife, Inés López. After Juan Manuel's death, they entered the household of López, who later married Pedro de Castellanos, one of Seville's public notaries. In López's dowry, the two women were valued at 30,000 maravedís, a significant sum. They stood together in the courtroom chamber of the Casa when they were declared "neither slaves nor free" during the 1543 inspection of slaves in Seville. Over the next two years, Isabel ministered to her household companion, Inés, as she struggled with a lingering illness, to which she finally succumbed. In the four years of life Isabel still had left in her own body, she shared her knowledge of Tabasco with Inés's three orphaned children, for whom she now cared. When Isabel was laid to rest, it was in the Church of Santa Ana in Triana, the same place where Inés had been buried.[106]

Indio slaves in villages like Carmona or in cities like Seville formed friendships and associations with people—also called indios—from a broad global swath.[107] Indigenous slaves from disparate parts of the West and East Indies labored and conversed together.[108] Inés was the servant of doña Aldonza de Manrique (the former governess of Margarita Island) and her daughter. To prove her origins while litigating for her freedom, Inés stated that she could still remember her native tongue of the Rio de la Plata region, but that "when I hear the [servants and slaves] from China and Malacca speak, I [also] understand them."[109] That may be because these were the people with whom Inés spent most of her time, servants with whom she might gossip or compare the different words for, say, *pail* or *mouth.*

Many indios formed partnerships with other indios, some from the same ethnic context.[110] Those who married considered themselves as having greater status than single male and female slaves. For indios, marriage was considered a higher calling in several regards. In principle, slaves could choose their partners, but in reality masters often approved and facilitated marriages.[111] To marry, one had to be Christian, which, also in principle, gave a person the right eventually to gain freedom. From their own perspective, married indio slaves formed their own conjugal unit (a circle within a larger circle of relations), the male indio being the head of his own family even if they lived with the master.[112] The story of Pedro and Luisa—two of some seven thousand to ten thousand slaves captured, branded, and sold while Nuño de Gúzman served as governor of Pánuco, Mexico (1527–1533)—illustrates slaves inhabiting more than one circle of relations. Pedro and Luisa had been selected to work in the governor's household in the village of Santiesteban (Pánuco). As Pedro explained in his opening statement, he was eleven years old when Gúzman "took [him] for his house."[113] Not long thereafter, Gúzman's *mayordomo* forced Pedro to marry Luisa, also a domestic servant in the household. Ten years later, in 1539, Gúzman was removed from his position as governor and returned to Spain, where he faced a number of lawsuits. Pedro and Luisa followed their disgraced master to Castile, where they continued working in the new household and "sleeping together as man and wife."[114] As Pedro stated, "Nuño de Gúzman has always treated us as free and his overseer made us marry, which Gúzman knew." Pedro reasoned that because they had been indoctrinated in the Catholic faith and lived in holy matrimony, and because others treated them as a married couple (and not as slaves), they should be free. All told, the couple remained in Gúzman's service for twenty-five years. Pedro and Luisa remained a part of his household, whether in Pánuco or in Castile. But they also formed their own household unit, one in which, as Pedro stated, they were never subject to "any type of bondage." They were persons, not property.[115]

Work

As victims of serial dislocation, indigenous slaves continually refashioned new relations with masters and other servants and slaves. Pedro and Luisa had formed a family, a smaller circle within the Guzmán household and the broader circle that linked family with community. They considered themselves to be servants rather than slaves because of their status as a married couple and Guzmán's treatment of them. But power manifested itself on slave bodies and minds in the daily routines of work as well. Day-to-day relations between masters and slaves revolved around the operation of the household economy. Chores and tasks produced goods that could be consumed or sold, and financial transactions enabled the household to survive and prosper. Although Castile was not a slave economy, slave and servant labor was fundamental to its survival and success. In fact, slaves and servants often performed similar tasks, which may explain why, when slaves were sold to other, perhaps more brutal masters, they complained that they had always been treated as free persons.[116] Their point of comparison would have been the laborers with whom they interacted regularly, and which would have included a range of free servants (criados) both Castilian and non-Castilian, adolescents hired on temporary contract (soldados), and servants and slaves from the Malabar Coast and sub-Saharan and northern Africa.[117] Some indigenous men apprenticed as artisans in a trade that could bring remuneration, security, and independence.[118] Two indios, Francisco Manuel and Francisco, followed their master, a merchant, as he peddled his wares (perhaps silk cloth) near Almería. There, the two slaves witnessed the transactions and exchanges of commodities between their master and the Granadan silk weavers and Genoese merchants.[119] Francisco, an indio slave who lived in Almendralejo, in Extremadura, declared that he was a "laborer who went to the fields of the village to hoe and plow, and the villagers all recognize[d] that he always went to work and to earn extra income as a day laborer like others who have their occupation."[120]

It is difficult to get a clear sense of the gendered division of labor among indios living in Castilian villages and towns.[121] After they had finished cutting, scraping, kneading, scrubbing, wiping, and serving food, women tended small vegetable patches; then, in their "spare time," they wove and sewed hemp or flax clothing. Were male indios generally muleteers or wheelwrights?[122] We can assume so, given what we know of Castilian commoners. But the documents do not say whether it was women or men who baked bread or biscuits for the table and market, who did the spinning and weaving in a particular village, who collected firewood from the communal woodlands, or who made charcoal from the hardwood shrubs in the mountainous regions. Slavemaster litigants named their professions, but only rarely indicate what type of labor they demanded of their indigenous slaves. It is never indicated what, for instance, slaves actually did on a day-to-day basis in working for papermakers, bellmakers, swordmakers, jewelers, buttonsellers, or innkeepers.

Thus, many slaves were not unlike the tax-paying commoners of Castile, many of whom performed a variety of tasks in addition to the trade or occupation for which they had been trained.[123] What was commonly referred to as agricultural labor involved a range of activities, including planting, weeding, harvesting crops, pruning olive or fruit trees, tending to animals, or processing wheat, barley, and other grains, which needed to be ground, placed in hemp sacks, and stored. Manuel, an indio, claimed that when he passed through Baeza, he saw his cousin Joan, who was also from Colima, working in the fields.[124] Another indigenous witness, Esteban of Cuzcatlán, who had lived as a slave in Baeza for nearly two decades, provided a more trenchant impression of Joan's arduous life.

> This witness saw that Joan, indio, served Catalina de Peralta in agricultural labor like irrigating the grapevines, plowing, reaping, harvesting grapes, and [baking?] her bread. At night [he would] soak and knead hemp and make ropes and panniers and mats. When he had nothing else to do, he carried water on an ass throughout the city of Baeza. From those for whom Joan would pour water he would earn two reales which he would [then] give to his master. This witness knows [about this] because it is the custom in Baeza that slaves give [their earnings] to their masters, being paid one-and-a-half reales, serving as a slave, renting themselves out in the city as a plasterer or upholsterer, of which this witness is a master, which is why I know how to answer this question.[125]

And how did the class or status of the master or mistress affect the lives that slaves led? How did it affect the social networks slaves formed with others? Certain slaves had a more "privileged" life, in the sense that the physical demands on their bodies were kept to a minimum. Male indios in the custody of a priest or friar, for example, sometimes learned the prized skills of reading and writing; it is almost certain that the lives of these indios were less grueling than those of fieldworkers.[126] When, in 1561, the master chef Cristóbal initiated a lawsuit, he was a tired old man no longer eager to make the stews and sauces that had tantalized his master's guests and family for over a decade. He worked for an elite household that had a kitchen staff of young maids, and the mistress complained that they now did most of the work.[127] And might an india employed by a marchioness be treated more like a governess than a servant? What, exactly, did Domingo do on a daily basis as he labored on behalf of Alonso de Torquemada, mayor of Trujillo? As he fulfilled his master's wishes, was he treated better than were the water carriers and tillers of the soil?[128] The answer to these questions is most certainly yes in terms of enduring a less harsh work regimen. Certainly, some masters trained their slaves to have marketable skills, hoping they would provide more lucrative income for the household. As was the case with other slaves, indios were rented out for their services on a short- or long-term basis; contracts varied according to whether the owner wanted the slave to learn a professional trade and to how much of their earnings the individual slaves could pocket for themselves.[129] Their paltry earnings might help feed their children or buy herbal remedies or, once a year, a new garment.[130] Whether they ever earned enough to buy their freedom is difficult to ascertain.[131]

Certainly there were jobs that no slave wanted. Slave owners wishing to punish recalcitrant indios for misconduct sometimes placed them with the hempmaker, who chained them ankle to ankle with slaves from Guinea or Granada, creating an immediate, visceral knowledge between heretofore strangers.[132] If they did not work the razor-sharp vegetable fibers of nettles, flax, or hemp quickly enough, the slaves would be beaten. Once the fibers had been separated, they had to be soaked or retted in water or dew, then placed in the sun until they were parched white. With their fingers, slaves would remove the fiber bundles from the woody core, break the stems with a breaker, separate the hanging fibers by scutching them with a sharp knife, and finally hackle or comb them to prepare the finer materials for spinning or making into ropes or baskets.[133] Some less fortunate slaves (perhaps without any family contacts) worked alongside other laborers in the salt mines of Tarfia or fashioned the highly prized black and white soaps in the workshop (*fábrica*) of the archbishopric.[134] The most dreaded labor punishment of all—a veritable death sentence—was to be sent to work as an oarsman on one of the Spanish galley ships that patrolled the Mediterranean.[135] There were also scenarios in which categories that distinguished one "type" of slave from another—Guinea, morisco, or indio—made no difference. They were all just persons in bondage, forced to endure the master's whip.

Mistreatment and Ruptures

Fragmentary evidence from the litigation suits shows that indigenous men and women worked in various capacities in the casa, in the shops and fields, and on the roads. However, it is difficult to address the psychological effects that mastery had on their bodies and their psyches, since most of what we learn about slave labor is derived from the segment of the litigation suit in which they sued their masters for back wages, and reluctant masters were prone to exaggerate their former slaves' lack of strength or minimal labor value.[136] Owners commonly accused indio litigants of being by their nature inherently idle and prone to evil.[137] Such assertions, stated out of anger and bigotry, do little to help us determine when slaves felt that a physical or psychic boundary had been crossed.

Time and again, indigenous litigants would state, almost verbatim, "My master treated me as though I were a slave." Such a blanket statement masks the very real materiality of power operating on their minds and bodies. It masks how slaves defined themselves internally and externally, how they might have fought to maintain a sense of dignity. Such a generalization—"as though I were a slave"—acquires more dimensionality in the telling of a story about changed expectations, because the specifics of the narrative reveal the underlying legal and cultural logic.[138] Since infancy, Isabel, originally from Tabasco, had lived in Triana with her master, Leonor Hernández, and another couple. (We are left to wonder whether Isabel knew the slaves Inés and Isabel, also from Tabasco.) Isabel's mistress claimed to have honored the decision to keep her as a naboría, "neither slave nor free," who could not be alienated as property but who was required to remain permanently under Hernández's control. Hernández treated Isabel well by providing her with dresses and shoes "as [she would] a daughter." But when the inspection of 1549 freed Isabel, Hernández appealed the decision.[139] The action of freeing of Isabel produced a rupture, revealing the true sentiments of absolute possession the mistress had toward her surrogate "daughter." For Isabel, ribbons for her garments or a better cut of meat were not enough; she wanted to be paid eight ducats of gold each year, like any free worker, and the 1549 decision helped her to realize that desire.[140] The appeal initiated by Hernández exposed her false consciousness of "good treatment" (*buen tratamiento*) and her cold logic of seeing Isabel as the "fruits" of a capital investment. The closing statement made by Hernández's lawyer, a response to the final verdict that rejected the appeal, was equally illuminating: "He or she who possesses [a slave] in good faith acquires the fruits of personal service of the slave, even if [s]he is free, since [s]he was acquired as a slave and with a title."[141] In other words, it was unlikely that Hernández would ever see Isabel as anything other than a person whose daily backbreaking labor produced benefits for Hernández herself. As long as she remained in the household, Isabel was marked for life.

Isabel's case was not isolated. After 1542, word spread in the plazas, along the main travel routes, and in the streets that indigenous peoples were free by their nature: the New Laws stated that illegal possession of indios would no longer be tolerated. Vassals in the major centers of imperial power such as Seville and Valladolid were probably the first to hear the news, but the word quickly radiated along main travel routes throughout Iberia. The following year, in 1543, a Crown official named Gregorio López traveled to Seville to conduct an inspection of indio slaves, resulting in the freedom of over a hundred individuals. Indios everywhere began to understand that these laws might mean justice for them and their children. In household after household, former slaves began to experience the disintegration of unspoken understandings of bondage and the meaning of "family." Digesting the change in status from slave to freedperson had its own process, which for former slaves often involved enduring broken promises, threats, physical mistreatment, and, above all, a backlash of paternalistic rhetoric. But for other slaves who had spent years tolerating the intolerable, they were no longer willing to do so once a window of opportunity presented itself. Once that had happened, they would not agree to reinstate the unspoken status quo.

Many slave owners maintained that the granting of freedom to their slaves actually interfered with and hindered the humane treatment of their property—in other words, that freedom would actually cause harm to the freedman or freedwoman. A freedman would no longer have a casa, a protective domain that sheltered him and facilitated his well-being. The casa was the only home and family a slave had known since arriving from overseas, and to cut those ties would be to create an unfettered vagabond. It would also mean that a slave, considered inseparable from the master, would become an individual, instead of a part of a collective whole. For some masters, the longing to maintain the terms of bondage—the slave self existing only in relation to the master—was refracted through the lens of good treatment and protection from the outside world.[142] Many owners had abstained from meting out severe physical punishments, as in the case of the aforementioned Nuño de Gúzman, who had "never shackled [Pedro and Luisa] about the ankle or neck."[143] In other words, Gúzman had never crossed the invisible line of too much punishment (mal tratamiento). But once the owners realized that such pleading was ineffective and that they would be required to pay their former slaves back salary, masters like Gúzman switched strategies. They began to emphasize instead how much it cost to maintain slaves, based on their food intake and energy expenditure. They also began leveling accusations that their slaves had stolen food, shirts, jewels, or sacks of grain, or claiming that slaves had mistreated or taken advantage of them. After detailing the costs of care and their own mistreatment, masters resorted to gendered representations of slave vices: male slaves were prone to drinking, gambling, running away, and disobedience, while female slaves were prone to running away, belligerence, and being "loose with their bodies." The assumption behind such claims was that because the former slaves in question were fatally flawed, had committed crimes, or had defamed their masters, they did not deserve wages and should not be emancipated.[144]

Men and women in bondage had to deal on a daily basis with being objectified as lesser beings: they were assumed to be unethical, intrinsically defective, and unstable. Another continuity experienced by slaves was bodily harm. Although it was more likely that mistreatment would go unnoticed in rural locations, where slaves did not have ready access to a local authority, it did not matter whether owners lived in Madrid or Almería: they felt it was their right to beat, flog, or otherwise harm slaves if they "misbehaved." As one slave owner proclaimed, "I only beat him when he deserved it, but no more."[145] The legal corpus called the *Siete Partidas* in fact sanctioned a certain amount of violence: "When a master has cause of complaint against his slave . . . he should exercise his rights over him by punishing him by reproof, or by blows, in such a way as not to kill or cripple him."[146] Moreover, what slave litigants could say about the daily violence and denigration they had experienced before deciding to litigate was circumscribed and had to be cast in a certain way. Unlike their masters, slaves could not resort to character assassination as a defense strategy. They could not describe a master or mistress as a compulsive liar, as lazy, or as prone to drink, nor mention that married male masters regularly came to their beds at night. Slaves could, however, call attention to their mistreatment through opaque or generic statements, as long as they did not directly claim that their masters were brutal. They could rely on the legal "idioms of harm," analyzed by the historian Brian Owensby for colonial Mexico, by presenting themselves as "suffering wrong or violence from others more powerful than they."[147] They could either rely on witness testimony or present their bruised and manacled bodies as irrefutable evidence of injury.[148]

Occasionally, more specifics on the form of torture were offered in testimony. Marina's master regularly whipped Marina and her daughter, or threw boiling lard (*pringandolas*) on them.[149] What Marina was being punished for was never specified, but in describing Marina's mistreatment to the court, Marina's lawyer placed a reprehensible action within the public domain. Whether throwing boiling lard was considered an unusual or excessive punishment is questionable, for the verb *pringarse* appears in a seventeenth-century dictionary.[150] In addition, certain kinds of bodily aggression went unmentioned because the court did not recognize them as violence. For example, female slaves did not ever use the terms *violación* (physical violation) or *estupro* (rape) to describe the sexual abuse they experienced from male masters or others. But the lack of any mention of violation in the litigation suits should not be taken as evidence of the absence of such practices. On the contrary, solicitors may have discouraged female litigants from making such an argument because they knew it would not carry sufficient legal weight.

Thus, there was tacit agreement in both social custom and law that certain punitive measures against the bodies of slaves were permissible. It was culturally acceptable to brutally inscribe the surface of the body with a hot iron, for example, or to strike it with certain forces—a pummeling fist, a blade—that might cause seepage, discoloration, or scarring. The extremities—eyes, ears, fingers, and toes—were all susceptible. Whipping slaves, locking them up, shackling them, or intimidating them with verbal abuse were the culturally sanctioned options for forcing a slave into submission when the expectations of the master were not being met.[151]

Indigenous slaves who were continually mistreated sometimes resorted to running away, which could have serious consequences. Many such incidents resulted in capture and severe retribution: the loss of a limb or permanent scarring from retributive whippings. In Castile fugitive slaves were considered criminals and forfeited their right to freedom. Indios throughout Castile heard horror stories about local authorities or the owner's henchmen pursuing fugitives, about fugitive slaves having to beg for scraps of food or volunteer to do the vilest of work, about recaptured slaves having to endure scaldings, prolonged beatings, and imprisonment in chains.[152] The cook Cristóbal, who ran away several times, once returned home in tatters, "all broken and in pieces, and near starvation."[153] Even that did not stop his master from severely castigating him.

Despite the repercussions, flight was a viable option for large numbers of nonindigenous slaves, particularly near Seville. To survive, they stole jewels, grain, money, and even mules, to facilitate hurried departures to coastal cities or into Portugal. But after 1542, given that the laws, the major legal tribunals, and King Charles and Prince Philip generally supported their petitions for freedom, many indios preferred to use the courts to seek justice. If they decided to flee their masters' homes, it was largely in the hope of reaching the courts in Seville, Valladolid, or Madrid.

New Masters

Excessive violence created a major rupture between masters and slaves, but a slave's experience of moving into a new household or of taking orders from a new master within the same household could also be traumatic. Looming in the background was the threat of being sold at a fair a week's cart-ride away from one's children or one's lover, or of being taken to a port where one would be transported to yet another diasporic site; or, worse, of being conscripted to work as a galley slave. Mothers occasionally expressed dread that their children would be taken away from them.[154] It wasn't just that slaves feared separation: they also faced the burden of having to reinvent themselves each time they entered a new household with a fresh set of relations and expectations. For them, consent was never an option. Even those who considered themselves to be free were never asked whether they wanted to be sold or transferred to a new family, since the assumption within the larger household was that they were property.

As an integral part of the "slippage of life" in a household, slaves found their status deeply affected when masters died or left for the Indies, when widowers remarried, or when sisters and brothers quarreled.[155] Often indios became someone else's property, whether due to a clause in a dowry, a power of attorney, a donation, or a will (or lack thereof).[156] Litigants often complained that the new masters treated them "as though they were slaves."[157] In different ways, indio slaves all experienced a loss of dignity and a rupture when a relatively tolerable (or less degrading) relationship with a master ended. It was all a matter of degree.

Another tipping point for many slaves occurred when they were sold to owners unrelated to their original masters. Not only did such sales place the true status of the individual slave in sharp relief—for instance, it was clear that he was considered a commodity, not a family member—but it meant the slave was forsaken and expelled from a known household with its attendant set of relations.[158] For masters, there were the cold calculations of whether it was worth keeping freed indios as salaried servants, especially as they faced increasing pressure from Crown authorities to do so, unless the slaves had legitimate documents. After being abducted in Guatemala, the india Monica came to Castile via Lisbon. For many years, she worked for a ropemaker and his mother in a section of Valladolid where used clothing was sold. When she decided to ask for a salary, in 1559, her owners branded her and tried to sell her. The ropemaker argued, "If [Monica] died, we would lose our investment [of what we paid for her]."[159] But then he added that she was like a "daughter and sister and [that they] love[d] and treat[ed] her as such."[160] These family sentiments and the fragile distinction between person and property surely did not factor into the decision to brand her illegally and sell her to someone far away, but the ropemaker did not consider his words and actions to be contradictory.

Even more difficult was when the Spanish partner of an indigenous woman died, and mother and children were transferred to a new owner. As the *Siete Partidas* stated, the *patria potestas* (power of the father) extended from the male head of household to the household's legitimate and illegitimate family members in a "bond of reverence, subjection, and castigation."[161] This hierarchical relationship included children born out of wedlock (*hijos naturales*) and indigenous partners who came to Spain with a Castilian father and partner. For a Spanish male of means, it was risky to reside with his indigenous partner, as he might be censured by villagers or subject to disapproving murmurs from other family members. But the arrangement was riskier for an indigenous female, since she did not have the legal rights she would have had if she were married to her master. Given that some of these women had been former slaves, it became necessary for them to maintain a "productive rapport" with their master-cum-partner once they arrived in Castile. Obedience and subjugation were integral to the intimacies between them.[162] An unmarried indigenous women cohabitating with a Spanish man could easily be vulnerable to his whims or to those of his capricious relatives. The male might decide to send the india mother back to America once he planned to wed someone else, leaving the mestizo children dependent on the father to ensure that they would remain free after his death.[163] A woman was especially vulnerable after her partner died; in several recorded instances, indigenous women who had been living openly with their partners were "passed on" to other family members who saw them as disposable property.[164] Children were also susceptible. The rule of patria potestas of a father over his mestizo children born out of wedlock was clear if he legally recognized them, but if he did not, other relatives could subject those children to servitude.

It might seem self-evident that mestizos would be considered free in Castile, even if the Spanish father and indigenous mother were not married at the time the india mother gave birth. But the situation was more complicated if the mother had been or was currently a slave or perceived to be a slave just because she was an india. The laws were never explicit about such situations, which gave slave owners ample room to argue that if the mother was a slave when the child was born, the child was also a slave.[165] Even before the New Laws of 1542 prohibited indigenous slavery, a law promulgated in 1534 stated that no women could be taken as slaves, but this law was not applied universally in Castile. If the Spanish father remained in America or did not play an active part in raising the child, the slave mother would live in fear that her children would be sold, for she had no proof, other than her word, that their father was a Spaniard.[166]

The case of the aristocratic Oropesa family of Cáceres poignantly illustrates the vulnerabilities of mothers and children. They owned a castle and fortress in nearby Plasencia, which was filled with servants and slaves who attended to their daily needs. When Pedro de Oropesa returned from Peru, he was accompanied by his indigenous partner, Isabel, their mestizo son, Lorenço, and an orphan boy, Gaspar Sánchez, whom Oropesa had decided to raise as a "Christian free vassal." Everyone assumed that Isabel, Lorenço, and Gaspar were free from bondage because Oropesa treated them as such.[167] For nine years, Gaspar lived as a free boy with his surrogate father, Isabel (who was considered Pedro's *amiga*, or concubine), and Lorenço, whom Pedro de Oropesa legally recognized as his son.[168] Four months before he died, Oropesa decided to marry a woman named Isabel Gutiérrez. Because he had never identified the india Isabel as a free woman, the safety of both mother and son was now at stake. With Oropesa's death, Isabel, Lorenço, and Gaspar lost their male protector; his understanding of them as free subjects vanished with his last breath. Pedro's new wife disapproved of his union with Isabel and was not inclined to "let the two [mother and son] enjoy their freedom," despite the fact that Pedro had left a bequest for Lorenço in his will. Isabel Gutiérrez also considered the young orphaned man, Gaspar Sánchez, to be a person in bondage. According to the deposition later made by Gaspar to his legal representative, Isabel Gutiérrez "treated him like a slave, calling him Moorish dog, and treating him like a black slave, throwing chains on him."[169] He was unaccustomed to such brutal treatment and resented being compared with the household slaves.

After consulting with supportive relatives, Gaspar and Lorenço approached the *corregidor* of Plasencia, who brought the matter to the attention of the Council of the Indies and ultimately King Philip. At stake for Lorenço was the status of his mother. Curiously, the lawyer representing Isabel argued that because she willingly had carnal relations with the unmarried Oropesa, she was free, and so was her son. She had told the lawyer that even if Isabel Gutiérrez chained her and locked her up, she was still free "because she had given birth three times." (Two of her children must have died.) Furthermore, even in the land of her birth, Peru, all the indios were free. When she arrived in Plasencia with Pedro de Oropesa, "she rode on a mule, seated on a pillow with a chain of gold around her neck." She brought a letter of freedom with her. After Pedro married, he apparently lost the letter, although, according to the lawyer's summary of Isabel's deposition, he tried to find someone who could get a copy. He also offered Isabel a dowry of 80,000 maravedís if she ever wanted to marry. After Pedro's death, however, she languished with a lock (not a gold chain) around her throat. In 1570 King Philip II ruled in favor of mother and son, ordering the opposing parties to pay the court costs and not to perturb the three litigants in any way. Isabel Gutiérrez was to adhere to the clause in Pedro's will that stipulated that his son Lorenço was to be paid an annual allowance of twelve ducats and was to receive instruction from a tutor. At the age of twenty, Lorenço was to receive the lump sum of 20,000 maravedís.[170] In a separate lawsuit, Gaspar was also freed. What is interesting about this case is that Isabel used the argument of having given birth three times while under the patria potestas of her partner and during a long-standing relationship of concubinage. In her mind, she was free because of motherhood and consensual union. However, this line of reasoning probably did not affect the king's decision; it is more likely that he relied on the laws that outlawed indigenous female slavery and, more generally, slavery in Peru to release her from Isabel Gutiérrez's custody.

In this case, a rupture occurred because Isabel, Lorenço, and Gaspar were dependent on the father; it did not matter, after his death, that he had determined by his treatment of them and legal recognition of his son that the mother and son were free. Isabel, Lorenço, and Gaspar were appalled to find that their new owner perceived and treated them as though they were slaves. They found it necessary to prove that they were not persons in bondage. Although ultimately a matter for a court (and the king) to decide, the rupture in the household came about because of the master's death. How fragile were the bonds of patria potestas; how important was perception in the maintenance of the casa with all its relations of dependency and with the presence of individuals from disparate parts of the world.

Deciding to Litigate

The very act of initiating a lawsuit or an appeal created a radical disruption in the pulse of daily household life. It stirred up seething anger and frustration. It exposed the rawness of power. Slave owners protested loudly against the implementation of the New Laws and the freeing of over one hundred indios in the inspection by Gregorio López, arguing that they had treated their slaves well, like members of their family, like daughters or sisters or sons. How could their slaves not appreciate all that had been done for them? How dare they petition for their freedom when they were practically free? In initiating lawsuits, indio slaves and servants revealed their feelings of betrayal, loss, and confusion. When they were passed or sold to another family member, they saw how easily the bonds of trust could be broken. Like other slaves in Seville, they may have expected that their masters might free them if they worked hard enough, since indios could not rely on relatives or social organizations to ransom them.[171] But after 1542, differences in the quotidian experiences of people in bondage differentiated as black, morisco, or indio were set in stark relief. Only indios now had recourse to laws that determined they could be freed if they had been unjustly enslaved.[172] Thus, it remains to be seen whether disparities in masters' treatment of these different subjects in the domain of the casa led directly to differences in governance over colonized subjects more generally. Focusing on the discord between and unrealized expectations of masters and slaves at the household level helps us to understand the intricacies of bondage and the fine line between freedom and slavery. A household rupture might occur after one too many lashings or the loss of a finger or ear. Knowing now that the laws generally supported their rights as free vassals, those indios who had assumed they were free realized at that critical moment that their masters saw them as commodities or expendable property. Each instance of radical rupture brought the realization that relationships were not as they seemed. Each instance also exposed the truth that indio slaves had theretofore been forced to live in silent conformity.

When indigenous slaves decided to litigate for their freedom, the tenuous bonds between masters and laborers became increasingly fraught. Tensions ran particularly high when masters were confronted with the possibility that their indio servants would initiate lawsuits against them. These were the bald truths, the layers of complacency or apparent trust falling away to reveal darker realities, and they often led to an escalation in violence. Indios might have thought they were safely ensconced within a family niche, within a circle of familiars who would look after them and their children, even if they were laborers. They worked alongside others who were free, performing the same tasks. In some instances, it was difficult to discern which came first: a master's attempt to sell the slave, or the slave's move to initiate litigation. What is of interest to the historian is that lawsuits forced owners to acknowledge the violent underpinnings of their power in a public forum.[173]

Lawsuits brought the testimony of the "street" together with the testimony of the "court," where sentiments, rationales, and behaviors were publicly exposed.[174] Lawsuits highlighted slave owners' assumption that the law would respect that indios were their property and members of the casa, where the law should have no jurisdiction.[175]

Once a slave began the litigation process, the brutality against them usually increased.[176] There are many stories of horror.[177] When Pedro, from Tierra Firme, sought his freedom, his master tied him to a post, whipped him severely, then wrapped him in chains. Responding to the accusation that this punishment was excessive, Pedro's master said, "If [Pedro] is imprisoned or chained up it is because he is a thief, a drunk, and a fugitive; [he is] incorrigible and a master is legally permitted to punish him."[178] His next recourse was to try to sell him. Fortunately, a friar named Francisco de Carvajal saw Pedro in the streets with a neck lock fastened to his throat. Carvajal approached him, saying, "Come here, brother indio, how is it that you, an indio, are wearing a lock and chains, since because you are an indio you should be free?" After a brief exchange, the friar advised Pedro to seek legal protection at the Council of the Indies.[179] And so Pedro became one of nearly 184 indios to enter the courtroom arena to seek legal and social justice.

THREE

Small Victories?

Gregorio López and the Reforms of the 1540s

When this witness [Francisco] told his mistress [Beatríz García] that he was free and did not have to serve her as a slave, [Beatríz García] told her brother-in-law, a swordmaker, what he, Francisco had said, and the brother-in-law then responded, "Give him to me and I will sell him two hundred leagues from here where he will never see anyone again."

—"Deposition, Francisco, indio," AGI, Justicia 1019, n. 5, r. 1, 6r

From the Crown's perspective, 1543 was a difficult but triumphant year, thanks to Gregorio López Tovar (1496–1560), an aspiring jurist on the Council of the Indies.[1] As a result of a months-long inspection he led to verify the legal status of the indios residing in the archbishopric of Seville, over one hundred slaves had been freed. This emancipation was unprecedented and sent a clear warning to slave owners who had collaborated, in one way or another, with the prolongation of indigenous slavery in Castile. López also benefited. He was paid a handsome sum to carry out his mission, and over the next decade his star continued to rise. By 1558, when the jurist decided to retire from the council, he had overseen dozens of litigation suits involving indigenous slaves. But such dedication to this and other legal causes came at a cost. After decades of clarifying and upholding the letter of the law, López found that his health had seriously deteriorated.[2] He returned home to Guadalupe, an important pilgrimage site where sixty years before Christopher Columbus had brought two Taíno indios to kneel and be baptized before an image of the Virgin.[3] López lived the last two years of his life there, in austere living quarters, surrounded by family members. Years later, when King Philip II visited the judge's humble quarters, he exclaimed, "A small cage for such a large bird!"[4]

Like Bartolomé de las Casas, López helped to free scores of indios who were an ocean away from home. This was a remarkable feat. But as López himself realized after arriving in Seville to conduct the inspection, altering decades of unlawful practices and striking at the widely held conviction that indios *should* be slaves required more than one man's efforts. Not only was Seville known round the world as a dynamic (*movido*) city, but the Casa, where the inspection took place, was notorious for its behind-the-scenes bribery, threats, and other abominable actions that benefited slave owners and humiliated indios. Many sevillanos with a stake in upholding slavery knew that López's stay was temporary and trusted that as soon as his carriage left the city, life would return to normal.

Indeed, evidence from litigation suits initiated after the 1543 inspection shows that the great jurist's efforts may not have been as effective as scholars have generally assumed. In April 1544, less than a year after López had left Seville, an anonymous man "who [was] aware [of the situation] and who wishe[d] to clear his conscience" informed Bartolomé de las Casas, who had just arrived in Seville, that a "great deal of evil and bribery" was occurring, whereby Spaniards were selling free indios for a small sum, then covering up the truth or threatening the indios if they complained to an authority.[5]

The warning issued by the unidentified man is corroborated by the litigation suits. Those indios who had dared to state before López in 1543 that they were free later endured beatings or were locked up in iron chains. Some were branded and sold to unsuspecting buyers as slaves of just war. Even more problematic was López's decision to declare a number of indios as "neither slaves nor free," since that new, liminal status afforded them few options. López may have reduced the extraordinary rate of illegal slave traffic and the bald-faced exploitation of large numbers of indios, but following his inspection, slave owners issued numerous complaints and hostility toward indios in Castile was patent. Six years after López's inspection, the Crown decided another inspection would be necessary.

In this chapter I examine the dismantling of the most egregious forms of slavery and how indigenous litigants deeply engaged with Castilian legal culture. I consider the implementation of a bureaucracy and legal apparatus designed to enforce the laws implemented in the 1530s against distinct aspects of indigenous slavery and the creation of legal indios in the heart of the Spanish empire) I analyze the politics of the inspections of 1543 and 1549 from the perspective of slave owners, who resorted to various means to retain their property, legally or surreptitiously. As slave owners responded to the rapid legal changes, freed and enslaved indios struggled to find a legal and social space for themselves in Castile. Meanwhile, council members and the king participated in simultaneously upholding and dismantling servitude in its various guises. Behind the scenes, theologians like Bartolomé de las Casas encouraged the implementation of a clear set of laws that would attack slavery from the moment an indio was captured in America. But this legalistic strategy did not have the effect Las Casas had hoped for. In short, the dismantling of indigenous slavery in Castile was neither straightforward nor easy, and new legislative practices only enhanced the liminal status of indios as neither free nor enslaved for decades to come.

At stake in the efforts of López and others was how to define the juridical status of the indio. The struggle for justice—combating indigenous slavery—involved deciding where indios fit in the natural and political order. In the 1540s and 1550s, jurists, lawyers, and slave owners living in Castile grappled with the philosophical contradictions inherent in indigenous slavery and eventually concluded that indios were not natural slaves, but neither were they to be completely free vassals. Rather than a clean break with the past, the new law reflected a gradual transformation in legal reasoning that sought to move away from indigenous slavery and servitude, but not to eradicate it. The resolutions reached at the time also established a framework for future discussions regarding the legal status of indios, their position in relation to Spaniards as a part of a separate republic, and their contributions to the colonial economy.[6]

Dismantling a slave system not only involved implementing laws and ordinances; it also meant exposing the paternalism that fed that system. Sentiments of loyalty and disloyalty, dominion and dependency, and intimacy and violence often structured the slave-master relationship. In that sense, it would be misguided to separate the legal codes from the attitudes that upheld and perpetuated indigenous slavery. The law was not an abstract set of principles placed above the values of patriarchy, paternalism, and privilege: it was cut of the same cloth. The creation and enactment of laws was a haphazard, contradictory, and cumbersome process, as the snail-paced evolution in attitudes about slavery worked in tandem with the legal codes driving those transformations. The enactment of laws may reflect a desire for change and order, but these prescriptive rules, as legal anthropologists have shown, do not reflect daily practices on either imperial or commoner levels.

The shift in legal practices toward indigenous slaves occurred at a key moment, when an awareness of a Castilian imperial "self" began to emerge. In a two-pronged approach, the Crown and the king's agents attempted to impose legal and administrative boundaries to distinguish Castile from other imperial powers while simultaneously exerting control over powerful vassals such as encomenderos and merchants who promoted and maintained indigenous slavery in Latin America. But as Bartolomé de las Casas liked to remind the king, Castilian tyrannies against the indios were not only widespread in Latin America, but also rampant in the economic heart of the empire, Seville.[7] Skilled and loyal administrators, he argued, were needed to develop a clear, forward-thinking policy ensuring that indios could live as free, but subservient, Castilian vassals. Such efforts had to begin in Castile.

The two inspections of 1543 and 1549 were part of a larger Crown strategy to effect some serious administrative housekeeping at home. As it became increasingly clear that the enforcement of decrees regulating or prohibiting indigenous slavery in Spanish America was going to be extremely difficult and time-consuming, Crown authorities decided to make a more concerted effort to police Castile. To implement laws protecting unjustly enslaved indigenous peoples and to monitor the inspection practices for ships, passengers, cargo, and slaves, Charles V began in 1542 with an inspection of the Council of the Indies and the following year of the Casa, the two political and economic linchpins of a growing but as-yet fragile imperial system.[8] But, as he soon realized, authorities there were not always as impartial or loyal as he would have liked. Not all council members and Casa officials exalted good governance over self-interest, as Bartolomé de las Casas liked to point out.[9] Another problem was that over a twenty-year period the jurisdictions of the Casa and the Council of the Indies had to some extent overlapped. The king hoped that enhancing the council's role as the superior body would allow it to serve as a distant but powerful watchdog over the more corrupt (and some would argue less professional) Casa.

In some ways Charles V's decision was like putting a thin bandage over a gaping wound. Since the Casa's inception, its officials had profited handily from their lucrative extra-officio transactions. Over the decades, Crown authorities with ties to Casa officials and members of the merchant community stood to benefit from the arms-length control over its administration. But by 1543, as news of scandals continued to reach the king, he decided to intervene directly to curtail some of the Casa's authority.[10] Specifically, he targeted the three officials—the treasurer, accountant, and business administrator—all of whom arbitrated as judges and decided which passengers and which goods could come and go.[11] The king wanted to put an end to their unscrupulous activities.

By opting to conduct a comprehensive inspection of the House of Trade, the king knew he had to choose a reliable official. The behind-the-scenes efforts of Las Casas, who regularly sat in on council meetings and regularly spoke with the king, may also have influenced the council's choice of Gregorio López to conduct the review of 1543.[12] A fresh face on the Council of the Indies, López was considered the perfect choice for a Crown-appointed inspector. He was rigorous, knowledgeable, and hardworking. For several years he and several other well-trained jurists had edited and created glosses for the corpus of royal laws being compiled, including the *Siete Partidas*.[13] The king favored him for other reasons. Not only did López show promise as a jurist—he knew the laws and juridical procedure well—but as one of the newest members of the Council of the Indies, he had not yet established personal ties with House of Trade authorities.[14]

The appointment of a loyal and scrupulous inspector was important because earlier inspections that had attempted to thwart the illegal commerce—including one by Licentiate Suárez de Carvajal, the bishop of Lugo, in 1536—had had little effect.[15] Although the Casa officials were under king's orders to inspect ships before disembarkation in Seville and to review the papers of indios brought into Castile, gross injustices occurred on a regular basis. Either indio slaves were brought ashore in nearby Palos de la Frontera or San Lúcar de la Barrameda, or Casa officials ignored faulty paperwork. Generally, when the portero (the official charged with inspecting the entrance of all goods) confiscated illegal slaves, he was supposed to grant them freedom and place them in deposit with reputable sevillanos, with whom they might live and earn a salary. However, many indios were instead left to fester or die in jail; those deposited in private homes were often branded and illegally sold to garner a profit.[16]

The 1543 Inspection

Corruption, faulty record keeping, and the improper treatment of indios were only a few of the issues that López faced when he arrived in Seville in late May 1543. By then, sevillanos were already on edge, but for other reasons. They had just endured two years of bread shortages and exorbitant prices for other basic foodstuffs.[17] The city was growing rapidly, perhaps too rapidly, and its population now surpassed fifty thousand.[18] The city's economic instability perhaps exacerbated the lack of probity in business matters, but it became clear to López as soon as he began inspecting the records (or the lack thereof) and interviewing officials at the Casa that corruption was rife on multiple levels. Over the course of eighty-four days, he and his notary, Juan de la Quadra, wrangled with the problem of governance of the Casa and wasted no time in attacking the problem of illegal slavery.[19]

Throughout the summer of 1543, indios were inscribed into a ledger, slaves in one section and free or freed persons in another. Masters were to appear in person with their slaves and freed servants and were required to bring documentation proving legal ownership. Failing to comply with the order meant risking a fine of 20,000 maravedís, the loss of legal authority over their property, and the immediate granting of freedom to slaves.[20] Appropriate papers included a title of purchase and evidence that slaves had been examined before being branded and as they embarked with their masters for Spain.[21] Missing or forged documents would result in the immediate release and freedom of slaves, some of whom had been in their masters' possession for decades. As the ultimate arbiter, López had the authority to decide each slave's fate. To speed up the inspection and sentencing processes, López was ordered by the king to act *sumariamente*—quickly and without a lengthy trial.[22]

While the inspection was proceeding, slaves were to remain in the owners' custody. Attempts to transport or sell them would result in heavy fines.[23] In clear cases of abuse or life-threatening danger, a slave could petition to be removed from a master's custody and placed with a court-appointed guardian. Even then, the owner could appeal the custody decision (a form of legal deposit), not only because absconding with his property was considered by many to be offensive (and illegal), but because wrangling over the bail bond could serve as a stalling tactic. Although the medieval legal code called the *Siete Partidas* stated that a third party who received property (a slave) because of a pending lawsuit was not obligated to return that property to the owner until the dispute was settled, nearly all requests to return slaves to the custody of the master—especially when the slave owner argued that needed income from the slave's labor was being lost—were honored.[24] Owners were required to swear that they would not take the returned slaves outside the city limits, or beat, punish, or attempt to sell them. They also had to ensure that the slave would have access to the procurador assigned to represent them and would not be denied access to proper legal counselling. From the perspective of the slaves, continuing to reside in the master's home while litigation proceeded was extremely awkward and, in some cases, dangerous. The intimidation, bullying, and inveigling that occurred at this delicate stage of the legal process sometimes had the desired effect for masters, although this is rarely documented. In such instances of abuse, humiliated slaves would withdraw their petitions for freedom and continue bearing the burden of bondage in silence.[25]

To compensate for the fact that many slave owners were unable to produce the correct documentation in a timely manner—and they complained vociferously that the time allotted had intentionally been made too short— they were allowed to draw up a set of questions for witnesses, who participated in a *probanza* (inquest, proof) to attest that the slaves had been acquired in a just and legal manner.[26] The probanza questions were clearly biased in favor of the slave owner, and witnesses were coached on the appropriate responses.

Slave owners lacking sufficient paperwork relied on an assortment of arguments, from credible to feeble, to prove ownership. Some reasoned that, as in a common-law marriage, the length of time the slave had been in the owner's custody—in some cases ten or twenty years—should be the equivalent of just title. Others asked why the slaves had not previously filed legal complaints or questioned the condition of bondage, why no paperwork had been required when the slaves had been bought, or why the laws were being applied retroactively. Many insisted that they had always provided proper food and lodging for their slaves, had taught them the rudiments of the Catholic faith, and had not abused the right to beat or use physical punishment when called for.

The probanzas drawn up by several slave owners also disclose another cut of truth. Witnesses disclosed underlying sentiments about slavery—some paternalistic, some bigoted—that many still openly embraced. For instance, Juana's master, Alfonso Baeza, asked his witnesses to answer the leading question "If they [the slaves] were free, they would be lost because they would be drunkards and thieves, [so are they] . . . better off with their masters?"[27] Testimonies also echoed arguments being made in judicial chambers throughout Spanish America, that if the slaves were not removed from their native habitats, they would incite rebellion and kills all the Christians.[28] However hollow the arguments—about the time of possession, proper care, and education, or around claims that indios were better off in the care of Castilians—they were nevertheless powerful rationalizations that had justified illegal and rampant slave trafficking for decades. Truly believing that indios were untrustworthy drunkards, thieves, and pagans, both slave owners and some Crown authorities had participated, tacitly and transparently, in maintaining the system of indigenous slavery for nearly fifty years.

So Crown authorities turned to laws and ordinances to bolster their changing position. One of the first orders of business for López was to reorganize and update the archive containing ordinances and decrees.[29] He did this to ensure easy accessibility to the cache of royal decrees for Casa officials and legal experts. In fact, much to the chagrin of slave owners, he drew on several previously enacted but rarely implemented royal decrees to bolster his decisions about the fate of slaves. One decree, issued by Queen Isabel on 16 March 1536, had been read out on the steps of the Cathedral of Seville, then inscribed in the Casa's ledgers.[30] It delineated the proper procedures to follow for enslavement and migration of slaves and indigenous servants to Castile. All slaves brought to Spain from New Spain and Santo Domingo required a letter from the viceroy, governor, member of the royal court, or the chief justice of a municipal council (*justicia mayor*). The decree also made it obligatory for these same authorities to review the documents, including the title of ownership, which had to state the origin of the slave and whether the current owner had acquired the slave through inheritance, donation, or purchase. For slaves designated as war captives, accompanying papers needed to prove the circumstances of captivity and that the slave had been examined and branded by a royal official. Authorities at the different Atlantic ports were mandated to ensure that paperwork was in order and to ask indigenous "slaves" if they truly were slaves and accompanying their masters to Spain voluntarily. Finally, ships were to be inspected before setting sail from American ports and once again when they docked in Seville.[31] If, at any stage of the migration process, authorities discovered any missing papers, they were to free the slaves immediately.

These procedural mandates had two effects—they increased the involvement and scrutiny of royal officials over the various stages of enslavement in America, and they made it incumbent on slave owners to prove just title of legal enslavement. In short, these laws bureaucratized slavery. Crucially for indigenous slaves, it hindered the massive enslavement that had gone unchecked for decades. It also ensured that the onus of proof no longer rested with the slaves. Reliance on these laws also made Gregorio López's job a little easier, especially since at least twenty slave owners decided to appeal his decisions before the Council of Indies (see table Intro.1). Once the appeal process had begun, the prosecuting attorney of the council, Licenciate Villalobos, did the heavy lifting for López.

It was in these appeals that clashes between past practices and present policies surfaced. Slave owners often complained to Villalobos that López lacked the legal authority to adjudicate in cases involving personal property; neither had he allowed them to seek proper legal representation. They maintained that each time López adjudicated, he always determined that his decision was final, which meant that their only recourse was to initiate an appeal before the Council of the Indies. To these complaints Villalobos usually responded that the law stated that indios were, by their nature (ingenio) free, that López had proceeded in accordance with the instructions given to his commission, and that according to the 1536 decree, neither a bill of sale nor a royal brand constituted legal grounds for servitude. In cases involving children or women, the fiscal Villalobos relied on a decree, issued in 1534 in Toledo, that prohibited the enslavement of women and of children under the age of fourteen. This was crucial because most of the indios had been abducted at a young age, and 48 percent of slave litigants in 1543 were female. Although not a foolproof guarantee of freedom, the decree certainly helped indigenous litigants win the appeals initiated by their masters in the wake of the 1543 inspection.[32]

What constituted admissible evidence now also changed. For decades, branding had been considered unquestionable proof of slavery, even if a royal authority had not been present. A number of slave owners presenting their slaves for inspection were astonished when the "R" brands on the chins or faces of their property were not automatically accepted as proof of bondage. But as the 1534 decree stated, too much "disorder" (desórden) had occurred in illegal and indiscriminate branding practices. Over the decades, reports had filtered up to Crown authorities that blacksmiths were fashioning their own brands, that the names of multiple masters crisscrossed the faces of slaves, and that the faces of free men and women were scarred as a form of punishment.[33] Given these practices, the Crown decided to respond, albeit only after hundreds of thousands of indios had been permanently disfigured. Different royal decrees stated that only royal officials could brand slaves (in 1528 and 1532) and that branding no longer constituted clear proof of slavery (1534). Unambiguous evidence of illegal branding would result in the automatic freedom of the unfortunate slave. "Just title" meant stating before a local authority why a slave had become a captive, at which point the notary would pronounce that individual to be a "slave."[34] Only then would the slave owner have the right to brand the slave and had to do so in the presence of a local justice who had the brand in his possession.

Finally, the controversial New Laws of 1542 provided the legal nail in the coffin for slave owners in Seville. Among the twenty three articles dealing specifically with the status and treatment of indios, slavery for just war and ransom, and even in cases of rebellion, was now strictly prohibited (although exceptions abounded).[35] Newly designated Audiencia members or governors were charged with inspecting all titles of slave owners and freeing any indigenous peoples who had been unjustly enslaved, while special legal representatives were now assigned to represent indigenous litigants in court.[36]

Slave owners who lost possession of their slaves in the 1543 inspection or in the consequent appeals were confused and irritated for any number of reasons. They complained that decrees cited during the litigation suits had only been sporadically enforced.[37] For decades, Crown authorities had been inconsistent (and lackadaisical) in enacting and enforcing legislation that prohibited indios from entering Castile. "Licenses" granted in America were often slapdash, deficient, and, in some cases, counterfeit.[38] Despite the 1536 mandate requiring specific documentation, many slave owners passed inspection in the Casa with what one Crown authority euphemistically referred to as "simple decrees."[39] Furthermore, the king continually allowed exceptions to his own rules.[40] The king was inconsistent in other ways: over the decades he had also promulgated, then rescinded legislation banning slavery. Even more irksome were the irregularities from one inspection to the next. Indios declared slaves during the 1536 inspection conducted by the bishop of Lugo were freed seven years later by López. If we view the 1543 inspection as a watershed event where royal will, bolstered by law, confronted "recalcitrant realities," we need to keep in mind that some of the "realities" of unmitigated slavery had had the explicit support of Crown authorities for decades.[41]

Although the 1543 register is now lost, it is deeply significant that over one hundred men and women were freed as a result of Gregorio López's inspection.[42] We do not know how many others were ordered to remain as "neither slave nor free" with their masters. Among all the appeals initiated by owners against the 1543 decisions to free their slaves, only one resulted in a slave remaining as "neither slave nor free" in the custody of his master, a priest. All other indios, with the support of the fiscal, retained their status as freedpersons (based on López's decision). However, responses from the council varied with regard to the slaves' compensation and future treatment. Unlike some of those who later brought lawsuits, none of these litigants received financial compensation. However, in some cases slave owners were ordered not to perturb their slaves or they would face a substantial penalty. In cases involving duplicity or damaging physical abuse, former slave owners faced even stronger penalties. One owner not only lost the appeal to keep his two slaves, but was obligated to pay the couple's return passage to Mexico and give them money for the care of their young child.[43]

Finally, the council tackled the issue of licensing the transatlantic travel of indigenous slaves. A royal provision iterated what had been said before: that Crown authorities were aware that Castilians had "general licenses" to bring free and enslaved indios to Spain and that the indios traveling with them always said that they had come of their own volition. López complained to council members that, with the exception of the 1536 decree of Empress Isabel, there were no laws on the books to prohibit or regulate indios from entering Castile.[44] In September 1543 (and once López had returned to his duties on the council in Valladolid), the Crown passed a decree stating that under no circumstances, not even with a license, were indios to be brought to Castile by anyone of any "station, status, or condition."[45] Anyone who aided or abetted in the process would be fined 100,000 maravedís, and complicit authorities risked losing their offices.[46] Crown officials also attempted to place a legal stranglehold on intra-American indigenous slave trafficking by passing legislation that prohibited indios from being removed from their provinces of origin under penalty of a 100,000 maravedís fine and the cost of returning the indios to their naturalezas.[47]

Because laws now dictated the terms of enslavement from the moment of capture to overseas travel, large-scale indigenous slavery became much more difficult. But it was one thing to enact legislation to limit new enslavement, and quite another to modulate the attitudes and actions of slave owners as they dealt with the slaves and freed indios who had labored in their homes for years, if not decades. For some of these indios, the 1543 inspection was a pyrrhic victory. Some never made it to the inspection. They were hidden or stealthily relocated to the independent domain of a count or to other parts of Andalucía. In one or two instances, Crown authorities were able to track down the slaves—including an india taken to the village of Baza, home of the *oidor* (a member of the royal court in Castile or Spanish America) of the Audiencia of Panama, known for his wholehearted support of Indian slavery.[48] But this kind of detective work was rare.

Not only were indios removed to remote villages, but they were chained and sequestered even in Seville.[49] In the case of one indio named Juan, his owner kept him prisoner by claiming that he was a "runaway." In fact, Juan's incarceration was meant to deter him from consulting with legal experts who were helping to advance his case.[50] Other slave owners did not bother to present their slaves at the inspection and, when questioned, claimed that they had not heard the town crier or that they had been so sick or indisposed that they had been unable to respond when the inspector's assistant or the constable showed up at their doorsteps with summons.[51] Another common ruse was for owners to tell slaves that there was no need to go before the inspector, because they were already free. But no sooner had López left town than those slaves would be sold to unsuspecting buyers as slaves of just war. Such transactions were relatively easy because Seville was a port city, and port cities were porous, exposed sites filled with new opportunities and old perils. Genoese, Portuguese, or Flemish slave traders regularly slipped in and out of the city with their human wares. According to the indios who confided their anguish to Bartolomé de las Casas, slave traders were everywhere, lying in wait.[52]

The initial jubilation that some indios felt when they heard the royal decrees read out on the cathedral steps quickly soured in the face of numerous and complex legal quagmires. The story of Francisco, from the province of Tlaxcala, illustrates how easily some indios could fall between the juridical cracks. In his initial deposition of 1540, Francisco stated that four years earlier, word had spread among the slaves that all indios from New Spain were free by their nature. But whenever he reminded the members of his mistresses' household in the village of Puerto de Santa María that he was being treated like a captive, they told him, " 'Look at the dog, what will the judges of the Casa do with it, you think they will favor [a dog] there?' "[53] When Francisco told his mistress he was free, she passed him off to her brother-in-law, who threatened to sell him " 'two hundred leagues from here where he will never see anyone again.' "[54] Francisco's greatest fear then came to pass. First the swordmaker took him to a barber in Seville, who branded his face. Next, the swordmaker convinced Francisco to accompany him to Cádiz, where he said he had to buy materials to fashion swords. Once they had reached the Atlantic port, he quickly sold Francisco to a merchant intrigued by the slave's sailing skills. Fortunately, because Francisco was able to find a sympathetic ear, he was placed in the custody of Gregorio López, then still in Seville conducting his inspection.

For some reason, however, the jurist did not adjudicate Francisco's status during that momentous summer of 1543. It took four additional years before Francisco was finally freed by the Council of the Indies, in 1548. Perhaps his paperwork had languished at the bottom of a stack, or perhaps Casa officials had listened too intently to the pleadings of his mistress. The slow pace of court bureaucracy and faulty communications between the Casa and the Council of the Indies might also help to explain the slow pace of Francisco's case.[55]

Francisco learned firsthand that attaining the life-affirming condition of *libertad* could be ensnared by bureaucratic nettles. The lengthy appeal process (initiated by masters) meant that indios might not gain their freedom for two, three, or even ten years.[56] Officials then made little effort to ensure that freedpersons could travel of their own volition, to help them find new employment, or to protect them from revenge-seeking masters. Reports filtered back to Crown authorities that angered and humiliated slave owners tortured and derided their freed indio servants as "slaves" and "dogs." According to Las Casas, indios were beaten and branded if they were absent from the master's home even for brief intervals, including those indios whom López designated as "neither slaves nor free."[57] Indios in Seville feared for their safety because the city was rife with *especieros*, individuals who traded spices for slaves, then boasted that they had acquired them in just war.[58] Thus, a combination of the legal system's slow pace, the lack of protection for freedpersons, and vulnerability to unscrupulous slave traders who saw indios as quick capital increased the anxiety levels among the indios living in Seville.

Despite these significant fears and obstacles, being granted freedom was a monumental transformation for former slaves. Those who continued to work in the homes or shops of their former masters might be given less demeaning tasks, provided with meager dowries to marry, or trained as artisans. Some now earned modest salaries. Others sought security in what could be a cut-throat environment; women and their children remained with their former masters, the children doing small chores when summoned. Their new status as freedpersons might not have been apparent to all, but it was a visceral, heartfelt transformation for many. Beatríz, who identified herself as a vecina, or permanent resident of Triana, said, "I worked for twenty-three years in the home of María Ochoa, and I was freed at the same time as [another slave named] Juan. I now reside in her [María Ochoa's] home and just because I eat bread like a free woman does not mean that I won't tell the truth."[59] Whether it was eating fresh, refined-flour bread or sleeping on a bed instead of a flea-infested mattress, such details allowed them to hold their heads a little higher, to consider themselves residents of the households in which they lived, and to cultivate a sense of belonging in Seville.

There is no doubt that López's 1543 inspection caused a major stir in Seville. It struck deep, raw nerves, triggering panic among slave owners and causing desperation and profound anxiety among freedpersons. The charged atmosphere was still palpable when Las Casas reached his home base of Seville in March 1544 to prepare for his last voyage to America. Newly consecrated as the bishop of Chiapas, Las Casas had recruited over fifty Dominicans to travel with him to do missionary work in America. Before embarking, however, he wanted to settle a few scores. Whether he was naïve or just extremely hopeful, Las Casas had thought the enactment of the New Laws and López's inspection in Seville the previous year would truly make a difference for the indios living in Castile. But the indios who, on learning that Las Casas would be there, flooded the visitor's parlor of the Monastery of San Pablo revealed another stark reality. Infuriated that so "many indios living in southern Spain are still unjustly enslaved," Las Casas dispatched a detailed account to Charles V on Passion Sunday. He began by saying, "[The Monastery of San Pablo] swells up with indios who believe I [can] take them [to America] or that I am able to do something about their captivity and [alleviate] the anguish they experience."[60]

To underscore the level of violence occurring on a daily basis in Seville, Las Casas recounted a disturbing event that had transpired that day. An indio had come to see him to complain that even though he carried with him a letter of freedom granted by López, his owner not only treated him like a slave ("le tenía por esclavo"), but worse than a slave. He was being forced to haul water with an ass, a duty he considered below his station. Las Casas wrote, "I told him to go directly to the House of Trade and there the officials would deal with the situation." Las Casas even dispatched a young servant to show the man the way. But somehow the owner found out and in a rage tore up the letter of freedom and demanded that someone look for a hot iron to brand "this dog." When the terrorized man jumped out of a window to escape, his master cried out, "Thief, thief!" Passersby in the street below heard the cries and stabbed the indio with a knife, then thrust a sword into his neck. The mortally wounded man somehow managed to make it to where some of Las Casas's attendants had gathered. They tried in vain to stop the bleeding. That evening, Las Casas wrote in a postscript to the letter, "He is about to die."

Although he lost no time in issuing a formal complaint, Las Casas received a cold response from unnamed authorities: "It does not surprise me that they kill the indios because they [the indios] steal and do other bad things." Las Casas ended his narrative by encouraging the king "to consider how impoverished they are of all favor" and to seek a remedy for the gross injustices that occurred regularly in Seville. In quintessential Las Casas fashion, he reminded the king that such tyranny was occurring right under his nose: "They dare to do this when in Seville. Just the other day a judge [jurado] knifed an indio to death."[61] Such brutish acts were unacceptable anywhere, but even less so on Castilian soil.

It was, as it turns out, exceedingly difficult for Crown authorities to enforce penalties and ensure the safety of freed indios. Before leaving Seville, López had drawn up a list of indios whose return passage former owners were to pay. The money collected for that purpose was to be held in deposit until the next flotilla could depart with the freedpersons. By December 1543, five months after the inspection had ended, reports filtered back to the council that only three or four indios out of the hundred who had been freed had in fact returned to America.[62] Some continued to be held in legal deposit either in the Casa jail or under the legal authority of Casa officials, because their former masters refused to provide the travel funds as required, or because the appeal process delayed (sometimes permanently) their return to America.[63] The new requirement may have been an example of magical thinking on the part of the Crown, for why would a spurned master pay the return passage of a former slave, and why should busy Casa officials follow through on time-consuming Crown mandates? It would mean tracking down scores of slave owners, one by one. Laws and ordinances could only go so far.

The reticence of former masters to conform to the law created other, equally formidable barriers for freedpersons. In the same April letter to the king, Las Casas complained about how his efforts to procure the freedom of one woman had been hampered by numerous and, in his opinion, unfair legal impediments.[64] He was referring to, among other things, the right of legal deposit. This form of deposit, as determined in the *Siete Partidas*, gave the property owner the right to place movable property—a slave—in the custody of a trustworthy individual for safekeeping, until the owner decided to retrieve his "goods."[65] A place of safekeeping, however, might turn out to be a musty, rat-infested jail. The case to which Las Casas referred had involved none other than the magistrate of Seville, Bartolomé Ortíz. He had failed to present his four slaves to Gregorio López in a timely manner. When he finally did, all three—Cristóbal (purchased in Santo Domingo), Pedro (from Santa Marta), and Catalina (also from Santa Marta)—were freed. A fourth servant, named Beatríz, from Cuba, was freed on 23 July 1543, and López ordered Ortíz to pay her return passage. The following day, Ortíz arrived at the Casa, the necessary papers in hand, to begin the appeal process. In his statement to the court, he remonstrated that since he had assumed the office of alcalde four months earlier, he had been so busy working in the service of His Majesty that he had neglected his own affairs. His rationalization about Beatríz was peculiar. He claimed that "without being asked to, I manifested her as 'free' before leaving Cuba and had taken her with me at the insistence of local authorities there. [I did this] for her and the vecinos' well-being and tranquility, and for being a worshiper of idols. I brought her [here, to Seville] and she is upheld in her liberty [amparada de su libertad]." This comment was confusing, so council members asked why Ortíz had deposited Beatríz in jail in Seville. "Because," he explained, "she was a runaway Indian who [had] wandered about the hills [of Cuba], trying to spur the indios [there] to start an uprising."[66] That answer did nothing to explain his behavior. Ortíz may have hoped that attributing to Beatríz negative cultural markers like *idolater*, *rebel*, or *runaway* would raise concerns about the dangers associated with her freedom of movement in Seville. It was unlikely that he really believed she might organize a slave revolt in Seville, and his histrionics, in any case, did not have the desired effect. López reconfirmed that Beatríz was indeed not a slave, and he ordered Ortíz to pay for her return passage. But when Las Casas arrived, in April 1544, Beatríz was still in Seville.

Neither Slave nor Free

Although left to languish in jail for eight months, Beatríz was still free. Many indios were not. López's liminal classification of "neither slave nor free" was deeply troublesome for many indios. They confided to Las Casas that they did not believe the judge had their best interests at heart; he merely confirmed their captivity, their *jaez*, or similitude to slaves. The new status did nothing to help them; slave owners hounded and tortured them. Even if they had lived with families for decades with relative protection, they were now afraid they would be sold or forced to leave behind children and kin. They were essentially trapped laborers with few options. Las Casas could not have agreed with them more. He had hoped that, after decades of effort, the Crown would have found a solution to the problem of indigenous slavery that was "finite, not infinite."

What in principle offered a clear, legal distinction between alienable (slave) and inalienable (naboría) property was much more porous in daily practice. Castilians saw nothing wrong in passing naborías from one family member to another, mistreating them when they were arrogant, or selling them if they proved to be too assertive. Several witnesses for slave owners pointed out that they had not asked their naborías (neither slave nor free) to work outside the home as day laborers (*jornaleros*), which they would have done if they had considered them to be slaves. Instead, naborías performed domestic tasks "not as slaves but as persons obligated to serve."[67] But enslaved and free laborers often performed similar tasks, so the distinction between bondage and freedom based on occupation might not always have been clear. Secular and religious authorities with experience in America had seen this blurring occur for decades. In his *Tratado de la esclavitud de los indios*, published in 1552, Las Casas wrote that *naboría* was nothing but a euphemism for "slave," except that it was more difficult to sell a naboría without incurring a fine.[68] The status was intentionally left vague, he added, basically serving as a way of holding indios against their will in a variety of ways. Others agreed. In his June 1543 report to Gregorio López, the cleric Luis de Morales, who had spent over fifteen years in various parts of America, described *naboría* as "a palliative word used so they [would] serve against their will, almost like slaves although they [the owners] could not sell them. In such a manner they had them deposited in persons who made use of their labor in their mines and estates. If they wanted to go out somewhere, they were not able to because they were called naborías."[69]

No sooner had López's carriage left Seville than indios, some fresh off the boat from the Indies, were sold to unsuspecting individuals. Even though the decree expressly stated that indios declared as neither slaves nor free could not be traded or sold without an express license from the king, court records indicate several instances where owners did so—as Alonso Álvarez, a clothing hawker, sold the india Inés—and then tried to cover it up.[70] Key to distinguishing unfree servants from slaves were the terms *traspasar* and *enajenar*, which meant, respectively, "to transfer ownership" and "to alienate property." Although women like Inés were now considered inalienable property, by law they had to remain in the custody of the owner. Inés's case would not have entered the judicial records were it not for the fact that one her master's debtors, a court notary named Antonio Clavijo, brought the matter to the attention of Diego de Pantoja, the public prosecutor of the Casa. Clavijo was acting not out of a sense of justice for Inés but in hopes of recuperating money owed to him. When Álvarez appeared as ordered before the prosecutor in early October 1545, he claimed that Inés "[had] left him with a man" some five or six months before. Why, Pantoja queried, had he not searched for her? Because, Álvarez responded, "she had stolen more than 300 ducados from him, and his life was better without a thief in his midst." Pantoja asked a question that pierced to the crux of the matter: "Did you try to sell her?" Álvarez denied that he had done so.[71]

Álvarez insisted that both the bishop of Lugo *and* Gregorio López had declared Inés to be his *slave* and that he was under no legal obligation to respond to the court summons. In his mind, the consecutive verdicts of neither slave nor free meant that he still had dominion over Inés.[72] Dominion meant ownership, and ownership meant that he could do with her what he liked. His opinion was shared by other slave owners and confirms what several indios had told Las Casas during his stay at the monastery in Seville. That they were no longer alienable property mattered little. The status only confirmed their jaez, or condition of permanent bondage. As the lawsuit against him progressed, Alvaréz did what many men backed into a corner would do: he attacked his victim. In an effort to divert attention from himself, Álvarez began a gendered character assassination of Inés, whom he called a thief, "very bad with her body," and irresponsible because she had tried to escape on many occasions.[73] (Runaway slaves forfeited their right to be freed.) Witnesses on his behalf confirmed these assertions by stating that Inés regularly stole from Álvarez, that she was a scoundrel, a whore, and a runaway.

Months later, a local constable found Inés and brought her to court at Valladolid for questioning. She began her tale: "Around seven years ago they brought me from Santo Domingo on the island of Española to Seville and they gave and sold me to Alonso Álvarez, a clothing hawker."[74] When asked if Álvarez had registered her during the 1543 inspection, she replied, "Yes, they registered me and Álvarez took me before the Licentiate [López]." But when asked if the licentiate had declared her to be free, she said she did not know. (Had anyone explained to her what the verdict of "neither free nor enslaved" would mean for her?) Because she was able to provide details about when and where the transaction had been legalized, authorities were able to locate the bill of sale identifying Inés as an india slave from Mexico City. [75] When confronted with this damning evidence, Álvarez responded that he had drawn up the "false donation" in order to frighten Inés "because she was such a thief." Intractable to the end, Álvarez received the maximum fine of 20,000 maravedís, as established by Gregorio López. However, Inés's fate remains unknown.[76]

Why had López not freed Inés in 1543? There was no documentation to prove just title. Álvarez claimed to have had the documents when he presented Inés before the bishop of Carvajal during the 1536 inspection, but to have since lost them. He had purchased Inés when she was seven years old from an anonymous lady in Triana. Álvarez was thus in clear violation both of the 1534 law, which stated that no females or children under the age of fourteen could be sold, and of the 1536 decree, which indicated the requisites for documentation. Even with these discrepancies, López had confirmed Inés's status as neither slave nor free.

Like any person, López was vulnerable, and he may have occasionally succumbed to a master's pleadings. But given the cultural climate, he perhaps thought he was taking a humanitarian stance by assuming that underage individuals who remained in their masters' custody would have a better chance of survival. Being cast into the streets might bring a worse fate to a young girl.[77] Seville was filled with many needy individuals who, although they worked, lacked the means to feed their families or to find adequate housing without social assistance or dependence on another individual.[78] In the sixteenth century it was customary for those of subordinate status—whether criados or slaves—to have masters that looked after them. An individual who wandered aimlessly without a family, home, employer, or master was considered a vagabond and a serious problem for society. Charles V once expressed his concern that the indios who were abandoned in Castile or no longer under the authority of a master had no way to earn their daily bread.[79] Indios in Castile were seen as subordinate, childlike vassals in need of a support system. Slave owners would certainly see continued bondage or servidumbre (in its broadest sense) in that paternalistic light.[80]

But what we might see as paternalistic impulses or even, more generously, as humanitarian rationales behind decisions to declare indios as neither slave nor free might also have been influenced by the case-based casuistic logic common in sixteenth-century legal deliberations. Casuistry was then a legal art used to resolve a moral dilemma. In the vein of his contemporaries, López, like the king, reviewed the specific details of each case and sometimes decided that the letter of the law did not apply. Although we are not privy to his musings or to which circumstances of the case tipped the balance in favor of his determining a liminal status for a number of indios, it is clear that he weighed each case separately and applied the laws at his discretion, in a nonsystematic manner. In 1543 it was not clear how Crown policies toward indigenous vassals were going to play out, since clearly the Crown (and López acting on behalf of the Crown) did not consider Christian indios to be on the same level as Spanish vassals.

Whether Las Casas's 1544 Passion Sunday letter had much effect is difficult to gauge. A few freedpersons crossed the Atlantic and returned to their homelands in the ships that carried Las Casas westward for the last time. Beatríz, the so-called idolater from Cuba, may have been one of those fortunate enough to be on board one of those vessels, since Las Casas had received permission to have released into his custody those freed indios who were still being held in deposit. Charles V had ordered him to see to it that they were returned "to the places where they had been taken," at the cost of their former owners.[81]

A few spotty efforts were made in 1544 to issue summons to recalcitrant slave owners who had failed to appear before López with the appropriate papers. If they did not appear before the tribunal at the Casa or the Council of the Indies in Valladolid within a specified time, their slaves would automatically be freed.[82] When pressed, a few masters who wished to avoid costly travel to Valladolid or Madrid or the steep fines and court costs decided to draw up legal documents, finally freeing their slaves. Prince Philip intervened directly to free several adult residents and children who had been brought to Seville illegally.[83] Casa officials did inspect some ships more closely, but slowly life returned to "normal," and slaves slipped into Seville without questioning.[84]

The 1549 Inspection

Within six years another royal inspection of all indios occurred, this time led by Hernán Pérez de la Fuente, canon of Zamora and a member of the Council of Indies since 1545. Like López, he was considered a good jurist, but his sour nature and harsh recriminations against law-breakers made him unpopular among Casa authorities.[85] Once again, Bartolomé de las Casas may have had something to do with the 1549 inspection; since his return from Chiapas in 1547, he had maintained his perch at council sessions and was known to have private audiences with the king.

Like his predecessor, Gregorio López, Pérez conducted the inspection during the hottest months of summer. He ordered slaves and free indios to line up with their owners, masters, or legal representatives and present the appropriate papers to the authorities. To help him arbitrate, Pérez drew on the same legislative cache available to López in 1543 and also cited subsequent decrees.[86] The inspection differed from the one of 1543 in several respects. Indigenous litigants now had a legal representative to tell them their rights and represent them during the inspection and appeal process. By 1549, Diego Pantoja, who had served first as the portero and later, in 1545, as a prosecuting attorney in the case against Álvarez, was now the court-appointed procurador for the Indians (procurador de indios). As the procedural expert, Pantoja was considered by the king to be "well versed in the things of the Indies."[87] The Casa now had a salaried attorney (*promotor fiscal de la contratación*), the licenciate Hernando Becerra, to replace the three main officials there (tesorero, contador, and factor) as the main arbiter in legal matters. In principle, he was there to represent the voice of the king in legal disputes.[88]

Because litigation suits involving indio slaves in Castile had increased dramatically, appeals now took much longer to resolve than those initiated in the aftermath of the 1543 inspection.[89] A more rigorous attempt to implement the letter of the law resulted in a backlog of cases, and the workload of the members of the Council of Indies and the Casa increased exponentially. Litigation and appeals suits mounted at a time when Crown authorities deliberated a series of issues related to more effective bureaucratic administration of the Indies. As the council increased its oversight of the Casa and handled appeals of various sorts, it became necessary to hire a permanent well-trained jurist (called the *asesor letrado*). The council appointed the licentiate Salgado Correa, who, beginning in 1554, began to oversee juridical matters of the Casa.[90]

Between 1543 and 1549, the legal discourse had also changed. In the lawsuits initiated by slaves around the time of the 1549 inspection, lawyers representing slaves began making arguments that echoed discussions taking place at the University of Salamanca among several Dominican and Jesuit theologians who had been influenced by Francisco de Vitoria (d. 1546).[91] Diego Pantoja advised indigenous litigants to make three separate but interrelated claims: that they were free by birth (*de su nacimiento*); that they were free by their "nativeness" (naturaleza), based on their place of origin; and that they were free by their ingenio, or capacity as rational beings.[92] The opening statements of litigants now included these arguments, which were chiseled into formulaic statements that would serve as blueprints in future cases. They iterated the basic rights of indios as free vassals upheld by natural law, the New Laws (of 1542), and the rapidly accumulating ordinances of the king and queen. It is at this point that we begin to see the development of a clear, logical ideology as the driving force behind these litigation suits.

Another notable difference was the appearance of the term *miserable*. At the beginning of one lawsuit initiated in 1549, the council-appointed lawyer Sebastian Rodríguez argued that he was speaking on behalf of Juan "because he is a legal minor and a poor and miserable (*miserable*) person."[93] Indigenous peoples had been designated as legal minors as early as 1512, and beginning in the 1520s, indios as "a whole people" were identified as *miserables*, people in need of protection against abusive Spaniards in America.[94] This concept had medieval precedents and jurists drew on the law code in the *Siete Partidas*, which identified those poor and wretched individuals, such as widows, orphans, and the impoverished, who were in need of protection against those more powerful than they. But although antecedents appear in earlier legislation, the term *miserable* did not enter Castilian legal discourse until nearly 1550, when defense lawyers began identifying their enslaved indigenous clients in such terms.

Another major change involved compensation. The defense attorney Pantoja encouraged indigenous litigants (whose masters appealed Pérez's 1549 decision to free them) to seek financial remuneration for the time they had served. Here we see a shift in logic, as the Crown began to support the notion of indios as wage laborers under the protection of the Crown. For Crown authorities it was important for former slave owners to understand the distinction between free and wage laborers, which is why they insisted that indios be paid back salary as a form of compensation; for some, this could be significant.[95]

Detailed instructions from Charles V to Hernán Pérez also reveal a rethinking of a key Crown policy. What had seemed like a good strategy in 1543—that is, to designate certain indios as neither slave nor free—had only prolonged their poor treatment and indeterminate status. It was, to paraphrase Las Casas, an infinite, not a finite solution. In his directive to Pérez in 1549, Charles V referred to indios as naborías, as free but permanent servants in need of the guidance of Spaniards.[96]

Although popular in America, this "palliative" term, as the aforementioned Luis de Morales called it, was only rarely employed in official documents generated in Castile, even though dozens if not hundreds of "free" indios came to Castile with their masters over the decades. They came because of legal loopholes.[97] Most naborías were children, and some were female, which meant they were legal minors and subject to the authority of Spanish masters even after they had reached adulthood. In principle, naborías should have been able to choose the person whom they wished to serve, but this was patently ignored.[98] Indias like Francisca, taken as a girl in the battles of the Yucatán and declared neither slave nor free by Gregorio López in 1543, had to wait until 1576 to be freed.[99] When Castilians returned to Castile, they brought with them not only young indigenous men and women, but also those ambiguities related to their status. In reality, the continued use of the category of naboría in Castile and in America reinforced some of the more insidious aspects of paternalism. It meant the continued subordination of indios, supported by king and commoner alike. It also meant viewing indios as malleable children, as evidenced in royal decrees and in the testimonies of former slave owners, who were appalled when they learned that their indigenous laborers were now completely free.

Considering "freed" indios to be personal retainers also revealed an attitude that considered indios childlike and in need of the guidance of Spaniards, especially since they were no longer in their natal environments. That attitude had deep roots in Spain and was inscribed in the *Siete Partidas* as one of the key aspects defining the relationship between a servant and his master. For servidumbre included both slavery and servitude (*estado de siervo*) in its definition. It meant that the master or head of the household had the right of patria potestas over servile family members. In Spanish America, because naborías had been uprooted and taken from the "useless islands" and elsewhere, they could not be designated as encomienda Indians, since they did not belong to that local village, nor were they under the authority of that particular cacique. The idea was that Spaniards would have patria potestas over them.[100] In Castile it was believed that because indigenous peoples had been uprooted from their homelands, they needed masters. In essence, however, the category of naboría was a way to garner additional personal laborers.

Thus, when King Charles iterated these same ideas in his instructions to inspector Hernán Pérez in 1549, he was not creating something new.[101] He was, however, drawing a new line in the sand with regard to slavery. He wanted Pérez to free the indios but ensure that they still had masters. Otherwise they risked become *vagamundos*, wandering aimlessly, without community ties and cut off from kin.[102] To see them as children in need of paternal guidance was a compromise attitude that was beginning to emerge in other legislative arenas and a discourse that would eventually replace, or at least mitigate, perceptions of indios as natural slaves. But even here, in the act of freeing them in Castile, the king could not quite see indios as completely free vassals or completely rational beings.[103] This manifestation of patriarchal doublespeak—free but not completely free—continued to dominate discussions well into the 1550s and served as the foundation for imperial laws regulating the wage and nonwage labor of nonelite indigenous peoples and providing them with special legal protection as inferior peasants (*rústicos*) or *miserables*.[104] On the other hand, this directive cemented a policy that said that indios as a collective abstraction were entitled to special legal protections.[105] Nevertheless, for several naborías, this second inspection provided an opportunity to be completely freed from bondage.[106]

After the two inspections and the appeals, the number of litigation suits that were not related to determining imperial status diminished. At issue in several cases of the 1550s was what it meant to consider or treat someone as a free subject. Here, as Brian Owensby has argued for a later period, the term *libertad* (freedom) began to acquire a new meaning, one associated with freedom from being treated as a slave. At issue for indigenous people was "that their labor not be taken without their consent."[107] Two main "idioms of harm" were used to support arguments on behalf of mistreated indios.[108] The first was *mala fe* ([in] bad faith), which meant that indios felt cheated, or that some legal or moral transgression had occurred. *Usurpar* was the verb that lawyers defending indigenous clients used most often; it meant "to usurp, deny, take away, or make off with something possessed by someone else." But what exactly did indigenous litigants think was being usurped or denied? How did they find language to explain those transgressions of power and authority? In 1560 Beatríz from Oaxaca went before the Council of Indies from Salamanca to claim,

> I and my husband [Alonso] were brought by deceit to these kingdoms by certain Spaniards from the province of Oaxaca, where we are from and those Spaniards turned us over to Antonio de Herrera, a vecino of the city of Salamanca. For many years, and in bad faith [mala fe] he has made us serve and continues to make us serve as though we were his slaves even though we are free by birthright. Now the said Antonio de Herrera has attempted to sell us as slaves because he knows we want to ask for our freedom.[109]

Antonio de Herrera responded by presenting a copy of a letter he had drawn up indicating he had given Beatríz her freedom seven years earlier.

> Having as a thing of his Beatríz, india, a natural of New Spain who was the wife of Alonso, indio, her husband, by just titles, in service of God our lord and for other reasons that move him I want to declare as free and I free the said Beatríz who is no longer under my legal authority [poder] as a free person who can do with her person what she wishes coming and living in the land, place, and house that seems best. I gave and give to Perico, the son of the said Beatríz, now absent from this city for more than four years, [his freedom] to do what he wishes.[110]

Beatríz was not specific about what had occurred in bad faith. In fact most indigenous litigants weren't always clear about how their "freedom" had been taken away or what exactly they had lost. We do not know what triggered Beatríz's decision to press for an acknowledgment of her freedom in court. It may be that her understanding of mala fe was vested in everyday practice and experiences, rather than in legal abstractions. The distinctions between free and not free were visceral but sometimes hard to put into words. If she had been declared to be free and her "freedom" was in some way compromised— usurped—she might feel the transgression even more strongly.

Conclusions

Despite the passage of numerous ordinances and the New Laws of 1542, it was not entirely clear whether indigenous slavery would ever be completely abolished, even in Castile. We tend to think of laws as encoding a sense of finality or conclusiveness, but this was not the case. The laws were strategic tools used as a buttress against the deeply entrenched attitudes of slave owners and Crown authorities toward indigenous peoples. Their implementation in specific cases and during the two inspections was meant to frustrate specific illegal practices related to slavery.

Gregorio López never declared outright the immediate emancipation of all slaves. That would have been too daring and risky, and authorities in Castile had already heard of the serious grumblings in America over the New Laws. We also tend to think of the law as an antidote to antiquated or "backward" practices and view it as representing more modern or advanced ideas. But paternalism was embedded in, or at least in dialogue with, the laws, not above or distant from them. These paternalistic practices were finely honed in Spanish America and migrated with masters and slaves returning to Castile. Finally, the careful and consistent implementation of laws required dedicated individuals, and those were far and few between. Many Castilians were willing to blatantly ignore royal summons, fines, and especially the declarations that their former slaves were now free.

By the late 1540s, at issue was not whether indios were slaves (in principle), but whether as legal minors who were not quite as human as Castilians, they required additional royal protection from the powerful.[111] Gregorio López, who knew the *Siete Partidas* as intimately as any jurist of his time, saw it as a way forward from the moral and theological dilemma of natural slavery or of the legality of the Spanish presence in America. Six years later, indios in Castile were to be considered wage laborers. Such dilemmas were being played out in the courts, in the council chambers, and in the homes of powerful and humble Castilians and among those indios who had crossed the Atlantic.

Unmistakably the meaning of *indio* had evolved from its initial usage to distinguish the people from the Indies into a category that included slaves. Whether they were truly human and not subject to natural slavery remained to be determined by the Crown, although the pope had taken a firm stance in 1537. Until the 1540s the noun *esclavo* preceded the word *indio* in much of the written documentation. There were, of course, other kinds of indios—naborías, for example, who were often categorized in Spanish America as neither free nor slaves because of specific circumstances.[112] Although legal experts and theologians debated furiously the social and legal implications of the category indio, many Castilians, especially those with experience in "the Indies," continued to view commoner indios as slaves or potential slaves. As the Crown reviewed its official position in the New Laws and iterated that by virtue of being indios, indios could no longer be enslaved, it took several decades for many Castilians to accept that in practice. Indios living in Castile would have to enter the courtroom, armed with law codes and supportive witnesses to prove who they truly were. But the bureaucratic and legal culture of the courtroom, which included procedure, evidence (including branding), the authority of documents, and the power of expert witnesses, also worked to create and maintain notions of legal indios. Documents were active sites of power upheld by the law and governance of slavery. But these truth-objects were also given relational value: by the ways slave owners and litigants interacted with or interpreted them. Slaves and masters objectified such documents as truth-telling evidence by also registering them with their own grains of truth.

FOUR

Into the Courtroom

✦

Martín, indio, had a small mule in a halter and while standing in a meadow the mule was startled and [the kick] made [Martín's] face bleed. I don't know whether [the kick] left a permanent mark but it [the mark] did not come from anything else [such as the king's brand].

"Testimony, Juan de Villa Santesteban," 7/III/1537, AGI, Justicia 1007, 22v

The piecemeal implementation of decrees, ordinances, and royal inspections in Castile through the 1530s and 1540s all contributed to the construction of the indio as a free vassal. The courts of the Council of the Indies and the Casa began to develop more efficient and potentially less corrupt ways of handling the plethora of litigation suits and appeals that began to emerge in 1543. But the legal process moved in fits and starts. Obstacles often arose, and lawyers found exceptions to prevent indios from gaining their freedom, especially in the context of the paternalism that had permeated every aspect of their lives for decades. Moreover, the Crown did not see nonelite indios as completely independent, and the debates over whether they should remain as permanent servants or be paid wages still had not been resolved by the early 1550s.

Indios entering the legal arena to deliberate their future status as free vassals worked within a formal template. There were procedures to follow, witnesses to gather, interrogation questions to draw up; for slave owners, there were documents to locate.

In this chapter I examine the physical evidence used in the courtroom—paper documents, brands, and witness depositions—that helped to characterize enslaved and free indios. Specifically, bills of sale, travel documents, brands on the bodies of slaves, and the typology of witnesses contained what Hayden White would call the "plot elements" used to bolster narratives justifying the slavery of individual litigants. In turn, these structural "elements" used to create a viable legal case also represented a kind of epiphenomenal truth (or fiction) about bondage that fit into a normative legal framework, itself a metanarrative.[1]

Historians tend to focus on the narrative contents of documents or witness depositions because the narrativity and use of language in those testimonials carried tremendous weight. But while these aspects were important to the creation of the legal indio, the creation, preservation, and physical presence of papers, physical markings, and "kinds" of expert witnesses were also "active sites of power" because of the authority vested in them.[2] In other words the documents, in tandem with how they were interpreted, had an objective authority in themselves.

In this chapter I consider the kinds of power that contemporaries vested in notarial and testimonial documents and the "truths" spoken by particular kinds of credible and expert witnesses. Rather than focus on the end result—the sentencing—and whether litigants and defendants won or lost their cases, I expose the underlying tensions between what were customary cultural practices related to slavery and enslavement and the ways that slave owners and slaves adapted to changing laws in Castile.[3] Court records show slaves and slave owners erasing, covering over, or reconstructing the past as they manipulated paper-generated documents and their readings of branded bodies in the legal present. An analysis of these processes has much to say about how indios were constructed.

Paper Trails

Accountability formed an integral aspect of each lawsuit. It meant providing proof that the indio in question had been legitimately acquired and transported across the Atlantic. At the beginning of each lawsuit, lawyers or advocates asked slave owners to present evidence that would indicate legal possession. Such evidence included documents demonstrating just title, inspections required for travel, and bills of sale, some perhaps dating back decades before the case began. These documents served the purpose of "bringing the facts and circumstances into a correct and valid written form."[4]

Once slave owners presented the appropriate legal authorities with their documents, they were transcribed, recorded, and arranged in a new, legal, and documentary context. Papers produced in vastly different political and cultural contexts were folded next to one another in a single "package" that collapsed time and space and left little trace of the actual historical production of the documents. In the timing of the presentation of these documents, or in their recontextualization and reinterpretation, we see the tissues of verities and lies of the past reconfigured and presented in a new documentary form. We see the making of a *slave*.

Paper trails were integral to the long-established bureaucracy of slavery in the Mediterranean region.[5] Slave merchants and owners were accustomed to accounting for the buying, selling, transporting, locating, and bequeathing of human merchandise in imperial and local contexts. Not all transactions were codified in writing (which might present problems later), but many were. Recordkeeping proliferated as the increased human traffic of the fifteenth and sixteenth centuries swelled Castilian homes and fields with laborers imported from around the globe. The production of different documents to identify and locate indigenous and other slaves in Castile also fit within a pattern emerging in sixteenth-century Europe that blended old and new ways of identifying migratory peoples.[6] Slave owners were required to identify humans held in bondage clearly and distinctly when generating documents related to travel, sales, or transference or bequeathal to a new owner. Local notaries and bureaucrats also now produced documents to verify the new status of large numbers of freedpersons.

The creation of documents related to slavery also responded to specific legal requisites that changed over time. What constituted "acceptable" evidence of possession in the courtroom had to match the shifting imperial logic that established legal mechanisms to protect indios who had been unjustly enslaved. The laws did not merely constrain who could own indigenous slaves and who could and could not be enslaved (for instance, after 1534, only indio males over the age of fourteen). The legal apparatus also created new kinds of procedures that slave owners had to follow to capture and transport a slave to Castile (see the 1534 law), and new guidelines regarding what constituted evidence of possession (see the 1536 law). What we observe in the back and forth of the paperwork is a wrangling over the power vested in the different kinds of documents. As the Crown determined a new regimen of evidentiary practice with regard to proving possession and legal enslavement, slave owners and indios articulated their own understandings of possession—I possess, therefore the person I possess is a slave—and the relevance that the documents should or should not have.

What is especially interesting from the ethnographic standpoint is that slave owners who entered the legal arena believed strongly in "papereality." For them, the action of creating a legal document (a particular form of representation) and the existence of the document (its physical attributes) denoted the reality of bondage. In many cases, the form of representation "took precedence over the things and events represented."[7] In Castile many slave owners authorized the buying and selling of slaves with a notarized transaction (except on those occasions when they were passing a slave to someone within the family). Castilians who traveled and lived in Latin America did the same. Questions regarding the legality of the initial capture or abduction (or the voice of the slave protesting at the moment of inscription) were effaced. In other words, the action of enslaving an indio unjustly did not matter (the past erased by the present), since the paper proved the condition of bondage and made it legally meaningful. The social object (the person made into a slave) was formed by the act of inscription and the creation of a notarized document. It did not matter what the documents said; it did not matter whether the individual indio had been unjustly enslaved.

We see this pattern in case after case, wherein an anxious slave owner presented the court with legal documents—a donation, a dowry, a bill of sale—which they claimed as proof of bondage. They believed that the presentation of the documents in the courtroom locus of enunciation carried weight because they represented recorded transactions, whether they were based on the reality or fiction that the human beings involved were or were not really slaves.[8] In the inspection of 1543, for example, one slave owner was permitted to keep his slave simply because he had followed all the directives and his "papers were in order." Thus, the increasing complexity of legal procedure (additional documentation for each stage in the process) sometimes worked to reinforce cultural assumptions about the importance of paper.[9] How, then, could indios protest against this form of "papereality," in essence, to regain the free status that they believed they had never lost? It is important to note that whenever slave owners presented documents, the courts assumed that the litigants were property until they could prove otherwise. Slaves who protested their bondage were required, unless the royal government determined that their lives were in danger, to remain in the master's possession. Paper had that much authority, which led to the tension between the power vested in documents presented in the court and the testimonial representations of the past by indigenous litigants.

It would be misleading, however, to say that the production and possession of legalized documents had value only for slave owners. Papereality also
resonated with freed slaves, whose status inevitably was tied up in the legal
bureaucracy of slavery. Freed men and women of African or indigenous heritage relied heavily on written documentation to affirm their newly acquired
status when it was questioned or when they wanted to travel to and from
America.[10] Testimonies found in various archival forums of freedpersons
with diverse life experiences share two common elements: the belief that the
letter of freedom embodied their freedom, and the fear that the destruction
of the treasured document in their possession would threaten that freedom.
At issue were their own self-perceptions, which were measured against how
others saw them. The reader may recall the story of the indio, freed by Gregorio López, whose angry master grabbed his letter of freedom, tore it up,
and asked that someone find a person to brand the man. (The indio died later
that day, after his master accused him, falsely, of being a thief and bystanders
summarily stabbed him with knife and sword.)[11] There was a brutal power
in the act of destroying the document that "held" the truth of that doomed
man's identity. How poignant to think that a piece of parchment could carry
that much more weight than the spoken utterance *Yo soy libre* (I am free).
But papers were necessary and were intended, in these and many other instances, to protect the underprivileged. As a matter of course, the Casa and
the Council of the Indies made certain to issue letters of freedom to successful indigenous litigants. A few freed (and cynical) indios were adamant about
ensuring they would receive written proof confirming their new status.[12]

As slave owners in the 1540s came to grips with the new documentary
requisites, they relied on whatever they had in their documentary stock-
pile to cover their tracks or to create believable ones, especially if they had
to demonstrate proof of title from ten, fifteen, or twenty years before.[13] Yet
prior to 1536, slaves were often sent to Spain by merchants, family members,
and others with little scrutiny and minimal paperwork. Hastily created descriptions were inconsistent and makeshift in both America and Castile. To
say that a slave had been captured in just war was common parlance in bills
of sale generated in Castile and America. Furthermore, until the 1540s, laws
and ordinances were irregularly enforced. In the Council of the Indies, during the lawsuit initiated by Pedro in 1538, his master had no title or bill of
sale, but the royal *R* and his master's name were branded on Pedro's face and
were enough to prove possession. What sealed his fate was his transatlantic
fugitive status: he had boarded a ship illegally in Santo Domingo and was
apprehended as a criminal as soon as he set foot in Seville.[14]

Just as the existence of the document carried a certain epistemological weight (representing truth and reality), so, too, did the language contained within the document. We might think that bills of sale produced as evidence in the courtroom would exhibit a somewhat formulaic and consistent vocabulary, similar to passenger lists, parish records, and other census-like materials generated by colonial authorities. After all, they dispassionately recorded the moment of transfer from one owner to another at a specific date and location. As well as name, age, place of origin, and price paid, a bill of sale might provide more specific information, such as whether the slave being sold was free from drink, disease ("could drink all waters"), and personality defects, or whether he or she was a *ladino* (familiar with the Spanish language), a Christian, or fresh off the boat (*bozal*).[15] Encoded in these documents were key words that conjured up a predefined narrative about the past—capture (*cautivo*) under legal circumstances (as a result of just war)—and a narrative of the present ("I state that this man, woman, boy, or girl indio standing before you is now a slave"). Any historicity—an event occurring at a specific moment in a specific cultural context—that complicated the narrative about the moment of inscription was folded into its "legal" venue.[16]

Such documents nevertheless operated within the "domain of memory," even if we cannot readily see the historicity operating through the formulaic language. What we can see is how the "language of slavery" used in contracts such as bills of sale evolved over time according to the cultural and historical moment of inscription.[17] For instance, in bills of sale registered before notaries in Mexico City from 1524 to 1528, notaries, buyers, and sellers assumed that *esclavo* referred to an indio slave, since the presence of enslaved African peoples was limited at that time. Occasionally, bills of sale used the qualifier "from this land" (*de la tierra*).[18] In Peru sale transactions for indigenous slaves (identified as indios esclavos) did not include the qualifier *guerra justa* until after 1539, when it was entered into the transactions as a matter of course to meet legal requisites and to qualify the conditions under which a slave had been legally captured. Then again, certain terms had different meanings depending on the cultural context. *Cautivo* had a particular resonance in Castile, as thousands of converts from Islam to Christianity (moriscos) living in Granada and elsewhere were being enslaved, and as peoples captured in Northern Africa entered the markets of Seville and elsewhere. To describe an indio as a captive within this cultural context could trigger subliminal associations with the morisco slaves living in Castile.[19] The point here is that the language used (or not used) in the bills of sale reflected specific presumptions about slaves that changed over time in tandem with the laws, and that also depended on the specific geographic, cultural, and demographic configuration of the site where the transaction was recorded.

Just as the presentation of documents in court cases showed a new form of authority and truth-seeking, a competing phenomenon was also evident, resulting in a kind of "piquancy in the uncertainty about truth in documents."[20] As several scholars have shown, forgeries and fraud increased in proportion to the new legal requisites for just title, registration, and identification.[21] Most slave owners presented papers that had been stored in trunks or that were readily available from the local notary, then hoped for the best. Others, more forgetful and perhaps less organized, tried sleight of hand. Some paid exorbitant prices to have documents falsified, while others submitted documents that blatantly contradicted one another. Because not all legal representatives were alike, slave owners might have hoped a poorly trained solicitor would overlook discrepancies in dates or agree that it really did not matter that the indigenous person's name on the bill of sale was Pedro instead of Francisco.[22] Then again, a blank parchment with a signature made it easy for a notary to fill in the appropriate blanks at the appropriate time, which made fact-checking in the court all the more vital.[23]

Lawyers at the court were keenly aware of the logic of papereality, which they used to support their arguments. In the 1549 inspection of slaves in Seville, thirty-year-old Pedro was declared free from bondage, but his former owner, the cleric Juan de Jaén, appealed the decision before the Council of the Indies, claiming to have all the appropriate paperwork. This included a straightforward bill of sale and a license from the king stating that three indigenous slaves could be brought back if they were examined first. A third document, dated February 1536, included Viceroy Mendoza's confirmation of the request to bring Perico, Francisquita, and Anica to Castile. A document from such a high-ranking official carried tremendous authority. However, the prosecuting attorney for the council, Diego de Pantoja, protested that the viceroy had not inspected or examined the three slaves to verify that they had been captured in just war, their place of origin, or that they were over fourteen years of age. This document contradicted the mandates of the king, which ordered an inspection—a paper from an even higher authority. Pantoja surmised that the document that was purported to be from the viceroy was fraudulent since the viceroy would not have allowed *any* male slave younger than fourteen years of age to leave Mexico. The appeal was denied.[24]

If a legal representative did not have a discerning eye, slave owners could get away with being slipshod with facts around their having inherited a slave. Because of the vast distance between America and Iberia, it was easy for family members to "appropriate" as their legal property the indigenous household servants of deceased relatives or *colegas* who had spent lengthy periods in America. If it became necessary, they could have a document drawn up later. Francisco was married to Juana, an indigenous woman from Guatemala. He lived in Ciudad Real and had been freed in 1545, when the local corregidor showed up at his doorstep with a decree. Nevertheless, Francisco had a difficult time convincing his former owner, Cristóbal de Cueto, that he should be permitted to live with his wife, Juana, who had also been freed. Cueto appealed the decision to free the couple before the Council of the Indies, arguing that he had inherited Francisco and Juana from his deceased brother and had received authorization to bring them to Spain.[25] As evidence, he presented a decree issued by the Crown in 1539 ordering the governor of Guatemala to allow him to transport to Castile two indigenous slaves, one male and one female, as long as he could demonstrate that he had inherited them from his brother's estate and could provide paperwork showing whether they were free or enslaved and had been captured in just war.[26] But when Pedro de Cueto, Cristóbal's brother, died in Guatemala sometime before 1533, Francisco was still a young boy. In fact, by 1533, Pedro de Cueto's half of an encomienda had already been awarded to someone else, and the king issued a decree to Guatemalan authorities in 1535 to allow the brothers' mother (in Spain) to handle Pedro's estate.[27] Nor was there any proof that Francisco and Juana had been Pedro's slaves in Guatemala (here the defendants argued that possession denoted bondage) or that Cristóbal was the intended beneficiary. The desperate assertion that Juana was the daughter of Pedro de Cueto's African slave and not an india had not been proved either. Francisco's lawyer pointed out that when the governor supposedly granted the license for Francisco to travel, Francisco was a boy, which went against the 1534 law prohibiting the enslavement of children under fourteen.[28] To cover up this discrepancy, Cueto had lied about Francisco's age. Changing the slave's age at the time of capture and saying that a slave was a descendant of an enslaved mother of African heritage were two ploys common among slave owners intent on keeping their slaves. But the falsification of a document was another matter. On close inspection, Francisco's lawyer determined that either the license had been fabricated or it referred to another slave. It had not been issued by the then governor, the conqueror don Pedro de Alvarado, but by the licentiate don Francisco de la Cueva, who was not at that time serving as the governor's second in command.[29] The use of this particular license, the lawyer argued, was a "joke, just like all the other *desórdenes* [decoys or distractions]" deployed to keep indigenous people from gaining their freedom.[30] Thanks to the lawyer's careful scrutiny, the council saw through the ploy and on 13 May 1549 declared Francisco, Juana, and their two children to be free. Within two months they had boarded a ship for Guatemala.[31]

There is no evidence that Cristóbal de Cueto's license from the governor's assistant in Guatemala or fraudulent bills of sale were forged, either before or after the trials had begun. Certainly, in Seville there were notaries willing to create believable documents for the right price. What is interesting here is the investment made by slave owners to create a viable documentary archive to legitimate the past under present circumstances, even though in all of the instances discussed, the efforts failed.

Even if they lacked proper papers to prove possession, many slave owners who entered the courtroom believed that they had another way to prove legitimate bondage: the brand. Stained and scarred skin was believed to be irrefutable proof, a flesh-and-blood testimonial. The act of branding, as the historian Sherwin Bryant has argued, was a "ceremony of possession" that commodified humans as objects.[32] As the lawyer for the Catalán slave owner Gerónimo Trías stated in his 1543 allegation, "Manifesting the said slaves branded with the brand of His Majesty is the main and most indubitable proof that can exist to know that they are slaves."[33] But in the courtroom setting, indigenous litigants with disfigured faces could argue against this logical grain, to prove their innocence *because* of the brand.

Stained and Scarred Skin

Inside and outside the courtroom, the flesh was a site where the discursive processes of colonial power could easily be read. In any Iberian city—Seville, Santo Domingo, Trujillo (Honduras), México-Tenochtitlán, Panamá, or Lima—passersby could look at someone's countenance, or arm or leg, and know if they were a slave. The text of servitude was imbedded in the bodies of thousands. Brands scarred and stained cheeks, thighs, and calves, distinguishing the free from the unfree and, in some cases, from the neither free nor enslaved.[34] More often than not, the surface of the skin exhibited the master's name, in effect saying, "I am you, not me."[35] Conversely, the absence of marking was a signifier of freedom. As the merchant Alonso Román, a vecino of Seville who had lived in Vera Cruz between 1523 and 1527, explained to the Spanish court, indios without a brand were assumed to be free: "Everyone accepts them as such."[36]

Slave litigants often recalled that the radical shift from free to slave began when their faces were seared somewhere in Latin America or the Caribbean. Catalina, a Pipil from Nonoalco (El Salvador), recalled some twenty-five years after the fact that she had been branded on the face by Sebastián de Benalcázar when she was eight years old, because Benalcázar had heard that her parents were searching for her.[37] Her history of mutilation fits within a long-standing and legally sanctioned pattern of marking males and females as indio commodities. As early as 1511, Ferdinand had authorized the use of the *carimbo*—the iron poker heated to orange-red—to distinguish from the Taíno natives those indios brought to Hispaniola from the Lucayas and elsewhere. These "foreign" slaves were marked on the thighs as slaves and on the calves as naborías.[38] With military incursions into Panama, the northern areas of South America, and Mexico, the use of the *R* and *G* became more popular. The *R* did not stand for the king (*rey*) as one might assume, but for *rescate*, which referred to those people who had previously been slaves or enslaved by other native peoples. *G* stood for *guerra*, or war, indicating a slave justly taken by military force.[39] The Crown would receive 20 percent (called the *quinto*) of the value of slaves captured or of the proceeds of the slaves' sale at a public auction. Antonio de Peramato explained that over the fourteen years he spent in Mexico, he branded a number of slaves, some with the *R* and others with a *G*, and that the slaves from just war tended to be sold in the public markets in larger quantities, since they were considered to be commodities like horses and other animals.[40]

By the 1520s, because the faces of so many indios bore the letters *R* and *G*, slave owners in America found a way to distinguish their slaves from others: they inscribed their surnames across the faces of their property. Pedro Armíldez Cherino, a royal inspector in charge of provisions (*veedor*), along with one of two lieutenant governors whom Hernán Cortés left in charge of the government while he was absent in Honduras, described practices in which Armíldez Cherino had participated in the 1520s. After the slaves sold in the town square (a public site) had been branded with the royal brand, Armíldez Cherino observed, the slave owner would sometimes put his brand on the other side of the slave's face.[41] Not only did this type of branding provide additional "proof" of ownership, but it served as a kind of "tracking number" in cases slaves were abducted and sold by other Castilians in need of funds. As Benito de Cuenca, a slave owner, explained,

> In the village of Tonacatepeque [*sic*, Tencontepeque] (Pánuco), they put letters [owners' names or initials] on certain indio slaves that they took

with them [on the road]. [Cuenca] said that a certain young slave girl had begged the cousin of Juan Romero with whom she was traveling to [brand her] with the name of her mistress, because her mistress had told [the female slave] that in Mexico [City] they stole slaves who did not have letters [*rótulos*] on them.[42]

In addition to these particular measures, each geographic location developed what was considered to be its own common practice and custom (*uso y costumbre*). In Nicaragua one document from 1527 explained that slaves branded on the face were those who had confessed to being slaves, whereas a brand on the thigh signified individuals considered naborías, permanent household servants.[43] In the 1530s and 1540s officials used the *V* to designate the broad territory of Venezuela. In Central America, as large groups of individuals were enslaved at once, some were designated as "branded slaves," some as "branded naborías," and some as "slaves about to be branded."[44] Still, slave owners took precautions to follow legal procedure and create a "paper trail" of legitimacy, which included documenting payment of the royal fifth to the Crown. That documentation would be useful in case they ever wanted to sell their slaves.

Taking better care to keep track of slaves may also have coincided with the enactment of an ordinance in New Spain (1528) specifying that slave owners had to show papers that proved the circumstances of captivity and that the slave had been examined by someone who spoke their native language and "confessed" to being a slave; slave owners also had to provide evidence that the slave had been branded by a royal official with the *R* or *G* brand.[45] But as Bartolomé de las Casas pointed out in his "Defense of the Indians," the so-called confession of slaves was a monstrous charade.[46] Rarely in formal investigations (*residencias*) of the 1520s and 1530s were authorities fined or punished for illegal slaving activities. Take, for example, an official investigation in 1533 of Francisco Gutiérrez, whose job it was to brand slaves in Santiesteban, Pánuco. As he deposed, his memory suddenly failed him: he could not recall whether an interpreter (*nahuatlico*) was present when slaves were questioned about their status. He did remember asking the group of indios whether their mothers and fathers had been slaves, then proceeded to brand them on the left cheek with an *R*.[47] The Crown's attempt to control illegal activities by creating another bureaucratic hurdle actually encouraged additional "legal theater." The actions merely served to reinforce the tautology that only someone who was a slave would be branded and that, because of the stiff penalties, no one would dare brand a slave who had not been taken in just war.[48]

While slave merchants and owners might comply with legal requisites, they learned to play the game of legal documentation by their own rules. It did not take long before bills of sale, powers of attorney, and donations incorporated the new required legal language stating that the indio had been branded by the appropriate authority with a royal brand and that she or he had been taken in just war.[49] These documents reinforced the legal fiction of branding, iterating in writing what the brand already said.[50] The two written documents—flesh and parchment—reinforced one another and afforded the condition of bondage greater authenticity. In dozens of sale documents, slaves about to be sold were identified by name, a vague place of origin, an estimate of age, and, at times, where on the body the mark could be read. Some bills of sale mentioned a marking—*un letrero*—and nothing else. A few rare sale documents included a minimalist drawing of the brand, such as "Antonia, branded on the chin with an ¬."[51]

Given the fluidity of practices throughout Latin America, it was not uncommon for an expert designated by the court in Castile to examine a slave litigant's face and see several brands traversing it, each one a mapping of a life-altering moment. Some faces bore clear inscriptions of the royal *R* or *G*; others did not.[52] Some bore the scars of homemade brands employed hastily during large military campaigns, when hundreds of people were apprehended at once.[53] Others bore the names of a former master—Vaca or Castro—scripted across their faces. There were those countenances that resembled a palimpsest: the letters of a former master's name partially erased or scraped off, and other blackened letters carved over the crevices.[54] How could slave litigants facing notaries, lawyers, and judges in Spanish courts five, ten, or even forty-five years after the fact prove they had been branded illegally? How could they possibly reconstruct the historicity of the different moments of inscription (as opposed to the end result—the evidence of the brand itself) in a Castilian court?

Rather than try to distinguish the multiple scars on multiple faces, the easiest course of action for lawyers representing indigenous litigants was to cite the numerous royal decrees, particularly that of 1532, which stated that a royal license was required and that the king discouraged branding on the face.[55] What occurred then were complicated arguments over what constituted a "legal" or an "illegal" brand. Indigenous litigants took advantage of the lack of precision to avow their own historical narratives about brands that had faded, been partially erased, or resulted from an accident. For instance, when Antonio Gómez, an ordained priest, spoke with the indio Martín before testifying, the litigant had explained to him that the mark on his left cheek came from a mule kick. Gómez did not believe him and accused Martín of having put herbs on his cheek to erase the brand (a common practice, apparently). Martín's other cheek was inscribed with the word *Vaca*, the surname of one of his owners.[56] At issue was whether the mark that had supposedly been made by a mule was really a legitimate brand, since the name Vaca was not. A witness on Martín's behalf confirmed that he had known the lad when he lived in a village near Granada in Spain. He remembered hearing that a harnessed mule standing in a field had startled and kicked Martín in the face, making it bleed. Whether the mark that remained came from this incident the witness could not say, but it did not resemble the *R* or *G* in any way. This same witness confirmed that Martín's other cheek bore the inscription *Vaca*. The vague marking on one side of his face and the illegal inscription on the other led the judges of the Council of the Indies to determine in 1537 that Martín should be free.[57]

To counter the power that these markings had to determine the course of someone's life, indigenous slaves developed techniques to diminish the size or depth of a brand. It was easier if a brand had been etched on a cheek when they were young, since at that point the skin was continually renewing itself. Such was the case for Juan, a slave litigant in the city of Ciudad Rodrigo who in 1549 was examined by an expert witness named Santos García for signs of a brand. García told the notary that he had spoken with Juan in both Spanish and his "proper Indian language," asking him if he was a slave, to which Juan had replied, "Yes, and that he had been branded as a very young boy in Mexico." When García could not find any mark on Juan's face and questioned him about it, the slave replied that because he had been branded when he was very young, "the mark had disappeared." This came as no surprise to García, who said he had possessed a number of branded slaves and servants in the Indies whose scars seemed to fade over time. On the other side of Juan's face, García identified the name of a former master, Pedro de Torres. Once again, it was the illegal brand that guaranteed Juan his freedom.[58]

It wasn't just that judges and witnesses were tasked with identifying facial disfigurement that had occurred across the ocean and under very different circumstances; they were also operating within the culture of Castile. If branding practices in Spanish America had their own logic and rhythm according to time and place, the same held true in Castile, especially in a city like Seville. In that international context, slaves classified by place of origin, religion, or color of their countenances (mulato or loro or blanco) walked the streets and congregated in plazas, around the fountains, and by city doors. The branded flesh of cheeks, foreheads, chins, or lips served as readily identifiable texts to be read at a glance as a slave stooped to buy the freshest fruit in one of the stalls in the plaza mayor or brushed past someone on the muddy streets. A face or an arm might be marked with a fleur-de-lis, a star, an S beside a nail (*clavo*) to spell out *esclavo* (slave), or a large *X* to signify the shape of the cross on which Saint Andrew was martyred. A face from Seville might say "DSA"—*de Sevilla*.[59] Diverse West African peoples might bear the mark of the Crown on their right breast or the particular brand of a trading company on their backs, whereas slaves from Portuguese India were branded on the face.[60] Given that indigenous peoples from Spanish America were not branded with the *S* and nail, it would have been easier to identify them as not indio. In an appeal initiated in 1560, Pedro de Hermosilla, a swordmaker, argued that his slave, Gerónimo, was not of the lineage of indios: he had been born near Jerez de la Frontera, the son of a captive female slave, and had the *S* and nail carved into the flesh of each cheek. Hermosilla was thereby implying that the place of Gerónimo's birth and the kind of brand that marked him proved he was the son of a morisca slave.[61]

Often the skin or flesh of the face was an all "too-visible surface" that disguised one's history, biography, or whatever is knowable about someone.[62] What a brand meant in one location and context could change in another. Even the word *libre* carried its own hidden provisos. In 1539 Esteban Vicente drew up a notarized document in Mexico City stating that after ten more years of service, Magdalena, his slave from Pánuco, would be free, as would any of her children. The document affirmed the meaning of the word *libre* that Vicente had recently branded across Magdalena's forehead. "Make no mistake," the document read, "this only means she is free after ten more years."[63] But once Vicente arrived in Medina del Campo in Spain with Magdalena and another female slave, everyone who read her face assumed that she was free. Not only did her face say so, but in 1544 she was living apart from her master in Valladolid with a male partner. Because the high court was readily accessible in Valladolid and authorities were actively prosecuting slave owners, Magdalena was easily freed, despite the "provision" in the document drawn up by Vicente in Mexico five years earlier. In the courtroom the layered meanings of the all-too-visible surface of her face were exposed: first, a one-sided agreement for conditional freedom; next, a branding to confirm the pact, followed by the interpretations of the word *free* by the townspeople of Medina del Campo, and finally the readings of the documents given by the Council of the Indies several years later. Magdalena's body registered a "sign" that contained different meanings according to the historicity of the moment and cultural ways of seeing.

Branding was not only a legal inscription; it could also be an act of violent retribution against a body no longer considered docile. From the slave owners' perspective, it was an effective and humiliating way to punish indigenous slave litigants who initiated legal proceedings; dozens of indios in Castile complained that this had happened to them. But it was also a commonsense, albeit knee-jerk response, since slave owners knew a brand on the face (with an S and a nail, or a master's name) might result in an easy, quick sale to an unsuspecting buyer who would assume the slave came from the Portuguese domains or was the son or daughter of a captive morisco or African. In major cities such as Seville, Madrid, and Valladolid, it was not difficult to find black-market barbers who would brand slaves for a good price and could easily fabricate a royal R or G. Despite severe fines for doing so, slave owners throughout Castile assumed that it was worth the risk; illegal brandings occurred in at least two dozen lawsuits, and as late as 1579.[64] For example, when Inés Carrillo realized that her slave, Diego, originally from Pánuco, had initiated a lawsuit before the Casa, she had a barber brand him on the face. She then humiliated him further by placing a collar around his neck with the sculpted inscription "Slave of Inés Carrillo, vecina of Sevilla." Carrillo defended her conduct saying that she branded Diego *after* he had become her slave and because he had run away.[65] Like many other slave owners, she did not consider branding to be either illegal or an act of extreme violence.[66] Her logic made sense within the cultural context. In Seville and elsewhere, runaway slaves, whatever their place of origin, were branded as a punishment and as a means of ensuring that if they were to run away again, they could be readily identified. That Diego was an indio did not matter to Carrillo.[67]

But branding an indio in Castile did break the law, and the action provided another form of evidence for indigenous litigants to present in court. Here was physical proof—a fresh wound, a still-enflamed lesion, or a crevice—and the story to go with it. Litigants told stories of horror and deception, of being duped into following masters into the back rooms of barber shops, where their faces were seared. Barbola provided details of how her branding had occurred: "Last week, while I was in the home of the jurado, Diego López [my master] of Seville, he gave the order to brand me and they branded me . . . and the barber who did it is the son of Castroverde who lives in Alfalfa. I ask the judges to order them to be apprehended, jailed and punished for the branding and because I am a free woman."[68]

As evidence, Barbola showed her two cheeks which read, from one to the other, "Slave of the jurado Diego López of Seville."[69] Although López and the barber both confessed to the deed, the slave owner tried to defend his behavior by saying that all slaves from Venezuela were branded with the royal *R* in Santo Domingo and that Barbola was no exception. In other words, because she (supposedly) had already been branded, it should not matter that he had branded her again. The judges were not impressed with his rationale: they freed Barbola and penalized López 30,000 maravedís, of which 10,000 were awarded to Barbola.[70]

In cases where a slave litigant accused a slave owner of illegal branding, the latter had to prove that the branding had occurred before the slave arrived in Castile.[71] The indio litigant Francisco, in claiming he had been branded by his mistress in Seville, thought history and his ethnicity were on his side. In his initial deposition he stated he was from "Tlaxcala, which is in New Spain," and that he was free "because all those of this land where I am from are free; no one is a slave." Witnesses on his behalf supported his argument: he was free by birth because the indigenous people of Tlaxcala had been rewarded with a special status because of their assistance in the conquest of the Mexica between 1519 and 1521. Not only could Francisco not be a slave but he could not have been branded before arriving in Castile. The slave owner tried to invert the argument by stating that Francisco could not possibly be from Tlaxcala because all indigenous peoples there were free. The king's brand on Francisco's face—witnesses were asked to verify its authenticity—was used only on captive indios, and only in America, never in Spain, and Francisco's face had a brand when he arrived in Spain.[72] In the end, it was his young age at capture (under fourteen) that won Francisco's case, not the brand's authenticity or the site where he had been branded.[73]

Deliberations over what brands signified were of course calibrated toward achieving a goal: continued bondage or freedom. But the logic employed within this legal context reveals underlying sentiments about brands as documents and as evidence. They could be read differently depending on who was doing the "reading" and when. In the case of Francisco, he countered the logic of papereality—because the brand exists, he is a slave—by arguing that no a priori branding had occurred on the other side of the ocean and that his place of origin precluded that from occurring. His master's lawyer argued that Francisco could not have been from Tlaxcala since he was already branded when he arrived in Castile. No one questioned that the brand represented some sort of "truth," but whose truth depended on the particular point of view. In the abovementioned cases, a witness, litigant, or defendant was required to do the reading, which is why witness testimony had a particular bearing on the presentation and interpretation of documentation in the courtroom.

Witness Depositions

Like written documents and brands, witness depositions were active sites of power. Generally, historians focus on how effectively the narratives bolstered the underlying legal arguments being made in the opening statements by litigants and in the responses crafted by defendants. The narrative aspect of witness testimony is, in itself, crucial to understanding identity politics. Of interest here is not the content of what was said, but the forms of truth witnesses embodied because of who they were. In other words, different "kinds" of witnesses—the content of the form—represented different kinds of authority.

Witnesses were selected and called forth to accomplish several tasks. Those who spoke on behalf of slave owners verified possession in the absence of documentation, or they provided information that supplemented or filled in gaps in the extant documentation. Witnesses could help to prove the ethnic or imperial origins of indigenous litigants.

The choice of witnesses involved a silent agency not readily apparent in the lawsuits. Supportive witnesses might be the only ones available within the time allotted for securing witnesses; on the other hand, they might have been eyewitnesses to an event or been considered "expert witnesses." For certain questions, friends and neighbors, merchants familiar with the sea routes and the peculiarities of the slave trade, or individuals who labored with the litigant or defendant contributed their stories and answered the contrived questions set forth in the interrogatories (*interrogatorios*). Supportive witnesses were not divided into clear-cut indigenous versus Spanish camps. Castilians with experience in America—some as slavers or merchants involved in the more heinous activities associated with slavery and branding—came forward to testify on behalf of an indigenous litigant, while in some cases indigenous slaves and servants supported the master's position against the slave.[74] In general, however, indigenous witnesses supported one another, and in general friars opposed slave owners. Litigants might be fortunate enough to have a star-studded cast of powerful friars testify on their behalf. The friars Thomas de Berlanga (bishop of Panama), Bartolomé de las Casas (bishop of Chiapas), Gregorio Pesquera, and Rodrigo de Ladrada provided key testimonies that verified the cultural origins of several indigenous witnesses, based on the deep linguistic skills and cultural knowledge they had gained by ministering to different indigenous groups over the decades. Even though some believed that servants and slaves should not testify because of the ignominy of their souls, and that women should not testify because they were inherently flawed, both groups testified on a regular basis.

Credible witnesses fell into several camps. There were those who could state that they had known the litigant and defendant for lengthy periods and could provide eyewitness accounts of events or circumstances surrounding an event. A second group of "expert witnesses" had authority to speak based on their own life experiences or because they represented a particular "type" of witness. Some of those in the first group could attest to the history of the litigant in America *and* in Castile, thus bridging the temporal and spatial gap of the Atlantic crossing. Indigenous witnesses might claim to have known a litigant in Mexico, Lima, or Santo Domingo. Occasionally, they could help determine that a branding had occurred illegally. Juan, who identified himself as an indio natural of Peru and subject to the cacique Nonaguana, claimed not only that he was free and not a captive, but that "Francisco de Cavallos, the man servant of Hernando Pizarro, with little fear of God and contempt for royal justice and the prohibitions of His Majesty, branded me on the face by his own authority."[75] His key witness, Pedro, a twenty-two-year-old from Chincha in coastal Peru, testified in 1544 that he knew Juan before and after he had been branded in Lima. "When he met him for the first time in Peru," the notary recorded, "he was not branded." Later, the notary continued, "he told me that Licentiate Pero Vázquez had branded him and another servant of his to have him as a slave."[76] In effect, Pedro was able to link the before and after moments of Juan's traumatic history of branding in Peru.

Witnesses might also enhance their credibility with the judges because they could demonstrate a camaraderie and trusted relationship with an indio litigant who had confessed his or her place of origin. Many such deponents were indios who had developed close relationships with other indios, whether in the crowded neighborhoods of Seville or in the corridors of the Casa or Council of Indies tribunals. Their depositions revealed details of intimate congress and firsthand knowledge of litigants' social networks, the languages they spoke, and the stories they told about their homeland over the decades. But indios were not the only ones who possessed this kind of expert quality: witnesses of all stripes could claim close relationships with the plaintiffs, thus enhancing their standing in the court. In their narrative accounts deponents would sometimes set the scene of where friendly parlays had occurred. The Castilian Diego López de Moguer explained that he was walking along the road when Manuel confessed to him that he was from the Indies of Portugal and not from the Indies of Castile. López then prodded him by asking, "Aren't the indios from the Portuguese kingdoms lazier than the others?" To which Manuel replied, "The slaves from the Portuguese Indies are better than those from Castile."[77] In addition, Martín de Padilla, an innkeeper, said that while visiting and staying in the home of Sebastián de Aguilar, he saw Manuel and another indio named Francisco there. He asked Manuel why he was a captive slave, while Francisco was not. Manuel responded, "Because Francisco is from Mexico and I am from Portugal."[78] Such confidences, whether fabricated or real, had a deliberate function: to convince the judges of the credibility of the witnesses based on the likelihood that such an admission would occur between confidantes in a specific setting.

Witnesses with a long-term direct relationship with the litigant or defendant might also help to establish what I call the "lineage of bondage," by filling in the documentary gaps of how a slave came to be in the possession of the current master. They could also verify how many years the slave had been with the current owner in willing submission to bondage (*quieta y pacíficamente*).[79] This was important because part of the underlying epistemological framework of slavery was based on the owner-slave relationship. Unless it was a question of mixed heritage, the natal genealogy of the slave litigant did not enter the written record, and court officials did not consider blood ties to be essential to their cases. Only rarely, and always later in the case, when additional proof of indigenous (and not African or morisco) identity was needed, did abducted litigants name their parents.[80] This was nothing new in Castile, for anyone of servile status, slave or servant, foreigner or Castilian, was inscribed in most records in a relational manner as a part of a family or linked to a master's name. Witnesses located slaves "genealogically" vis-à-vis the merchants, shipmasters, or family members who transported them from port to port.

As a part of the epiphenomenal "truth" that a slave existed in genealogical relationship to a master, the opening statement of each case set the stage by listing the sequence of merchants and owners from the first to the last sale. Eyewitnesses recounted tales of how a slave had been transferred from a merchant to an owner, thus sealing his or her fate as a slave. By doing so, the witnesses employed a circular and tautological logic: because a slave was sold by merchant x to agent y, and then transported by agent y to owner z, he or she *must* be a slave. Gonzalo Hernández knew in 1549 that he lacked sufficient written documentation (specifically, just title), but decided nevertheless to appeal the sentence that had freed his former slave, Isabel. To build his case, he called on witnesses who corroborated his own version of events, which traced her "lineage" from the moment of the initial transaction in the public plaza of Vera Cruz more than twenty years before. He identified the exchange of Isabel from an unnamed merchant who had just left Campeche and Tabasco to his agent, a stockingmaker named Hernando Morzillo. Morzillo testified that he had fulfilled Gonzalo Hernández's request for a slave by buying Isabel and other slaves from the merchant. The detail that the merchant had come from Campeche and Tabasco did not bolster Hernández's case—he did not make the just-war argument—but it helped situate Isabel in the violent historical context of the first of several major Spanish military incursions into the area in 1527. Morzillo then ordered his agent (*factor*), who was about to board a ship for Spain, to tell Juan de Palma, a trusted representative whom he called a *compañero* awaiting instructions back in Seville, to deliver Isabel to Hernández.[81] Other witnesses who had observed the transactions or exchanges then attested that Isabel had remained peacefully with the Hernández family in Seville for over twenty years. The clear lineage of bondage and long-term possession thus proved, so the argument went, that Isabel was and should remain Hernández's slave. But the year was 1549, and Hernández had built a case on anachronistic and faulty logic: possession (and especially long-term ownership) no longer constituted de facto bondage. Isabel did not testify, and so what we learn of her history is reconstructed through the warp and the weft of her lineage of bondage, which entered the archival record as a verifiable representation of her status.[82]

The statements of the second type of witness, the "expert witness," were accepted as "truthful" because of their having been present there—"there" meaning somewhere in the Indies—vested them with an authority to speak the truth. Truth-telling involved a "moral truth," which did not involve actually having been an eyewitness to the "event" of abduction or moment of enslavement (the beginning of the story of bondage verified by the first type of witness).[83] The facts might be wrong or have nothing to do with the litigant's particular situation, but the generalities the witness spoke of bolstered the case.[84] Clues to understanding why this kind of authority carried weight in these particular legal circumstances may come from medieval French law. Andrea Frisch argues that "compurgation or oath-helping" was an important feature of some witness accounts in late medieval France. An eyewitness considered by the community to be upstanding was willing to swear an oath in a juridical context to support the defendant's moral integrity. Rather than bearing witness to an event or knowing a specific truth based on experience, these eyewitnesses offered solidarity to the person for whom they testified and spoke.[85] In other words, the moral standing of the witness counted more than what they said—the content of the form, as opposed to the content of the story.

Castilian and other nonindigenous eyewitnesses often began by revealing the amount of time they had spent in the Indies, the variety of locations to which they had traveled, and whether they were vecinos of a particular Latin American city or town. Several witnesses had been conquerors or professional slavers and could claim twenty or even thirty years' experience in Santo Domingo, Mexico, Peru, or the Rio de la Plata area.[86] As *hombres sabios*, veterans of wars, treacherous expeditions, and slave-raiding enterprises, men like Sebastian de Benalcázar, Martín Alonso de los Ríos, Nuño de Guzman, or Gonzalo de Salazar were accustomed to narrating their heroic deeds in the *probanzas de méritos*, in which they sought rewards for services rendered, or in residencias, the judicial reviews of colonial authorities, where much finger-pointing, covering up, and revenge-seeking occurred.[87] But it wasn't just that these notable and not-so-notable men had been in the Indies. For them, experience equaled having "been in many parts of the Indies of His Majesty" ([*ha*] *estado en muchas partes de las Indias de su Magestad*) and having seen different "kinds" of Indians in different geographical settings.

Most witnesses had never seen the litigant in his or her place of origin, but their own presence in similar locations gave them the ability to read the specific physiognomic features present in the indio litigant who stood before them. They were considered experts because they ostensibly had the capacity to pinpoint the place of origin of an indigenous litigant in a specific imperial and geographic location. This is why in 1577 Melchior de Villagómez, a procurador of the Audiencia of Santiago de El Estero, boasted to the court that the slave Alejo looked like the "Peruvian" indios he had seen when he walked more than six hundred leagues throughout those provinces and in Chile.[88] A typical response, however, would be less dramatic and would go something like this: "I have spent ten years in Rio de la Plata, and I am familiar with the Indians there as well as those of Tierra Firme and New Spain. I have observed the litigant and he has the features of an Indian from the area of Rio de la Plata and is not from the Indies of Portugal." Some expert witnesses referenced diasporic sites where indigenous peoples converged to be sold or used as laborers. Merchants who had spent time in Puerto Rico, Santo Domingo, or Lisbon claimed that they could situate the imperial or cultural status of a litigant because the variety of indios they had seen in those locations gave them a comparative perspective.[89] In some cases witnesses would hedge their bets by arguing that although the litigants did not look like they were from Brazil (i.e., the Portuguese domains), they, the witnesses, could not say definitively whether the litigants came from a specific location in the Spanish domains. Testimonies of this sort allowed plaintiffs and defendants to invent, to distort, or to practice what in psychotherapy is called "transference"—projecting their experiences onto another person and hoping their arguments would persuade the judges.[90]

Conclusions

The content of the form—the document, the brand, the quality of a witness— carried weight in the courtroom because of its normative value. The form of representation was thought to take precedence over the people and events being represented, and these documents and witnesses were believed to contain some sort of knowable truth related to the condition of bondage. The documents were powerful and active sites of power upheld by the law and in the practices of slavery. But these truth-objects were also given value in a relational manner: by the ways in which individuals saw, interacted with, or interpreted them. Whenever the history of an inscription on a parchment or body was introduced in the courtroom—such as being dragged into a barber shop or kicked by a mule, bearing the word *free* across one's forehead, or claiming the place of "origin" of the brand—it raised doubts about its veracity. Slaves and masters objectified such documents as truth-telling evidence by also registering them with their own grains of truth.

FIVE

Narratives of Territorial Belonging, Just War, and Ransom

I, Pedro Gutiérrez de los Rios, sixty years of age, as governor and in the name of his Majesty . . . in 1526 or 1527 . . . brought indio slaves, many of them by request, and those we brought from Nicaragua were slaves [of just war] and those brought [to Panama] were sold. Once in Nata [Panama], this witness bought fifty or sixty slaves [who had come] from Nicaragua, and I sold some, others I gave away, and some died.

—"Testimony, Governador Pedro Gutiérrez de los Rios," 8/I/1540, AGI, Justicia 1162, n. 6, r. 2, s.f.

It must have been strange for indigenous litigants to listen to depositions that detailed stories *about* them, or to realize that fragments of conversations held long ago—while carrying water, or plucking a chicken—would fit into certain ordered truths about *who they were.* Because the litigation process afforded documents and witness depositions the weight of truth, recorded words became binding representations of a verifiable (and effective) past, in this case the litigant's past. Although none of the indigenous litigants ever commented on the process, they participated in a bizarre legal theater where their identity as indios was determined by legalities such as just war (guerra justa), ransom (rescate), and territorial belonging (naturaleza), and even by the documents themselves.

The storytelling element of the opening statement was the most important phase of the trial because it could help persuade a judge that an illegal victimization had occurred and that the case could proceed on solid legal grounds.[2] But the opening statement was key to the litigation suit in other ways. It framed the litigants' history of bondage into a recognizable legal form, utilizing key terms that situated litigants in a body of established law and legal precedent. It was an "enforced narrative" of the sort discussed by the historian Carolyn Steedman in her study of eighteenth-century English servants, in that they were telling a story of a contrived indio self.[3] The "legal" stories told by litigants followed a particular pattern of conveying what was "already there," waiting to be told in this particular context, rather than of telling of a life lived.

In the previous chapter I considered how the documentary forms of legal procedure informed what was deemed important or necessary for judges and litigants to be able to assess bondage or freedom. But the stories conveyed in opening statements were also crucial to the judicial process. While indigenous identities as enslaved or free subjects were determined in part by a legal template that changed over time, the litigants' scripted stories are just as crucial in illuminating the perceptions, motives, and conflicts that contributed to larger narratives about slavery. The opening statement recounted by a litigant (or lawyer) presented a life story of sorts, sketching out a bare-bones narrative of deracination and displacement, beginning with the litigant's "origin" in a geographical, ethnic, and cultural context.[5] Such statements often began with a stock phrase: "While being in my nativeness [*estando en mi naturaleza*], a Spaniard [or Portuguese] took me by deceit [*engaño*] to the Spanish kingdoms."[6] In this context, "nativeness" was defined as a particular community or cultural habitat, presumably in Spanish America.

As Tamar Herzog has demonstrated, Spaniards living in the kingdoms of Spain in the sixteenth century regularly employed the term *naturaleza* to distinguish an individual who belonged to a specific community from an outsider or immigrant.[7] In the legal locus of the courtroom, *naturaleza* as it was applied to indio slaves, was both the homeland and the place where the act of enslavement occurred.[8] The site of deracination could be as vague as "New Spain" or as specific as a cacique's name. Emphasized here was that an indio's movement away from the site of origin was based on *engaño*, a false premise. Most of the trial then revolved around proving that the litigant was truly from a particular naturaleza. Litigants had to convince the judges that they were autochthonous to a particular region and, more important, were vassals of the Spanish Crown. This task required selecting—sometimes in a strategic and conscious manner, and other times in an ad hoc, random way—geographic and linguistic references to the homeland. In sum, the naturaleza was the location from which all other events unfolded.

In the opening statement and the defendants' written response (recorded later), one immediately senses the tension between two competing versions of the past. Indigenous litigants never used the terms *just war* or *rescate* to identify how they came into bondage, but instead emphasized being from a habitat, or naturaleza, where by birth they were free, and that they had been taken by force, engaño, illegally from that place of origin. By contrast, the defendant's rejoinder or accusations nearly always drew from the legal hatbox to situate the beginning of bondage in terms of how they had followed the legal requisites of just war, ransom, or determinants of cannibalism. But also embedded in these legal rationales was the belief that certain habitats and territorial domains produced the kinds of bellicose or defective indios who could be enslaved. Thus, for slave masters and their deponents, naturalezas became imagined geocultural arenas associated with human bondage.

Thus far we have seen how indios were redefined as they crossed the Atlantic and had to reorder their past to reconcile it with their present. We have seen how slaves entered into relationships with masters and the masters' kin, which were often filled with disillusionment, intimacy, and violence, and where the expectations of patronage were fragile at best. As men and women appeared before judges to petition for their freedom, they grappled with the paperwork that defined them as commodities and determined when they had been marked on the flesh or sold. They relied on newly established Crown requisites that protected them against improper practices of enslavement or treatment.

I now explore how the construct of indioness depended on legal codes that defined the circumstances under which legal slavery could occur. Specifically, I turn to witness depositions to focus on how litigant and witness courtroom narratives utilized three key legal concepts to define indios: naturaleza, rescate, and just war. I emphasize the "constructedness of the stories" that litigants, defendants, and witnesses told about indios and "the rhetorical means they use[d] to persuade others" that they had been captured legally and deserved to remain slaves or be freed.[9] To expose how forced migrations and on-the-ground realities could be effaced by indistinct legalisms such as *just war* or *ransom*, I consider the dilemmas faced by three litigants: Martín, from the central valley of Mexico, who contested his master's understanding of rescate; Francisco, from the "province of Nicaragua," who denied having been captured because he (and, by extension, his people) refused to accept Christianity; and Catalina Nicolasa, a Chorotega from the area comprising southern Honduras, Nicaragua, and Costa Rica, who also denied being a slave from a bellicose territory.

Peppered throughout decrees and ordinances, the terms *just war, ransom*, and *cannibalism* are often taken at face value by scholars who assume that these terms had fixed meanings across time and space. While it is important to show how these carte blanche terms helped turn slavery into a thriving business with the collusion of caciques, rarely do we see how they are contested or given dimensionality by legal experts, indigenous litigants, witnesses, and slave owners. The three case studies I discuss in this chapter bring backstories to the fore. The case studies provide the experiential element of the usage of legal terminology and show how past practices informed present circumstances. While courtroom narratives about just war, ransom, or cannibalism should not be considered true or fundamentally different from laws and ordinances (juxtaposing de jure versus de facto perspectives), neither were the decontextualized experiences of just war and ransom as relayed by slaves and slave raiders flat or one-dimensional. Rather, it is in the polemics over the possession of human beings as reconstructed in the courtroom context where we can begin to disentangle the debates and understand the assumptions that gave meaning to the construct *indio.*

Naturaleza

Most scholars, theologians, and jurists of the time agreed that applying the Aristotelian notion of natural slavery (servidumbre natural) to indios had no legal or theological basis. Those who disagreed believed that the people labeled as indios lacked humanity, and that those who were little more than bestial animals could be enslaved.[10] The Castilian Crown determined early on that indios were humans and fell within the governance of natural law. By the 1540s, the opening statements of litigation suits declared that the petition for freedom of indigenous litigants was justified because all indios had rational capacity (ingenio) by their nature as Indians (por naturaleza).[11] Here, *naturaleza* was equated with humanness and the indios' capacity to understand and accept Christianity because of their innate condition.

Proponents of indigenous slavery argued that certain indios were natural slaves based on where they were born; they were formed in accordance with their naturaleza. Particular environments, according to Galenic principles, formed slaves—that is, persons who were warlike, uncivilized, and incapable of understanding or accepting Christianity. Depending on the areas where they were born, some indios were assumed to lack ingenio, or the capacity to reason; they were inferior to Europeans and were more like children than adults.[12] Being born into an environment with too much sun and humidity was thought to explain why some indios were inclined to practice bestial and barbaric acts such as cannibalism. As the decades progressed, certain human geographies were also naturalized by Spaniards as habitats associated with fierce and bellicose temperaments that were difficult to control.[13]

Because naturaleza was linked to justifications for enslavement in certain areas, it was critical in courtroom depositions for indigenous litigants to locate themselves in a geographical context where slavery was no longer or had never been condoned. One's habitat determined the kind of indio one was. Thus, in the courts, the term *naturaleza* identified diasporic people who had been removed from their homelands and were later reterritorialized as having an identity associated with a specific environment defined by the laws governing the legality or illegality of slavery. Of course, indigenous litigants followed the protocol of all deposing litigants and witnesses, identifying themselves by name, age, and place of origin. But they then followed the advice of solicitors to make a general statement that they were from "New Spain," a territorial and political entity where slavery based on naturaleza had not been permitted since 1542. By following the ebb and flow of laws and ordinances, litigants might identify themselves as being born free (*en mi naturaleza*) in an area where slavery was no longer permitted.[14] Thus, the conflicting "courtroom" narratives revolved around establishing the litigant's place of origin as one that produced either slaves or friendly indios or had been declared by official decree to be a site where just war or rescate could occur. Litigants also emphasized before-and-after scenarios related to the moments in which they had been exchanged or abducted—nuanced aspects of slavery that often fall under the radar.

Caribs

Queen Isabel may have qualified indios as free vassals in 1501, but within three years she designated, by royal decree, that *indios caribes* (Carib Indians) from islands in the Caribbean and the coast of modern-day Colombia could be captured as slaves. The designation *Carib* was not entirely based on fiction. When the Spaniards arrived in the 1490s, a distinct ethnocultural group of caribes existed. They lived in various habitats throughout the Caribbean and Orinoco basin and spoke Arawak and other dialects.[15] The Taíno inhabitants of Hispaniola greatly feared these brave and aggressive people, who came in large fleets of pirogues to attack and make off with their people.[16] While the category "caribe" encompassed a broad ethnic group, it was also a European invention (and stereotype) used to describe a wide variety of peoples thought to have barbaric tendencies, the worst of which was to consume human flesh. Even before 1500, Castilians had already begun to distinguish "good" (*guatiao*, "adoptive brothers" in Taíno) Indians from "bad" (*caribe*, "cannibalistic") ones.[17]

As Spanish merchants, miners, and local authorities gained licenses to enslave indios caribes in large numbers, they purposefully left the cultural geography defining Carib territory vague. This vagueness allowed for an exponential expansion of the territories consisting of "Carib" peoples and ensured a steady supply of indigenous slaves for the Castilian inhabitants of Santo Domingo, Puerto Rico, and Cuba. Additionally, certain islands of the Lesser Antilles and sections of northern South America were designated or redesignated as caribe according to when extractive resources such as pearls were discovered, and when the Spaniards decided they needed an in situ labor force. The islands of Margarita and Trinidad, both initially designated as Carib islands, became "Castilian-friendly" islands when merchants from Santo Domingo decided to use them as bases of operation for pearl extraction and the coastal Venezuelan slave trade.[18]

A blatant example of establishing a carte blanche geopolitical rationale for enslavement of indios caribes came in a declaration made in 1520 by the residencia judge Rodrigo de Figueroa. He stated that any islands unoccupied by Castilians were inhabited by "barbarous Carib Indians," except for Trinidad, Lucayos, Barbados, the Gigantes, and Margarita, all strategic for the Spaniards at that time.[19] But as the 1503 declaration of Queen Isabel also made clear, the enslavement of the circum-Caribbean caribe peoples could also occur because of their active resistance to Spanish incursions or their attacks on Spanish settlements.[20] The resistance of the Carib people in eastern Puerto Rico and raids on Castilian settlements there and on Margarita, Dominica, and other islands actually escalated slave-raiding enterprises throughout the region well into the 1570s.[21] Resistance bred violence, which led to further resistance, perpetuating a vicious cycle.

By the 1530s, the bellicose indios caribes peoples were not limited to the Caribbean basin, nor were they all cannibals. As Patricia Seed has noted, the designation *indio caribe* extended into the Chichimeca area of northern Mexico, the territories of Charcas, Popayán, the interior of the New Kingdom of Granada, and parts of Argentina and Chile—all habitats of peoples, some nomadic, who fiercely resisted Spanish incursions into their polities.[22] For instance, in the instructions for reading the Spanish Requirement issued in March 1533, Charles V referred to those rebelling against Spanish rule in Peru (*alçados*) as "the Carib Indian rebels of the province of Peru."[23] As late as 1580, the Real Audiencia of Guatemala determined that "because the Chontal indios are Caribs and consume human flesh," they should be declared slaves.[24] Into the seventeenth century, colonial writers like fray Pedro Simón expounded on why the Pijao people of the New Kingdom of Granada were bestial cannibals.[25] The term *indio caribe* became a comprehensive term used to justify legally sanctioned military actions and subsequent enslavement long after the News Laws had been passed and in areas where peoples were not ethnically Carib.

The fantastic mystique surrounding the caribes did not help matters, and tales of cannibalism circulated widely in Castile and elsewhere.[26] Pieter Martír's *Decades of the New World*, a Latin account published and disseminated in 1511, afforded the "Caribs" a territory larger than continental Europe, which may have helped to broadcast the idea of their geographical breadth. Such was the fascination and abhorrence toward them that, according to Fernández de Oviedo's account, a curious Charles V requested that some be brought to Spain so he might see what cannibals looked like.[27]

Given the propensity to label vastly different resistant peoples as cannibals and the carte blanche licenses awarded to capture indios caribes, it is surprising that the referent appears only in a few of the lawsuits analyzed in this book.[28] One instance occurred in 1554, when Sebastian Vázquez, a lawyer arguing on behalf of his client, tried to portray Magdalena, the female slave his client had purchased eighteen years earlier as "of the Caribs." How he could state with authority that the unnamed individuals who captured Magdalena followed all the requisites necessary when war was waged on her unnamed people is unclear.[29] The original bill of sale, presented as additional evidence and dated from 1535 in Mexico, said nothing about the under-aged Magdalena being "of the Carib people." Fortunately, when she was questioned "in the Mexican language" by two witnesses—Francisco, a carpenter, and his wife, Ana de Alfaro—Magdalena explained to them that she came from Jicalango (Xicalango), a coastal village in Campeche familiar to Ana, where "cannibalism" was not practiced. Magdalena's specific place of origin, confirmed by these two witnesses, and her ability to say a few words in the "Mexican tongue" ensured her freedom.[30] In this and other cases slave owners conflated cannibalism with a warlike nature in order to gain an advantage in categorizing the origins ("Nicaraguan," "Brazilian," or "of the Caribs") of their slaves. Implied in the assertions made by slave raiders who captured indios caribes was that they were in fact rescuing indio caribes from themselves and others.[31]

Although stories of cannibalistic indios circulated widely in Europe and served as the raison d'être for enslaving thousands of innocent people, two other legal categories—esclavo de rescate and buena guerra—reinforced a typology of difference among slaves and created a power regime "that was at once micro-political and monumental in scale."[32] Both *buena guerra* and *rescate* were used to distinguish people held in bondage from free indios based on contextual contingencies having to do with warfare, resistance to "civilizing missions," the failure to accept Christianity, or preexisting conditions of slavery and slave exchange.

Rescate

The legitimizing term *rescate*, or ransom, had a long history, both in the Mediterranean and in Spanish America. In principle, rescate transactions occurred between a local cacique or lord and a Spanish buyer, authority, or encomendero who exchanged indios already held in bondage for goods. In other instances, so-called pagan people being held captive were rescued (ransomed) by the Spanish and brought into the Christian fold. The practice also expanded on local customs of barter, on taking captives in warfare or raids, and on experiences of captivity practiced by different ethnicities in different ways throughout the hemisphere. What we don't know, and what deeper ethnographic regional research would reveal, is how different local practices of rescate changed as the presence of Europeans became a permanent reality.[33] Investigations of different regions of Western Africa show how kinship and affinitive relations, hierarchies of social relations, the nature of trade, barter, and the commodification of human beings changed over time as African warlords and kings increased contact with Europeans, acquired new commodities, and tried to expand or maintain their regional power-bases.[34] Scholars of early Spanish America could draw from these methodologies to move beyond the victimization model of rescate still prevalent in the scholarship and explore how, in the sixteenth century, the exchange in human beings served as a tool of survival and expansion for local ethnicities.

To some degree, Spaniards viewed rescate as a civilizing practice, or at least that is how they portrayed the bureaucratized system of exchange in the written record. In the scores of licenses awarded by the king to individuals setting out on expeditions (*armadas*) to ransom or rescue (*rescatar*), the contracts covered the exchange or trading of goods between the designated Europeans in a broad geographical area. Licenses also involved the exchange of commodified humans, especially in areas such as Honduras and Santa

Marta, where slaves provided the main source of profit for Castilians.[35] The terms generally depicted (from the Spanish perspective) a person, already a slave, who was exchanged for goods or bartered to lessen labor or tribute requirements. Through being brought as slaves into the Christian fold (the redemptive dimension), indios would escape the ravages of paganism and would benefit from Spanish patrimonialism. Given the different connotations embedded in the terms, the noun *rescate* and verb *rescatar* involved both the notion of an economic exchange and the idea of saving people already in bondage from their own culture. Rescate was a legally sanctioned practice based on the premise that the Spanish mission in America was to bring indios into the Christian fold.

Contracts between the Crown and merchants, however, were also motivated by profit. In order to accommodate all possible contingencies, licenses to take rescate slaves referred to vague geographical spaces such as "Tierra Firme," "Paría," or the provinces of Santa Marta or New Toledo (Peru).[36] But certain procedures had to be followed. Much like a modern-day accountant, the veedor, a Crown-appointed official who generally accompanied expeditions of rescate, was charged with keeping track of goods bought and sold and taxes to be collected for the Crown.[37] Although veedores were to ensure that proper procedure was followed, many were canny businessmen who profited from the multiple transactions in human merchandise.[38] Another Crown authority, usually the lieutenant governor, was also supposed to be present at the transaction and was charged with determining from the indigenous lord or cacique that those who were being taken were legitimate slaves according to local customs and that they were being released into the custody of the slave traders voluntarily, not under duress.[39]

The granting of individual licenses and the overgeneralization of particular naturalezas as spaces where "trade" could occur had two effects. The first was to compartmentalize rescate as an activity that took place in vaguely defined geocultural arenas based on royal policies that were applied piecemeal and gave vast powers to individuals. The second is that legally sanctioned rescate was always connected in some way to naturalezas rather than to specific ethnic groups, which explains why several of the litigants accused of being slaves of rescate found it necessary to argue against the grain of place rather than against a specific culture. In other words, rather than claiming to be, for example, Cumanágato or Warao (groups that had been enslaved unjustly by the Spaniards in the 1530s), litigants would argue that they were from a broad terrain such as Tierra Firme, which would make it more difficult to prove that they had been ransomed slaves.

The main justification for granting rescate licenses rested on the assumption that Spaniards were simply continuing a long-standing practice.[40] While it is certainly true that forms of slavery already existed in specific areas of Central America and northern South America, the expansion of the Spanish slave trade exacerbated and strained local practices of slavery that served other purposes and that, prior to the arrival of the Spaniards, were not motivated by economic profit. The pressure on caciques to provide slaves to their encomenderos only increased over the decades, and there were serious consequences if they did not.[41] Some caciques profited from watching their enemies' people being rounded up and enslaved, while others saw their own wives, sisters, and brothers taken from their huts at night.[42] Striking a balance between navigating local geopolitics and placating the Spanish intruders was precarious and delicate at best. Moreover, most rescate slaves traded by the Spanish did not remain in their homelands. They were loaded onto ships and taken to other ports to be sold, despite royal prohibitions against ransoming indios from outside their jurisdiction.[43]

Given the widespread enslavement of indigenous peoples under conditions of rescate, how did indigenous litigants and slave owners create scripted courtroom narratives to fit into a legal framework but also reflect their own experiences? In 1536 the slave Martín took the bold step of petitioning for his freedom before the Council of the Indies. He hoped to prove that the exchange that his owner Salazar called rescate had, in fact, occurred under duress and was based on the false expectation that Martín would serve him as a free manservant (paje). His action was daring for several reasons. For one, no major legislation had yet been passed completely eradicting indigenous slave practices in New Spain or elsewhere. A 1530 royal decree banning slavery by rescate or just war was revoked in 1534, on the grounds that these slaves would be forever lost to Christianity if rescate slavery did not continue. As the royal provision said, "It would be inconvenient not to allow the continuation of the exchange of indio slaves by means of rescate," because "experience has shown that those slaves who remain in the control of the same naturales reside in idolatry and other sins and abominable practices."[44]

The timing of Martín's petition was also risky because his master, Gonzalo de Salazar, once an all-powerful political figure in post-conquest central Mexico, still had strong allies in Castile. Several accounts reveal that in 1524 the silver-tongued Salazar had convinced Hernán Cortés—then about to depart from Mexico/Tenochtitlán on what would turn out to be a two-year difficult expedition through the *selva* of Petén to Honduras—to let him serve as *factor*, or manager of Crown financial transactions and royal properties in his absence. While the marquis wended his way through the mosquito-infested terrain of Honduras, nearly dying in the process, Salazar, according to the many enemies he developed in that short period, transformed into a despot.[45] To consolidate his tenuous hold on power, Salazar proclaimed himself to be governor and *capitán general* and proceeded to murder his enemies and foment rumors that Cortés had succumbed in Honduras and would never return.[46]

Not only did Salazar revoke and redistribute encomiendas to his supporters, but he recklessly enslaved thousands of indigenous people from the central valley of Mexico and Pánuco before the authorities finally, in 1526, ousted him from his position and placed him in jail.[47] Martín was one of hundreds if not thousands of indigenous peoples whose lives were profoundly affected by the competitive machinations of Spaniards like Salazar and by the shifting political winds. Yet the circumstances surrounding Martín's deracination and eventual journey to Spain were uniquely his own.

By 1535, as lawsuits against Salazar piled up in the Council of the Indies, conditions favored Martín's chances of winning a lawsuit.[48] Still, as he was far removed from the location where his initial rescate had occurred, Martín found it necessary to redesign the past, creating one that would convince the judges that he was from the region he claimed as his place of origin and that he had been unjustly appropriated by force (engaño) and in violation of both Nahua and Spanish practices of barter or rescate.[49] He would have to explain how the "exchange" had occurred and convince the judges that he had had a particular identity before the circumstances of colonial rule irrevocably changed the political landscape of the central valley of Mexico.

To do so, Martín explained that he had been an Indian held in the trust (encomienda) of the factor Gonzalo de Salazar in the town of Tenayuca along the northwest shore of Lake Texcoco.[50] "I am a free man," he explained, "the son of free parents, and I did not commit any crime to warrant enslavement." It had been some time since his people had succumbed to Mexica rule, and they were familiar with different forms of labor dependency or slavery (*tlatlacotin*) in its various guises.[51] Throughout the central valley of Mexico, certain individuals were born "dependents" by naturaleza (being from a subjugated polity, or *altepetl*), were war captives, had committed a crime, or had been sold into slavery by their parents.[52] Mexica buyers regularly went to the nearby city of Azcapotzalco to choose slaves for domestic service, as burden bearers, or as future sacrifice victims.[53] But the early colonial situation in the central valley was radically different. Martín was well aware that in the immediate post-1521 period many of his people became slaves of rescate, as caciques or lords negotiated favorable conditions with the Spaniards who now occupied their altepetls and controlled their laborers. Early on, Cortés endorsed the right of encomenderos to receive slaves from their caciques, which further systematized the exchange of unfree individuals by caciques who now served as intermediaries with the Spaniards. By 1525, rescate had become a thinly disguised rationale for blatant kidnapping. More often than not, the victims were women and children.

In Salazar's truth-telling deposition, he pinpointed Martín's "origins" as an esclavo de rescate not to a geographical location or ethnicity, but to a time when his archrival, Córtes, had governed New Spain. He claimed to have possessed Martín for at least twelve years, since 1524. It was common, Salazar explained, for indigenous authorities to exchange boys like Martín for goods or to diminish labor service requirements or tribute; many leaders were threatened with violence if they did not adhere to the requests made by Spaniards. According to Salazar, the 1520s represented a period in New Spain when it was common practice (*uso y costumbre*) for these types of negotiations and terms of enslavement to occur. It was as though Salazar felt he had to remind the Consejo judges that the essence of rescate slavery was based on a preexisting condition among the indigenous peoples of the central valley of Mexico, one that had nothing to do with Spanish practices.[54] In other words, he repeated the legal mantra that the Spaniards were not exploiting the indigenous peoples; they were literally saving them by bringing them into the Spanish fold.

Witnesses in Martín's trial and soldiers like Bernal Díaz del Castillo noted how the native lords kept multiple slaves, who served them in the fields and in domestic service; these lords also sold slaves publicly in large numbers in the town square.[55] Spaniards like Salazar called on the rationale, used by the king himself, that rescate slaves like Martín would derive greater benefit from servidumbre under a civilized master who could guide them in the rudiments of Christian doctrine.[56] The truth was, however, that many rescate slaves sold at public auction were taken to the mines or sold on the *entradas* into war zones, or were forced to carry goods (as *tamenes*) and perform collective hard labor.[57]

To counter the arguments made by Salazar, Martín's lawyer interrogated witnesses using carefully formulated, leading questions that included rare but crucial information specifying Martín's condition before he was taken into bondage. They began by establishing his lineage and ethnicity, key aspects to identifying his specific naturaleza. Witnesses were asked if they knew "that the said Martín [was] the natural son of Viçil and Silosur, his father and mother, that they [were] vecinos of Tenayuca, one league from Mexico City, that his parents were . . . free from all servitude and [were] not slaves, and that they raised Martín in their home calling him son and he [calling them] parents."[58]

An indigenous witness named Francisco Martín (who in a later litigation suit identified himself as Francisco Manuel) testified before a notary on the litigant's behalf. Originally from Santiago near Manzanillo, Mexico, he claimed to have met Martín while he was still in Salazar's possession and that he had learned about the circumstances surrounding Martín's seizure from two lords of "Tenayuca[n]," named Tacatecloe and Tezcacoatl. They had told him that Salazar had asked Martín's parents and the *principales* of the village if Martín would serve as his page (*paje*, a Spanish term generally associated with free individuals of high status or calidad). Here, the element of asking permission from both the parents and the principales is a strikingly different arrangement than a simple barter of commodities.[59] Salazar may have had his eye on the boy—Martín was around nine or ten at the time—as a servant for his son, Pedro, since Salazar had arrived in Mexico with a large family in tow.[60] Francisco Martín then argued that because Salazar already had a reputation for being vengeful and overbearing, Martín's terrorized parents decided it would be in their best interests to donate their son.[61] From the Tepaneca perspective, this was not rescate, but a choice forced on them, and it would therefore fit neatly into the Spanish legal argument of protecting indios against engaño, or deception. Still, the idea that Martín would serve temporarily as a page for Salazar's son might have been considered an acceptable solution; at least he would not be sent to the northern mines. Moreover, for a young man from a higher class, entering into such a service might have been seen as an honorable transaction.

Unmentioned was the probability of Martín's noble heritage; perhaps he was even a high-ranking *pipiltin*, which could be why the lords took the discussion so seriously and why they were careful to distinguish him as a handpicked personal paje. Surely he would not have been considered a *macegualli*, someone who owed service to a noble, or even a temporary *tlacotli*, or household slave, although Spaniards often did not bother with such subtle distinctions.[62] For them, the only analogous Spanish terms were *paje* and *criado*.[63] It seemed, however, that these categories mattered very little, because, once Martín was in Salazar's possession, a henchman named Vaca was given orders to brand his cheek with a "V." Because the Nahua did not regularly mark or burn the flesh, instead using clothing and yokes to distinguish slaves, the branding must have been a deeply stigmatizing event for the child and an unanticipated affront to his parents. Martín never mentioned the *V* emblazoned on his cheek. Other witnesses confirmed that it stood for Vaca, the man who had supposedly ransomed him. For Salazar and his supportive witnesses, it was somatic evidence that proved beyond a doubt that Martín was a ransomed slave.[64] Any brand on the face, readily visible and easily read, was considered a legal document and irrefutable proof of servile status. The fact that it was not a royal *R* (for *rescate*) was inconsequential to Salazar. Not only did the brand disfigure Martín, but it marked him as a slave for life.

Conditions improved for Martín when a disheartened Cortés returned to Tenochtitlán to find that Salazar had usurped his lands and slaves and turned his house in Coyoacán into a veritable fortress. Cortés dealt swiftly with his enemies, and Salazar was imprisoned. With Salazar in jail, Martín jointed the Cortés household as an interpreter, considered a position of status and honor.[65] Martín would now have to rely on his new master for sustenance and protection and some sort of stability, despite the turbulent times. His life also crisscrossed with other indigenous men who would later reappear in his life. It may be then that he met Francisco Martín (Manuel), also an interpreter, who would later serve as a principal eyewitness on his behalf.

In a brief span, Martín's life had changed radically. But in 1528, as soon as Cortés departed for Spain, Martín's luck reversed again: Salazar regained mastery over him. Then, sometime in late 1529 or early 1530, Salazar also decided to journey to Castile. How horrifying the journey eastward toward Veracruz must have been for Martín; he would have beheld some of the over two hundred Tepetlaoztoc Indians laden with Salazar's goods languish and die en route.[66] Once on Spanish soil, his life was not much easier. Even though Salazar still considered Martín to be his property, over the course of the next six years Martín was passed off to caretakers in the disparate locations of Seville, Granada, and Segovia.[67]

Martín waited fourteen years and served several masters before he was able to tell his version of events. Yet, despite the detailed testimony and presentation of credible witnesses, the judges in Spain paid little attention to the clear violation of pre-invasion Nahua practices and the strained conditions under which his parents negotiated his status as a servant. Instead, they based their decision to free Martín, on 28 March 1537, on the lack of an official brand (since he bore a *V* instead of an *R*) or of appropriate papers, which, they emphasized, Salazar should have had. In the end, the *V* emblazoned on Martín's cheek served as evidence that legal protocol had not been followed.

But, for our purposes, what is most interesting about Martín's case is not that the evidence of an illegal brand helped to free him, but the ways by which contested versions of the past stood side by side in the record. We often consider these courtroom narratives as a part of a linear trajectory leading to the goal of achieving a favorable verdict. But these exchanges, albeit scripted ones, also provide clues to working notions of rescate that do not appear in ordinances and other prescriptive materials. Indigenous litigants like Martín identified themselves as being born free (*en mi naturaleza*) and considered it an essential quality of being.[68] They were referring to local ethnic customs that designated certain peoples as free or enslaved by birth, customs that pre-dated the arrival of the Spaniards in many locations. Martín's main witness, Francisco Martín, carefully linked naturaleza with his understanding of the kind of service a member of the nobility would likely provide a Spaniard. Martín's testimony also exposes the raw and unequal power dynamics embedded in processes of "exchange" and dependency whereby different expectations could easily be rendered inconsequential later by a facial brand.

Just War

Castilian law differentiated between natural slaves and the civil slaves who, over the course of human history, had been placed under the dominion of others for various circumstantial reasons. War was one such rationale. After taking war captives, Roman emperors spared them from death by keeping or "guarding" (*servare*) them as servants. Some were born of individuals who were already servants; and some were willingly sold by a third party.[69] In the case of the indios, the Crown had allowed the taking of captives of just war if they resisted the predication of the Catholic faith or responded with force after reading the Spanish Requirement, which "required" the people to become Castilian subjects. But habitat was also a large part of these rationales. Some indios lived in a naturaleza where rulers had previously resisted Spanish forays or where the Crown of Castile had designated that enslavement could occur simply because Spanish agents had negotiated favorable terms. In the 1520s, for instance, Spaniards eager to profit from the active slave trade between Central America and Panama and from the Atlantic coast to Santo Domingo argued that certain parts of Central America harbored bellicose and barbaric peoples. According to the chronicler Fernández de Oviedo, the people of "Nicaragua" were a "very barbaric and ignorant" people.[70] Slave raids authorized for just war only enhanced the violence in a given area, since they incited the people to rebel, which in turn gave Spaniards the authority to ship hundreds of captives to other provinces.[71] The collusion between Crown representatives and individual merchants or conquerors was tremendous. Despite laws to the contrary, governors, local justices, and others commonly profited from the economy of slavery.[72]

It was common parlance for litigating slave owners to insist that their "slaves" had been captured and branded in "just war" and were from a terrain inhabited by bellicose and cannibalistic peoples. They connected the term *naturaleza* with just war by insinuating that the people of a given territory were brutal, inhuman, and incapable of mastering Christianity. This was the prevailing assumption in the litigation suit of the indigenous slave, Francisco, who had escaped from his master, Martín Alonso de los Rios, a caballero of the Order of Santiago, and a member of one of the prominent conquest "families" of Central America and Panama. Francisco made his way to Madrid in 1539, where he initiated a lawsuit before the Council of the Indies.[73] In 1540, two years before the implementation of the New Laws, Francisco's owner and supportive witnesses gave their sworn statements before a notary and iterated the truism that in the late 1520s a group of captured Indians from Nicaragua, Francisco among them, had resisted Spanish rule and refused to become Christians (thus not following the tenets of the Spanish Requirement). Diego Gutíerrez de los Rios, city magistrate (regidor) of Panama (City) in 1529 and the cousin of Francisco's owner, testified as to why certain Indians of the province of Nicaragua, including Francisco, had been enslaved.

> They defended themselves and did not wish to come into the service of His Majesty and . . . they killed and ate some Christians and some Indians ate other Indians. . . . This witness knows for certain that the said Francisco, indio . . . was given as a slave because if he were not a slave the governor and officials of His Majesty would never have consented to allow the said Francisco to leave that province. This witness knows and saw that [the officials] did not allow any Indians to leave the province without looking them over, examining them, and taking the [royal] fifth for His Majesty. [After that] Francisco was taken by Diego de Herrera [to Panama].[74]

The narration touched on each of the legal tenets of proper procedure: Francisco was captured in a territory harboring rebellious and cannibalis-

tic people; after he was examined, the governor, a Crown authority, authorized his removal from that territory; the governor would not have done
so if Francisco were not a slave of just war. In the courtroom the witnesses
knew what to say because the laws dictated how Francisco's enslavement
should have occurred. But once again it was the procedure itself, executed
in a proper manner, that created the slave, not vice versa. Witnesses on behalf of the slave owner also detailed the circumstances surrounding Francisco's abduction, which was authorized by a Crown authority. Around 1526,
the governor of Honduras, López de Salcedo, authorized Pedro Gutíerrez
de los Rios, the slave owner's uncle and lieutenant governor of the licentiate
Francisco de Castañeda (Rios was named the governor of Panama in 1526),
to take a number of slaves on his ship to Panama to sell. As Gutíerrez de los
Rios had just been ordered by López de Salcedo to leave Nicaragua, the
license may have been a compensatory olive branch. Salcedo hoped to avoid
further internecine conflicts among Spaniards, like Gutíerrez de los Rios,
who were eager to carve up Tierra Firme and Central America and claim
specific areas as their domains.

Everyone leaving Nicaragua, the lieutenant governor explained to the
legal assistant, brought indigenous slaves with them. Such an overgeneralization was probably, in fact, true, since in the 1520s and 1530s slavery was the primary economy of Central America. Francisco was among two shipments of
180 men, women, and children placed on a small vessel bound for Panama.[75]
After their capture, the slaves had been marched in chains southward along
the Nicoya Peninsula, a practice sanctioned by the local cacique, who profited from such ventures. Once they reached the island of Chira, they boarded
a vessel—in Francisco's case, commanded by Diego de Herrera (the future
Audiencia judge)—and traveled to Panama, where they were distributed and
sold.[76]

Francisco's age at the time of his abduction is uncertain, but he was likely
under fourteen when his life took this radically different course. He may
have been ethnically Chontal and have come from the interior of Nueva
Segovia, the area in Nicaragua that borders Honduras, but available documents do not contain these details. By then, Pedro de Alvarado had already
done much to promote the idea of the Chontales as perverse and bellicose
people to justify enslaving them in his campaigns of 1524 and 1525.[77] Francisco was likely among a large group of captives, because slaving expeditions between 1525 and 1535 throughout Central America involved taking
scores of indigenous people at a time. Such raids were quietly authorized

(and sometimes underwritten) by different governors. In this case, López de Salcedo, who was known for his rapacious and excessively brutal conduct toward Indians, endorsed the shipments of large numbers of indigenous peoples to Panama and Santo Domingo for sale. Francisco was never branded with a *G* (for *guerra justa*), because at the time of his shipment, according to Diego Gutiérrez's testimony, no brand was available.[78]

No one, including Francisco, elaborated on the circumstances of his capture or his ethnicity. Throughout the lawsuit, Francisco claimed in his depositions, with some authority, to be a free servant (his lawyer called him a naboría), rather than a slave captured in just war. As he stated, "I am not branded nor have I committed any crime to warrant enslavement."[79] What, we wonder, was the crime to which Francisco referred: resistance, or some act he himself would have considered illicit? As some slave owners themselves iterated—and contrary to the testimony of Diego Gutíerrez de los Rios—proper inspection by Crown authorities of the captured slaves was not required until 1528, and branding was, up until that time, considered the responsibility of the individual who purchased the slave.[80] Official brands were not always on hand when slaves were loaded onto private vessels at Chira. As the defendant and his supportive witnesses stated, Diego Gutiérrez purchased Francisco from Diego de Herrera while they were aboard the vessel sailing to Panama, then, several months later, exchanged him for a fancy chair and 500 pesos, while he and his cousin Martín Alonso de los Rios, the new owner, stood in the plaza of Panama to conduct the transaction. There was no notary on hand, no document to guarantee the deal. It would not at that moment have occurred to Martín Alonso de los Rios that twelve years later a lack of a legal brand or legalized document would work against him. For him, the informal exchange of goods in a public space was enough.

Nor would he have guessed that a judge would inquire whether Francisco had been born free or whether his parents were slaves. Did he, the judge queried, consider the possibility that Francisco might be a naboría when he purchased him?[81] In response, de los Rios resorted to circular logic, claiming that he would never have purchased Francisco if he were a naboría, because that would have meant he was not a slave of just war. Why Francisco only had one witness on his behalf is never explained, but when Tomás de Berlanga, bishop of Tierra Firme, spoke, he borrowed the logic used by many friars working behind the scenes at court: "I do not know whether [Francisco] is free or where he is from but I consider him and all other indios to be free until they are proven to be slaves of just war."[82] In other words, Francisco was innocent until proven guilty. The judges determined that the narrative constructed about Francisco being from "Nicaragua" was not enough to prove the status of bondage, and he was freed.

Although a lack of evidence of legal branding was crucial to the verdict, as it had been in Martín's case in a different way, what is interesting about Francisco's trial is how the subtexts of "free" or "not free" were contextualized by litigants and witnesses. Even though he supposedly came from a habitat—"Nicaragua"—where de los Rios argued that slaves of just war could be taken, many of the children and women "taken" were then labeled naborías, who were not permitted to be enslaved. As the 1534 royal decree stated, if indios were taken captive during battle, governors, captains, or subjects could keep them as naborías.[83] It may be that Francisco fit into the legal narrative of not-slave-but-not-free, which his lawyer would have emphasized, but another possibility is that the witness Diego Gutiérrez, speaking on behalf of de los Rios, was telling the truth: that the scores of "slaves," including Francisco, were loaded on the ship destined for Panama without having been branded because a brand was not available at the time or because authorities thought they could do it later. Serendipity may have also been a factor. In any case, the deponents on behalf of de los Rios attempted to rescript the past to fit present legal requisites, but the "past"—a lack of branding under circumstances we will never understand—came back to haunt them. A fabricated naturaleza was not sufficient evidence to prove Francisco's guilt.

Francisco's case transpired before the passage of the New Laws. But even into the 1540s, lawyers for the Council of the Indies were clear that if documentation demonstrated that an indio had been captured in just war, then his or her enslavement was considered legal and would be upheld by the court.[84] Litigants like Catalina Nicolasa had to be careful about how they identified their naturalezas. When her attorney related Catalina Nicolasa's captivity account in his opening statement before the Council of the Indies in 1548, he reported that she was a Chorotega Indian who had lived on Diego de Alvarado's repartimiento in Nicaragua.[85] It was well-known that entire populations of repartimiento Indians were sold to provide the capital for the South Seas ventures.[86] It was also well known that Alvarado's brother Pedro and others had unjustly enslaved Chontal people simply on the grounds that they were considered bellicose, while the Chorotega people were considered "friends" of the Spaniards.[87] But in his haste to gather together thousands of indigenous people, Alvarado had paid little attention to ethnicity. As the case progressed and Catalina Nicolasa was called in to testify, she emphasized different details of her history. She said she was thirty years old and a natural of Cuzco; she had been baptized there, which was why she was now called Catalina.[88] She may well have been telling a half-truth, leaving out the first part of her story of bondage—that she was ethnically Chorotega and among the three thousand "Guatemalan" slaves abducted by Pedro de Alvarado and placed on ships bound for South America.[89] Or she may have been taken from the Nicaraguan village of Ayatega, under the control of the afore-mentioned Pedro Gutiérrez de los Ríos and dangerously close to the Pacific port of Realejo, where Pedro de Alvarado docked temporarily before sailing southward.[90] When asked who had brought her to Spain, she replied, "A caballero named [Alonso de] Alvarado."[91]

Hoping that her ancestry would provide more clues about her natura-leza, the council judges asked Catalina to name her parents. She replied that she could not remember because they had died when she was very young. Later, when queried about her mestiza daughter Marequita, who stood by her side—even in the 1550s, discussions of whether the condition of slavery passed on through the indigenous mother were still ambivalent—Catalina reported that the father was named Francisco, that he was from Vizcaya, and that "while in my land of Cuzco I became pregnant by him."[92] Marequita also testified, repeating what her mother had said, but adding that there were three people—"a Spaniard named Vecerra, his Indian [su indio] named Juan, and an African slave"—from the town of Toro (the Castilian village where she and her mother had lived for a brief period) who could verify that they had once been in Cuzco.[93]

Catalina's case was aided by the royal decree of 1534 that stated that no women of any age, even if captured in just war, could be enslaved. By the time Catalina entered the courtroom, the New Laws had gone into effect, but she did not wish to take any chances. If she were to state that she was ethnically a "friendly" Chorotega, she would make it possible for her owner to claim that she had been taken in just war, since such ethnic distinctions could easily be blurred in the courtroom context.[94] Even in the 1550s, there were slaves from "questionable" war-ridden areas who were not being freed, and prosecuting attorneys would seize on shadow-of-a-doubt regions to construct a viable counter-defense. The fact that Catalina had been a repar-timiento Indian and a Christian did not seem to make much difference. We can only deduce that her lawyer advised to change her naturaleza because it was easier to claim that she was from Peru, where Indians could not in principle be enslaved. In the end, however, Catalina's case remained unresolved because of legal technicalities.

Conclusions

In those cases involving just war, slave owners made blanket statements about certain naturalezas, like Nicaragua, Santa Marta, and Honduras, that harbored bellicose and barbaric peoples. Hundreds of thousands of indios became victims of such gross overgeneralizations. But the terms *naturaleza*, *rescate*, and *just war* encompassed so much—too much, in fact—that they were formidable and dangerous weapons. It was easy to create a narrative that would fit the legal paradigm and determine a "false positive." Slave owners could draw on witnesses who had experience in the entradas and slave-raiding ventures of Central and northern South America, experiences that could easily be labeled as just war. In such circumstances, no indigenous witnesses stepped forward to argue for ethnic specificity or that their people were not at war with the Spaniards. To prevent themselves from being labeled Chontals—a code word for warlike and bellicose people—slave litigants generally did not claim to be, for example, Nicarao or Chorotega. For this reason, Catalina Nicolasa quickly changed her story to hide her Chorotega ethnicity. Why litigants like Catalina Nicolasa thought such ethnographic detail would not aid their cases is unclear. More than likely, the Castilian legal advocates were unfamiliar with the cultural geography, or there were no available witnesses, especially friars, to provide more specifics. Judges or legal assistants may have felt pressured to act as ethnographers-on-the-fly vis-à-vis indio litigants like Catalina.[95] But each litigant and his or her legal advocate employed different legal strategies and sometimes in ambiguous ways. Martín countered the assertion that he was a slave of rescate by providing a witness who could explain where he was from, who his parents and ethnic lords were, and why the conditions of his "service" did not involve the exchange of goods for a slave. The litigant Francisco remained mute on the circumstances surrounding his capture and failed to mention his naturaleza. Instead, he emphasized that because he had not been branded with a "G," he was a naboría (a lifelong servant), not a slave. Catalina Nicolasa had to counter the detrimental possibilities of being identified with a particular territory or naturaleza by proving she came from a peaceful area or by inventing a new home. Perhaps her lawyer counseled her to do so because the terms *just war* and *rescate* encompassed such broad territories that he thought it best to emphasize other details of her diasporic history.

More generally, these cases answer some questions but raise others. Did legal advocates hope that a lack of evidence from the opposition would trump other experiential details about historicity, cultural location, parentage, or deceit? A successful lawsuit seemed to depend on the kinds of circumstantial or eyewitness evidence that supportive witnesses could offer, as well as on the timing of the litigation suits. The narrative content was not so much about revealing a truth related to cultural geographies or naturalezas, but about which argument made the most sense within the dynamics of a particular case. Sometimes, as in Martín's case, local historicities may have influenced the judges' sentence, even though we are not privy to their deliberations.

Analysis of the deposition narratives of Martín, Francisco, and Catalina Nicolasa reveals the kind of competing claims that were made to counter the effects of such powerful terms sanctioned by law as *rescate* and *just war*. Martín did so by calling on the indio witnesses Francisco Martín, whom he either had known in America or had merely claimed to know there. He provided crucial details about Martín's "past" on the other side of the Atlantic. But since such transatlantic connections were uncommon, deponents often used other criteria to identify indios as being from a particular region or imperial domain. These forms of identification included physiognomic descriptors such as coloration, head shape, and bodily markings, as well as sonic identifiers such as language.

SIX

Identifying *Indios*

✦══✦

I, Melchior, moreno, and vecino of Carmona, and fifty years old, state
that I do not know the language of the indios of Mexico nor of those of
[the kingdoms of] Portugal because I have never been in these places,
but I do know that in [their] gestures and coloration they are different
because the indios from Mexico are better formed and whiter than the
indios who come from the kingdoms of Portugal.

—"Testimony, Melchior, moreno," March 1564,
AGI, Justicia 783, n. 3, pieça 3, im. 336

Of the more than two thousand people categorized as indios
who traveled to Castile in the sixteenth century, a handful pa-
raded before royal officials dressed in colorful regalia and wearing feathered garments and bearing weapons. Some posed for
curious artists. Others came in the entourages of indigenous
elites who sought diplomatic or political favors, retribution for
their subjects, or titles and privileges from the king. Europeans
returning from the Indies shared their ethnographic observations about indios and displayed artifacts from America that
stirred the cultural imagination of royal authorities and others.
If the Castilian royal court was a site where different visual and
living representations of indios from around the globe converged, how did Castilians in villages and cities grapple with the
ethnographic observations of returning travelers, the images of
feathered men and women, and the incredible tales they heard
about so-called brutish peoples? How did they reconcile this

cultural imaginary with the flesh and blood indio slaves and servants in their midst?[1]

The majority of the indios who appeared in Castile did not carry spears or adorn their bodies with feathers. They were children and adult slaves and freedpersons who wore tattered garments and performed grueling labor daily in the homes, shops, and fields of Castilian villages and cities. They did not journey to Spain as part of a diplomatic entourage or as living artifacts, but as the victims of a prosperous and active slave trade. They were identified in relation to masters or the other slaves in their midst, by documents, including brands, that consigned them to a particular status, or by the histories they told about the circumstances under which captivity had occurred. But there were yet other ways to identify indios, which not only determined the free or enslaved status of an individual, but also exposed sixteenth-century methods of discernment.

Vanita Seth has argued that "to make alterity familiar, intelligible, it needs to be translated into categories that are commensurable."[2] There is no question that the physical presence of indios toiling in the villages and cities of Iberia aided in the mutual process of sense-making. An analysis of the litigation suits reveals Castilians and individuals who identified themselves as indios comprehending one another through a "lexicon of resemblance" based on physiognomy (which included physical attributes in relation to geographic context), one's nation (nación), and lineage—all means of differentiation that had been employed throughout the Mediterranean for generations.[3]

In assessing identity we must pay closer attention not only to the cultural experiences of witnesses, but also to the particular bureaucratic and archival locus of enunciation, which, it is clear, heavily influenced how notions of difference were constructed. For instance, scholars have identified contexts, such as the Casa and the Inquisition, in which authorities gathered documents, drawn up by local magistrates, that ascribed labels and descriptive phrases in an increasingly regimented way to identify passengers and aspirants from that particular locality who wanted to prove purity of blood.[4] But that does not mean that Castilians, particularly those who had traversed the globe, identified the indio slaves in their midst in the same way. Until the 1580s, Castilians continued to depend heavily on physiognomic models to determine indios' imperial status, nation, or lineage. They also relied on sonic criteria, especially language. The court records, while clearly circumscribed in formulaic and legalistic ways, allowed witnesses, who were less distanced from the litigants than a bureaucrat would be, to speak about their notions of identity and identification.

Our usage of descriptors—particularly color—to identify indios and others also requires careful historical, geographic, and demographic contextualization. In the bills of sale and travel licenses that sold indigenous peoples into bondage and transported them across the Atlantic, color was one of the most significant markers of indio identity. Although we are now more sensitive to the complexities of color as a marker of status, we should not assume that by the sixteenth century Castilian notions of physical difference and body color were already immutable and that they remained stable in their transfer to vastly different contexts throughout Latin America. In sixteenth-century Castilian society, where individuals were identified and differentiated legally by noble, commoner, or slave status, color descriptors such as black (*negro*), white (*blanco*), and laurel (*loro*) were sometimes used in travel documents and bills of sale as synonyms for servile, if not slave, status. Before the sixteenth century, the word *esclavo* was not always used to qualify a person's legal status in bondage. But color was. In Seville and southern Castile someone described as blanco in these particular documents was assumed to be a slave.[5] The descriptor also served as a synecdoche for someone of the Muslim faith. Given the historical contingencies of when military invasions occurred, where the slave trade expanded, and how the color coding of slaves developed, it is understandable that litigants relied heavily on descriptors already in use to identify indios by color in the Castilian courts. Like the pre-1492 Mediterranean vocabulary, the descriptions of indios found in many of the 127 litigation suits were multivalent; they shifted over time, and both indigenous litigants and slave owners strategized and manipulated those constructs to influence the outcome of each lawsuit.

The assessments of indio identity taking place in sixteenth-century Castilian courts highlight what some Latin Americanist and Iberian scholars have been arguing: we need to unfix "race" as a construct to explain how colonial vassals, whether free or enslaved, distinguished one another in the sixteenth century. Others disagree with this position and note a hardening of racial or protoracial labels during that time.[6] Color was one of several physiognomic determinants used to identify the individual characteristics of an indio who was held in bondage (whether slave or naboría) and who was not free to travel of his or her own volition or to draw up a will. Simply put, color, which is usually associated with post–eighteenth-century conceptions of race, was not in the sixteenth century considered a sign of fixed biological or cultural traits associated with particular groups of enslaved peoples. Color was a marker of individual "geohumoral" traits and status, determined by context, demography, and, increasingly after 1550, lineage.[7]

As a lexicon for reading others, physiognomy (of which coloration was one of several readable aspects) distinguished and categorized—sometimes arbitrarily and politically—different enslaved individuals for the purpose of either discriminating against them or providing them with legal protection.

The criteria used to determine the identities of indios as slaves also depended on specific historical contingencies, which included religious faith, the volatility of the slave trade, and changes in legislation that limited or prohibited enslavement under certain conditions. The first criterion, confessional heritage, which with each passing decade became increasingly paramount to the social status and position of Old Christians, is what most often comes to mind when we think of categories of difference (and the anxieties they created) in late fifteenth- and sixteenth-century Castile. Some have argued that, because physical differences among Jews, Muslims, and Castilians were minimal, genealogical investigations into the lineage of conversos (Jewish converts to Catholicism) and moriscos became compulsory. Perhaps nowhere are these tensions more palpable than in the restrictions implemented by the Casa. There, authorities interviewed potential emigrants and probed genealogies to detect purity of blood (*limpieza de sangre*) and, in principle, allowed only Old Christians to cross the Atlantic.[8] Then again, not only did Christian heritage determine status, position, and the ability to migrate, but confessional faith had for centuries been the raison d'être in Christian Iberia for the enslavement of non-Christian enemies dwelling in lands not subject to Christian rule (infidels), who, once captured, were labeled as captives of just war. As several scholars have shown, identifying the jurisdiction of such captives could be strategic and calculating.

These records show that, although witnesses, plaintiffs, and defendants might have wanted to essentialize the indio litigants, the purposeful manipulation of the descriptors used to identify indios in documents and depositions were by no means standardized or fixed. In short, courtroom evidence did not point to any sense that indioness represented a reductive biological inalterability. Litigants and witnesses iterated and navigated changing notions of indioness, depending on the timing of observations and the past experiences that witnesses brought to bear at the moment of archival inscription. For, although legal circumstances of the 1540s (the New Laws) and beyond framed the discourse of how indios were marked, the past (an inscription at another time and place) was also clearly present in the bills of sale and other documents used as evidence in the courtroom, as well as in the minds of witnesses whose experiences twenty or even thirty years before informed their interpretations of present contingencies. Not only were descriptions conditioned by a familiarity with different sites throughout the globe, but they were sometimes influenced by the demographic critical mass of "foreigners" living in the village, town, or city of a given witness. By the sixteenth century, some Castilian villages and towns—such as Carmona, where Beatríz and Felipa had lived—were heterogeneous settings constituted by the continents of Africa, Asia, Europe, and America. Just as the cultural environment influenced the intense sense-making that was occurring, each individual relied on a familiar lexicon related to notions of geography, physiognomy, and imagined corporate communities as he or she fashioned arguments about indios.[9] Thus, the process of constituting indios both inside and outside the courtroom revealed how perceptions of difference changed as the world of sixteenth-century Castile became more complex.

The identification of free and enslaved individuals revolved around three important and interrelated terms related to belonging and status— *naturaleza*, *nación*, and *calidades* (physical and moral qualities)—notions that had circulated throughout the Mediterranean for centuries. Because humans inhabited different geographic zones (distinguished by proximity to the sun), they acquired distinct characteristics that helped identify them as naturales, belonging or pertaining to a particular naturaleza or habitat. The science of physiognomy taught that the geohumoral nature of the environment (whether cold, warm, dry, or humid) and its proximity to the sun helped determine the calidad, complexion, and health of its people. The consumption of foods produced in a given context also determined bodily difference.[10] This ordering principle informed the thinking of sixteenth-century Castilians, particularly Bartolomé de las Casas, who relied heavily on the science of physiognomy to develop his argument that the indios of America were capable of reason and a part of civil society.[11] As the renowned Dominican elaborated in the *Apologética historia sumaria*, "The body and its complexions are subject . . . to the qualities of each place and region and the disposition of the land . . . as well as to the air currents that flow there."[12] For instance, people from an extreme northern climate had white humoral complexions because they were cold and moist and, therefore, phlegmatic and stagnant, whereas those with black complexions were dry and hot. An observer could assess an individual's character and physiognomy by "readable" features, which included the complexion—the changeable external features subject to climatic and other variations determined by a balance (or imbalance) of the internal humors as well as language, marks, and other signs that corresponded to the environment. An appraisal of these external characteristics would help determine a person's naturaleza and calidad.[13]

If *naturaleza* evoked ideas of belonging in a physical and physiognomic way, the term *nación* involved more of a sense of an imagined corporate community, with its own sets of laws and privileges. The term *nación* was used by Castilians to distinguish foreigners, or non-Castilians—including Flemish, Genoese, and Portuguese—who were part of a collection of inhabitants in a province, country, or kingdom. It could also refer to an abstract political, cultural, or geographic sense of belonging, akin in meaning to *naturaleza*. However, it was clear from the testimonies in indigenous court cases (which were occurring in Castile) that the Castilian nación was the barometer against which everyone else was measured. Even in the fluid Atlantic world context, at sea and on land, merchants and others distinguished one another by nación, but not necessarily in an antagonistic way, since many commercial and familial enterprises were intermeshed and interdependent.[14] A young sailor once explained it in practical terms: "When some ship passed by the coast of Brazil in need of provisions, water, or firewood, we gave it to the members of all naciones, whether Spanish, Portuguese, or French."[15]

Castilians and others also employed the concept of nación to distinguish non-European foreigners living in their domains and under their legal authority. Castilians referred to the people of the naciones of moros (Moorish peoples), negros (usually, but not always, from sub-Saharan African habitats, identified as black or dark brown in coloration), or loros (people identified as brown), which after 1453, when access to the Black Sea slaving trade was cut off, entered the canon as a means to distinguish (and homogenize) uprooted North and West Africans who had been forced into bondage and were now living in Castile. Unlike the geographic and political connotations of "Genoese" or "Flemish" naciones, these more abstract groupings were also based on religious differences (that is, Islam versus Christianity) and geohumoral references (that is, black). One can find expressions such as *de la nación negra* (of the black nation) or *de la nación mora* (of the nation of Moors) in documents generated in Seville and Granada.[16] As the slave and freed population grew increasingly diverse in late fifteenth-century Seville, the number of naciones expanded to include the *nación de berberiscos* (Berber peoples from northwestern and northern coastal Africa), *nación de loros*, and *nación de canarios* (Canary Islanders).

To provide the people of these nations with legal representation, the Castilian Crown created the legal position of *mayoral* (steward) and judge of all the free and captive slaves who belonged to the negro and loro naciones. Each nación was also assigned a special lawyer (procurador) to represent the people's legal interests and help them obtain their freedom, especially if they were being held in unjust bondage or were being abused.[17] But it was one thing to define the legal parameters of each nación and quite another to distinguish one's place within those somewhat arbitrary classifications. The historian Aurelia Martín Cásares cites a poignant example of a freed sub-Saharan man named Alonso Sánchez, who lived in Granada (the exact date was not specified) and testified in the beatification hearings for Juan de Dios. When questioned about his patria (homeland) and nación, Sánchez expressed his confusion in a "forceful manner." The scribe wrote, "He [Sánchez] says he is negro by nación, but his patria is in this city of Granada because he was born here."[18]

It therefore made sense that various witnesses, testifying on behalf of indigenous litigants or their masters, would repeatedly refer to the nation of indios as the inhabitants of the Indies, distinguishable from people of other nations by their physiognomic nature. A Castilian named Pablo Collado argued in 1567, "I have seen many male and female Indians of different provinces and it is well known that the said Indians are different from Spaniards and [the people of] other nations."[19] In 1544, when "Pedro Márques, of the Indian nation," identified himself as part of a collective imaginary, he and the lawyers and judges in the Castilian court understood why he would do so; Pedro went on to qualify his indio identity by stating that he was a natural of Mexico City.[20] This, too, was common—to express a sense of belonging to the nation of indios, but then to qualify it with a regional, local, or ethnic indicator.[21]

Given the lack of clarity, witnesses and lawyers went to great lengths to determine the imperial nación of an indio litigant. This more ubiquitous sense of the term nación is evidenced in the 1562 case against the deceased indigenous slave Felipa, whose daughter, Barbola, and supportive witnesses all claimed she was from Mexico. Barbola needed to prove that her mother was free in order to erase any stain of bondage from her and her children's lineage. Local politics in the globalized village of Carmona, however, made this process exceedingly difficult. There, the indios of Calicut and Mexico faced off against one another by strategically constituting the notion of nación in ways that proved that Felipa was from the nación of indios of the kingdom of Portugal, not from the nación of indios of the kingdom of Castile.

Many deponents relied on the geocultural sense of the term nación to pinpoint someone's indio identity. Over time, however, authorities, litigants, and witnesses came to believe—and testimonies of the mid-sixteenth century bear this out—that *nación* could also refer to a genus or group of distinguishable peoples, such as moros, negros, loros, and indios, with distinctive characteristics based on lineage. This neologism (which has antecedents as a referent to Jews and Basques) may be related to the seeping influence of sixteenth-century bureaucracies such as the Casa and the Inquisition, which focused so insistently on parental lineage. It may also be connected to the etymology of the term *casta*, which in common parlance referred to distinct groupings based on religious lineage, geography, or culture.[22] We see this shift in the midcentury testimonies of several Castilian witnesses who employed the terms *nación* and *casta* interchangeably. In 1553 Don Diego Sarmiento de la Cerda, the mestizo son of the count of Salinas y Rivadeo (from a municipality near Ciudad Real), was deeply affronted that his two slaves, Francisco and Sebastian, would sue him for their freedom by falsely claiming to be "indios" from New Spain. On the contrary, he stated, "the said individuals are of the casta de moros . . . and as slaves they have carried and carry the marks of slavery [brands]. One can tell by their aspects that they are not indios nor of the casta de indios but of the nación de moros."[23]

Perhaps don Diego's complex positioning in his own aristocratic family gave him a particular sensitivity to such matters. His conflation of *nación* with *casta*, however, also reveals how perception and experience—in locales throughout Castile and the vast Ocean Sea—had more to do with how Castilians and others saw the indios living in their midst. On his family's estate, don Diego probably lived in proximity to laborers and slaves who represented an increasingly global mosaic. It also reveals a moment of archival inscription when a powerful slave owner "created a new singularity" from *casta* and *nación*.[24]

What, then, were the specific indicators that could help determine the imperial identity or nación of an indio litigant? One could certainly express an innate sense of knowing another's nation, but in the courtroom context more specific methods of verifying the imperial identity of indios were crucial to the success of a case. To that end, expert witnesses who knew about the Indies and their inhabitants were called in to scrutinize the litigant (*por vista de ojos*). They employed their "physiognomic eye" to determine the aspect, qualities, or signature characteristics of litigants that could help identify their nations or imperial contexts.[25] The expert witnesses noted movements, semblance or shape of the head and face, overall coloring, facial expressions, demeanor, hair, quality of the skin, gestures, and body build. Sonic criteria, such as how the voice sounded, were also a part of the physiognomic intelligence available to be read.[26] The sum total of the observable features would determine the calidades of the litigant, which in turn established where he or she "fit" in the social order or body politic. The judges then weighed the testimonies of expert witnesses for the defense and prosecution against one another and alongside any documentary evidence presented before reaching a verdict.

As the anthropologist Joanne Rappaport has argued, because expert witnesses wanted to see the person as an indio, they described him or her in a way that fit a vague idea of what an indio of the Spanish or Portuguese domains should look like. To that end, their responses were often generic (and predictable).[27] Thus, when Pedro Gutiérrez, a vecino (permanent resident) of Santo Domingo, was asked "if a young man [mozo] named Thomas Rodríguez," whom Gutiérrez had scrutinized, "seem[ed] to be an Indian or of which nation he pertain[ed]," the witness answered that, based on Thomas's "aspect and the particularities of his face and person," he had determined that he was a "natural indio" (indio natural).[28]

Sonic Criteria and Body Markings

Sonic criteria—vocabulary words and tone—and accompanying gestures were important identifiers that helped reinforce the "truth" about a particular litigant. For instance, in trying to determine the imperial status of Beatríz, an indigenous witness with the same name stated that she had known Beatríz since the Empress Isabel had died (in 1539). They had crossed paths in Carmona and Seville, and she had always assumed that Beatríz was a natural of Malacata, in the province of New Spain. She explained to the scribe how she recognized the litigant Beatríz even though they spoke different languages.

> This witness is a natural of Mexico, and given that the language of Mexico is different than the language of Malacata, people know very well who is from Mexico and who is from Malacata. Just like those who don't know the language of the others—[for instance], that Castilians recognize Portuguese and Flemish and other nations by their aspects and other traditions even if they don't know how to speak their language—and so [it is the same for] this witness. Although I do not know how to speak the language of Malacata, I can recognize the said Beatríz as being from Malacata just as a Castilian can recognize a Portuguese.[29]

Noticing that another indio spoke an indigenous language unfamiliar to the listener was a common occurrence in Castilian cities where slaves from different parts of the world converged. Like Beatríz, other indigenous witnesses reported hearing indios speak "the indio language" without understanding them.[30] Even some children born of indigenous slaves in Castile could not understand their mothers when they chanced upon someone who spoke the same natal tongue. Then, too, as slave owners realized they had to be more scrupulous about the *kinds* of indios they were buying (Portuguese rather than Spanish), they might assess the language of the potential slave before proceeding with the sale. In 1572 the comptroller for the Queen of Portugal, Francisco del Villalpando, brought with him a servant who knew "the language of Brazil," to ensure that the slave he was buying was from Brazil and was a legal purchase.[31]

But what exactly *was* the indio language, and how did it become common parlance? Why did indios and other Castilians sometimes not use more precise markers, such as Nahuatl, Pipil, or Quechua? Were these languages purposefully conflated into an indio language by the court scribes, or did these more precise identifiers not matter in Castile as they did in America? There are several possible explanations.

The phrase "language of indios," which was in common parlance in the courts of Castile, might have referred to a patois that developed as indios learned snippets of different languages during their travels. Although a former slave named Esteban de Cabrera, who testified on behalf of an indio litigant named Gaspar in 1561, was originally from Cuzcatlán and thus spoke or understood Nahuatl and Pipil, he had picked up some of the language spoken by the "indios of Santo Domingo," presumably Taínos, during his stay there. Thus, "this witness asked [Gaspar] in his language which was that of the city of Santo Domingo . . . and he responded in his language and [by using] words that they have and many other [words] that this witness spoke, naming many things that the indios from there name and come across [*topan*]."[32] Even then, local Taíno dialects might come into "contact" on the other side of the ocean. When Esteban's friend Juan, who was also from Santo Domingo conversed with Gaspar, he was at a loss to identify certain vocabulary words, because of differences between the dialect(s) spoken in the city of Santo Domingo, which had a large diasporic indigenous population (especially of multilingual Carib and Arawak peoples), and those spoken in the rest of the island.[33]

Survival meant learning Spanish, other indigenous dialects, or even Portuguese, especially if slaves had spent any time in Lisbon. Polyglot indios, particularly those who knew some Portuguese, had to be cautious when they entered the courtroom because lawyers and judges were not always willing to take into account the complexities of deracination and the permutations of the illegal slave trade that many had experienced. Knowing, for instance, how to prepare certain Portuguese dishes or the Portuguese words for certain foods could be used in the courtroom as evidence against the slaves.

If the very nature of the diasporic experience of indigenous peoples complicated the court's reliance on language to identify a litigant's place of origin, the fact that many indios had left their homelands as young children made it only more difficult. Litigants might remember their place of origin, but when queried could not recall words in Guaraní, Nahuatl, Pipil, or other languages.[34] On many occasions when Castilians questioned indio plaintiffs in the "language of indios," they would answer in Spanish.[35]

Despite the incongruities and fallibilities in assessing a litigant's native language, judges asked witnesses to interview litigants in different languages.[36] Some witnesses did specify that they had interviewed litigants in Guaraní or in the "Mexican language" (Nahuatl).[37] But the problem was that many indios from "New Spain" did not speak Nahuatl. From the court's perspective, it must have been difficult to find available witnesses to speak the numerous Mayan dialects. In one instance, when a witness queried an india in the "Mexican language," and she gave signs that she did understand, the witness then speculated that she *looked* Guatemalan even though she could not speak "Guatemalteca."[38] Still, there were times when a witness who only knew Nahuatl but had direct experience in a specific environment where Nahuatl was not spoken could query a litigant about historical or geographic features. Francisco de Castellanos, who had been the treasurer of the province of Guatemala, interviewed Catalina from Nonoalco (in coastal Central America) in the "Mexican language" and asked her the name of the cacique of her village. When she answered, "Don Juan," Castellanos confirmed that what she said was true.[39]

How indigenous plaintiffs were questioned about their language also depended on the questions posed in the interrogatory. When slave owners framed the question about language in a vague and generic manner, they got vague and generic answers. Interrogatories were also structured so as to provoke a set response that mimicked the question. In the case of Inés, witnesses testifying on behalf of her slave owner were asked to confirm that neither she nor her parents knew how to speak the language of indios.[40] In another lawsuit, witnesses stated that Francisco and Quintin could speak only the language of their place of birth (presumably Brazil), and not the Mexican language or that of the Indies of Spain.[41]

In several instances where the imperial identity of an indio plaintiff was in doubt, the Council of the Indies called on available court interpreters, experts "in the Brazilian language" or in the more generic language of indios of the kingdom of New Spain, to interrogate the person.[42] Witnesses might ask specific questions such as "Where are you going?" or query about specific vocabulary words.[43] But some of the questions were anachronistic. When the friar Gregorio de Pesquera queried Esteban, he asked him in the Pipil language about certain words and what they used for currency in his land. Esteban answered, haltingly, "bread," "rock," "fish," and "chicken"—the last a term that did not exist prior to the early 1520s in that area. Most often, however, lawyers relied on witnesses who could speak in generalities about the litigant's manner of speaking (*habla*) and language (*lengua*).[44]

What seemed particularly awkward was the assertion made in several lawsuits that a witness and litigant spoke the same imperial language, as though people from Goa, the Moluccas, or China could understand one another. Of course many indios learned the "imperial" languages of Castilian or Portuguese, but that is not what these witnesses meant. To strategically emphasize that they were "one people, "either of the Spanish or Portuguese nación, indigenous deponents—some from the Americas and others from South and East Asia—might state that they understood one another as one people. They sometimes conjured up this notion because they were motivated to side with their masters, who claimed that their slaves came from the Portuguese domains where indio slaves were not free by law. But deponents made these statements under oath, which leads one to think that these sweeping imperial abstractions were credible beliefs circulating at the time. Still, there is something fantastic about the claim made under oath that people from either the Portuguese or Spanish Indies were "one."[45]

Like the spoken language of slave litigants, specific markings such as piercings or tattoos could be very helpful in pinpointing imperial identities. Occasionally, a witness would provide culturally specific details or describe a flattened nose (*nariz chata*), the curve of the cheekbones, or markings such as pierced ears in order to declare with full confidence that the litigant had been born in, for example, New Spain (a very broad territorial domain).[46] Bills of sale might be presented to corroborate unusual features. In 1554 a merchant from Antwerp, in temporary residence at the Spanish court in Valladolid, sold the eighteen-year-old Martín, "from the land of Brazil," to Francisco Bravo, a resident in the village of Palacios. The bill of sale recorded Martín's "lineage of bondage," his place of origin, and a description of his physical features—that he was of medium height, the color of quince, and that he had "a small cleft at the bottom of his lower left earlobe and a marking in the indentation of the chin below the lips."[47] Another bill of sale from 1544 described the litigant Juan as the color loro and with "ornamentation of indios on his wrists."[48]

Again, having a witness who could point to specific cultural markings could mean the difference between continued bondage or freedom. In a case from 1574, Rui Pérez de Osma initiated an appeal against Antonia, who had been declared free by the Council of the Indies, claiming that she was from the Portuguese domains. Interested in protecting her four children from perpetual bondage, Antonia presented an autobiographical account, stating that she had been purchased as a young girl in Peru and had been bought and sold many times in Castile. Although she was now free, she and her children continued to serve her former owner, Pérez de Osma, "as though [they] were his slaves."[49] Witnesses on her behalf were asked if they could identify the litigant as being from Lima or Trujillo, farther north. Don Sebastian Poma Laquito from Cuzco, who was present at the court in Valladolid, came forward to testify on her behalf, saying that she looked like the Indians from Peru and that he had spoken with her on numerous occasions, concluding, "I take her to be an india."[50] But he offered no further specifics. The next witness, Gregorio González from Cuenca, was more forthcoming. During his nineteen-year tenure as a judge in Lima, he had traveled to the district of Trujillo, where he observed that the people there "maintain the custom of marking their arms with lines and black or blue markings like the ones Antonia displayed."[51] "By her semblance and coloring," he continued, "this Indian woman appears to be from the nation of indios and from Trujillo, where they are called Mochica indios."[52]

Color as a Physiognomic Attribute

In the cases of Antonia and others, identification of the markings, language, head shape, or nation of the litigant, in combination with the quality of the witness testimony, helped inform the outcome of the indigenous litigation suits. But so, too, did coloration. As the sixteenth century progressed, the most common color used to describe indios in Castile was loro—a brownish hue akin to ripened wheat. Occasionally, however, slave owners referred to their individual slaves as black (which encompassed the colors black and dark brown), baço (brown inclining toward yellow), white, or other intermediate hues, including mulato (brown) or membrillo cocido or cocho (cooked quince).[53]

The use of this color palette fit preexisting Mediterranean patterns in several ways. For example, descriptions of slaves often linked geographic place (invented or real) and color because of the belief that complexion and disposition derived from the proximity of the habitat (and its inhabitants) to the sun. Second, for centuries slave traders throughout the Mediterranean had attempted to naturalize and link certain colors with the peoples of particular geographic places, to no avail. Instead, as the slave trade expanded to newly invented areas such as "Guinea" or "Berbería," geographic neologisms were intermeshed with other cultural descriptors to "identify" captives as slaves. For instance, the sixteenth-century use of the category *moro* (Moorish) exemplifies how geography, religion, and complexion were conflated, as new renditions were layered over older ones. Embedded in the label *moro* were various interrelated etymological strands related to body color, confessional faith, geography, and cultural group or nación.[54] Thus, a term such as *moro* or *Guinea* could selectively and simultaneously refer to a vague or precise geographic location, culture, ethnicity or nation of people, person of Muslim or non-Christian faith, or someone with a certain physiognomic aspect. These previously established practices and admixture of usages influenced how the term *indio* was used and manipulated in sixteenth-century Castilian courtrooms as a geohumoral and physiognomic referent.

Frequently we look to documents generated by Spanish Crown officials or theologians to detect late medieval and early modern discourses on physical descriptors of slaves. In fact, it was often the Genoese, Portuguese, and even Flemish merchants (or corsairs) who influenced the terminology and how decisions were made to categorize or invent slave identities in cities such as Seville. The use of adjectives to identify the coloration of slaves—*lloro* (Catalan), *laurus* (Genoa), *loro* (Seville), and *louro* (Lisbon)—reveals that Portuguese, Flemish, Castilian, and Genoese merchants, working in tandem, often set the descriptive agenda of terms used to mark newly conquered or enslaved peoples. As slave-raiding forays into new territories increased during the fifteenth century, thousands of unsuspecting peoples were identified as loros (with no geographic place of origin listed) when they were sold in Seville and elsewhere. But politics also influenced the term's shifting application. Whereas before 1453 the color laurus (laurel) described Saracen slaves sold in Genoa and Barcelona, after that date, when Constantinople submitted to Ottoman rule and access to the Black Sea was cut off, it referred more frequently to North African and Iberian (from Málaga or Granada) slaves (moros loros).[55] By the sixteenth century, the term *loro* was fairly ubiquitous in identifying a range of slaves in Castile.

Colorizing slaves as loros in bills of sale also directly correlated with the timing of military incursions into specific areas, including Fez (Morocco,

1480), the Canary Islands (1480s), Cabo Agadir (1499), Alhama (1503), and Oran (1508). As the Portuguese established trading outposts and abducted people from Calicut, Cochín, the Moluccas, and other parts of South and East Asia, the color classification loro accommodated these slaves, some of whom were sold in Seville. This explains why two slaves, twelve-year-old Antonio of Malucca (1514) and eighteen-year-old Pedro from Calicut (1515), were described as loros in their bills of sale.[56]

Although some slave owners might have hoped to essentialize one color descriptor per nation or group of people, in reality this did not occur. For instance, Saracen slaves (a broad category) were classified as white, black, and *llor* in Valencia and Barcelona. The color white (blanco or *albi*), which described Bulgarian, Russian, and Tartar slaves sold in fourteenth- and fifteenth-century Italy and Aragon, later became a popular descriptor for berberisco slaves captured in the naval and military incursions into northern Africa, many of which were launched from the Canary Islands, where captives were also taken. Bills of sale in Granada and Seville, however, also show "Berber" slaves and Canary Islanders being described as loro, membrillo, or black. In Seville and Huelva, the color white was sometimes used to describe someone of mixed black and white heritage.[57]

This lack of fixity has several explanations. The first is that color referred to the overall body (not specifically skin color), which in turn reflected the expression of the circulation or excess of any of the four humors, which depended on the individual's habitat and proximity to the sun. This may be why a scribe, reflecting on the slave standing before him, might see a person who exhibited a little bit of brownness (bile) and whiteness (phlegm) and so ascribed to him or her the label "blanca casi lora."[58] As Jack Forbes has argued, "We cannot know what a Spaniard of 1560 meant by 'stewed quince' color or what an Italian of 1530 meant by 'olive-ish' color. Nor can we know if there was any agreement among people about such terms or, more importantly, about the colors in the mind conjured up by such terms."[59] The bills of sale in various locations and the litigation suits of indigenous slaves indicate clearly that classification was still a subjective art, not yet a science based on the hard-and-fast logic of naturalized differences.

A second explanation is that by 1480 Seville was already a cultural and physiognomic mosaic with large Castilian, foreign, free, and enslaved populations and with a legal infrastructure that enabled captive slaves to obtain their freedom and form their own households. Trying to fit "new" peoples into an extant color code was a messy business, which could involve spontaneity as well as discrimination. To colorize a person demonstrated the raw imbalance of power, since, in most cases, slaves were not the ones affixing the labels. But the captives arriving at Seville from other locations and categorized as loro, blanco, or negro were sometimes of mixed heritage and already culturally and ethnically hybrid. They might come from other sites of cultural and sexual intermingling, such as the coast of northern Africa (Berbería), Santo Domingo, Panama, and elsewhere. We cannot ascertain, without knowing the parents' place of origin, whether slaves described with a specific gradation of color—"black like loro" or "black nearly loro"—were of mixed heritage or merely individuals with unique complexions.[60] The answer may be both, because the peoples from northern Africa labeled as berberiscos were ethnically diverse, owing in part to the continual movement northward of captured peoples from sub-Saharan Africa.[61] Thus, although the terms used to indicate various color gradations of loro, like *membrillo cocido* or *mulato*, did not always indicate mixed heritage, they were certainly used to indicate individuals of diverse West African and Arabic or Castilian heritage. Thus, the son of the "black" María in Seville was described as "loro, nearly white" and men and women journeying to America and identified as loros might have a Castilian or Italian father and a black African or "lora" mother.[62] *Loro* is, therefore, a clear example of a pliable intermediate descriptor that adapted to the increasing ethnic pluralism in Seville and elsewhere after 1480.

The association of the color loro with the recently acknowledged peoples of the Americas (Indies) was first made in the carte blanche contracts (asientos) given by the Crown in 1500 to Alonso Vélez de Mendoza and Rodrigo Bastidas. Color and servitude are linked in the authorization to take black and loro slaves from the Caribbean and northern South America "who in the kingdoms of Castile were held and reputed to be slaves."[63] Although the eminent nineteenth-century Cuban historian José Antonio Saco states that a lack of geographic and cultural knowledge explains why the Crown described the people of the Indies inaccurately, it is likely that in these instances they used the terms *loro* and *black* loosely to mean people who *could be taken* as slaves. This left open the possibility that people *like* the loro and black slaves they were already familiar with (a lexicon of resemblance) would be found in America and could be enslaved. On the other hand, it might have been an open invitation (consciously or not) to "see" indios as loro or negro, which is what happened. In any case, the language used in early contracts offers clear examples of merchants and explorers seeing indios based on what was already known. However, the heterogeneity of cultural backgrounds of the Genoese, Portuguese, Flemish, and Castilian explorers and slave traders also dictated how the lexicon of resemblance operated. If Rodrigo Bastidas saw the indios he enslaved as loro or negro in 1497 because the contract determined that was how he should see them, Amerigo Vespucci identified the indigenous people of París (Venezuela) as having a "reddish cast to their flesh like that of lions," with flattened faces "similar to those of the Tartars," because in his youth in Florence he had seen Tartars hunched over their tasks.[64] After 1500, Portuguese merchants with experience in the West African trade who navigated the coast of Brazil saw the indios there as black, which might be why in 1509 a Valencian scribe heard what the merchant standing behind him said and inscribed a ten-year-old boy named Martín into his ledger as being from Brazil, the land of blacks (*terra de negres*).[65] Seeing the coloration of indios in this period was not just a matter of describing individual features; it was also related to their enslaveability, based on the pseudo-geographic conflict zones (zones of just war) and other rationales long at play in the Mediterranean slave trade. The connection of color to enslaveability may explain why the color loro was the most common marker of indios in official documents, bills of sale, and litigation suits in Castile until the mid-sixteenth century.[66] But slave owners and others did what they had done before: they created neologisms and recognized *indio* as a color. It explains why Balthasar was described as the color indio when he was being sold in the village of Almagro in 1541 or why twelve-year-old María was identified as such in a death certificate drawn up by a doctor in 1566. Just as the categories of loro, blanco, and negro were used to identify persons in bondage, the color indio became synonymous with slavery.[67]

In the courtroom setting, the color coding of indios could be highly charged and dependent on changing legal requisites. Records show that, until the 1540s, the use of the descriptor *loro* to identify an indio in bills of sale or travel permits was unproblematic.[68] After 1542, when the indios of Spanish territories were declared to be free vassals, using *loro* to describe slaves sold in Castile began to impair the slave owner's case, since for decades so many distinct peoples had been marked as loros. For instance, in 1548, as district authorities began a closer inspection of indio slaves throughout Castile, Francisco de Rueda, from Toro, decided to sell Catalina Nicolasa and her daughter. Knowing he was holding them illegally might have inspired him to cut his losses and lower their price. In the bill of sale he drew up with the innkeeper Gonzalo de Tarán, the two females, who had been described as "loras" in the sale document to Rueda, were now described as "blancas." Tarán continued to insist they were "white slaves" when local authorities began to pressure him to bring Catalina Nicolasa to court to verify whether she and her daughter were in fact indias. By describing them as "esclavas blancas," Tarán might have hoped that authorities would assume they were Berbers or moriscas and leave him alone. When mother and daughter finally appeared in court with the Corregidor, nearly ten months later, they were identified as indias. According to one expert witness, Catalina's indioness consisted of being "*morena* [brown], wide in the face, with wide and large nostrils . . . and the color india."[69]

Not only did indios change from loro to white from one bill of sale to another, but as the color black became increasingly associated with the juridical status of slavery over the course of the sixteenth century, indigenous slaves transformed from loro to black as well.[70] When in 1560 a high-ranking *comendador* from Toledo named Perafán de Rivera questioned Pedro's assertion that he was from Tierra Firme, Rivera presented two bills of sale as evidence to the contrary: the first identified the twenty-seven-year-old Pedro as a "loro" slave (never mentioning that he was an indio) captured in just war; the second identified him as a "black" of medium height with an iron chain around his neck.[71] Although neither bill of sale specified Pedro's geographic place of origin, Pedro's lawyer and supportive witnesses argued that, because the people of Tierra Firme were not black, they could not be slaves. For them, the category black distinguished slaves of western Africa, Calicut, or Cochín from the berberisco (white) slaves of northern Africa. In addition, Portuguese and other merchants regularly used the category black (read "slave") to identify Tupinamba slaves from Brazil, a territory in dangerous proximity to the broad expanse of Tierra Firme, which is why some Castilian slave owners, like Rivera, attempted to blacken their so-called Brazilian slaves in the bills of sale.[72] To convince the judges that Pedro was an indio, Friar Francisco de Carvajal testified that the first time he saw Pedro, he said, "Come here, brother indio, why do you have those locks and chains if you are an indio and free by your nature?" He described Pedro's hair and beard as very black, but not tightly curled in the manner of the blacks and mulatos (individuals designated as brown in coloration or of mixed heritage) whom the friar had seen in the New Kingdom of Granada. Pedro's face color was darker because "the faces of indios near the sea coast, which is *tierra caliente* [hot land], are more bronzed [*tostada*]."[73] Unfortunately, because the defendant's depositions are missing from the file, we do not know how the opposing side constructed its arguments. In the end, Pedro was declared not free.

Because Pedro's place of origin might determine his black or *indio* identity, witnesses described his aspect in a political and highly charged way. Although in most cases the relationship of coloration with geographic location was completely arbitrary, litigants trying to prove imperial status went to great lengths to distinguish the less-black peoples of the Rio de la Plata area (Spanish territory) from the blacker peoples of Brazil (Portuguese territory).

As the political winds shifted, so did the questions attorneys asked of potential litigants. Determining whether a litigant was from the Portuguese domains remained standard before the court decided to take on a case, but after 1560 lawyers probed whether a litigant could remember if either parent was a mulato slave. This shift has several explanations. As the sixteenth century progressed, the presence of slaves in Iberia increased tremendously. In Seville (by 1565), one of every fourteen inhabitants was a slave. Some were of mixed heritage, or their owners claimed they were. In such cases debates in the courtroom centered around physiognomy *and* lineage, especially the mother's heritage, because laws stated that the status of slavery passed through the mother. Just as slave owners began to avoid the category *loro* because of its ubiquity as a descriptor, slave owners also began to describe *indios* as "mestizos" or "mulatos" (thus replacing the term *loro*) to emphasize their partial West or North African heritage. This practice may explain why lawyers included a question about the litigant's lineage in their questionnaire for prospective witnesses.[74]

The transition from the use of the descriptor *loro* to *mulato* to describe indio slaves becomes evident in a litigation suit that began in 1568. It involved an indigenous litigant, Jorge, who had recently fled his master, the regidor (councilor) of the town of Martos (near Jaén, in Andalusia), in order to reach Seville and initiate a lawsuit before the Casa. While Jorge was being held in jail (as authorities attempted to verify who his master was), he was identified as the "color indio and branded on the face." Once the lawsuit was under way, the bills of sale presented by his master, Hernando de Rivas, identified him as the color loro, without specifying his place of origin. But Jorge's lawyer was quick to point out that the bill of sale in Seville identified Jorge as loro, and not as mulato or black, as Rivas contended. Rivas countered the assertion that Jorge was an "indio loro":

> The bills of sale regarding Jorge do not declare Jorge's nation, but it is not necessary to state the place of origin of the slave nor [is it justified] to say that because he looks indio that he *is* an indio. There are many slaves who are the same color [loro] as Jorge, and they are neither indios nor assumed to be so. They are slaves, just as Jorge is [a slave], and they [their owners] sell and transfer them from one person to another.[75]

Because his identification as loro was no longer sufficient to prove Jorge's indio identity—and the judges remained uncertain after having inspected him—Jorge's lawyer tried a different tack. He argued that Jorge was "born of an indio father and an india mother from Santo Domingo and so is free by his birthright [*nacimiento*] and generation [*generación*], and his mother was named Isabel García, india."[76] However, it was not clear whether Isabel García was in fact his mother, since one witness claimed that Jorge had been taken from Isabel some twenty-three years before, when they disembarked in Sanlúcar de Barrameda, and she had only found him recently (when the case began). But when Sarmiento, the procurador de indios (legal representative of Indians), requested that the testimony of Isabel García be admitted to the court, the head judge, Salgado Correa, refused to comply. Perhaps it was because Salgado Correa was cozy with the slave owner, Rivas, or because the judges doubted that Isabel was really Jorge's mother. In any case Jorge was unable to prove that he was an indio from Santo Domingo, and he was not freed.[77]

Jorge might have gone to extremes to "adopt" an india mother to help his cause—there are other such instances in the documents—because of the increasing pressure to prove lineage rather than physiognomy or naturaleza. Yet because in most instances proving a slave litigant's parentage was nearly impossible, color coding still formed an essential aspect of the strategic game of identification in the cases presented after 1560. In another telling case, which began in 1575, Lucia claimed to be from Panama. When her owner, Agustín Sánchez (from Madrid), purchased her in Spain in 1567, the bill of sale described Lucia as a slave of just war and the color of cooked quince. No mention was made of her geographic or cultural origin. Sánchez and his witnesses took advantage of the indistinct descriptors in the bill of sale to make what had become a standard argument: Lucia was not an india, for she had been born in Portugal and was the daughter of an Arab man and a black woman. To trace her trajectory of bondage, one witness vaguely recalled that Lucia had been brought from Portugal to the fair at Zafra, where she was sold and then transported to the mines of Guadalcanal, where Sánchez purchased her. Witnesses noted that the demonstrable qualities of her body, face, physiognomy, and manner of speaking provided clear evidence of her mixed heritage. She was a mestiza slave, they contended—half Arab and half black—which would mean she had no recourse to freedom on either side of her genealogy.[78]

As in other cases, identifying Lucia depended on what each witness wanted to see, sometimes based on personal experiences of capturing, seeing, or owning slaves.[79] For instance, Doctor Mathias de Huerta Sarmiento, the alcalde of Cartagena (in Murcia), identified Lucia's mestizaje through his own experiential lens: "I have seen many Indian slaves, and I have never seen an Indian like Lucia. Generally, they have very different bodies, mouths, eyes, cheeks, and hair, and manner of speaking. . . . [W]ithout a doubt she is not an india because her hair is different from the indios—long, bland, and flat—and the mouth ugly, and the cheeks sunken, and [her] coloration very different from the indios born in the Indies." All signs indicated to Huerta Sarmiento that Lucia had been born "in these parts," meaning on *his* side of the Atlantic.[80] His eighteen years of administrative, military, and slaving experience in Oran and Mers el-Kébir, along with his ownership of dozens of mestizo slaves, gave him the authority to claim that Lucia was part Arab. He explained to the court that the slave raiders from Oran had captured black slaves and brought them across the Sahara in military operations called *cabalgadas*. He failed to mention that Castilians regularly financed and participated in such expeditions (fifty-nine of which originated from the Canary Islands in the sixteenth century), sending large numbers of horses and men, and that to recover their investments they captured between forty and seventy slaves per expedition.[81] The centuries-long active slave trade had turned various places in northern Africa into diasporic sites, where uprooted, culturally diverse peoples congregated and ethnogenesis occurred. According to the witness Huerta Sarmiento, when the Arabs, Berbers, and Moors "mixed" (*envuelvan*) and impregnated the black women, their children had the same coloring as Lucia. He ended his testimony by saying that he had heard, at court and among people working in the silver mines of Guadalcanal (owned by the Fugger family, who employed large numbers of slaves to extract the ore), that Lucia was the daughter of a black woman and an Arab. He never explained how Lucia or her parents had reached Guadalcanal from Oran (via Portugal). He did, however, think it was curious that until then Lucia had never said she was an india; it was only because indios were being freed by the Crown, he suggested, that she was claiming this new india identity.[82]

But Castilian witnesses with experience on the other side of the Atlantic saw Lucia differently. To Captain Pedro Bravo de Paredes, who had held the office of corregidor of Chayanta (Bolivia) and had just returned from serving in military expeditions to Chile, Lucia was too black to be an Indian. She had the features of the daughter of a black woman and an Indian from Peru. Another witness, Juan Arias Maldonado, the mestizo son of Captain Diego Maldonado and Luisa Palla of the Cuzco nobility, could not remember having seen an Indian "as black in color or with the same form of [her] factions, especially being from Panama, as Lucia [said] she [was]. [He had] seen the people of that land and those of [the island of] Taboga and [did] not remember having seen anyone with the color and proportions [*talle*] of Lucia."[83]

Judges rarely recorded rationales for their decisions, so we do not know how they weighed such drastically different accounts to determine, in December 1575, that Lucia should be freed. However, we can draw several conclusions from this and the other examples. Clearly, the in situ applications of descriptive terminology were by no means standardized in Spain. Sixteenth-century Castile was a highly globalized society, in terms of both the diversity of peoples living there and the worldly experiences of its inhabitants. For a Castilian who had spent time in Seville or northern Africa, the terms *mestizo* and *mulato* identified individuals with a combined African, Arab, or Castilian heritage. For Castilians with experience in the Latin American context, particularly in Peru after the 1550s, the descriptors *mulato* and *mestizo* could indicate individuals of Spanish and African or African-Spanish and indigenous lineage, respectively, or could instead identify coloration.[84] Moreover, in the Castilian courtrooms after 1542 it would not have been logical (or fruitful) for a slave owner to accuse a litigant of being a mestizo slave with indio heritage on the mother's side. That did not, however, prevent a few slave owners from claiming that the mestizo children of their former india slaves should remain in bondage—but only rarely were they successful.

If experiences abroad in different imperial domains gave added weight or complexity to witness depositions, the increasing globalization of Castile allowed peoples who had not traveled outside its domains the chance to compare and contrast peoples of different cultures living in their midst. Castilians made sense of indios in their midst and in their memories within a rapidly changing demographic and increasingly globalized context. As slaves from different imperial settings converged in towns and cities, and as Castilians returned from ventures in northern Africa or Latin America and interacted with Genoese or Portuguese merchants living in Seville and elsewhere, perceptions of non-Castilians shifted. A gradual emphasis on geohumoral attributes *and* lineage emerged, used especially to pinpoint enslaved status. But these descriptors had not yet hardened into exclusionary categories that would translate into the more rigid system of classification known as the caste system, as some scholars argue. These litigation suits, as well as bills of sale and other records, reveal that in fact Castilians did not yet have a homogeneous set of terms to denote individual physical differences or a template that established hard-and-fast distinctions among identifiable groups of people in bondage.

Given such a globalized, imperial context, it is important to note that indios in Castile were held in relief against peoples from other places of the world, not only against Old Christians. Although it is crucial to elucidate how the standards of limpieza de sangre (a genealogical continuum of Christianness) gradually became the blueprint for determining the lineage and qualities of Spanish vassals, we should also pay more attention to how the status of slave or laborer influenced the use of descriptors such as *black*, *white*, *mestizo*, and *mulato* to identify the mother's heritage and to prove or disprove slavery or tainted heritage both in Castile and in Latin America. Why, for instance, were certain terms related to enslaveability used in some imperial locales and not others? Until the 1550s, slave owners in Castile commonly adopted the descriptor *loro* to describe indios living there, but it was exceedingly rare to identify an indio as loro in documents generated in Spanish America. Many scholars assume that Castile was the site from which all physical descriptors emerged, but documents from these cases show that that was not always true.

The construction of indioness based on identifiable sonic and physical criteria was key to determining whether someone was in fact an indio and to which imperial domain he or she belonged. But the notions that indios originated from a particular territory because they looked a certain way or that they were slaves because they inhabited a particular naturaleza deemed to be bellicose or contaminated were further complicated by contested Portuguese and Spanish imperial claims of sovereignty in distinct parts of the globe.

SEVEN

Transimperial *Indios*

The *indio* [Francisco] does not look like he is from New Spain but from Rio de la Plata or Brazil, which are two conjoined provinces and all one land we call *"firme."*

— "Testimony, Bartolomé de las Casas," 30/VIII/1557,
AGI, Justicia 1023, n. 2, r. 2, pieça 8, s.f.

As the decades progressed, into the 1550s, 1560s, and 1570s, slave owners unwilling to relinquish their property made strategic decisions about their indio slaves' imperial status. Attorneys and supportive witnesses began to argue that slaves had originated from the Portuguese domains—Brazil most commonly, but occasionally Portuguese outposts in what is now the subcontinent of India, in the coastal cities of Goa, Cambay, Calicut, Cochín, and Diu. Or, as access to East Asian territories became a reality, slaves were said to have come to Spain from the Moluccas, Myanmar (Burma), or China. In turn, enslaved indigenous men and women from some of these sites also began to argue deliberately that they originated from Spanish territories, because that imperial status allowed them by law to litigate for their freedom.

In the cases of Beatríz and Felipa, several deponents for both the plaintiffs and the defendants argued that these two indias conformed to an abstract sense of groupness or community (nación) based on imperial affiliation. To convince the judges, deponents relied on sonic and physiognomic criteria to fix the two women to a particular location. They also iterated a discourse found in documents, laws, and legal language that constructed indios as a single legal entity, with a particular kind of monolithic identity since the label increasingly collapsed and effaced ethnic, generational, and geographical differences. The fact that the floating construct indio could identify someone from America or Asia was also based on expanding access by Spaniards and Portuguese to disparate parts of the globe. Thus, based on their experiences in some of these places, some deponents argued that Beatríz or Felipa came from Mexico, while others said they came from Calicut or elsewhere. Even legal advocates in a Castilian court could just as easily label a person from Guatemala as indio as he could someone from what is now mainland China or India. This combination of mobility and the enormous geographical and ethnic scope of the indioscape sometimes made it easier for litigants to argue that they were from a culture other than their own.

In the globalized context of Carmona, indias, like Beatríz, from Spanish America and the Caribbean were held in relief against peoples from other places of the world. In the wrangling, invention, and negotiation that took place in the written evidence presented to the judges, witnesses and litigants transformed the discourse about what it meant to be an indio. They imagined the spatial trajectories that slaves might have followed from their places of origin to Castile because these pathways were within their cognitive framework. In other cases, litigants questioned monolithic assumptions about physiognomy, nation, geographical location and natural slavery, or the inherent enslaveability of all indios. But the application of the label *indio* as a legal abstraction could transcend the notions of nación and of belonging to a group in other ways. In such instances it became important to decide on the imperial affinity of those indios who metaphorically fell into the borderless, "entangled" domains Portuguese and Spanish authorities imagined themselves to possess.[1]

Key to these discussions was the notion of sovereignty. Although both Crowns claimed broad swaths of territory and, by implication, the people inhabiting those lands, the reality was that their physical dominion over those territories and people was limited. As the legal historian Lauren Benton has argued, "It is misguided to see empire building as a series of treaties that consolidated order and stability on a global scale."[2] To assert legal claims of sovereignty, Portuguese and Castilian officials applied various means to redesign geographical knowledge of and control over the apportioned globe. The Crowns sanctioned official expeditions ready to exert military force over other European powers if necessary and establish small outposts with settlers. They encouraged merchants to launch commercial networks in desirable territories. At home they relied on firsthand testimonies of ship crew members and others who had traveled and lived in contested areas and hired talented mapmakers to redraw boundary lines to suit imperial designs. Chroniclers on the Crown payroll studied these maps and absorbed travelers' accounts. They rendered this information into rational imperial narratives about conquest and fait accompli dominion, thus contributing to what Rolena Adorno has identified as the "polemics of possession."[3] Claims of sovereignty over territories and people could therefore be expressed by drawing up treaties, by exercising military control, through the physical presence of merchants and settlers, and by the manipulation of knowledge about those areas embedded in maps and chronicles.

In this chapter I examine three cases in three distinct imperial sites, where claims of imperial sovereignty and possession dominated the discourse taking place in Castilian legal venues. The first case involved an india named Aldonza, and took place in the 1520s and 1530s in the Moluccas, known then as the Spice Islands (today the Maluku Islands) and located in the eastern section of the larger Indonesian archipelago. The second case concerned four anonymous male indios captured in the 1540s in the borderlands of Brazil and the Rio de la Plata, the coastal area of South America, between what is now Rio de Janeiro and Buenos Aires. The third case is that of Pedro, originally from Pegu (now called Bagu), located in what we now know as Myanmar (Burma), but who also lived as a slave in Diu, a port in northwestern India in the 1550s. Each case reveals how the litigants who appropriated the *Spanish indio* label for calculated reasons relied on the murky geographical knowledge of or disputed imperial claims over these territories to reach a favorable outcome for themselves. The Moluccas, Brazil, and even Pegu were, in different ways, borderlands where European settlers, merchants and indigenous peoples interacted and circulated among one another without always defining clear parameters of who was and who was not an imperial subject. On another level, each case reveals conceptualizing and coming to terms with the complexities of different domains that were imagined to form part of a larger imperial sphere. Each case shows how space was not only a physical environment to be controlled, but a continuum of epistemological possibilities (and dreams) of Atlantic and Pacific exchanges and movements of people and goods. Each case shows how, as Serge Gruzinski has argued, people, some of whom had never traveled to these imagined territories, were "thinking the world." The journeys of Aldonza, the four Brazilians, and Pedro disclose tentative colonial contacts in parts of the Western

Hemisphere and South and East Asia, connecting East to West and West to East. They show how the "four parts of the world," including the continents of Asia, Africa, Europe, and America, were now united in a contest for sovereignty, both anticipated and real.[5] Transimperial indios helped make the early modern world what it was imagined to be.[6]

As the physical boundaries of the Spanish and Portuguese imperial domains expanded during the sixteenth century, people inhabiting areas as discrete as the Moluccas, Brazil, or Myanmar, who might have once been labeled with another moniker, were identified in Castile as indios according to abstract notions of territoriality and possession. Precisely because determining the imperial status of a liminal indio was not a straightforward process, it presents an opportunity to examine the margins of empire from one of its presumably stable centers: the Castilian courtroom. In that setting, witnesses, lawyers, and litigants wrangled with the boundaries of what constituted territorial possession and ethnic belonging in places far from where these imperial interactions occurred. Each of the participants helped come to terms with who was, and who was not a vassal of the Spanish Crown, despite the heterogeneity of the "conquered" people and the tentative nature of European possession. Through these litigation suits, we, the historians, can gaze at these deponents "stepping on the shadows of empire."[7]

Counter to the tendency to see imperial empires as disconnected and European "encounters" with other European powers as clashes or confrontations, the historian Sanjay Subrahmanyam suggests that it might be better to see them as expressions of contained conflict or careful mediation.[8] Furthermore, although the kingdoms of Castile and Portugal considered themselves to be distinct, and historians write about them as though they were, they were far more interrelated dynastically, politically, and culturally, even before the union of Crowns took place in 1580.[9] While witnesses and litigants would argue otherwise, the Portuguese and Spanish "empires" were not, in fact, separate and inviolable, but interconnected in different contexts, whether in the frontier area between Extremadura and the Algarve, in cities like Cádiz or Seville, or in outposts in other parts of the world.[10] European merchants, sailors, and conquerors journeyed to areas that were contested and dangerous, where Europeans had to rely on each other for resources and crucial information. Under such circumstances, they would refer to themselves as fellow Christians, rather than by their nation. It was only in the courtroom where deponents, many of them merchants from different nations, unscrambled borderland areas where they came in contact with, competed with, and constituted one another.[11] Despite their assertions that the territorial and ethnic boundaries where they exchanged goods with indigenous peoples were clearly demarcated, these sites were not preconceptualized, naturalized, or even self-contained.

But where did indios fit into the liminal space between geographic imagination, legal treaties, and interimperial commercial enterprises? How did deponents and litigants in each of these three case studies, some of whom had never been at the contested site, give narrative weight to these discussions? How were their trajectories constitutive of imperial boundaries? Castilian jurists and lawyers no doubt pondered these questions in determining to which empire the indio slave Martín Quintín belonged. As a boy, he was sold, in May 1544 in Valladolid, by Baltasar Schetz from Antwerp to Francisco Bravo, a Castilian from Palacios. The bill of sale, which could falsely codify an individual's place of origin at the stroke of a pen, described Martín as being from the "land of Brazil" despite his claim—supported by the testimony of Bartolomé de las Casas—that he was from the Rio de la Plata area, supposedly Spanish territory. His lineage of bondage established that Schetz had bought Martín from a German named Juan Vanhelst (also spelled Van Helst), residing in Lisbon with agents in Brazil.[12] Was possession determined solely by his place of origin or was imperial sovereignty—due to his residing in the contested territory of the Rio de la Plata—a consideration? In dispute in Martín's and other cases were concepts of belonging to a unified and politically determined social body; of being "Spanish" or "Portuguese" or "French" or, in the case of the indios, belonging to a specific ethnicity; or of being "friendly" or "unfriendly" to the Europeans.

The subject-making of transimperial indio slaves like Martín Quintín occurred in a rapidly transformative world where geographical, commercial, and cultural borders were in flux. They were transimperial because European litigant-owners both claimed them as their subjects—as Portuguese, French, or Spanish—and sought to prove how and why they were. Many of the witnesses in cases involving imperial status were peripatetic merchants or subjects of Flemish, Norman, or Portuguese origin residing in Valladolid, Seville, or Cádiz who wanted to protect their commercial interests despite imperial claims.[13] But the indio litigants were also adept at arguing that they came from specific locales in the Spanish domains or were possessed by individual Spaniards. These indios were mobile border crossers: traveling the world from place to place with merchants from different nations. They embodied the changing geopolitical landscape by virtue of the seas they had traveled and the continents they had traversed. But they were also residents of Castile and in most cases lived at least part of their lives in the heart of the empire. Because indios were so dependent on witness testimony to prove their origins, their transimperial mobility could serve to deceive authorities or hinder the opposition's ability to prove their origins. But they also hoped to achieve an imperial fixity, demarcated by clear imperial boundaries that distinguished them as Spanish vassals. In other words, indios crossed borders by virtue of their ethnicity, geographic location, and association with various Europeans, but as juridical subjects in the courtroom, they became symbolic boundary markers of imperial differences for legal advocates, witnesses, and defendants hoping to solidify claims of sovereignty.[14] Indios were emblems of imperial sovereignty.

Border Crossings

Border crossings involved vital interactions and modes of relating based on shifting assumptions about imperial differences, both real and imagined. These constitutive exchanges began at home in Castile, especially in commercial relations. The porous land-based border separating the kingdoms of Castile and Portugal enabled wealthy Castilians to send agents to Lisbon or elsewhere on a regular basis to buy slaves and transport them across Extremadura. That open expanse of land made it possible for the Castilian Vicente Yáñez Pinzón to buy the nine-year-old Loarte, from Calicut, in the Algarve from a Portuguese merchant in 1513, or nearly two decades later for Beatríz to travel by cart across southern Portugal through Extremadura to join the Cansino household in Carmona, Spain.[15] In turn, Portuguese merchants regularly crossed the border and traveled to the *ferias* (fairs), including the one in Zafra, due east of Lisbon, to peddle their wares and sell young slaves fresh off caravels arriving from Brazil and elsewhere.[16]

In their depositions, slave owners could easily point to the entangled nature of Portuguese–Spanish business relations in Seville. The labyrinthine streets and various neighborhoods of this cosmopolitan city harbored Flemish, Genoese, French, German, and Portuguese merchants, tradesmen, and travelers whose international connections facilitated the passage of silks, spices, and especially slaves through the city.[17] They came to the city because they were business partners in companies or because they had drawn up short-term contractual agreements to buy or transport African, Indian (from India), and Brazilian slaves, by land and by sea, to Castilian ferias and ports.[18] Some of the same merchants who captured American indios and transported them from west to east profited from bringing deracinated northern and sub-Saharan African peoples to the peninsula.[19] Genoese merchants involved in buying and selling slaves were particularly well entrenched in Seville, with networks dating back to the thirteenth century.[20] Because of King Charles V's close association with merchants in his native Flanders, Flemish merchants based in Seville were awarded contracts to operate between Seville, Lisbon, Brazil, and the Rio de la Plata.[21] Entire streets in Seville were dominated by Portuguese families, some of them conversos with ties to Spanish New Christians.[22]

As the sixteenth century progressed and trade with markets in South and East Asia began to prosper, the connections among merchants from different nations plying commodities and capital became even broader and more deeply enmeshed.[23] Peripatetic merchants with bases in Seville cultivated economic associations in a broader swath of the globe, traveling from the Mediterranean to cities where the Portuguese had established outposts in Calicut, Goa, and further east, in Melaka, the Moluccas, and into China.[24] Parts of the Western Hemisphere became increasingly connected to broader global markets.[25] Goods moved in larger circles and followed progressively more intricate routes. By 1558, a Portuguese merchant could procure a contract from the Spanish king to bring an herb renowned as a strong dye from the kingdom of Cambay or Gujarat (in northwestern India, near Diu), instead of acquiring it from the French, and then to transport it to Santo Domingo, where indio laborers would use it to dye the bolts of cotton and wool cloth a luscious blue.

Such international merchant contacts increased the chances that a slave like Martín Quintín, who was presumably from the Rio de la Plata region, might come in contact with German, Flemish, Portuguese, and Spanish merchants in the course of his travels. Despite a papal bull prohibiting "foreigners" from entering Spanish territories, the seas were wide open for European merchants to form alliances and commercial ties across time and space.[26] But these chances were also enhanced because Castilian laws prohibiting the sale of foreign indio slaves in Spanish territory were unclear and irregularly enforced. Prohibiting indios from Portuguese territories from entering Castile was contradictory and piecemeal; it was never clear whether those laws applied to indios from the Portuguese domains sold in Spanish territory, particularly where sovereignty had not been clearly established.[27] But the sale of Brazilian indios throughout the Western Hemisphere had long been a reality. From the earliest days of exploration along the northern coast of South America, slaves from the as yet unclear boundaries of Brazil were captured and sold throughout Latin America and the Caribbean.[28] Most of the Brazilian Indians went to the islands of Hispaniola, Puerto Rico, Margarita, or

Cubagua, but spotty evidence points to other destinations in Latin America as well.[29] The majority of these victims of the slave trade fell beneath the archival radar. We know that entrepreneurs based in Santo Domingo established connections with the Spanish settlers on the islands of Cubagua (est. 1509) and Margarita (the Guaiquierie or Guayquirí people allowed the Spaniards to settle there, beginning in 1524). Those islands, in turn, served as bases of operations for slave-raiding ventures along the South American coast and into Portuguese territory.[30] Such enslaving operations in the area of Tierra Firme "called the coast of Brazil" were openly sanctioned in the 1520s by governing authorities in the city of Santo Domingo.[31] It is uncertain how many years this slave trade endured or how many Brazilian indios actually came to the island, but clearly an interimperial and inter-American slave trade in Brazilian indios was a reality.[32] Such an open trade endured until the mid-1550s, when the traffic in Brazilian slaves that had so benefited merchants and landowners in the Greater Antilles was curtailed by Charles V, who was no longer willing to tolerate illegal interimperial commerce. In a decree he ordered that all indios from foreign domains taken to Spanish territories should be freed.[33]

What is also clear is that these and other mandates involving indio slaves from Portuguese territories were never applied systematically. Evidence from the indigenous lawsuits in the tribunal of the Casa and Council of the Indies supports the argument made by Lauren Benton that laws did not establish a stable legal order, as some scholars have argued, but rather laid the basis for ad hoc exchanges and (dis)agreements between different imperial powers.[34] Moreover, the political dynamics between Portugal and Spain changed over the course of the sixteenth century. As Esteban Mira Caballos has argued, the union of the two Crowns (in 1580) only increased the number of indio slaves from the Portuguese domains coming to the peninsula, some of whom went to Castile.[35]

The creation of transimperial indigenous subjects was made possible because of the intermeshed nature of commercial transactions, the lax legal codes regulating the interimperial slave trade, and individuals who crossed borders on a daily basis in the shops of Seville and Lisbon and on the ships of merchants and explorers. Evidence of the intertwined nature of interimperial relations could be found in the Castilian courtroom, at the commercial fairs, and in the peripatetic lives of merchants, slave owners, and indio slaves. Indios placed in bondage by merchants in contested outposts and settlements traversed the connected seas and oceans until, eventually, they arrived in Castile. Once some of those slaves entered the courtroom, their imperial status came into question. The first of the three case studies, an early example of border crossings that transpired in the Moluccas during the 1520s, involved disputes over territoriality, possession, and sovereignty, and a questioning of the imperial identity of a slave named Aldonza.

The Moluccas

In the 1520s possession of an island or a portion of an island in the Moluccas (see map 7.1) on the east of the larger Indonesian archipelago might be based on a claim of sovereignty or by the physical presence of men literally holding down the fort for longer than did other European parties.[36] Assertions of imperial sovereignty also rested on tenuous alliances with competitive sultanates in the small archipelago. On his 1511 journey Ferdinand Magellan (in Portuguese, Fernão Magalhães) claimed the Molucca Islands for Portugal. Nearly a decade later, in an attempt to circumnavigate the globe, he traveled westward, this time on behalf of the Spanish Crown. He was killed near Cebú, in the Philippines, in 1521, but the expedition continued under the charge of Juan Sebastián del Cano, touching on and claiming parts of the Moluccas before returning to Spain, in September 1522. At the time, the Europeans were mainly interested in the clove-producing islands of Ternate and Tidore in the northern part of the archipelago.[37] The kingdom of Tidore and the sultan of the village of Jailolo offered shelter to the Magellan expedition, but once the Spaniards departed, the people of Tidore were ruthlessly attacked by the islanders of Ternate, who were their enemies and allies of the Portuguese. Eager to make commercial inroads into the volatile area, the Spanish king, Charles V, ordered a trading post be established at Tidore as early as 1525, hoping it would serve as a base from which merchants could access the cloves and sail further northward and trade on an ad hoc basis.[38]

Throughout the 1520s, the Moluccas continued to be contested by the Spanish and Portuguese. Although Charles V argued that Magellan's first voyage did not constitute imperial possession of the Moluccas, the Portuguese king, John III, contested this absurd claim; the Portuguese had been there since 1511. To resolve the matter two imperial delegations met in 1524 on a bridge that separated Spain from Portugal. The Spanish delegation included survivors of Magellan's first voyage and teams of mapmakers, including the Portuguese cartographer Diogo Ribeiro, now employed by the Spanish Crown. Several stunning maps produced by Ribeiro and presented at the meeting placed the Moluccas squarely in Spanish territory.[39] Notwith-

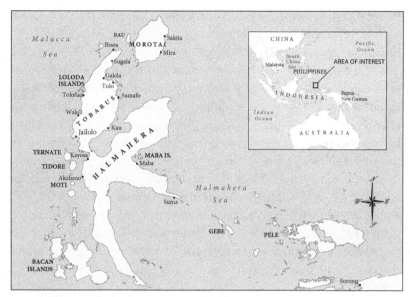

MAP 7.1: Spice Islands (Moluccas). Designed by Sarah Bell.

standing the manipulation of cartographic knowledge by world-renowned geographers and under-the-table attempts at bribery, the two sides failed to reach an agreement over the demarcation that divided the globe into two hemispheres based on the Treaty of Tordesillas (1494).[40] Following the failed conference, Charles V decided to bolster Spanish claims to the Moluccas. To do so, he set a goal of outfitting annual expeditions to the area, including one in 1525 that comprised seven ships and 450 men commanded by García Jofre de Loaísa. Over the next few years, Loaísa, who died at sea in July 1526, and his successors succumbed to disease or were murdered, and Hernando de la Torre became the fourth person named as commander and governor of the Moluccas by the king of Spain. From the outset, the Spanish claim to Tidore was tenuous and de la Torre and his men remained ensconced in a fort there beginning in late 1526 or early 1527.[41] Over the next three years, the greatly outnumbered Spanish contingent relied on its indigenous allies in Tidore and Jailolo and resorted to strategic guerrilla warfare to maintain possession.[42] They became entangled in the wooing and machinations of the different kings and queens in the Moluccas archipelago, some of whom played the Portuguese against the Spanish to gain an advantage over their enemies.[43] On a European imperial level, the situation became more complicated when Charles V married his cousin, the Portuguese infanta Isabella, in 1526. After a few years he realized that more peaceful relations with

Portugal were desirable and that expenditures in East Asia—he was borrowing heavily to finance the expeditions—outweighed the benefits. Besides he needed money to finance other European military campaigns.

In April 1529, in exchange for 350,000 ducats, Charles V signed the Treaty of Zaragosa with John III, relinquishing Spanish control over the Molucca Islands to the Portuguese and reaffirming the line of demarcation that separated the two imperial claims. Later in the year, word reached Hernando de la Torre that the Portuguese now possessed the Moluccas. The commander found himself facing annihilation unless he was willing to yield all claim to the island and ally himself with the Portuguese.[44] He signed a *capitulación* on 28 October 1529, and the Spaniards were removed from the fort at Tidore and dispersed to different islands.[45] In February 1534, after de la Torre had spent nine years in the Moluccas, the Portuguese granted him and his party safe passage to Lisbon aboard a Portuguese vessel.[46] A young india named Aldonza and an unnamed indio boy, both servants of de la Torre, were on that ship.[47]

These details were not in the lawsuit that Aldonza initiated in 1549. According to her deposition and supportive witness testimony, after reaching Europe Aldonza had remained with de la Torre for five years, first in Lisbon and then, beginning in 1536, in Frías (Burgos) until he died, apparently intestate. She then labored for his brother, who sold her to Diego de Alfaro, a solicitor for the royal court of Valladolid, for whom she worked for nearly ten years. When Alfaro was murdered, she served his wife, Catalina de Valdés, whom Aldonza claimed held her against her will and bragged publicly that Aldonza was a slave when she was not.[48]

The 1549 interrogation questions on behalf of Catalina de Valdés asked witnesses to comment on Aldonza's lineage of bondage—to whom she was sold and when—and to affirm that she had been a slave for more than fifteen years based on a legal bill of sale drawn up in good faith. But several of the questions revolved around issues of territorial sovereignty and possession of a slave, which those with direct experience in the Moluccas would have been able to answer. Did witnesses know that in 1525 Captain Hernando de Torres (a permanent resident of Frías, in Burgos, Spain) had spent some years in the Molucca Islands and a few years in Portugal? Did they know that on the Molucca Islands, possessed by the king of Portugal, male and female slaves were captured and sold among the people who lived there? Did they know that Torres had bought Aldonza, and that before he bought her, she was already a slave? The only eyewitness to the events that had transpired fifteen years earlier was Aldonza herself.

Embedded in each question were issues related to imperial sovereignty, the transimperial identity of Aldonza, and whether she was considered a slave or a servant before she entered the de la Torres household—presumably at the fortress at Tidore or while de la Torres was in Portuguese custody in Jailolo. Also at issue was whether Aldonza was a legal dependent of a Spaniard being held prisoner in territory now occupied by the Portuguese.

To address the argument of territorial sovereignty, Aldonza's lawyer argued that because she was de la Torre's free servant when several of the islands of the archipelago were being contested by the Spanish, she should be considered a free vassal of the Spanish Crown. The opposition countered by saying that de la Torre had surrendered (by capitulación) to the Portuguese and was no longer in Spanish territory when Aldonza entered his household. Gone was any prior claim, however fragile, that the Spaniards had had over the island of Ternate. Neither side could give specific dates or provide witnesses who had been there, which made it impossible to prove whether Aldonza had entered de la Torre's household (Spanish territory) *before* or *after* the surrender had taken place.[49] Four years is a long time when imperial imbroglios are concerned, and each side chose to segment the periods of Spanish (1526–1529) versus Portuguese (1529–1534) control differently to support their own narratives.

Then there was the issue of Aldonza's condition of bondage before de la Torre acquired her. The lawyer representing Valdés claimed that, because of Portuguese dominion over the Moluccas—here, he was assuming that all people of the Moluccas were Portuguese subjects, which was not true— the Portuguese had the legal authority to buy and sell slaves. Aldonza, by her nature, he argued, was already considered a slave before de la Torre possessed her. This argument assumed the generic enslaveability of the diverse peoples of those islands. At no point did anyone mention Aldonza's ethnicity—whether she was from the island of Tidore or from Jailolo (on the big island of Halmahera), both areas that had resisted Portuguese rule. Nor was there any discussion of the diverse sultanates and complex kinship system, or whether she might have been enslaved as a non-Muslim captive and taken to Tidore. Because she was such a small child—five years old— when she entered de la Torre's household, she might have been a gift to him from one of his Moluccan allies. But none of these details mattered, having little bearing on which side of the imperial divide she fell.

The defense also asserted, without a shred of evidence, not only that de la Torre had purchased Aldonza—a legal transaction—but that when he traveled to Lisbon he brought another slave with him. The implication was that because he brought another indio on the return voyage to Lisbon, he must also have purchased Aldonza. This was pure speculation.

Aldonza's testimony did not resolve the timing issue (pre- or post-1529) or her imperial or ethnic identity. Instead, without offering any details, she drew on her past as a free child. Whether coached or not, she was emphatic that she had not been considered a slave while serving Catalina Valdés or her husband for over eleven years. About de la Torre she said little: "The captain was on the island of Maluco [Molucca], but she could not remember when, only that she had heard several times that he had been there fourteen years and that when he left there he brought this witness and she was in Frías."[50] To the accusation that he had brought along another slave she countered, "Yes, the captain brought another indio from the island, but he did not bring him as a slave or sell him before he died."[51]

Although the witness testimony did not resolve the thorny dilemma of the status of a young girl caught in between two imperial rivalries and a casualty of local politics in Molucca, the Council of Indies declared on 7 September 1549 that Aldonza was free because Catalina's legal representatives had failed to follow proper procedure and did not have the appropriate legal documents. Catalina de Valdés and her children were condemned to perpetual silence on the matter.[52]

Hernando de la Torre was a Spanish vassal, but between 1529 and his return to Spanish soil in 1536, he remained in a liminal position as a prisoner of the Portuguese, who now had legal dominion (by treaty) over the Moluccas. By virtue of being his servant and in his possession, Aldonza had been placed in a precarious position. Her former identity as belonging to a specific sultanate was erased when she entered his household, and her transimperial positionality was questioned in a court in 1549, decades after the fact. At play were questions of what constituted possession of the Moluccas, the shifting sands of imperial control as the Spanish relinquished control over one portion of Ternate in 1529, the vulnerabilities of the different sultanates involved in the imperial machinations, and what it meant to possess a female slave who had crossed several imperial borders. As feeble as the arguments on both sides were, they exposed the instabilities of nascent colonial rule in an area where no Europeans yet dominated, despite treaties to the contrary. They also exposed the vulnerabilities of children labeled by the Spaniards as indios, who were caught in these interimperial entanglements. Like many slaves in Spanish America, I have thus far discussed, Aldonza was possessed by a Spanish vassal. Unlike those slaves, however, her possession as an india occurred in an area contested by Spaniards and Portuguese.

Questions of sovereignty over a particular territory informed overstated courtroom arguments about Aldonza's imperial identity in order to affect a favorable outcome for the defendant or litigant. Those arguments also revealed larger truths about the tentativeness of Portuguese-Spanish interactions in the late 1520s and that the process of marking imperial boundaries and subjects in that region was still ongoing fifteen years later.

The Rio de la Plata and Brazil

Probably the most vulnerable region on the planet in the 1530s and 1540s was the coastal territory comprising the Rio de la Plata and Brazil. It was an area rife with slave-raiding activities justified by the principles of just war and ransom.[53] Before 1560, the jurisdictions that separated the imperial domains of the two areas were unclear. Part of the problem stemmed from a lack of agreement on where the north-south line of demarcation intersected the South American continent. According to the Reinel Map (1519), which the historian Alida Metcalf calls a "dream of possession," the entire Amazon basin and then southward past the mouth of the Rio de la Plata River (the site of what is now Buenos Aires) pertained to the Portuguese.[54] The Spaniards, however, claimed that the line fell farther east, which would have given them the territory from Rio de Janeiro to the site of Buenos Aires. As in the case of the Moluccas, the creation of politically sensitive maps helped to promote different imperial claims of possession and to render known what had been unknown.[55] In the Rio de la Plata area, the demarcation issue was further politicized when the famous Spanish cosmographer Alonso de Santa Cruz (1505–1567) traveled to the area. Santa Cruz had studied under Sebastian Cabot, the pilot major of the Casa, then followed Cabot on an expedition attempting to repeat Magellan's trajectory and circumnavigate the globe. By the time they reached the stopover point in the Rio de la Plata area, their ships were no longer seaworthy, and they could not continue. Santa Cruz spent the next five years mapping the South American coastline and interior domains, developing a deep knowledge of the area.[56] His atlas of the world, finalized in 1542, granted Spain significant territory and determined that the imperial dividing line fell between what is now Rio de Janeiro and São Paulo, and included São Vicente, the settlement established by the Portuguese in 1532.[57]

As cosmographers and Crown officials wrangled over jurisdictional limits at their respective courts, Europeans from a variety of nations lived, traded, and freely navigated the coastal waters between São Vicente and the

Rio de la Plata estuary, claiming and reclaiming coastal enclaves and islands as their own. The island of Santa Catalina was a main stopover point for European vessels traversing the shoreline eager to trade. Different Spanish explorers would lay claim (*tomar posesión*) to that island as they traveled between São Vicente and the Rio de la Plata.[58] Sebastian Cabot was there in 1527, and Alvar Nuñez Cabeza de Vaca's armada, which departed from Cádiz in 1540, landed there and proceeded to claim the island again for the Spanish Crown.[59]

Often indispensible to the establishment of fragile settlements were the European castaways who chose to reside in Brazil or the Rio de la Plata area permanently. Some were French, others German, Portuguese, or Spanish— and, as the historian Alida Metcalf has shown, they provided food or safe haven, helped with navigation, served as translators with the Tupí and other peoples, and cultivated diplomatic exchanges.[60] Imperial identities were not always foremost on the minds of Europeans as they dealt with famine, diseases, and the uncertainties of whether the indios they encountered would be their allies or enemies. Some of the early Spanish accounts make it clear that those who stayed to establish families with the Carió and Tupinambá peoples were fundamental in times of need.[61] They acted as crucial intermediaries between Europeans and the indigenous peoples interested in trade. But European go-betweens could also profit handily from the active slave trade in Brazilian indios, which was exacerbated by the arrival of the Portuguese and, later, of the Spanish and French. For instance, by 1548, João Ramalho, married to the daughter of a powerful Tupinikin chief, had supplied six hundred settlers of São Vicente with three thousand slaves, captured enemies of the Tupinikin.[62]

Because of the contiguous borders, interimperial conflicts that involved slave raiding in the Rio de la Plata area often pitted the Spanish and Portuguese Crowns against one another.[63] Portuguese merchants, explorers, and commercial go-betweens would sometimes invade the island of Santa Catalina or points farther south—such as Biaça, Paquiri, and Paraná, in territory the Spaniards claimed as a part of the Rio de la Plata—to capture hundreds of slaves and then take them to São Vicente.[64] But other Europeans present in the area also commiserated over slave-raiding practices and aided one another by testifying in a Castilian court. In such instances, Portuguese, French, Flemish, and German merchants were not interested in representing their nation, but in preserving their commercial interests.[65]

Thus, issues over sovereignty—as fragile as territorial claims were at the time—could collide with commercial ones, and the question then became a matter of determining the imperial status of indio slaves caught in the interstices of competing interests. A lawsuit initiated in 1547 reveals deponents manipulating the construct indio, relying, in some cases, on established tropes, such as friendly or unfriendly, to reinforce different claims of sovereignty. In August 1547 Dionisio Molón, a merchant from Rouen, France, purchased four Brazilian indio slaves in Harfleur, in Normandy, and took them to Cádiz to sell.[66] Someone alerted the local magistrate of Cádiz to this fact, and Martín de Orué, by now the procurador general of the provinces of the Rio de la Plata, was apprised. Orué decided to press charges against Molón, claiming that the sale of the four indios had broken Spanish imperial laws and ordinances that prohibited bringing indio slaves to Castile; therefore, the four Brazilian indios should be freed.[67] An initial hearing before the corregidor took place in Cádiz in October 1547. Molón's deposition claimed that he brought the slaves to Cádiz since he had business dealings there. The truth, which Molón did not admit, was that slaves who entered France could be freed.[68] Two months later, on 2 December 1547, the corregidor ruled in Molón's favor, but Orué appealed to the Council of the Indies, which began its review nearly a year later.[69] While the case was pending, Dionisio Molón attempted to sell the four men in Cádiz, but Orué intervened and paid Molón one hundred ducats (twenty-five for each slave) to maintain them in his possession, with the understanding that the money would be returned to Orué if the four were freed.[70] Throughout the trial, the indios remained in deposit with Orué, who put them to work carrying stones and limestone and tending the vineyards in the adjacent village of Puerto Real. Orué's enemies argued that the lawsuit was merely a ruse to keep the indios in Orué's service so they could function as interpreters on a future expedition to the Rio de la Plata. The case dragged on, but the four men were eventually freed, on 30 August 1550. Unfortunately, by then one of them had already succumbed to disease.[71]

As Orué began to frame his arguments and questions for the interrogatory, his imperial agenda—how to deal with the French—became more obvious. It was so obvious, that throughout the lawsuit the names of the four indios—Martín, Sebastián, Pedro and Tomás—were only mentioned once, in the final verdict granting them their freedom. Instead of humanizing their stories, albeit in the minimal and telegraphic manner common to many indio petitions for freedom, their voices were never heard. Instead, they were portrayed by Orué and other deponents as indios in ways that fit into the larger arguments about imperial jurisdictions and the relationship of the different indigenous groups *to* Europeans. Depending on the arguments being made in the court, the four indios were either the friends or the enemies of Christians. The individuality of the four men did not matter; they represented all Brazilian indios, friend and foe, in the abstract.

In this case the indios were not described as Tupinambá, the allies of the Spanish and French, or Tupinikin, who supported the Portuguese and were the enemies of the Tupinambá. Instead, Orué deployed the term *generación* (variously defined in dictionaries as "generation," "lineage," "genus," or "type") to describe the four unnamed indios who represented the kind of Tupinambá indios who inhabited Brazil—that is, who knew no imperial boundaries, but were the friends of all Christians.[72] They were "of the generation of Tupinambás who are and dwell in the confines between the conquests of His Majesty our Emperor and Lord and the king of Portugal, and in one part and in the other part of the said conquests live the generation of the said indios, who are the friends of Christians."[73]

Orué portrayed the Tupinambá as friendly coastal indios whose territories traversed the invisible imperial boundaries as though the Tupí had no conceptions of territoriality and space. According to the depositions, the Tupí knew no geographical or imperial boundaries in their assistance to all Christians whom they wanted to befriend, since they were eager for European goods. Whenever European ships navigated the waters near their villages, the Tupí accommodated Spaniards, Portuguese, and Frenchmen with water, firewood, and other provisions.[74] They were of a generación—in this instance, of a type—of friendly indios, and opposed to the native Brazilian enemies of the Europeans.[75] The Tupinambá, as the interrogatory on behalf of Orué stated, "have always been and are friends of Christians, and they have lived among them and treat them well, even [among] those [Christians] who live in São Vicente and Puerto Seguro and in other parts of the coast populated by Christians."[76]

Witnesses emphasized that Portuguese and Spanish sailors traveled the coast and engaged in trade with the "friendly" Tupinambá, who sold their enemies in exchange for prized goods like axes.[77] Some Tupinambá, Orué continued, even expressed a cautious interest in boarding the ships and traveling to Europe to trade, as long as they would be returned to their homelands. As Juan Alfonso, a Portuguese pilot explained in a later deposition, the Portuguese usually had on board an indio interpreter who could communicate with the indios who met them when the Portuguese put down anchor on the Brazilian shore, and he remembered that, on the two trips he had taken, those who came aboard were well treated by Spaniards and Portuguese.[78] Such depictions of amicable and trustworthy relations between indios and the Portuguese may have been only partially true, in this instance in order to juxtapose the "good" Portuguese and Spanish against the "bad" French.

Here, we are reminded of a similar story told to Orué by the Tupí woman Francisca who in litigating for her freedom seven years later, in 1553, accused the Portuguese of abducting her and her male relatives by force. When Orué interviewed Francisca, he questioned her in Guaraní and she answered in Tupí. Through an interpreter, she told Orué "she was from a river that is next to Cabo Frío [just east of Rio de Janeiro,] which is the land of Brazil and subject to the most serene King of Portugal." When asked who had brought her to Spain, whether she was from the interior or the coast, and whether she had been captured as a result of war between the Indians of the interior and the coast who imprison and eat one another, Francisca responded, that "she was from along the sea coast and that when a caravel of Portuguese arrived, [her people] coming in peace, as they usually did to bargain and exchange their goods with the Christians, whether Castellanos, Portuguese, or French, they made her and three or four brothers and other relatives enter the ship. Once they had them inside, they did not want to let them leave, and so they brought them to the Kingdom of Galicia, where they sold them."[79] To the third question Francisca answered, "The coastal people were not hostile to the Christians and they are not captive [slaves] but free, because the Portuguese, who cautiously travel up and down the coast looking to exchange goods, sometimes tricked people into coming on board their ships, and then once they are aboard they take them to different provinces to sell, where it is impossible to verify the truth."[80] After surviving the long journey to Galicia, Francisca and her male relatives disembarked on the dock in the tiny village of Marin (near Pontevedra). They were lined up like cargo, shivering amid the squawking parrots and logs of brazilwood, waiting to be bartered and carted off to different locations in Castile.[81]

But in 1548 it was the French, not the Portuguese or Spanish, who were being accused in the high court of Spain of behaving unethically and threatening the vulnerable coastal indios by their manner of slave raiding. Once their vessels were loaded with merchandise, Orué's deponents argued, the French lured indios on board with promises of riches in Europe, then violated that fragile trust and kept them there by force. It seemed that much was at stake. Taking away the wives, sons, and relatives of the Tupinambá allies caused anger and internal turmoil, then attacks against and cannibalism of the entire "generation of Christians," because the Tupinambá did not know how to differentiate one European from another.[82] Once trust had been breached, the Tupinambá captured all Europeans they encountered, asking them, "Why did you not bring back my brothers and sons?," and committing atrocities against them, including cannibalism.[83]

Orué concluded that further trouble could be prevented and the fragile interimperial balance of power restored if the French were refused entry into the territory possessed by the king of Spain. Such an argument may have resonated with both the Spanish and Portuguese Crowns, who were interested in curtailing the activities of the French, who were eager to establish a permanent settlement near current-day Rio de Janeiro. Orué wanted to teach the "foreigner" Molón a lesson, requesting that he pay the maximum penalty of 100,000 maravedís and the costs of return passage for the four indios to their homelands. Orué hoped that freeing the indios would send a clear signal to the French that they were no longer welcome along the eastern shores of South America. To deny the indios their freedom and to allow Molón to walk away without penalty, Orué asserted, would endanger Spanish relations in the entire Rio de la Plata region. Too much was at stake.

Molón and his supporters, many of them from Harfleur, had a different perspective. They claimed that the indios were captives of just war taken licitly by the French and that they belonged to the French king. Rather than employ an argument of imperial sovereignty based on territoriality, Molón resorted to the argument more commonly used against indios from Spanish America who were enslaved under the terms of just war. Not only were all Brazilian indios bellicose but Molón had bought them on French soil from a French merchant (which would have been illegal by French law), then brought them to Cádiz to sell. He possessed the slaves as a French vassal. None of this was new or noteworthy information. For decades, Norman interpreters with families among the Tupinambá had acted as go-betweens in trade relations among the French and the Tupinambá.[84] Mariners and merchants from Rouen, long involved in commercial operations in eastern South America, now hoped to make further inroads into the Rio de la Plata territory claimed by the Spanish.[85]

Even though relations with the Tupinambá were relatively peaceful, thanks to Norman interpreters, the merchants who supported Molón in a Spanish court defended the enslavement of indios by arguing that all Brazilian indios ate human flesh and made war on and killed all Christians. According to Juan Mota, a Frenchman who had helped capture indios in Brazil, "all [of them were] enemies of the Christians."[86] Another witness from Harfleur, Nycolas Oybiço, cautioned that all Europeans in Brazil had to be careful. While in Brazil he had heard that "the indios" had killed seven or eight French Christians, as well as a few Englishmen aboard another ship attempting to establish trade in the area. Here Oybiço also used the long-standing argument, common to slave traders throughout Spanish and Portuguese America, that the captured indios were already slaves because "the indios of Brazil were always making war on each other and capturing slaves."[87]

Molón and his witnesses stressed the imperial right to capture indios who were already slaves, as well as their right as French merchants to be in Brazil despite Spanish and Portuguese territorial claims. But there was one other dimension to the case that becomes evident in a close reading of the depositions. Several of the merchants who testified on behalf of Molón and Orué were uncomfortable with all the imperial finger-pointing. These were men from Castile and Normandy and Lisbon who had worked hard to develop contacts in Cádiz and hoped to continue doing business there in a favorable climate. For thirty years, the fifty-year-old Jacome de Vieira had witnessed indios from Brazil being brought to Portugal and Cádiz for sale: "With my own eyes I have seen them being sold [here in Cádiz]. In days past I [myself] bought a Brazilian slave."[88] To him, there was nothing remarkable about the fact that a Frenchman had brought four Brazilian indios to Cádiz to sell. No doubt the merchants breathed a collective sigh of relief when the corregidor, probably with a vested interest in the matter, ruled on behalf of Molón. The Cádiz merchants were plainly nervous that the appeal had gone before the Council of the Indies. From their perspective, the enmeshed nature of commercial and social relations among merchants in Iberia, other parts of Europe, and Brazil was reason enough to leave things as they were. As Jorge Gómez, a Portuguese merchant with his own caravel who had been in Brazil for five years, stated, "I would like this lawsuit to end for the good of the indios and everyone involved."[89]

Despite the victory by Orué, several years later the French Crown began to express an interest in establishing a "French Antarctic" in Brazil, where they, too, could capitalize on a more regular trade in brazilwood.[90] The Molón case may have temporarily halted the small trade in Brazilian indios to Cádiz (and illegally via France), but it would be several more decades before the French would lose interest in establishing a permanent colony in Brazil.[91] The four freed Brazilian indios had survived an Atlantic journey and three difficult years in Cádiz, until one of them died. Whether the rumors were true that the three survivors accompanied Orué as interpreters on an expedition that left Sanlúcar de Barrameda, in August 1555, bound for the Rio de la Plata, we will never know.

Pegu-Perú

The third case of imperial entanglement did not involve territorial disputes or the designation of indios as friendly or unfriendly. Instead, it highlighted geographical misunderstandings and ignorance, and arguments about the imperial domain to which an indio slave named Pedro, supposedly captured by non-Christian enemies, belonged. In a broader sense, the last case best exemplifies sovereignty as a longing to possess others, as the complainants imagined the world in new interconnected ways. Pedro went before the Council of the Indies in 1557 to petition for his freedom from Antonio Baéz, a Portuguese clerk in the high court of justice (*escribano de cámara*) of Princess Juana (the widow of John III, king of Portugal, whose young son, Sebastian, had become king).[92] Baéz had crossed the imperial border, traveling with the royal entourage to Madrid on official business. But according to the lawyer who spoke on behalf of Baéz, "Pedro never said in public that he was from the Spanish Indies, or from Peru or China, until he initiated this lawsuit. And now he says it by the induction of one [Cristóbal de] San Martín, a servant of the prosecuting attorney [of the Council of the Indies] and because of the other indios in this village [of Madrid] who cannot [possibly] know Pedro's place of origin."[93] Pedro, stated one witness who had lived in the Rio de la Plata, looked "more Moor than indio."[94]

But after counseling from legal advocates at the Madrid court, Pedro, "the Moor," insisted on proceeding with the lawsuit. He decided to call himself an indio (we do not know how he was labeled in Lisbon). Despite his master's efforts, he wanted to be taken for a free vassal of the Spanish Crown. His initial statement read,

> Pedro, indio, and a natural from the province of Burma, which is next to the province of Peru and China of the Indies of the Ocean Sea, says that he was taken from his *naturaleza* by deceit while still a small child and of a very young age, by a Spaniard, approximately eight years before [1549]. [This Spaniard] brought Pedro to these [Spanish] kingdoms, where he was sold, as though he were a slave, to Antonio Baéz, a Portuguese, who is [residing] in this court. Pedro has served and serves Baéz without any title and in bad faith because he is free by birth, and now the said Antonio Baéz has tried to sell him as a slave. Because he knows that [Pedro] wishes to ask, as he is asking, for his freedom before your Majesty, he mistreats him.

This opening statement touched on what were by now formulaic arguments being made by lawyers at the Council of the Indies: that he was free by birth, taken by deceit as a child from the Spanish territories by a Spaniard, and brought to Castile and sold illegally without title or proper documentation. Pedro claimed he was being mistreated and prevented from pursuing justice. His case merited review by the court based on natural and imperial laws because he was from the Spanish territories of Peru and China.[95]

The defense lawyer for Baéz, Iñigo de Mondragón cited several reasons why the case should not go forward. Pedro, he argued, was not from Burma, as he alleged, but from the Indies of the king of Portugal, in the province of Diu (in what is now northwestern India, and a Portuguese outpost since 1509). The Council of the Indies therefore had no jurisdiction over this case, which should be reviewed by other judges with better knowledge of the case. The prosecuting attorney did not have the right to intervene based on the laws that he invoked. Mondragón added that in the province of Diu indios had been taken as slaves since time immemorial and ever since the said province had been won by the Portuguese. Pedro had consented to being sold numerous times, further legitimizing his lineage of bondage. His previous owner was Manuel Fernández, a Portuguese, who sold him to Baéz for 25,000 maravedís in Lisbon.[96]

Why the judges of the council decided to assess the case is unclear, since in the sixteenth century the territory of "Burma" (present-day Myanmar) had never been under Spanish control. Wayward Spaniards or merchants usually stopped farther south in Malacca, on the Malay Peninsula, and ventured no farther north. But, more important, it seems that the case had been misclassified because, as some would later admit, "Pegu," the name of a southern coastal city of Burma, sounded very much like "Peru." Even the cover of the litigation suit was misleading: "The prosecuting attorney on behalf of Antonio Baéz, Portuguese, royal notary of Princess Juana, over the freedom of an indio whom he brought from Peru."[97] Thus, someone knowledgeable about Portuguese colonization could state with some assurance, "I have never heard Pedro say that he was from Peru, but from Pegu, near China in the East Indies, where the Spanish have never had any commerce."[98]

Unlike the case involving Aldonza and the Moluccas, it would have been difficult for a Castilian lawyer to argue on Baéz's behalf that Pegu in Burma, or even Diu in northwestern India, was a site contested by the Spanish. Why the prosecutor argued that Pedro was from Diu instead of Pegu is somewhat curious. Someone behind the scenes with a keener sense of East Asian geography may have been aware that the inhabitants of the province of Pegu resisted Portuguese incursions and had not yet been subjugated by them when

Pedro was captured.[99] Why Mondragón may have counseled his client to say that his slave was from Diu is unclear.[100] That Pedro had traveled the merchant circuit from Pegu to Diu and eventually to Lisbon would be plausible, since trade networks between Burma and parts of India were long-standing.

Consequently, in the interrogatory, witnesses on behalf of Baéz were asked an absurd question: whether they knew that Pedro was a natural of the island of Diu, which was next to the province of Pegu, and which pertained to the king of Portugal. Diu was hardly "next to" Pegu, but the defense was trying to paint the geographical terrain in broad strokes to convince the judges that it formed a single imperial domain. In the courtroom it was also easier to make sweeping claims about who pertained to the Portuguese. Witnesses would make overgeneralizations: "On these islands and in all of the Indies of the king of Portugal generally the indios are captives, and it has been that way for ten, twenty, thirty, forty and longer years."[101] This was part of the desire to possess: connecting discontinuous domains into flowing narratives about sovereignty.

In addition to the several staff members (criados) working for the princess of Portugal, a doctor named Juan de Almaçen stepped forward to testify.[102] He was at the Spanish court attending to King Philip II's medical needs, and revealed that Pedro had told his story to him. He embellished Pedro's story with his own geographic expertise, which he had gained by reading chronicles. Pedro, Almaçen claimed, was a natural of Burma in the province of Pegu, proximate to the kingdom of Malacca. From there, moros who had come from the straits of Mecca had abducted him from his homeland and treated him as a slave while they traveled the seas, eventually arriving in the city of Diu, which was in the province of Cambay [Khambhat, India], and subject to the king of Portugal. There, Almaçen stated, Pedro had served several other owners, whose names he could not remember. Almaçen then qualified the confusion about Pegu and Peru.

> Pegu is a kingdom that is very different from Peru. It borders the kingdom of Malacca, which the ancients called Aurea Chersonese, and farther along the same coast, one can navigate to China, all along the coast toward the east by the southern sea. All this is [a part of] the Portuguese conquests in which the Portuguese maintain contact and commerce, and in other areas, dominion and lordship [señorío] similar [to that] in Dio [sic] and Malacca and Ormuz and Goa, all of which were conquered by military force. The others, like China, and Calicut, and Cochín and many other [places] are where [the Portuguese] have [established] contact.

And with the indios with whom [the Portuguese] maintain a friendship, they do not capture or take slaves, but they are accustomed to capturing the bad Moors and the indios who are bad or are allied [with the Moors] or with whom the Portuguese are at war. Moreover, in the Indies of Africa they even sell their own people, who are friends, as slaves.[103]

Almaçen admitted that he had acquired his knowledge through conversations with Portuguese travelers and by reading manuscripts or recently published writings by João de Barros and Fernão Lopes de Castanheda.[104] To converse with those who had traveled the globe was not an unusual experience; many travelers described what they knew about exotic places in the world to others, inside and outside the court. But in this instance two epic narratives of Portuguese expansion were being deployed in the courtroom to verify imperial truths about possession and imperial geography.[105] These illusions about sovereignty and control had been enshrined in books that glorified providential conquests and omitted arbitrary, chaotic, or compromising information. There was nothing in these narratives that indicated alterity or uncertainty; in them was only a production of uncontested order and truth about possession and being possessed.[106] They were, as Rolena Adorno has argued with regard to several Spanish American chronicles, works that were constitutive of events, because the polemical style was specifically intended to "influence readers' perceptions, royal policies, and social practices."[107] Clearly, Almaçen referred to these chronicles as documenting a reality that could influence the outcome of a court case involving a slave. Just as maps, with their carefully constructed agendas, embedded a certain logistical truth about empire, chronicles did the same. Almaçen situated Pegu within a grand master narrative that collapsed distinct histories, cultures, and processes of contact, "possession," and exchange into one succinct paragraph. In his monologue, he used the ubiquitous term *Moor* to make vast generalizations about those who could be enslaved. He explained rationales of enslaving "bad Moors" (anyone who was Muslim, basically) and indios who were associated with the "bad Moors" or who were in situations of just war or rescate (the exchange of their own people for goods). Pedro, a "Moor," would fit one of these criteria.

The legal representative of Pedro, Cristóbal de San Martín, insisted that Pedro was from the Rio de la Plata area and asked interpreters who specialized in Guaraní or experts who had spent time in that area to question him. But Pedro could not answer the questions posed to him in Guaraní. By then, the council had realized that it had made a mistake and that Mondragón was correct: the lawsuit should be transferred to the proper legal jurisdiction, where judges could better rule on the matter. Pedro's efforts to cross imperial juridical boundaries had failed. He had hoped to fashion an identity as a Spanish indio from Pegu or the Rio de la Plata area in the supportive Madrid court. It is likely that he returned, with the imperial entourage, to Portugal to live his remaining days in bondage.

Conclusions

The cases involving Aldonza, the four anonymous Brazilian indios, and Pedro revealed the ethnocentrism and arrogance of Europeans whose perspectives of territorial possession and ethnic belonging subsumed them into a grand epistemological paradigm. In these lawsuits, identification of the ethnic and cultural nature (naturaleza) of the indigenous inhabitants was not at issue. Rather, these lawsuits emphasized proving the assertion—however questionable—that slave owners had legal possession of indios by virtue of those indios having inhabited a territory under Portuguese or Spanish control. In these cases, territoriality and possession defined who was an indio, although the French tried to argue against this grain. In each of the three cases, territorial dominion was expressed in terms of military occupation or commercial dominance, or as a coveted domain, linking broad swaths of territory and peoples.

In the case involving the four Brazilian indios, the Frenchman Dionisio Molón, and the Castilian Martín de Orué, imperial goals of establishing clear territorial demarcations contrasted with the more fluid commercial relations involving Normans, Flemish, Castilians, and Portuguese, all of whom had a stake in maintaining a certain status quo in Cádiz and in the Rio de la Plata area. The defense and prosecution could not have presented more disparate depictions of the Brazilian indios. Orué's deponents cast them as a generation friendly to *all* Christians and as unable to distinguish one nation from the other. He demarcated a difference between friendly and enemy indios. Molón's witnesses, on the other hand, avoided arguments around territorial sovereignty and instead portrayed all Brazilian indios as enemies of Christians, bellicose, and as cannibals. From this perspective, all indios were enslaveable, whether Tupinambá, Guaraní, Tupinikin, or Carió.

The timing of accusations against a particular imperial power was strategic, and constructions of difference among the indios were calculated to favor each nation's cause. Seven years after the four Brazilian men were freed, Orué used some of the same arguments around unethical conduct against the Portuguese to argue for the freedom of Francisca, who admitted that she was Tupí and from Cabo Frio, in Brazil. It is likely that, in other chambers, the Portuguese were doing the same. The case of the four Brazilian indios illustrates the complexities of different kinds of imbroglios in different imperial sites, and the attempt by men of different nations to create distance from those complications when it behooved them to do so. The geopolitical stakes in a region in the process of becoming an imperial domain were high for the Spaniards, who had only a meager foothold in the area, which is why Orué chose to attack the power base in Cádiz to accomplish his goal.

Pedro was not from the Spanish terrains, although his lawyer made a feeble attempt to assert that he was a Guaraní indio from the Rio de la Plata. In the Castilian courtroom, deponents and the lawyer on behalf of Baéz argued, absurdly, that the Portuguese territories formed a unified entity, and that Pegu and Diu were proximate kingdoms. In this case, notions of territoriality were broader, even imperial, and almost global. Distinct domains were represented as being proximate (Peru to Rio de la Plata, Diu to Pegu), connected domains. The assumptions of possession were further supported by relying on information in recently published chronicles, themselves constitutive "events" in the process of empire building.[08] Pedro's case was less about military conflict, which had occurred in the Moluccas, or about commercial interactions, as in Cádiz and the eastern coastline of South America, than it was about segmenting the world into imperial portions and stating that it was so. It was about suggesting that Portuguese imperial history was already written and that establishing imperial sovereignty was fait accompli. Pedro, whether an indio or a Moor, was the object of debates about imaginary royal turf.

More broadly, these cases show how these indios were constituted as transimperial subjects. Pedro was from Pegu, but his Portuguese captors associated him with Moors and thus rendered him as more Moor than indio. In another location, the Madrid court, legal advocates attempted to render Pedro as a Guaraní indio. His trajectory from east to west encompassed long-connected commercial routes, but was now circumscribed by Europeans in a new way. Aldonza left her sultanate in the Moluccas with a Spanish master captured by Portuguese soldiers, later traveling to Portugal, and finally settling in Castile with other masters. She crossed many seas and imperial borders, but claimed Spanish imperial fixity. The four Brazilian indios had come into contact with Frenchmen who then crossed an imperial border and attempted to sell them in Cádiz. These tales of transimperial border-crossings are not anomalies or fantastic stories about unusual globetrotters.

Moreover, those who crossed from one imagined domain into another were individuals whose knowledge of areas previously inaccessible to Europeans entered the discourse of the courts. They were both subjects and objects of history making.

These particular indio litigants were not tributaries or inhabitants of a given community in Latin America with a cacique at its head. A discussion of their histories and struggles for justice, however, is equally relevant to deliberations over imperial belonging and the mapping of social position in distinct global locations, Spanish and Portuguese America included. A consideration of how indios became transimperial provides a more nuanced view of the mobilities constituting the early modern world. Musings over transimperial identities held expectations for slave and master regarding what the future of empire could contain and how indios fit into an established, abstract legal and social order. As constituent members of empires that were in the process of becoming, these cosmopolitan subjects embodied the continents of North and South America, Asia, Africa, and Europe in previously unfathomable ways. They were border crossers because there was no stable imperial center, and they were boundary markers because of how they defined themselves and were calibrated by others. It was the indio slaves who brought the world into sharper focus and whose global experiences permeated imperial dialogues.

Finally, these three cases reflect different ways of conceptualizing the world more broadly. Considered individually, each case seems simply to illustrate a local power struggle being played out in a Castilian courtroom. Juxtaposed, however, they reveal distinct ways of articulating abstract notions of territorial demarcation and ethnic belonging. By placing three cases that involved three continents over three decades into the same analytical framework, we are able to understand empire as a process of becoming and sovereignty as articulated in multiple ways. We can see individuals—indio slaves, merchants, kings, doctors, and lawmakers—grappling with the demarcations and shadows of empire, caught in the act of "thinking the world" and attending to the parameters of the ever-expanding indioscape.

Conclusions

✦

In this house there was another *india* girl thirteen or fourteen years old who called herself María Madalena and said she was from the village of Majes. . . . On this occasion Felipa de Vargas [her mistress] said that the *india* was from Santa Cruz de la Sierra and was the daughter of Chiriguanas [*sic*] and she had been given to her by doña Inés Chirinos de Loaysa, wife of don Alonso Mariño de Lovera, saying that [Madalena] was the daughter of their Chiriguano *indio* slaves from the war zone (*tierra de guerra*). And [Madalena] replied that was not so but rather, Majes [was her place of origin].

—Miguel Contreras, *Padrón de los indios de Lima en 1613*

In the opening scene of this volume, we encountered twenty-year-old Catalina de Velasco, awaiting an interview with Bartolomé de las Casas after having managed to escape a kind of house arrest in her mistress's palace. Like dozens of other indios, Catalina relied on the support of the bishop of Chiapas and others to affirm her identity as a free vassal. Her body bore no marks of legal branding, and she argued that she originated from Mexico, in Spanish imperial territory. The sketchy and circumscribed tale recorded by the court notary is one of loss and of resolve, but it also reveals larger certainties about paternalism and bondage and what it meant to be a legal indio in an increasingly globalized world. And this story isn't just about Catalina; it is but a fragment of a whole, a refraction of a constellation of similar moments recorded by other indio litigants relying on expert witnesses to testify on their behalf.[1]

Powerful men like Las Casas worked to establish and maintain a legal infrastructure that eventually dismantled indigenous slavery. But struggles like Catalina's were also important in advancing that process. Without romanticizing or giving such litigants too much agency, I have argued that indigenous slaves in Castilian households, courtrooms, and taverns contributed significantly to the gradual psychological and legal dismantling of indio enslavement and to the transformation of legal practices of justice.

The 127 court cases (with 184 litigants) I have analyzed disclose the desires of slave owners to keep things as they were, unable and unwilling to see indios as anything other than a reflection of their own desires. They also show some slave owners and former slave raiders letting go of a brutal past. They reveal concrete moments of inscription—on faces, in documents, and in recorded language—that defined indios as free by their naturaleza or as slaves of just war or ransom. They show the lived experiences of bondage and the eagerness for things to be other than they were. The courtroom testimonies recorded over five-and-a-half decades also demarcate a period of transition, from viewing indios as slaves to understanding indios as free vassals akin to legal minors.[3] More broadly, these case histories of bondage are a part of a situated knowledge in a given locale while also relating to the larger Atlantic and global palette of the times. These small-scale perceptions, desires, imaginings, and assertions helped shape the indioscape.

With the chronological and thematic arc of this book I have charted the course of indios' lives in bondage: from their abduction and placement onto ships, to their arrival in Seville, to their incorporation into households, to their entrance into the Castilian legal system. As the passage of various laws regulating indio slavery increased, the courts became a locus where deponents navigated the murky waters of proving legal possession. Certainly by the late 1540s, at issue was not whether, in principle, indios were slaves, but documenting that the capture, branding, enslavement, oceanic transport, and sale in Castile had followed legal requisites. Thus the lawsuits reveal an evolution in the strategic thinking of slave owners and indios, whereby past customs and current legal frameworks dictated how arguments were being made. Over time, the belief that particular habitats harbored bellicose indios faded, and just war rhetoric diminished; the documents also reveal a palpable erosion of confidence in the papereality of written documents and brands, as the designation of indios as legal minors (miserables) who were assigned a special legal representative took hold. Into the 1550s and beyond, litigants began to rely on creative contradistinctions about Spanish or Portuguese imperial designations and on arguments related to sovereignty, territoriality, and imagined possession as they designated indios as slaves or free from bondage.

Witness depositions, paper documents, and brands defined indios by their places of origin, genealogy of bondage, and, occasionally, ethnicity or parentage. The use of physiognomic markers and descriptors to identify indios was also central to how arguments about place of origin or enslaveability were being made. Changes from the 1530s to the 1580s in the use of color descriptors such as *loro*, *blanco*, and *indio* reflected concerns in Castile with religious heritage, enslaveability, and differentiating who was whom as the kingdom became increasingly globalized. The use of such descriptors also reflected the experiences of highly mobile Castilians and others who had come into contact with different peoples, whether in Castile or in another setting.

For the men and women discussed in this book, slavery involved physical dislocation, greater mobility than they had previously known, and entering new households with new expectations. Surviving bondage in Castile required establishing intimacies with others who had also been displaced and who were also called indios, whether they had come from Goa or the Moluccas or Brazil. In the courtroom, surviving bondage entailed being perceived as someone one was not or as someone one wanted to be. For Castilians who had experienced or heard about different habitats, it meant constructing stories about bondage that relayed certain kinds of truth about boundaries and possession and that which they could not classify. Recreating the conditions of enslavement involved collapsing time and space into a legible narrative and calling forth imagined imperial boundaries. It necessitated recalling a moment of inscription as a slave that had occurred ten or twenty years before. Being indio in sixteenth-century Castile connected the worlds and individual histories of Castilians and others by means of journeys, brandings, the play of descriptive terminology, the power of documentation, and the ways perception and cultural conceptions could constitute selves and others.

The dismantling of indigenous slavery in Castile was neither straightforward nor easy, and new legislative practices only enhanced the liminal status of indios as neither free nor enslaved for decades to come. The majority of indios who crossed the Atlantic or circulated as commodities throughout the Western Hemisphere began their treks as young children. But this most likely did not influence perceptions held by Crown and church authorities, including Bartolomé de las Casas, that indios were the childlike, innocent victims of brutal atrocities rendered on them by so-called Christians. The impression that indios were in need of Crown protection, as Anthony Pagden and others have argued, had other roots, both theological and legal.[4] Still, the paternalism that drove the continued enslavement of children and the categorization of indios as neither slaves nor free in Spanish America, even after the passage of the New Laws, needs to be investigated further, since it has profound implications for understanding ethnogenesis and the relationship between Spanish paternalism and indigenous family formation in the early colonial period.

The passage of the New Laws, which was due in part to the efforts of Las Casas, has been considered a decisive moment in early colonial Spanish American and Spanish history. But these laws were severely tested in the courts of Spain and in other ways in Spanish America. Many of their tenets were rescinded or ignored. The Crown never issued a retroactive emancipation proclamation, nor was there a complete and protracted elimination of indigenous slavery in the sixteenth century. Even in Castile, where vassals of the Spanish empire were the first to hear the town crier report the news that the indios were free by their nature, many continued for decades to assume that indios were slaves. In Spanish America the passage of the New Laws brought little immediate relief for those unjustly enslaved. It took the arrival, in 1548, of a Crown servant, Licenciate Alonso López de Cerrato, to free thousands of indio slaves being held illegally in Central America.[5] Even after the spotty Crown efforts to free slaves were completed by the early 1550s, indios remained as legal minors under the tutelage of the Crown, with conditional freedom commensurate with performing required labor and paying tribute to a new master.[6] Many complained that indios had merely switched owners. As the Crown gradually extended its control over the distribution of indigenous laborers to Spaniards throughout Spanish America, it also exacted its pound of flesh from the native peoples as producers of goods and services.

Once they had gained their freedom to be treated as sovereign subjects, indios in Castile and Latin America no longer had to wrestle with the conundrum of being both property and a person; they were free to move where they wanted, serve whomever they wished, and earn a meager salary, at least in principle. Trained as carpenters or domestic servants, some migrated to Seville or other cities, where they could find gainful work and attach themselves to new employers with new expectations. No doubt many remained in the employ of their former masters, as moving elsewhere and insinuating themselves into new households would have been too daunting, especially for those who had children and spouses in tow.

Becoming a free vassal was a lived practice, not just a legal pronounce-
ment. For the female litigant who stated that she now ate her bread like any
free woman or the witness who identified herself as a vecina (a permanent
resident), their new status brought daily perquisites and feelings of rootedness. For others, it was a shallow victory. While some freedpersons received
back payment for their years of service, others did not. The archives include
references to women like Antonia, freed in 1574, who then had to request a
donation of four ducats from the Crown to finance her long journey back to
her children in Cáceres, in southwest Spain.[8] Though she was now a royal
vassal with the legal right to protection as a miserable, the barriers of economic and social paternalism still severely compromised her mobility and
limited her options.

The stigma of having been an indio slave also carried over to the next
generation. Freed mothers protecting their children from a fate similar to
theirs sometimes relied on archival repositories to represent the "truth,"
sometimes to no avail.[9] Records kept by notaries or housed in the archive
of the Casa were sometimes lost, requiring sworn statements of authorities
that a particular slave had, in fact, been freed.[10] But even when there were
pieces of paper representing "reality," they were not always enough to bring
justice.[11] The right to be treated as free and the assumption that one was free
depended on the active participation of former masters and slaves and the
surrounding community. Even documents housed in the archival repository, which historians generally see as constant and formidable, could succumb to dust and oblivion. After all, the archive was only viable because of
those who made it so.

If, in some instances, freed indios could rely on paper or local authorities
to implement justice, the Crown, too, had to fulfill its obligation to protect
indios as legal minors by issuing decrees compelling former masters to pay
the return passage to their places of origin.[12] There were successful instances
of families of freed indios returning to their homelands, occasionally petitioning the king for financial and legal assistance.[13] Gaining one's freedom,
however, did not guarantee that former slave owners would relinquish their
desire to control bodies and fates. The records show a few Castilians who
went to great lengths to resist the wishes of indio servants to return home,
relying on deep-rooted discriminatory attitudes or assumptions about the
submission and possession of indios, the association of indioness with inferior characteristics, and the ambiguous meanings of "freedom."[14]

Did freedom for indios in Castile resonate differently than it did for their
counterparts in Spanish America? The answer is not entirely clear, although

research in Lima, Peru, shows former females slaves from Central America establishing solid networks based on new labor and kinship affiliations.[15] Archival forays in other locations may demonstrate how former slaves navigated the fine line between bondage, free servitude, and the lived experiences of liberation, especially in areas where slavery persisted.

Although narrative accounts of early colonial Spanish American history portray the New Laws as a defining moment for indigenous people, it is less well known in the literature that the commodification of indios in both the Spanish and Portuguese domains continued well into the seventeenth century. Just-war forays by the Spanish against the Chichimecas, Pijao, or Araucanians continued, as did the capture and sale of hundreds of enemy peoples by different indigenous ethnicities in the littoral of northern South America.[16] After 1565, as Spaniards learned to navigate the Pacific currents, and as the Iberian Union (1580–1640) enhanced commercial links between Portuguese and Spanish merchants in South and East Asia, countless numbers of slaves from South and East Asia (and, most notably, from the Spanish and Muslim Philippines) who were categorized as "chinos" began arriving in Mexico and elsewhere. They mainly served as domestic laborers and artisans.[17] Although many had originated from the Spanish domains of the Philippines, authorities in Mexico purposefully avoided labeling these "chino" slaves as *indios* for more than one hundred years so that they could not petition for their freedom as Spanish vassals protected by the New Laws. In fact, it was not until 1672 when a Spanish royal decree declared them to be free indios.[18] Works such as Tatiana Seijas's *Asian Slaves in Colonial Mexico* remind us of how central ambiguous identifiers—whether *indios of just war* or *chinos as not-indios*—were to the process of creating slaves and prolonging slavery in both urban and so-called frontier areas of the Spanish empire long after the New Laws had been implemented.

Despite laws prohibiting indios from being removed from their homelands in the Spanish domains, many continued to be deracinated and moved stealthily to other locations. In areas of the Spanish empire where slavery and deracination persisted, the color and category indio retained connotations of enslaveability as well as freedom. Although the numbers pale in comparison with the plight of African diasporic peoples in bondage, indio slavery did persist into the seventeenth century. Indigenous bondage must therefore figure into our discussions about what constituted indio identification not only during the conquest and early colonial era, but throughout the mid-colonial period. Indios were free tribute-paying subjects, but they were also slaves, and historians could deepen their explorations of colonial relations by studying how these colonial vassals experienced the unfree-free labor continuum in rural and urban settings.

In different ways, the works of Matthew Restall, Tiya Miles, James Brooks, and Rachel O'Toole, among others, remind us that we need to put individuals distinguished as "blacks" or as "Indians" into the same analytical framework.[19] This is especially relevant when considering the ongoing slaveries and forms of dependence, servility, and coerced labor of both African and indigenous people in colonial Spanish America. Such a methodological receptivity enables us to better understand the complex social and cultural interrelationships of subordinated colonial subjects, how laws and regulations revealed fears about and expectations of those subjects, and how labor relations and experiences of bondage and freedom were constituted by subordinated people utilizing laws and customary practices to navigate difficult circumstances. Understanding these relations, whether in colonial Spanish America or Castile, in a constitutive manner also illuminates colonial governance not as an abstraction, but as intimate, negotiated practices.

While it is important to understand how the practices of indigenous bondage in Spanish America resonated with concurrent slaveries elsewhere in the world, the stories of the displacement and dispersal of indios from Portuguese and Spanish America to the European continent are important because they help us understand the global unfolding of what it meant to be an indio in the early modern world. The construct indio was more diffuse a signifier than readers might imagine. Not only was it imposed by Spaniards on a variety of distinct people (or purposefully *not* imposed on slaves such as the "chinos" who went to Mexico), but as a lived practice the label came to have different meanings depending on its cultural and legal context. Yet, as malleable as the construct was, people did fully inhabit the category indio for strategic and identification purposes. Just as twenty-first-century people continue to struggle with the question "Who is an Indian (indio)?"—especially when navigating the tense interface between individuality, community, and the "state"—indigenous people of the sixteenth century also grappled with the tensions and advantages of being associated with the label in the courtroom context, by claiming it in different ways.[20]

But if the category *indio* was multifaceted in its expression in Castile throughout the sixteenth century and into the seventeenth, what might it tell us about how the construct changed in different locations in Spanish America? How, for instance, did the introduction of a new construct, naboría (neither slave nor free), influence interethnic relations on Hispaniola? How did naborías from the Bahamas (the Lucayos), the Gulf of Paría, Brazil, and the

Lesser Antilles, some marked with brands on their legs rather than on their faces, complicate the significations of the term *indio,* which at that point included free and unfree laborers who were not assigned to encomenderos? What about the changing nature of ethnogenesis, as thousands of foreigners labeled by the Spaniards as indios migrated involuntarily to Santo Domingo, Mexico City, Guatemala, Panama, or Peru? How did that intra-American mobility change the cultural and demographic landscape? Important ethnographic works have shown how seasonal migrations and relationships to the environment and to labor demands helped constitute ethnicity and social relations among some indigenous groups. But we have to dig deeper still to complicate nonbureaucratic usages of the construct indio. For instance, how did the early colonial processes of deracination and slavery, so often ignored by historians, elucidate what it meant to be a member of a household, a community, or an ethnicity?

Although I have focused on the historical processes that constituted indios in Castile, the identification of indios as slaves or free based on documents, physicality, and place of origin was also occurring concurrently in different legal venues throughout Spanish America. When I first came across a document about a pock-faced man named Francisco, trained as a chairmaker and originally from Tenochtitlán, who was accused of being a branded slave in Lima, Peru, in 1546, I decided that it was an interesting example of the power and fragility of paternalism in master-servant relations. Especially relevant to my assessment was the fact that Francisco had become extremely vulnerable to mistreatment once his benefactor, the governor Francisco Pizarro, was assassinated, in 1541.[21] Francisco was called a slave of just war, but witnesses on his behalf argued that the pockmarks on his face were the result of disease, not of a royal brand, and he insisted that he had come from Mexico as a free man. What struck me later was how similar the processes of identifying Francisco were to those being used by complainants and defendants on the other side of Atlantic. With my "skilled vision" now honed from reading Castilian documents, I realized that Francisco's story had a larger scope: it was both locally and imperially relevant.[22] It could be simultaneously "located" in the context of civil war in Peru and as a part of the dismantling of indio slavery that was taking place in different locales of the Spanish empire.

A later archival source, a 1613 census of Lima, taught me a similar lesson about the enduring importance of place of origin in determining one's slave or free status, about the arbitrariness of labeling, and about how slavery was a reality for many indigenous vassals. In that door-to-door listing of the city's indigenous inhabitants, I located the act of registering a fourteen-year-old india slave named María Magdalena. When the census taker Miguel Contreras asked her place of origin, she said that it was Majes, a peaceful area of Arequipa. But her mistress claimed that she was from Santa Cruz de la Sierra, a war zone associated with Chiriguanos deemed by law to be enslaveable. María insisted on being inscribed in the archives as she originally stated, and Contreras obliged her.[23] The point here is that the disputes over naturalezas and marked bodies I have analyzed in this volume can help us to better understand the broader legal, geographic, and cultural contexts within which circumscribed indios in Spanish and Portuguese America were also being identified and identifying themselves in the sixteenth and seventeenth centuries. This, too, is a part of the indioscape: how the contents of indioness "held" within documents are not necessarily spatially bound to that particular moment of inscription, but also have a relationship to other archivally inscribed moments occurring elsewhere. Such revelations help expose some of the more insidious aspects of colonial governance.

Much like the variety of usages, practices, and imagined perceptions that occurred in different sites in Castile, each American locale—whether in Bogotá, Lima, Mexico City, Nueva Galizia, Panama, or Soconusco—employed the legal and cultural category of indio distinctly and developed its own contextual rubric to distinguish indios from the other peoples there. It was a legal category that enabled Crown authorities to exact tribute and labor obligations, but it was also a construct that could have other contextual meanings and applications. In situ definitions and practices of identification developed and changed, as in the cases of Beatríz and Felipa in the village of Carmona. These notions were transformed by the larger continuities and interactions among the Mediterranean, Pacific, and Atlantic worlds, perpetuated, in part, by those involved in the slave trade or by the many Castilians who had experienced different parts of the globe before taking up a post or trade in Latin America. Given these local and imperial confluences, we should be very cautious in how we employ an empire-wide system of classifying and naturalizing indios in colonial Spanish and Portuguese America. By considering the displacement of thousands of indigenous people, we can begin to disassemble our own geographical containment of arenas like "Mesoamerica," the "Caribbean," or "Latin America." Instead of atomizing these artificially constructed geopolitical regions, studying diasporic indigenous slaves can help us see that "Latin America" was not only part of a broader Atlantic and Pacific world, but that it consisted of territories, people, and cultural arenas that were simultaneously local and global. Just as some

African scholars would like us to move away from a strictly Atlantic-centric and European-driven way of conceptualizing the African diaspora, I argue that considering indigenous slavery in a decentered manner will carry us beyond hemispheric confines and into other oceans, continents, and territorial realms. By decentering the center, we can uncover histories of rupture and displacement that provide a fresher sense of the intricate breadth of early colonial rule.

On the other hand, the construct indio is so large, so geographically all-encompassing of so many distinct parts of the world, that the articulation of its nearly boundless parameters can serve as a metaphor for early colonialism: the desire to possess that which has not yet been possessed, but which should not be possessed by other European powers; or, conversely, the desire to inscribe peoples and territories as not-yours. Just as kings and lawyers and members of the Council of the Indies wanted the label *indio* to take on a worldwide cast(e), individuals from China, the Moluccas, Brazil, and Peru litigating in Castile wanted to be viewed as indios because they equated the term with freedom. And just as certain people in Spanish America wanted to be categorized as indio in order to avoid paying the sales tax (*alcabala*), to avoid being interrogated by the Inquisition, or to benefit from legal privileges associated with the corporate category, some individuals in the Castilian courtroom were eager to be labeled indio, since it meant freedom from bondage.[25] Thus, the indio construct was not a fixed essence or an end result, but a process of identifying oneself or someone else for particular purposes.[26] An analysis of these litigation suits begs scholars to examine more carefully the processes of identification taking place in different contexts and documentary loci, and not to assume an Iberian set of fixed, stable descriptors related to enslaveability and identity.

At the same time, however, the desire to establish colonial governance meant creating taxonomies that named, labeled, characterized and distinguished colonial subjects. As a comparative knowledge about non-Castilians grew, attempts were made, in the latter part of the sixteenth century, to establish a normative and universalizing order based on belonging and difference. This was key to establishing and maintaining colonial rule.[27] Part of that process involved creating bureaucracies that structured identification in particular ways. The witness depositions and documentary evidence I have analyzed were presented in Castilian legal contexts with their own sets of expectations and ways of framing discourse, which changed over the course of the sixteenth century. Further research might reveal how (and whether) particular forms of documentation and documentary contexts—

the Inquisition or idolatry records, parish registers, chronicles, passenger licenses, paintings, or bills of sale—created and sustained particular processes of sense-making or their own universalizing discourses about how to describe or codify differences or capture an indio essence.[28] Such research might help better contextualize the vast dissimilarities between the identification and appropriation of distinct identities by those who toiled in the fields and homes of Castilians throughout the Spanish empire and the stylized legal imaginary on which they depended.

Finally, I ask readers to reimagine an indioscape that integrates mobility and the cultural imaginary into our analytical explorations of the early modern world. Many of the stories told in these litigation suits are of "globetrotting" movements and pathways associated with deracination. But like the presence of sailors, merchants, and even pirates, the presence of indio slaves on board the ships that navigated the Atlantic, Indian, and Pacific Oceans served as a reminder of the continual lack of fixity of imperial borders and as evidence of expanding geographic and commercial trajectories.[29] In the courtroom, indio litigants constituted the pathways of the world in dynamic and creative ways. On land, the presence of slaves in village and city dwellings exposed a *histoire croisée*—a crisscrossing of peoples from different cultures violently uprooted and relocated as a consequence of business enterprises, many of them illegal.[30] We have only to turn to the rich scholarship on the African diaspora to see how the forced mobility of millions from west to east and from east to west radically altered the cultural, historical, and historiographic landscape.

But in this volume I not only track the mobility of indios themselves, but also show how sense-making notions about being indio circulated— how mobility influenced changing itineraries of knowledge and perceptions about the peoples and territories of the broader world. Whether indios were characterized as inherently free or as rebels, uncircumcised Jews, moriscos, or cannibalistic heathens, or identified by a particular coloration or association with barbaric habitats, the construction of indioness was always relational to other local and global experiences and to other people in bondage. Such conceptualizations moved and circulated and also deeply permeated the cultural landscape of Castile, so much so that in Europe, the term *indio* came to connote savage-like peoples, which included peasants, Sicilians, and Asturians who had deviated from Catholicism.[31]

The displaced indios who litigated in the courtroom were a part of a complex spatiotemporal web of attachment, migration, perception, and legal ascriptions on both sides of the Atlantic; they were connected by inscribed social relations as they moved from one social space to another and shared their legal and cultural knowledge about how to be indio. Litigants and witnesses actively reconstructed and constituted the world through their perceptions of what it meant to be an indio in the sixteenth century. Inside and outside legal venues, they constructed an indioscape that connected the four parts of the world.

This leads to the larger issue of how we can better integrate overlapping spatiotemporal conceptualizations into our assessments of the involuntary and voluntary circulation of people and ideas in the early modern Iberian world.[32] A consideration of the lives of deracinated slaves provides an excellent way to decenter paradigms of center-periphery and Iberian-American imperial formation. It is also a more useful way to consider knowledge-making about colonial subjects as nonlinear, indirect, and fragmented. When we think of mobility, the ideas of changeability, instability, and inconstancy often come to mind. But mobility in an imperial context is also about both creative transformation and the ongoing desire to control others. It is not only about the physical movement of people from one context to another, but also about how perceptions and desires were reconstituted into narratives that established prerogatives, fixed boundaries, and mythologies.

As a consideration of these cases has shown, there was no self-referential Castilian "system," no clear-cut epistemology in the metropolis about self in relation to other on which discussions about indioness hinged. There was no center from which all things Iberian emerged and transculturated to the colonies. Knowledge moved within local and global settings. Legal wrangling and cultural exchanges in the chambers of the Casa and the Council of the Indies were transformative to the individual and collective lives of indigenous people elsewhere in the globe. Being indio meant conspiring with other indios and with scribes and legal advisors to change perceptions of indios as unfree laborers and not-quite-human-beings, and to recalibrate the category in small but significant ways.

Some of the migration stories told by litigants were true, but many were lies that revealed deeper truths. One of those truths is that a core arena of empire—the courtroom—represented the most peripheral symbols of empire itself: indio slaves. Over the decades, the deterritorialized margin became the center, exposing what was wrong with colonial governance as it had existed for fifty, sixty, and seventy years. Ultimately, these small stories of displaced individuals pay humble tribute to the lost stories of hundreds of thousands of dispossessed others who also left their naturalezas to cross land and sea and empires.

NOTES

Preface

1. Doña Inés de Pimentel was the wife of Don Fadrique Osorio de Toledo, marquis of Villafranca.
2. AGI, Justicia 1178, n. 4.
3. "Testimony, Bartolomé de las Casas," AGI, Justicia 1178, n. 4, s.f.
4. For Esteban, see AGI, Justicia 1023, n. 1, r. 1, 112v; for Martín Quintín, see AGI, Justicia 1023, n. 2, r. 2, pieça 8; for Baltasar, see AGI, Justicia 1038, no. 2, 33r.

Introduction

1. See the recent, revisionist treatment of Las Casas in Castro, *Another Face of Empire*, 2. The list of works on Las Casas is enormous. Several of the key studies are by Friede and Keen, *Bartolomé de las Casas in History*; Giménez Fernández, *Bartolomé de las Casas: Delegado de Cisneros para la reformación de las Indias*; Giménez Fernández, *Bartolomé de las Casas: Capellán de S.M. Carlos I*.
2. Throughout this volume, I use the term *indigenous* to refer to the native people of colonial Latin America.
3. See also Hanke, "Bartolomé de las Casas"; Hanke, "More Heat."
4. Yannakakis, "Indigenous People and Legal Culture."
5. The figure of 650,000 is an estimate, and probably on the low side. Given rampant illegal slave-raiding activities and the lack of accurate records, it is difficult to accurately determine the numbers of indigenous who were deracinated from their homelands. Estimates for the Lucanas people of the Bahamas range from thirty thousand to forty thousand (Sauer, *The Early Spanish Main*). Karen Anderson-Córdoba calculates that some 34,000 "foreign" slaves (including Lucayos) were taken to Hispaniola and Puerto Rico ("Hispaniola and Puerto Rico," 10, 268). Enrique Otte estimates that six thousand slaves were taken from the northern coast of Venezuela, Trinidad, Curaçao, and Cubagua, but that seems low to me (Otte, *Las perlas del Caribe*; Otte, "Los jerónimos y el tráfico humano en el Caribe"; and Mira Caballos, *El indio antillano*, 391–99).

For Honduras, Linda Newson claims that 150,000 slaves were taken (Newson, *The Cost of Conquest*; Newson, *Aboriginal and Spanish Colonial Trinidad*). For information about the Nicaraguan and Central American indios (estimated at 300,000–450,000) who were deracinated to Panama and South America, see Radell, "The Indian Slave Trade"; Sherman, *Forced Native Labor*. Bishop Zumárraga's total estimate is fifteen thousand; he suggests that nine thousand were taken from Panuco and six thousand from throughout New Spain; see Chipman, "The Traffic in Indian Slaves." The deracination of peoples *within* the domains of New Spain, the Andes, Brazil, the Rio de la Plata, and Panama must also be taken into account. The historian Brett Rushforth estimates that in the Western Hemisphere between two and four million Indians were enslaved from the late fifteenth century to the mid-nineteenth (*Bonds of Alliance*, 9).

6. Foreman, *Indians Abroad*; Floyd, *The Columbus Dynasty in the Caribbean*; Deive, *La Española y la esclavitud de los indios*; Deive, *Heterodoxía e Inquisición en Santo Domingo*.

7. On freeing those indio slaves brought to Castile, see "Real Cédula," 20/VI/1500, in Konetzke, *Colección de documentos*, 1:4. On their status as laboring vassals, see "Instrucción a frey Nicolás de Ovando," 16/IX/1501, AGI, Indiferente General 418, libro 1, 39r–42r; "Real Provisión," Medina del Campo, 20/XII/1503, in Konetzke, *Colección de documentos*, 1:16–17.

8. By 1504, Isabel was dead, and massive enslavement ensued, as did the inconsistent, contradictory, and piecemeal enactment of legislation that lasted for decades (see Mira Caballos, *Indios y mestizos americanos*, 50–57). The scholarly literature on the legal and theological status of the Indians of the Spanish territories in the sixteenth century is enormous. Seminal works include Zavala, *Servidumbre natural y libertad Cristiana*; Hanke, *The Spanish Struggle*; Pagden, *The Fall of Natural Man*; Seed, " 'Are These Not Also Men?' "

9. In this book I do not address the indigenous slaves in the kingdoms of Aragón, Granada, and so on. The historian Esteban Mira Caballos has calculated that 2,442 indigenous slaves went to Castile from 1492 to 1550. This number, as he admits, does not consider the illegal traffic of slaves, the majority of whom were shipped to Spain before 1520 (Mira Caballos, *Indios y mestizos americanos*, 142–43). See also Julián, *Bancos, ingenios y esclavos*, 17–58.

10. "Indios americanos en Sevilla, siglo XVI," Historia de Sevilla (blog), 2 March 2010, http://historiadesevilla.blogia.com/2010/030207-indios-americanos-en-sevilla-s.-xvi-.php.

11. I borrow this term from Rothman, *Brokering Empire*, 2–15.

12. See the map designed by Esteban Mira Caballos that depicts the towns and cities in Castile where indios resided with their masters (Mira Caballos, *Indios y mestizos Americanos*, 175–76).

13. O'Gorman, "Sobre la naturaleza bestial del indio americano," 143–44.

14. Rumeu de Armas, *La política indígenista de Isabel la Católica*, 341–42; Pagden, *The Fall of Natural Man*, chaps. 3 and 4.

15. "R. Provision para poder cautivar a los canibales rebeldes," Segovia, 30/X/1503, in Konetzke, *Colección de documentos*, 1:14–16; iterated in the Laws of Burgos (1511), "R. Provision . . . los indios caribes se puedan tomar por esclavos," Burgos, 23/XII/1511, in Konetzke, *Colección de documentos*, 1:31). Francisco de Vitoria later argued (1526–1529) that the anthropophagic tendencies of the Caribs did not justify their enslavement (see Pagden, *The Fall of Natural Man*, 65, 80–86; Castañeda Delgado, "La política española con los caribes," 115).

16. Frederick H. Russell argues that medieval notions of just war derived from Augustine, whose conviction was that "war was both a consequence of sin and a remedy for it" (*The Just War in the Middle Ages*, 16).

17. Zurara, *Chronica do descobrimento de Guinea*; Wolf, "The 'Moors' of West Africa," 455; Constable, "Muslim Spain and Mediterranean Slavery"; Muldoon, *Popes, Lawyers*, 193 n. 14. The neologism *Guinea* encompassed the Wolof peoples to the north of the Senegal River and the Mandinga peoples to the south.

18. On the determination that the people of the Canary Islands were Christians, see Rumeu de Armas, *La política indigenista de Isabel la Católica*, 37–38.

19. Muldoon, *Popes, Lawyers*, 140–42.

20. Seed, "Taking Possession and Reading Texts," 203.

21. Quoted in Guitar, "The Requirement," 2:545, who quotes Hanke, *The Spanish Struggle*, 33–34, who quotes from Fernández de Oviedo y Valdés, *Historia general y natural*, lib. 29, chap. 7, 131–32.

22. Queen Isabel's application of the legal term *just war* occurred first against the "rebels" of the province of Higuey, whom she ordered to be enslaved ("Real Cédula," Burgos, 30/IV/1508, in Konetzke, *Colección de documentos*, 1:17–18).

23. For a consideration of debates over the enslaveability of the Chichimecas, see Cook, "Forbidden Crossings," chap. 3.

24. See las Casas, *Apologética historia sumaria*, 1:chaps. 23–39.

25. Real Academia Española, *Diccionario de autoridades*, 5:591.

26. Until 1492, Muslims living in Al-Andalus engaged in the practice of ransoming captives taken by the Christians (see Marín and El Hour, "Captives, Children, and Conversion").

27. Sherman, *Forced Native Labor*, 19.

28. On the commerce of slaves in Castilla del Oro, see "Real Provisión," 6/IX/1521, in Konetzke, *Colección de documentos*, 1:71–72. On the freedom of indio slaves, see "Real Provisión," 1/XII/1525, in Konetzke, *Colección de documentos*, 1:78–80. On the freedom of *indios* of New Spain, see "Real Cédula," 9/XI/1526, in Konetzke, *Colección de documentos*, 1:87–88. On the prohibition of slavery, see "Real Provisión," 2/VIII/1530, in Konetzke, *Colección de documentos*, 1:134–36. On the conditions under which slaves of just war and ransom could be taken, see "Real Provisión," 20/II/1534, in Konetzke, *Colección de documentos*, 1:153–59. For additional legislation prohibiting or qualifying different aspects of indio slavery, see Encinas and Gallo, *Cedulario indiano*, 4:361–77; Puga, "Carta al Virrey," Valladolid, 16/IV/1550; *Provisiones, cédulas, instrucciones de S.M.*; *Recopilación de Leyes de los Reynos de las Indias*.

29. By 1514, naborías were being distributed to lower-ranking Spaniards, on His-paniola and in Puerto Rico, who had not received an allotment of *repartimiento* indigenous laborers (Arranz Márquez, *Repartimientos y encomiendas en la Isla Española*; "Real Cédula," 27/IV/1514, in Konetzke, *Colección de documentos*, 1:60–61).

30. Because laws and ordinances did not clearly define the parameters of a guard-ian's legal power over a naboría until 1539 (and even then they were ignored), many naborías were treated like property and sold. Royal legislation reveals this ambivalence (see "Real Cédula," Madrid, 19/IX/1539, in Konetzke, *Colección de documentos*, 1:194–96; "Real Cédula," Madrid, 5/IX/1540, in Konetzke, *Colec-ción de documentos*, 1:197–98). Morella A. Jimenez G[raziani] points out that on Hispaniola masters paid small amounts of money for each naboría, which would have monetized these nonslave indigenous peoples (*La esclavitud en Venezuela*, 125).

31. The term *naboría* probably had legal antecedents to the term *servidumbre* in medieval Castilian law. Under the legal terms of servidumbre, a laborer (siervo), either male or female, was awarded by contractual agreement by one lord to another to work for life with remuneration of some sort. The master could not sell or remove the servant from his place of origin. On the differences between siervos, *criados*, and *esclavos*, and on how historical context, rather than laws, often defines relationships of dependency and bondage, see Stella, "Travail et dépendances au Moyen Age"; Martín Cásares, "Domestic Service in Spain," 194, 196.

32. Indigenous people labeled as naborías were taken from islands designated as "useless" (e.g., the Bahamas) or from locations where Spaniards could not find gold (Sauer, *The Early Spanish Main*, 159–60; "Real Cédula," 21/VI/1511, in Konetzke, *Colección de documentos*, 1:26–27).

33. For Cuba, see "Real Cédula," Madrid, 5/XI/1540, in Konetzke, *Colección de documentos*, 1:197–98. For Guatemala and Honduras, see "Real Cédula," Talavera, 11/I/1541, in Konetzke, *Colección de documentos*, 1:198–99.

34. Hanke, *The Spanish Struggle*, 91.

35. Muro Orejón, *Las Leyes Nuevas de 1542-43*, 10.

36. Rumeu de Armas, *La política indigenista de Isabel la Católica*, 141; Ramos Pérez, *Audacia, negocios y politica*, 480–81, 500–501.

37. Walter Johnson, "Inconsistency, Contradiction, and Complete Confusion," 407.

38. On slaves and servants as military auxiliaries, see Matthew and Oudijk, *Indian Conquistadors*. On naborías as status-seeking military auxiliaries in Oaxaca, see Yannakakis, "Allies or Servants?"

39. On the vulnerability of children to enslavement, see Campbell, Miers, and Miller, *Children in Slavery*. See the example of Catalina, from Santa Marta in Colombia, who was enslaved as a child, brought to Seville, and sold in 1537 as a "slave of just war" ("Venta de esclava," 4/I/1537, AGI, Justicia 1153, n. 2).

40. "Real provisión," Toledo, 20/I/1534, in Konetzke, *Colección de documentos*, 1:153–59.

41. The Portuguese historian António de Almeida Mendes reported that children and women constituted more than 70 percent of slaves coming from Senegambia to Lisbon between 1499 and 1522 ("Child Slaves," 23).
42. Patterson, *Slavery and Social Death*.
43. On the importance of children as historical subjects, see González and Premo, *Raising an Empire*, 238–45. See chapter 2 for further discussion of household formation, intimacy, and violence.
44. On moriscos in Seville, see Pike, "An Urban Minority," 369; Morales Padrón, *Historia de Sevilla*, 91; Fernández Chaves and Pérez García, *En los márgenes de la Ciudad de Dios*, esp. 38–39, 42–45, 83–140, 521; Domínguez Ortíz and Vincent, *Historia de los moriscos*, chap. 4.
45. The population of Seville nearly doubled, from 55,000 in 1534 to 100,293 in 1565, and then increased to 120,519 by 1585. See Esteban Mira Caballos, "El padrón de vecinos de Sevilla y su tierra de 1571," Historia de Sevilla (blog), 3 February 2010, http://historiadesevilla.blogia.com/2010/030205-el-padron-de-vecinos-de-sevilla-y-su-tierra-de-1571.php. Antonio Dominguez Ortíz has argued that the archbishopric of Seville included nearly fifteen thousand slaves by the end of the sixteenth century (*La esclavitud en Castilla*, 369). On "the endless globe," see Pérez-Mallaína Bueno and Phillips, *Spain's Men of the Sea*, 1.
46. Pike, "Seville in the Sixteenth Century"; Pike, "Sevillian Society in the Sixteenth Century"; Franco Silva, "El indígena americano"; Franco Silva, *La esclavitud en Sevilla*. On West African slaves in Seville, see Peraza, *Historia de Sevilla*, 71; Lansley, "La esclavitud negra."
47. Torres Ramírez and Hernández Palomo, *Andalucía y América*, 249–74. For a detailed discussion of the various routes that slaves from Portuguese territories took to arrive in Seville, see Fernández Chaves and Pérez García, "Las redes de la trata negrera," 8. By the 1570s, more than one thousand slaves were sold in Seville on an annual basis, with 90 percent of them remaining for local or provincial use (Fernández Chaves and Pérez García, "Las redes de la trata negrera," 20).
48. Smallwood, *Saltwater Slavery*; Rediker, *The Slave Ship*.
49. Northrup, *Africa's Discovery of Europe*; Spicer, *Revealing the African Presence in Renaissance Europe*; Earle and Lowe, *Black Africans in Renaissance Europe*.
50. Bryant, *Rivers of Gold, Lives of Bondage*, chap. 2; Smallwood, *Saltwater Slavery*, chap. 4.
51. Moreno Navarro and Burgos, *La antigua hermandad de los negros de Sevilla*; Phillips, *Slavery in Medieval and Early Modern Iberia*; Gómez, *Exchanging Our Country Marks*; Chambers, "Ethnicity in the African Diaspora."
52. Gómez, *Reversing Sail*.
53. Werner and Zimmermann, "Beyond Comparison"; Mason, "Reading New World Bodies."
54. The papal bulls were *Illius qui* (1442), *Dum diversas* (1452), *Divino amore communitati* (1452), and *Inter caetera* (1462). For a discussion of indio slaves in sixteenth-century Brazil, see Schwartz, "Indian Labor and New World Plantations." In the Portuguese imperial context, indios were also referred to as

gentios, a term that Portuguese chroniclers used to mean non-Christian peoples (Castanheda, *Ho primeiro livro da Historia do descobrimento*, vol. 1 and 2:459, where he refers to trade with the Maluku gentios). In Brazil, indios were called gentios or *negros da terra* (see Nóbrega, *Cartas do Brasil*, 82; Monteiro, "The Heathen Castes of Sixteenth-Century Latin America," 704–5).

55. In 1570 King Sebastian declared that the Indians of Brazil (gentios) were, by their nature, free ("Lei de 20 de Março de 1570 sobre a liberdade dos gentios," in Georg Thomas, *Política indigenista dos Portugueses no Brasil*, 221–22). However, pressure from the Portuguese inhabitants of Brazil led to a "softer" royal decree, in 1573, that allowed indio slavery to continue, except in cases of blatant abuse (Mauró, *Le Portugal et L'Atlantique*, 149; Miki, "Slave and Citizen in Black and Red").

56. Owensby, *Empire of Law and Indian Justice in Colonial Mexico*, 24, after O'Gorman, *The Invention of America*. Early (1500–1505) Portuguese, German, and Venetian letters discussing the "discovery" of Brazil did not use the term *indio* to identify the native inhabitants, but rather *gentes* or *homens da terra* or, occasionally, *animais racionais* (rational animals) (Amado and Figueiredo, *Brasil 1500*, 133–35, 277, 286, 314).

57. Lowe, "The Intimacy of Four Continents."

58. Smallwood, *Saltwater Slavery*, 49–52, 67–72.

59. The construction of blackness, and especially its conflation with slavery is beginning to receive attention from Africanist scholars (Ware, "Slavery in Islamic Africa," 50–51; Miller, "Beyond Blacks, Bondage and Blame," 9). On the construction of blackness in colonial South America, see Bryant, *Rivers of Gold, Lives of Bondage*. On the constitutive relations between "blacks" and "Indians" in northern Peru, see O'Toole, *Bound Lives*. See also Sweet, *Domingos Álvares*, 3–7; Northrup, *Africa's Discovery of Europe*; and Walter Johnson, *Soul by Soul*, which have been particularly influential for my study.

60. Miller, "Beyond Blacks, Bondage and Blame"; Stella, "Introducción," 5–6.

61. Northrup, "Becoming African"; Penningroth, *The Claims of Kinfolk*; Sensbach, *Rebecca's Revival*; Anderson, *The Betrayal of Faith*.

62. Walter Johnson, *Soul by Soul*; Brown, *The Reaper's Garden*.

63. Appadurai, "Global Ethnoscapes," 464–65.

64. Gilroy, *The Black Atlantic*, 3.

65. Appadurai, "Global Ethnoscapes," 471.

66. Take, for example, how the scholar Lhoussain Simour, in "(De)slaving History," examines the ways in which the Moroccan Al-Azemmouri's journey to North America and his identification have been analyzed by Al-Azemmouri's contemporaries and in current historiography.

67. Ware, "Slavery in Islamic Africa"; Toledano, "Enslavement in the Ottoman Empire"; Chatterjee and Eaton, *Slavery and South Asian History*.

68. Saunders, *A Social History of Black Slaves and Freedmen in Portugal*; Stella, *Histoire d'esclavages dans la péninsule Ibérique*.

69. Ginzburg, *The Cheese and the Worms*; Ginzburg, "Latitude, Slaves and the Bible"; and Ginzburg, "Microhistory."

70. AGI, Justicia 1021, n. 3, r. 1, 19v.

71. Jijón y Caamaño, *Sebastián de Benalcázar*, 1:13.

72. Trujillo, *Relación del descubrimiento del reyno del Perú*, 47–48.

73. "Carta de obligación," AGNP, Protocolos, Libro Becerro, 10/VIII/1533, 57f.

74. Lockhart, *The Men of Cajamarca*, 395.

75. Two notable exceptions are Emma Anderson's *The Betrayal of Faith* and Jace Weaver's *The Red Atlantic*. "Globetrotting" comes from Games, "Atlantic History."

76. Among the 184 litigants were children of mothers who were the primary complainants. And there were certainly more than 184 litigants; for instance, the verdicts listed by year in Escribanía de Cámara 952 and 953 name several freed slaves whose records have been lost. References to cases no longer extant include a lawsuit between the indio Francisco and Cristóbal de Villacastín ("Compulsoria," AGI, Indiferente General 424, libro 22, 292r–v); a lawsuit between Isabel and Leonor Hernández in Seville ("Carta ejecutoria," 24/XII/1554, Valladolid, AGI, Indiferente General 425, libro 23, 125r); the testimony of Diego Cercado, where he refers to his own litigation suit ("Testimony, Diego Cercado," 9/IX/1553, AGI, Justicia 1023, n. 1, r. 1, 78r); and the case between Alonso Chaves, the cosmographer of the Casa, and the india Catalina ("Comparecencia," 14/II/1546, Madrid, AGI, Indiferente General 1963, libro 9, 337v–338r). Although litigation suits continued after 1585 and into the seventeenth century—several are analyzed by Tatiana Seijas in her book *Asian Slaves in Colonial Mexico*—I did not consider cases beyond 1585 because the slaves who litigated after that date came mainly from the Philippines.

77. For example, see "Pleito de Diego Manrique de Mexico," ARCV, PL Civiles, Pérez Alonso (F), Caja 546, 6, 1546/47.

78. Mira Caballos, *Indios y mestizos americanos*, 111–13.

79. A few slaves appear in sale records in the Archivo de Protocolos de Sevilla for the early period. See, for example, the sale of the twenty-year-old Costança, from Hispaniola, for 10.365 maravedís ("Venta Diego Sánchez Bravo a Juan Rodríguez," 21/IV/1509, in Archivo de Protocolos, *Catálogo de los fondos americanos*, 2:11).

80. For key works on indigenous slavery in Latin America, see Saco, *Historia de la esclavitud*; Zavala, *Los esclavos indios en Nueva España*; Zavala, *El servicio personal de los indios en el Perú*; Sherman, *Forced Native Labor*; Newson, *The Cost of Conquest*; Newson, *Indian Survival in Colonial Nicaragua*; Newson, *Life and Death in Early Colonial Ecuador*; Deive, *La española y la esclavitud de los indios*; Jiménez G[raziani], *La esclavitud en Venezuela*; Whitehead, "Indigenous Slavery in South America." A broader hemispheric perspective is taken by Gallay, "Indian Slavery."

81. On slaves in sixteenth-century Spain, see Stella, *Histoires d'esclavages dans la péninsule Ibérique*; Cortés López, "La esclavitud en España." On indios and Spanish legislation, see García Añoveros, "Carlos V."

82. For two examples, see Cook, *Demographic Collapse*; Newson, *Life and Death in Early Colonial Ecuador*.

83. Hartman, "Venus in Two Acts," 10.

84. Clifford, "Diasporas," 302; Cohen, "Was There an Amerindian Atlantic?" Until recently, overviews of slavery in the Americas did not focus on indigenous bondage. See, for instance, Eltis, Lewis, and Sokoloff, *Slavery in the Development of the Americas*. However, this is beginning to change. See Eltis and Engerman, *The Cambridge World History of Slavery* (which includes Neil L. Whitehead's "Indigenous Slavery in South America"). See also Gallay, "Indian Slavery."

85. Robert I. Burns, *Las Siete Partidas*; Owensby, *Empire of Law and Justice in Colonial Mexico*, 55–56; Benton, *Law and Colonial Cultures*, 44.

86. The Crown had set a precedent in 1477, when it determined that the people of the Canary Islands were free vassals and could not be enslaved. Yet this was after more than eighty thousand Guanches had been brutally enslaved and shipped to Castile or exterminated. Lobo Cabrera, *La esclavitud en las Canarias*; Cortés Alonso, *La esclavitud en Valencia*, doc. 99, 232; Mendes, "Child Slaves," 25; Rumeu de Armas, *La política indigenista de Isabel la Católica*.

87. In February 1552 a plaintiff named Francisca, who claimed to be from Guatemala, was waiting in one of the chambers (*salas*) adjacent to where the council met, when she was harassed by the prosecuting attorney to testify that she was from Brazil ("Question for witnesses against Juan de Oribe," II/1552, AGI, Justicia 1022, n. 1, r. 1, 35r).

88. On Brazilian slaves who crossed the border at Extremadura and were sold at Zafra, see Periáñez Gómez, "La esclavitud en Extremadura en la Edad Moderna," 61–62.

89. On the use of the term *naturaleza* to distinguish Spaniards from one another, see Herzog, *Defining Nations*, 8, 64–66; Real Academia Española, *Diccionario de autoridades*, 4:651.

90. Cristina Grasseni articulates skilled vision as "a capacity to look in a certain way as a result of training" ("Skilled Vision," 41). I would like to thank Joanne Rappaport for this reference.

91. On Seville, see Silva, *La esclavitud en Sevilla*, 63–72, 140–53. On Málaga, see Ladero Quesada, "La esclavitud por guerra," 63–88. On Valencia, see Cortés Alonso, *La esclavitud en Valencia*.

92. The *Siete Partidas* stated that a slave could bring a lawsuit against a master but could not represent himself in court since he was not his own master (Robert I. Burns, *Las Siete Partidas*, part 3, title 2, law 8, 3:539). Richard Kagan identifies abogados as university-trained legal experts, procuradores as procedural experts, and solicitors as agents who ensured that the lawsuit proceeded smoothly and that all paperwork was in order (*Lawsuits and Litigants in Castile*, 52).

93. For an example see AGI, Justicia 727, n. 9, 1538.

94. On the fiscal, see *Recopilación de Leyes de los Reinos de las Indias*, book 2, title 5, law 1; Bayle, *El protector de indios*; Schäfer, *El Consejo Real y Supremo de las Indias*, 119–20.

95. Schäfer, *El Consejo Real y Supremo de las Indias*, 85. Before his appointment as the first procurador de los indios, Diego Pantoja had served as a low paid

portero (literally "doorman," but referring to a person in charge of receiving and registering goods and legal complaints).

96. For an example of legal representatives observing how another, concurrent case was evolving, see AGI, Justicia 1028, n. 4, r. 3.

97. de la Puente, "Into the Heart of the Empire," 32.

98. Sweet, *Domingos Álvares*, 111–12.

99. Benton, *Law and Colonial Cultures*, 125–26.

100. Owensby, *Empire of Law and Indian Justice in Colonial Mexico*; Yannakakis, *The Art of Being In-Between*, 129–30; de la Puente, "Into the Heart of the Empire," 18; Lockhart, *The Nahuas after the Conquest*, 327–73.

101. The *Siete Partidas* specified the conditions under which property could be deposited (from the Latin, *depositum*). When two parties were engaged in a legal dispute involving property, in this case a slave, he or she was required by law to be placed in the "hands of some trustworthy person" and committed "to his charge until the controversy has been settled in court" (Robert I. Burns, *Las Siete Partidas*, part 5, title 3, law 1, 4:1017).

102. AGI, Justicia 1164, n. 6, r. 1, im. 61.

103. AGI, Justicia 831, n. 6.

104. See, for example, "Emplazamiento contra Catalina de Ragama," 22/IX/1561, AGI, Patronato 286, r. 85.

105. "Statement, Beatríz, india libre," AGI, Justicia 757, n. 3, 98r, im. 95. See also Carmona García, *Crónica urbana del malvivir*, 189.

106. "Deposition of Catalina Nicolasa, india," X/1548, Justicia 1037, 27v.

107. Geertz, *Local Knowledge*, 215.

108. Zerubavel, *Time Maps*, chaps. 1 and 2.

109. Owensby, *Empire of Law and Indian Justice in Colonial Mexico*, 7.

110. For simplicity's sake, I will use the term *courtroom* throughout the book to refer to the judicial tribunals of the Casa and the Council of the Indies, which, technically, were not courtrooms.

111. Gowing, *Domestic Dangers*, 42.

112. Gowing, *Domestic Dangers*, 52–53.

113. Gowing, *Domestic Dangers*, 53; Snedaker, "Story-Telling," 15–45.

114. Excellent historiographic overviews are found in Trigger, Washburn, and Adams, *The Cambridge History of the Native Peoples of the Americas*.

115. Baber, "Categories, Self-Representation and the Construction of the *Indios*," 27.

116. Owensby, *Empire of Law and Indian Justice in Mexico*, 55.

117. Yannakakis, *The Art of Being In-Between*; O'Toole, *Bound Lives*.

118. de la Puente Luna, "Into the Heart of the Empire," 158–216; Cahill, "Colour by Numbers."

119. Almorza Hidalgo, "Género, emigración y movilidad social en la expansion Atlántica."

120. Johnson, "On Agency," 115–16.

121. de la Puente Luna, "Into the Heart of the Empire," 164–68.

122. Subrahmanyam, *Three Ways to Be Alien*, 176.

123. See Li, "Articulating Indigenous Identity in Indonesia"; Tavárez, "Legally Indian."
124. Scott, "Small-Scale Dynamics of Large-Scale Processes," 478.
125. "Talking back" comes from hooks, "Marginalizing a Site of Resistance," 340.
126. Ginzburg, "Latitude, Slaves and the Bible," 679; Putnam, "To Study the Fragments/Whole," 615–17.

1. All the World in a Village

1. Auke Pieter Jacobs calculates a rate of six to twelve miles per day on foot and a much faster rate by horseback ("Legal and Illegal Emigration from Seville," 66–67). I thank Amelia Almorza Hidalgo for the research she conducted in the municipal archive of Carmona, which aided in the completion of this chapter.
2. Pescador, *The New World inside a Basque Village*. Also useful are the microhistorical approaches taken by scholars toward village life, the most famous being Emmanuel Le Roy Ladurie's *Montaillou*, Carlo Ginzburg's *The Cheese and the Worms*, and Alain Corbin's *The Life of an Unknown*.
3. Altman, *Transatlantic Ties in the Spanish Empire*.
4. Pescador, *The New World inside a Basque Village*, xiii, xviii.
5. By demographic measures, Carmona was a small town or city, with nine thousand permanent residents by 1587, but the townspeople still referred to it as a village. I defer to the usage found in the documents. Beatríz and Felipa's lawsuits are the only two I found for Carmona, even though a few local indigenous witnesses stated they had been freed by the court. The phrase "four parts of the world" was used contemporaneously and has been explored by Serge Gruzinski, in *Las cuatro partes del mundo*.
6. Rothschild, *The Inner Life of Empires*, 7.
7. Gruzinski, *Las cuatro partes del mundo*, 262–63.
8. See, for instance, Yuen-Gen Liang's *Family and Empire*, a fascinating study of the Fernández de Córdoba family, whose kin and clients connected disparate territories of the Spanish empire.
9. Steedman, *Labours Lost*, chaps. 1 and 2.
10. Articles in the volume *Translocality: The Study of Globalizing Processes from a Southern Perspective*, edited by Ulrike Freitag and Achim von Oppen, have helped me to formulate some of my ideas.
11. Mira Caballos, "La segregación de La Campana," 4–5.
12. González Jiménez, "Carmona hace 500 años," 20.
13. Anton van den Wyngaerde reported in 1567 that Carmona had nearly 25,000 inhabitants, with 5,557 *vecinos* (permanent residents vested with particular rights and privileges), more a town than a village, although the walled quarters contained fewer people than did the sprawling vicinity below. See Kagan, *Spanish Cities of the Golden Age*, 336–37; Montaño Requena, "La población de Carmona en las series parroquiales," 103. The van den Wyngaerde figure diverges considerably from the tally calculated by Esteban Mira Caballos, who says that the population was as follows: 8,048 (1466), 8,756 (1533), and 9,216 (1587) (*La población en Carmona*, appendix 6, 135). In another publication Mira

Caballos states that Carmona reached 8,048 inhabitants in 1587 (Mira Caballos and Nogales, *Carmona en la Edad Moderna*, 343).

14. The Rueda, Quintanilla, and Caro families held the position of chief justice (*alcalde mayor*) for decades, and for centuries a long line of male Góngoras were regidores.

15. González Jiménez, "Carmona hace 500 años," 19.

16. During the plague of 1581, Carmona prohibited anyone from Seville from entering its borders. Cook and Cook, *Plague Files*, 95. The Ordenanzas of Carmona (1533) and the royal Tasa de Salarios (1552) regulated the salary being paid to jornaleros for agricultural labor, based originally on a flat fee for remuneration of their labor (1533), then later by the kind of work they did (1552). Puntas and López Martínez, "Mercado de trabajo y migraciones en Carmona," 144–45.

17. "Probanza hecha por . . . Alonso Guzmán," 1579, AMC, Pleitos y Procesos, leg. 715, n. 7, s.f.

18. For instance, the inventory of the widow Ana Gómez included her loom, which had helped her to earn needed income. AMC, Protocolos, Juan Fernández Mendoza, Oficio 6, Protocolo 167, 599r.

19. González Jiménez, *La Carmona medieval*, 99. Although his figures are probably imprecise, Tomás González noted that in 1530 Carmona had 1,394 vecinos, 459 widows, and 39 minors—a significant ratio of women (*Censo de población*, 84).

20. "Concierto," AMC, Protocolos, Juan Romi, Oficio 1, Protocolo 359 (1567–1568), 652r; Vassberg, *The Village*, 151.

21. "Pleito sobre la moneda forera," 1560, AMC, Pleitos y Procesos, leg. 717, n. 1; Vassberg, *The Village and the Outside World in Golden Age Castile*, 86–97.

22. In the census of 1508–1511, 10 percent of registrants were pobres de la solemnidad. González Jiménez, "Carmona hace 500 años," 19.

23. Pardo Molero, "Conflicto cultural y conflicto militar," 301, 303.

24. Lobo Cabrera, *La esclavitud en las Canarias*, 72.

25. "Pleito de Fernán Gómez de Sotomayor con Sancho Caro," 1549, AMC, Pleitos y Procesos, leg. 716, n. 9. Six years earlier, in 1543, Caro had participated in an unsuccessful attack—which the Pope called a crusade—on the city of Tlemcen, in northwest Algeria. According to his deposition, Caro nearly lost his life. In 1554 the kingdom of Tlemcen became a protectorate of the Ottomans. Juan de la Milla owned an india from Mexico at one point. "Testimony, Antón Aragones, color negro, liberto," 26/VII/1562, AGI, Justicia 783, pieça 3, im. 344.

26. "Testamento de Luis de Rueda," 1555, AMC, Protocolos, Juan Cansino, Protocolo 448, 163r. Rueda claimed that he was still owed back salary of over 300,000 maravedís from when he was stationed in Oran. He named Sancho Caro, married to Inés Méndez de Sotomayor, as the executor of his will.

27. In concrete numbers, 59 Carmonenses emigrated in the first half of the sixteenth century, and 41 during the second half. Mira Caballos and Nogales, *Carmona en la Edad Moderna*, 341.

28. Mira Caballos and Nogales, *Carmona en la Edad Moderna*, appendix 1, "Lista de Carmonenses emigrados a las Indias, s. XVI al XVIII," 362–65, 374–76.

29. Mira Caballos and Nogales, *Carmona en la Edad Moderna*, 343. Céspedes received an encomienda in Lima, but died young; his wife had a difficult time recuperating his estate.

30. Mira Caballos and Nogales, *Carmona en la Edad Moderna*, 350.

31. Mira Caballos and Nogales, *Carmona en la Edad Moderna*, 353–57.

32. Mira Caballos and Nogales, *Carmona en la Edad Moderna*, appendix 1, "Lista de Carmonenses," 337.

33. Mira Caballos and Nogales, *Carmona en la Edad Moderna*, 340.

34. "Demanda de Beatríz, india" 17/V/1558, AGI, Justicia 908, n. 1, pieça 2, 3r.

35. "Testimony, Gonzalo de la Vega," AGI, Justicia 908, n. 1, 173r, im. 391. How Vega, a regidor of the village in 1572, might have known this is an interesting question.

36. "Confession, Beatríz, india," 9/IX/1558, AGI, Justicia 908, n. 1, pieça 2, 11v–12r.

37. Given that the Muslim population of Portugal was not expelled until 1497, it is within the realm of possibility that Beatríz was born there. However, the dates of Beatríz's age at the time of her death vary; some said she was seventy-five, others that she was seventy, the latter of which would have placed her birth in 1501, after the expulsion of the Moors from Portugal.

38. "Testimony, Juan Cansino," 30/IX/1558, AGI, Justicia 908, n. 1, pieça 2, 14r–16v.

39. Cansino branded Catalina on the face as proof of her bondage and most likely in retribution for Beatríz's lawsuit against him.

40. "Respuesta de Juan Cansino a la demanda," 3/X/1558, AGI, Justicia 908, n. 1, pieça 2, 18r–v.

41. "Testimony, Silvestre de Monsalve," AGI, Justicia 783, n. 3, 1v, 5v; "Testimony, Pedro de la Peña," 1559, AGI, Justicia 783, n. 3, im. 172, 208r. On slave prices in Andalucía, see Franco Silva, *La esclavitud en Andalucía*, 82–87.

42. "Interrogatorio," AGI, Justicia 783, n. 3, im. 244–45.

43. "Ejecutoria del pleito de Silvestre de Monsalve," AGI, Patronato 289, r. 53.

44. "Testimony, Pedro Martín Cadenas," VII/1572, AGI, Justicia 908, n. 1, 132r, im. 309. "Testimony, Juana Ponce," AGI, Justicia 908, n. 1, 137v, im. 320.

45. Juana Muñoz, a butcher's wife who was originally from Carmona, stated that she had known Beatríz for over twenty years and her children since they had been born. She had not been to Carmona in over a year when she saw Catalina now bearing a brand on her face. "Testimony, Juana Muñoz," V/1558, AGI, Justicia 908, n. 1, pieza 2, 4r–v. María Rodríguez, the *lora* widow of Cristóbal Coracosta, claimed vecino status in Carmona even though she was currently residing (*estante*) in Seville. "Testimony, María Rodríguez," V/1558, AGI, Justicia 908, n. 1, pieça 2, 6r–v. Pedro Gómez, a loro shoemaker born in 1523, had been living in Seville for only four years when he testified on behalf of Beatríz.

46. Fernández y López, *Historia de la ciudad de Carmona*, 327; González Jiménez, *El consejo de Carmona a fines de la Edad Media*, 256–57.

47. "Listado de personas," 1583, AMC, Pleitos y Procesos, leg. 719, exp. 25, 1583.

48. "Testimony, Pedro Martín Cadenas," VII/1572, AGI, Justicia 908, n. 1, 132r, im. 309; "Testimony, Juana Ponce," AGI, Justicia 908, n. 1, 137v, im. 320. The first in-

digenous slaves to arrive in Carmona from Latin America for whom documentation exists were María and Inés, probably from the eastern part of Hispaniola or the Gulf of Pária, where slave-raiding ventures had become common. Mira Caballos, "Dos bautizos de indias en Carmona."

49. "Carta de venta," 1567, AMC, Protocolos, Juan Romi, Oficio 1, Protocolo 359 (1567–1568), 195r, of Catalina, color mulata, twenty years old; "Inventario de los bienes," 1568, AMC, Protocolos, Juan Romi, Oficio 1, Protocolo 359 (1567–1568), 473, includes an eight-year-old girl named Barbola, color mulata; "Venta," 1568, AMC, Protocolos, Juan Romi, Oficio 1, Protocolo 359, 644v, of Mateo, twenty-three years old, color mulato. On the new kinship and economic ties (especially owning property) developed by former slaves in the nineteenth-century United States, see Penningroth, *The Claims of Kinfolk*, 86–91.

50. An inventory taken in 1567 lacks the names and signatures of the parties involved, but lists the household slaves a man left to his second wife: "Una esclava, 30.000; Otra esclava, 37.000; Otro esclavo varón, 30.000; Otro esclavo, 18.750; Otro esclavo, 11.250." See "Inventorio," AMC, Protocolos, Juan Romi, Oficio 1, Protocolo 359 (1567–1568), 1r.

51. For example, the slaves Miguel and Marina, identified as the color loro, were passed from father to daughter as part of the daughter's dowry and joined the matrimonial household of the oligarch Alonso de Becerril and Ana Barba. "Carta de Dote," 15/XII/1548, AMC, Protocolos, Juan Cansino, Protocolo 203, 102r.

52. Ladero Quesada, "La esclavitud por guerra."

53. "Testimony, Melchior, moreno," AGI, Justicia 783, n. 3, im. 336.

54. "Testimony, Juan Muñoz," 23 de julio de 1562, AGI, Justicia 783, n. 3, im. 324, pieça 3, 12r.

55. "Questions for the interrogatorio," 19/VII/1572AGI, Justicia 908, n. 1, 131v, im. 308.

56. The butcher's wife María Sánchez recalled: "When they pronounced [in 1542] that certain *indios* from a certain island were freed, Felipa, who was with Pedro de Rueda, a cleric ordained to say mass who is now a friar in the monastery, told me 'I am from that island,' but Felipa did not say the name of the island, and if she declared herself [before the authorities] I do not recall. She also told me, 'Why should I try to free myself since I am in a house where I do what I want and I am more than free?'" "Testimony, María Sánchez," III/1561, AGI, Justicia 783, n. 3, n. 3, im. 259.

57. "Testimony, Leonor Gómez," AGI, Justicia 783, n. 3, im. 332–33.

58. Fernández y López, *Historia de la ciudad de Carmona*, 273.

59. Carmona Ruíz, "La ganadería en Carmona durante la Baja Edad Media," 307.

60. "Testimony, Leonor de la Milla," 24/III/1561, AGI, Justicia 783, n. 3, im. 78.

61. "Testimony, Ana, esclava," 1561, AGI, Justicia 783, n. 3, im. 269–70.

62. "Questions for the Interrogatory on behalf of Barbola," 15/VII/1563, AGI, Justicia 783,n. 3, pieça 3, im. 321.

63. On Gracia being identified as a "negra morisca de berberia," see "Tachas a los testigos," AGI, Justicia 783, n. 3, im. 187, 223.

64. "Testimony, Catalina de Vilches," 24/III/1561, AGI, Justicia 783, n. 3, im. 83.

65. "Testimony, Catalina de Vilches," 24/III/1561, AGI, Justicia 783, n. 3, im. 82–85.

66. "Testimony, Juan Muñoz," 23/VII/1562, AGI, Justicia 783, n. 3, pieça 3, im. 325; "Testimony, Antonio de Quintanilla," 24/III/1561, AGI, Justicia 783, n. 3, im. 85–87. On Monsalve's accusation against him in the tachas, see im. 187, 223. "Testimony, Polonia Gutiérrez," AGI, Justicia 783, n. 3, im. 261–62.

67. Earlier in the century, Méndez de Sotomayor's father had fought in Tlemcen and Oran, and had supplied horsemen for Ferdinand and Isabel's army. For his services, he was named a councilor of Carmona. See Cebreros, *Vida del Señor San Teodomiro mártir*, 41–42.

68. Some of these agents were "foreign" Muslims from Cairo, the Red Sea region, and other areas. See Bouchon, "A Microcosm," 44–45; Bouchon, "Calicut at the Turn of the Sixteenth Century"; Pearson, "Brokers in Western Indian Port Cities," 463–64.

69. "Testimony, Juan, indio," AGI, Justicia 783, n. 3, im. 102–3.

70. All told, six men from Calicut, all between the ages of forty-five and fifty-five, either testified or were mentioned.

71. "Testimony, Lisuarte, indio," AGI, Justicia 783, n. 3, im. 104; "Testimony, Antonio, indio," AGI, Justicia 783, n. 3, im. 111–12; "Testimony, Andrés, indio," AGI, Justicia 783, n. 3, im. 122–24.

72. "Testimony, Antón de la Milla," AGI, Justicia 783, n. 3, im. 114; "Testimony, María Gómez," AGI, Justicia 783, im. 116; "Testimony, Pedro de Rueda," AGI, Justicia 783, n. 3, im. 120; "Testimony, Blasia de Baeça," (india from Portuguese territorios), AGI, Justicia 783, n. 3, im. 126–27.

73. "Testimony, Juan Muñoz," 26/VII/1562, AGI, Justicia 783, n. 3, pieça 3, im. 327.

74. Vassberg, *The Village and the Outside World in Golden Age Castile*, 12–13.

75. Periáñez Gómez, "La esclavitud en Extremadura en la Edad Moderna," 125, 426; "Diego, esclavo blanco de 19 años," 20/X/1555, AMC, Protocolos notariales, leg. 3908, s.f.

76. Maier Allende, "Los moriscos de Carmona," fig. 3, 91.

77. Over two hundred came from the Albaícin quarter of the city of Granada; later 732 came from the village of Tolox (in Málaga province) when it was completely emptied of its morisco inhabitants, Fernández Chaves and Pérez García, *En los márgenes de la ciudad de Dios*, 189–90; Maier Allende, "Los moriscos de Carmona," doc. 3, 114–16.

78. Maier Allende, "Los moriscos de Carmona," 88.

79. For most of the moriscos living in Carmona, it was only a temporary stay. Within two years they were moved again to Seville, despite the protests of the Carmoneneses, who wanted them to remain as agricultural laborers. Fernández Chaves and Pérez García, *En los margenes de la ciudad de Dios*, 189–93. Of the hundred or so who remained in Carmona after 1571, a few later tried to escape. See "Poder, Doña Luisa de Céspedes mujer que fue de Juan de Parraga para cobrar un esclavo a Jerónimo de la Milla colegiado," 1581, AMC, Protocolos, Juan Fernández Mendoza, Oficio 6, Protocolo 167, 598r.

80. Over time, some moriscos adapted to life in the village. See "Deudo, Miguel Gutiérrez, morisco, á Alonso de Mendoza," 1581, AMC, Protocolos, Juan Fernández Mendoza, Oficio 6, Protocolo 167, 586r.

81. Questions for the Interrogatory, 19/VII/1572, AGI, Justicia 908, n. 1, pieça 2, 131v.

82. "Deposition, Beatríz," 15/III/1559, AGI, Justicia 908, n. 1, pieça 2, 71v–73r.

83. "Testimony, Francisco de Alinis," AGI, Justicia 908, n. 1, pieça 2, 133v–134v, im. 312–14.

84. Between 1481 and 1485, nine *conversos* from Carmona underwent investigation by the Inquisition. Several fled, three were jailed, others reconciled (confessed to heresy), and one was burned. González Jiménez, *Carmona medieval*, 117–21.

85. "Probanza de limpieza de sangre de doña Jerónima de Escamilla," 1584, AMC, Pleitos y Procesos, leg. 715, n. 9.

86. "Testimony, Juan de Ubeda," AGI, Justicia 908, n. 1, 208r, im. 467.

87. Nirenberg, "Race and the Middle Ages"; Nirenberg, "Was There Race before Modernity?"

88. "Testimony, Hernan Gómez Caro," AGI, Justicia 908, n. 1, 187v, im. 420.

89. "Testimony, Pedro Romero de la Barrera," AGI, Justicia 908, n. 1, 193v, im. 432.

90. On Ana, see the "Interrogatory for the tachas," AGI, Justicia 908, n. 1, 185v–186r.

91. Pagden, *The Fall of Natural Man*, 97–98.

92. "Deposition, Gómez Caro," AGI, Justicia 908, n. 1, 189v, im. 424.

93. "Statement for the *tachas*," AGI, Justicia 908, n. 1, 186r, im. 419.

94. "Questions for interrogatory on behalf of Catalina Hernández," AGI, Justicia 908, n. 1, 217v, im. 480, 215v.

95. "Questions for the interrogatory on behalf of Catalina Hernández," IX/1572, AGI, Justicia 908, n. 1, 218v. The Monsalve family used similar tactics, giving witnesses on behalf of Barbola limited hours to testify and making it difficult for women who remained at home or men who worked long hours to comply.

96. Kathryn Burns, *Into the Archive*.

97. "Testimony, Catalina Hernández," AGI, Justicia 908, n. 1, pieça 2, 24v–27v.

98. "Testimony, Catalina Hernández, india," 1558, AGI, Justicia 908, n. 1, pieça 2, 26v.

99. "Testimony, Juan Díaz," AGI, Justicia 908, n. 1, pieça 2, 28r–v; "Testimony, Martín Sánchez," AGI, Justicia 908, n. 1, pieça 2, 29r.

100. "Testimony, Andrés Nuñez, maestre," X/1558, AGI, Justicia 908, n. 1, pieça 2, im. 30v–33r.

101. "Testimony, Juan Ruíz," X/1558, AGI, Justicia 908, n. 1, 32r–v.

102. "Conclusions of Lawyer for Juan Cansino," 10/XII/1558, AGI, Justicia 908, n. 1, 56r.

103. "Testimony, Marina Hernández," 28/III/1572, AGI, Justicia 908, n. 1, 86v–87r, im. 217–18; "Testimony, Catalina Sánchez," 28/III/1572, AGI, Justicia 908, n. 1, 87v–88r, im. 219–20.

104. "Testimony, Catalina Sánchez," 2/VII/1572, AGI, Justicia 908, n. 1, 117v–118r.

105. "Testimony, María Fernández," 5/VII/1572, AGI, Justicia 908, n. 1, 120v–121r, im. 291.

106. "Testimony, María Fernández," 5/VII/1572, AGI, Justicia 908, n. 1, 124v, im. 294.

107. "Sentence, Council of the Indies," 22/I/1574, AGI, Justicia 908, n. 1, pieça 1, 15r.
108. "Testimony, Pedro Gutiérrez Ferrer," 1572, AGI, Justicia 908, n. 1, im. 349.
109. Rothschild, *The Inner Life of Empires*, 279.

2. Crossing the Atlantic and Entering Households

1. See Guha, "Chandra's Death."
2. Guha, "Chandra's Death," 36.
3. Guha, "Chandra's Death," 37.
4. Sweet, *Domingos Álvares*, 231.
5. Northrup, *Africa's Discovery of Europe*; José Luis Martínez, *Pasajeros de Indias*, 190–91.
6. Chatterjee, *Gender, Slavery, and Law in Colonial India*, 10; Miller, "Introduction," in Campbell, Miers, and Miller, *Children in Slavery*. Records of slave sales of indios in Seville between 1470 and 1525 show that 24 slaves (out of 31) were under the age of twenty. Franco Silva, "El indígena americano," 34, cuadro n. 2.
7. Before 1550, biological mestizos were sometimes called indios. See "Real cédula a Juan Martín Pinzón para traer un hijo suyo indio," 16/II/1533, Madrid, Mexico, AGI, Justicia 1088, L. 2, 208rv.
8. See, for example, the request made by Diego de la Peña, residing in Venezuela, to send four slaves (two male and two female) to his father in Illescas (Castile). "Real cédula al gobernador de Venezuela y Cabo de la Vela," 9/III/1537, Valladolid, AGI, Caracas 1, L. 1, 36r–v. See also Mangan, *Transatlantic Obligations*.
9. "Real Cédula a la Casa de la Contratación," 5/X/1540, Madrid, AGI, Indiferente General 1963, L. 7, 194r–v.
10. "Real Cédula dando licencia a Alonso Pérez de Valer," 15/II/1528, Burgos, AGI, Panama 234, L. 3, 73v–74r.
11. "Real Cédula," 1/III/1527, Valladolid, AGI, Indiferente General 421, L. 12, 25v–26r.
12. See "Licencia a Juan de Eguibar," 30/XII/1532, Madrid, AGI, México 1088, L. 2, 186v; "Licencia a Francisco Botello," 13/X/1518, Zaragosa, AGI, Indiferente General 419, L. 7, 166v [im. 242] and 773v im. 419; also cited in Gil-Bermejo García, "Indígenas americanas en Andalucía," 544–45.
13. See "Real Cédula a Pedro de los Rios, governador de Tierra Firme," 8/XI/1527, Burgos, AGI, Panama 234, L. 3, 23v–24r; "Licencia para traer indios a Catalina Álvarez," 18/X/1539, Madrid, AGI, Panama 235, L. 7, 77v–78r im. 164–65.
14. AGI, Justicia 832, n. 2, im. 19.
15. For examples, see "Real Cédula a la Casa de la Contratación," 27/XII/1542, Ocaña, AGI, Indiferente General 1963, L. 8, 97r–97v; "Devolución de una esclava," 8/XI/1538, Toledo, AGI, Panama 235, L. 7, 19v–20r; "Real Cédula al Doctor Villalobos," 14/VII/1540, AGI, Panama 235, L. 7, 162r; "Libertad de los indios del Doctor Robles," 4/IV/1542, AGI, Panama 235, L. 8, 11v–12r.
16. Las Casas, *Brevísima relación de la destrvycion de las Indias*.
17. On the distribution of slaves as part of "booty," see Góngora, *Los grupos de conquistadores en Tierra Firme*, 46–50.
18. Solar y Taboada and Rújula y de Ochotorena, *Servicios en Indias*, 16.

19. "Testimony, Pedro de Valencia," 5/V/1548, AGI, Justicia 831, n. 1, im. 27.
20. Franco Silva, *La esclavitud en Sevilla*, 40.
21. Guitar, "No More Negotiation," 3.
22. Sauer, *The Early Spanish Main*.
23. *Yucaya* is a misspelling of *Lucaya*, which refers to Amerindians from the Bahamas archipelago.
24. "Instrucciones . . . a Nicolás de Ovando," Burgos 30/IV/1508, AGI, Indiferente General 1961, L. 1, 31–36v; "Carta del rey al governador Ovando," 29/I/1509, Medina del Campo, Pacheco, *Colección de documentos inéditos*, XXXVI, 271; Sauer, *The Early Spanish Main*, 159.
25. "Real Cédula a Clara Martín de la Peña," 20/VII/1521, AGI, Indiferente General 420, L. 8, 297v–298r.
26. Smallwood, *Saltwater Slavery*, 8.
27. Walter Johnson, "On Agency," 115. See, for example, "Diego de Platas," 14/VII/1540, AGI, Lima 566, L. 4, f. 54.
28. For examples of slave owners emphasizing that they would teach migrating slaves the Catholic faith, see "Real Cédula al obispo de Venezuela . . . Diego Ruiz de Vallejo" (to bring two *indio* slaves), 6/IX/1538, AGI, Caracas 1, L. 1, 53r; "Real Cédula al gobernador de Venezuela y Cabo de la Vela . . . Gutiérrez de la Peña, regidor de Coro" (to bring four indio slaves), 5/IX/1539, Madrid, AGI, Caracas 1, L. 1, 73r.
29. Mira Caballos, *Indios y mestizos americanos*, appendix 1, 141–43.
30. On the confiscation of an indio slave, see "Desembargo de [un] indio de Francisco Corbalán," 5/VII/1527, Valladolid, AGI, Indiferente General 421, L. 12, 155v.
31. Bermúdez Plata, *La Casa de la Contratación*, 9.
32. Franco Silva, *La esclavitud en Andalucía*, 59. On the linkages among Portuguese, Genoese, and Italian merchants, see Renouard, *Les hommes d'affaires italiens du Moyen-Age*, 313; Foreman, *Indians Abroad*, 12; Deive, *La Española y la esclavitud de los indios*, 67–68.
33. See also Franco Silva, "El indígena americano," 27. On Portuguese merchants in Seville, see Studnicki–Gizbert, *A Nation upon the Ocean Sea*. Slaves also came to Seville from Valencia, where there were reportedly several hundred in the sixteenth century; Graullera Sanz, *La esclavitud en Valencia en los siglos XVI y XVII*; Hamann, "Inquisitions and Social Conflicts," 142. A small community of indios from the Americas were living in Algiers in 1580; Hamman, "Inquisitions and Social Conflicts," 238.
34. Jacobs, "Legal and Illegal Emigration from Seville," 69–75.
35. As early as 1511, a royal decree prohibited bringing an unlimited number of indios from Santo Domingo to Castile without a special license. "Real cédula a Diego Colón," 21/VII/1511, Seville, AGI, Indiferente General 418, L. 3, 91v–92r. Also see a later prohibition in "Real Cédula de Doña Isabel a los lugartenientes . . . en la provincia de Quito," 26/VI/ 1538, Valladolid, AGI, Lima, 565, L. 3, 15v.
36. "Licencia Diego Caballero," AGI, Justicia 741, n. 3, pieça 16; "Licencia, Antón Cordero, cuatro esclavos ['que tiene desde pequeños']," 3/V/1532, Medina del

Campo, AGI, México 1088, L. 2, 85v; "Licencia, Juan Barbarán, cuatro eslavos," 31/V/1541, Talavera, AGI, Lima 566, L. 4, 187r; "Licencia, Francisco Barrionuevo, governador, seis indios, unos esclavos otros libres" 23/XI/1537, Valladolid, AGI, Panama 235, L. 6, 141r–v; "Licencia . . . llevar cuatro esclavos," 1/XI/1535, Pardo, *Prontuario de reales cédulas, 1529–1599*, 59.

37. Machín's master, Andrés de Areiza, was desperate to leave Panama; he had become persona non grata there, and the situation had deteriorated dramatically when one of his enemies torched his home. See "Real Cédula al corregidor . . . Tierra Firme," 22/VII/1547, AGI, Panama 235, L. 8, 155v–156r. For Machín's opening testimony, see AGI, Justicia 1044, n. 7, r. 2, 1548, 1r.

38. AGI, Justicia 1019, n. 5, r. 1, 1548. For another example see, AGI, Justicia 727, n. 9, im. 25, 42; Franco Silva, "El indígena americano," 29 n. 13.

39. Góngora, *Los grupos de conquistadores en Tierra Firma*, 10–38.

40. AGI, Justicia 716, n. 4; AGI, Justicia 1019, n. 5, r. 1; AGI, Justicia 1021, n. 1, r. 2; AGI, Justicia 757, n. 3; AGI, Justicia 1173, n. 3; AGI, Justicia 741, n. 3, pieça 16.

41. "Testimony, Ginés de Carrión," AGI, Justicia 741, n. 3, pieça 16, 34, im. 795.

42. Sweet, *Domingos Álvares*, 231.

43. "Registro Santiago, Pero Sánches," León, 17/VII/1543, in Vega Bolaños, *Colección Somoza*, 7:39–40.

44. Radell, "The Indian Slave Trade."

45. Smallwood, *Saltwater Slavery*, 104–5, 115–18, 188–89; O'Toole, *Bound Lives*, chap. 2.

46. Then, too, there were the surprising indigenous intra-American migrations. The india Antonia testified in 1573 that she was from Lima and that her parents had brought her to Mexico. From there she was brought by a soldier to Spain. Why she had initially traveled with her indigenous parents to Mexico, we are left to wonder. See "Testimony, Antonia, india," 8/I/1573, AGI, Justicia 446, n. 2. r. 7, 5r.

47. Smallwood, *Saltwater Slavery*, 8.

48. Smallwood, *Saltwater Slavery*, 8.

49. Smallwood, *Saltwater Slavery*; Martínez, *Pasajeros de Indias*, 105–8.

50. AGI, Justicia 1153, n. 2, r. 1, im. 49; "Asiento, Rodrigo de Bastidas," 5/VI/1500, in Pacheco, Cárdenas y Espejo, and Torres de Mendoza, *Colección de documentos inéditos*, I, 2, 38, 362–66, 433–38.

51. "Venta de esclava," 4/I/1537, AGI, Justicia 1153, n. 2.

52. Whitehead, "Indigenous Slavery in South America."

53. On the merchants of Santo Domingo, see Otte, *Cédulas reales relativas a Venezuela*, xxvii. On various royal decrees, see "Licencia a Nicolás de Ovando y Miguel de Pasamonte," 1509, AGI, Indiferente General 1961, L. 1, 117v–118 and l39v; "Licencia," 1511, AGI, Indiferente General 418, L. 3, 211v and 213–214v.

54. Góngora, *Los grupos de conquistadores en Tierra Firme*, 35–38; Francis, *Invading Colombia*, 1–18. Throughout the 1530s and 1540s, as inroads into new terrain occurred, the just-war rationale continued to be used to authorize licenses. The trading posts of Santa Marta (1525) and Cartagena (1538) served as bases of operation for slave-raiding forays into the interior. For an example of a slave affected by these operations, see AGI, Justicia 741, n. 3, pieça 10, 20r, im. 485.

55. AGI, Justicia 1153, n. 3, r. 3, 1544. See the testimonies of Cristóbal de Arenas, Gonzalo Bello, and Martín Sánchez de Xerez, which confirmed the statement made in the interrogatory.

56. By the end of the sixteenth century, this had changed, as the Pijao people of the upper Magdalena River Valley were enslaved and exterminated by Spaniards for having been accused of practicing cannibalism. Bolaños, *Barbarie y canibalismo en la retórica colonial*, 156–69.

57. AGI, Justicia 741, n. 3, pieça 10, 20r, im. 485.

58. Juan might have been captured when Manjarres accompanied Governor Alonso Luis de Lugo to Santa Fé de Bogotá, by way of the Valley of Upar.

59. "Real Cédula de la reina Da Isabel al Licenciado Juan de Vadillo," 11/III/1531, Ocaña, AGI, Santo Domingo, 1121, L. 1, 73r.

60. AGI, Justicia 1173, n. 4. On the active slave market between the northern coast of South America, Cubagua, and Santo Domingo, see Otte, *Las perlas del Caribe*; Deive, *La Española y la esclavitud de los indios*.

61. AGI, Justicia 1153, n. 3, r. 3, 17r, im. 16.

62. The geographical construct "Tierra Firme" distinguished a solid land mass from an island. Until the mid-sixteenth century, many explorers thought that the territories of the Western Hemisphere were islands.

63. Games, "Atlantic History," 755.

64. Rothschild, *The Inner Life of Empires*, 6–7.

65. "Testimony, Marina, india," 9/III/1557, AGI, Justicia 1132, 6bis, 1r.

66. Walter Johnson, *Soul by Soul*, 14.

67. As persons, slaves had the right to gain manumission, could marry with the permission of the master, were protected from excessive punishment, and could initiate lawsuits. Robert I. Burns, *Las Siete Partidas*, book 4.

68. For a rich discussion on the organizing principle of familia as a way to include or exclude relatives and nonrelatives, see Premo, "Thinking beyond Lineage."

69. Altman, *Emigrants and Society*, 140. Ehud Toledano considers the household to be a "unit" of attachment, which includes broader economic and social relationships. His model transcends the nuclear family model previously favored by historical demographers. Toledano, *As If Silent and Absent*, 24, 27–28. See also Carmona García, *El extenso mundo de la pobreza*, 42–44.

70. Chatterjee, "Testing the Local," 215–24; and Toledano, *As If Silent and Absent*.

71. Gaunt, "Kinship," 261.

72. Particularly influential are Walter Johnson's *Soul by Soul*, Michael A. Gómez's *Exchanging Our Country Marks*, and James H. Sweet's *Domingos Álvares, African Healing, and the Intellectual History of the Atlantic World*.

73. Toledano, *As If Silent and Absent*, 25; Martín Cásares, "Domestic Service in Spain," 190.

74. In a recent article on women's petitions in the Spanish courts, Bianca Premo has argued that the "context" of a lawsuit should consider what happened both inside and outside the courtroom ("Before the Law," 263–65).

75. Chatterjee, "Colouring Subalternity"; Ghosh, *Sex and the Family in Colonial India*, esp. 107–32; Finn, "Slaves Out of Context"; van Deusen, "The Intimacies of Bondage," 15, 24–26, 30–32; Blumenthal, *Enemies and Familiars*, 149–53; Franco Silva, *La esclavitud en Sevilla*, 213; Phillips, "Manumission in Metropolitan Spain," 40–43.

76. Steedman, *Labours Lost*, 9.

77. Walter Johnson, *Soul by Soul*, 22.

78. The term "not-you-but-me" is adapted from Trinh T. Minh-Ha: "You and I are close, we intertwine; you may stand on the other side of the hill once in a while, but you may also be me while remaining what you are and what I am not" (*Woman, Native, Other*, 90). See also Natalie Zemon Davis, "Boundaries and the Sense of Self," 54.

79. Miles, *Ties That Bind*, 44–45; van Deusen, "The Intimacies of Bondage."

80. For instance, the fair at Zafra, discussed in Mira Caballos, *Indios y mestizos americanos*, 129.

81. Mira Caballos, *Indios y mestizos americanos*, 175. The masters also came from Lisbon. See "Testimony, Beatríz Alvarez," 10/VI/1575, AGI, Justicia 1133, n. 3, r. 2, 31r–v.

82. Toledano, *As If Silent and Absent*, 60.

83. Morales Padrón, *Los corrales de vecinos de Sevilla*, 9–15, 37–39; Carmona García, *El extenso mundo de la pobreza*, 45–46.

84. "Entrega de cinco niños indios a Francisco Guerrero, clérigo," 3/X/1533, AGI, Santo Domingo 1121, L. 1, 173v. Franco Silva notes that ecclesiastics commonly held slaves in Seville ("El indígena americano," 31).

85. Cook and Cook, *The Plague Files*, 47.

86. AGI, Justicia 1013, n. 2, r. 4.

87. AGI, Justicia 757, n. 3, 113r, im. 110.

88. Carmona García, *Crónica urbana del malvivir*, 36.

89. "Francisco Rodríguez, sastre," IX/1553, AGI, Justicia 758, n. 4, pieça 2, im. 97. See also "Questions for Interrogatory on Behalf of Pedro de Castellanos," AGI, Justicia 758, n. 4, im. 94.

90. Carmona García, *El extenso mundo de la pobreza*, 158; Cook and Cook, *The Plague Files*, 8–9, 62–65.

91. AGI, Justicia 831, n. 1, im. 38–40.

92. Steedman, *Labours Lost*, 11–12.

93. This section has been influenced by Carolyn Steedman's *Labours Lost*, esp. 35, 352–56.

94. Steedman, *Labours Lost*, 348–54. See also Riello, "Things that Shape History," 24–47; Joyce, *The Historical Meanings of Work*, 1–30.

95. "Real Cédula" (a Teresa de Aldana), 11/III/1536, Madrid, AGI, Santo Domingo 2280, L. 2, 83v; "Testimony, Catalina Nicolasa, india," AGI, Justicia 1037, 27r.

96. "Testimony, Leonor, esclava," 10/VI/1575, AGI, Justicia 1133, n. 3, r. 2, 30v.

97. "Testimony, Francisco, indio," 7/I/1540, AGI, Justicia 1162, n. 6, r. 2, 3r.

98. "Testimony, Inés, india," 21/XI/1573, AGI, Justicia 1133, n. 3, r. 3, 20v.

99. "Testimony, Juan García, indio," 3/III/1551, AGI, Justicia 757, n. 3, 113r, im. 110.

100. Toledano, *As If Silent and Absent*, 29.

101. The regidor of the city of León once saw the indio Hernando hit the slave Madalena so forcefully in the head that she was bedridden for days. "Testimony, Bernaldo Ramírez," 1574, AGI, Justicia 1133, n. 4, 25v–26r.

102. Miles, *Ties That Bind*, 44.

103. Cortés López, *La esclavitud negra en la España peninsular*, 19.

104. Miles, *Ties That Bind*; O'Toole, *Bound Lives*.

105. Herlihy, "The Making of the Medieval Family," 143. See the example of Juan de Olivares and Beatríz, in AGI, Justicia 757, n. 3, 113r, im. 110.

106. AGI, Justicia 758, n. 4.

107. For over ten years, Cristóbal (from New Spain), Pedro (from Santa Marta), Catalina (from Santa Marta), and Beatríz (from Cuba) lived in the same household with Bartolomé Ortíz, the future alcalde of Seville. AGI, Justicia 1153, n. 2.

108. For an example, see AGI, Justicia 1022, n. 1, r. 2, pieça 3, 4r.

109. "Testimony, Inés, india," 21/XI/1573, AGI, Justicia 1133, n. 3, r. 3, 20v.

110. See AGI, Justicia 1022, n. 5, r. 3, 1557; AGI, Justicia 1173, n. 4. Himmerich y Valencia, *The Encomenderos of New Spain*, 6; "Real Provisión," 18/IX/1538, AGI, Audiencia de Mexico 1088, L. 3, 206v, lists Trías in a group of *pobladores*. Occasionally, slave couples like Magdalena and Teresa and their husbands, Andrés and Alvarico, crossed the ocean with one of the first post-conquest settlers of Mexico, Juan Trías, a Catalán. Teresa died en route—although Magdalena and Teresa's lawyer suspected that she had been sold before arriving in Europe—but the others were eventually freed.

111. The *Siete Partidas* states that slaves could marry against the wishes of the master (Robert I. Burns, *Las Siete Partidas*, part 4, title 5, law 1, 4:901). See also Franco Silva, *La esclavitud en Sevilla*, 214.

112. AGI, Justicia 741, n. 3 (1543); Himmerich y Valencia, *The Encomenderos of New Spain*, 6; "Real Provisión," 18/IX/1538, AGI, Audiencia de Mexico 1088, L. 3, 206v, lists Trías among a group of pobladores.

113. "Opening Statement, Pedro," 19/VIII/1549, "Pedro y Luisa con Nuño de Gúzman," AGI, Justicia 1021, 1r.

114. "Opening Statement, Pedro," 19/VIII/1549, AGI, Justicia 1021, 2r; Chipman, *Nuño de Guzmán and the Province of Pánuco in New Spain*, 246–47, 277–80.

115. AGI, Justicia 1021. Pedro and Luisa were freed in December 1549.

116. Pollock, "Parent-Child Relations," 207–8; López Beltrán, "Estructura de los grupos domésticos," 94; Herrero, "Mozas sirvientas en Zarazoga"; Serrano, "El servicio doméstico en Córdoba"; de la Llave, "El papel de la mujer"; López Beltrán, "La accesibilidad de la mujer al mundo laboral"; López Beltrán, "El trabajo de la mujeres"; López Beltrán, "El prohijamiento y la estructura oculta"; Martín Casares, "Domestic Service in Spain," 202; Mira Caballos, *Indios y mestizos americanos*, 74–80.

117. Martin Casares, "Domestic Service in Spain," 194, 196.

118. "Testimony, Alonso Martín," 1560, AGI, Justicia 1024, n. 1, 15v.

119. AGI, Justicia 1022, n. 1, r. 2, pieça 2, 6r.

120. AGI, Justicia, 1022, n. 4, r. 1, 53–53v; also cited in Mira Caballos, *Indios y mestizos americanos*, 77.

121. Aurelia Martín Cásares argues that in domestic service, females always performed the least valued tasks (*oficios menores*) ("Domestic Service in Spain," 203).

122. Vassberg, *The Village and the Outside World in Golden Age Castile*, 48–57; Franco Silva, *La esclavitud en Sevilla*, 194.

123. Vassberg, *The Village and the Outside World in Golden Age Castile*, 36.

124. "Testimony, Manuel, indio," 13/X/1553, AGI, Justicia 994, 40v–41v.

125. "Testimony, Esteban, indio," 9/I/1554, AGI, Justicia 994, 43r–v.

126. AGI, Justicia 1037, n. 6, r. 2, 1553; AGI, Justicia 831, n. 7, 1549; Vassberg, *The Village and the Outside World in Golden Age Castile*, 159–61. On the grueling nature of labor, see Shammas, "The Domestic Environment in Early Modern England and America."

127. AGI, Justicia 1013, n. 2, r. 4.

128. AGI, Justicia 1132, n. 6, 1561.

129. AGI, Justicia 1019, n. 5, r. 1, 1548, 11r.

130. AGI, Justicia 727, n. 9, 1538, im. 53–54; AGI, Justicia 1164, n. 6, r. 1.

131. Franco Silva, *La esclavitud en Sevilla*, 194–97.

132. Smallwood, *Saltwater Slavery*, 120.

133. AGI, Justicia 825, n. 3, r. 2, im. 23; AGI, Justicia 928, n. 8, im. 11.

134. Franco Silva, *La esclavitud en Sevilla*, 200; Otte, *Sevilla y sus mercaderes a fines de la Edad Media*, 64, 97–98.

135. "Petición de Juan, indio liberto," AGI, Justicia 741, n. 3, r. 15, 35, im. 737; Pike, *Penal Servitude in Early Modern Spain*, chap. 1.

136. "Question for the interrogatory," AGI, Justicia 758, n. 4, im. 121.

137. AGI, Justicia 1038, n. 2, 29r.

138. Gowing, *Domestic Dangers*, 128.

139. AGI, Justicia 832, n. 2, 1550, im. 19.

140. "Sentence," 27/X/1553, AGI, Justicia 832, n. 2.

141. AGI, Justicia 832, n. 2, im. 65.

142. See, for example, the testimony of Pero Gutiérrez about his slave Nycolao. "Question for the interrogatory," AGI, Justicia 1028, 29v–30r.

143. "Testimony, Gaspar de Oviedo," 30/X/1550, AGI, Justicia 1021, n. 1, r. 2, pieça 2, 7r.

144. Robert I. Burns, *Las Siete Partidas*, part 4, title 22, law 9, 4:984.

145. "Testimony, Ana de Herrera," AGI, Justicia 928, n. 8.

146. Robert I. Burns, *Las Siete Partidas*, part 3, title 2, law 8, 3:539.

147. Owensby, *Empire of Law and Indian Justice in Colonial Mexico*, 55.

148. "Testimony, Francisco, indio," 7/I/1540, AGI, Justicia 1162, n. 6, r. 2, 3r.

149. "Testimony, Marina, india," 9/III/1557, AGI, Justicia 1132, 6bis, 2r.

150. That the term appears in the *Diccionario de autoridades* indicates that it was a practice common enough to merit an entry. Real Academia Española, *Dicciona-*

rio de autoridades, 5:382. See also Pike, *Penal Servitude in Early Modern Spain*, 350.

151. Toledano, *As If Silent and Absent*, 80.

152. Alonso Franco Silva notes that between 1470 and 1525, approximately 295 slaves were listed as fugitives (*La esclavitud en Sevilla*, 204). On stealing for survival, see Franco Silva, *La esclavitud en Sevilla*, 206; on punishments, see Franco Silva, *La esclavitud en Sevilla*, 209. On one instance of severe beating, see AGI, Justicia 1038, n. 2. See also AGI, Justicia 1024, n. 1, 29r, which documents an incident in which the slave Gerónimo escaped his master and was found begging for work. See also "Testimony, Licentiate Diego Florez de Carpio," 1557, AGI, Justicia 1022, n. 5, r. 1, 8r.

153. "Testimony, Bernardino de Castro," AGI, Justicia 1013, n. 2, 30v.

154. "Ejecutoria del pleito litigado por Gaspar Sánchez, indio," 24/XI/1570, ARCV, Registro de Ejecutorias, Caja 1193, 42. For examples of single mothers litigating on behalf of their children, see AGI, Justicia 446, n. 2. r. 7; AGI, Justicia 1164, n. 6, r. 1; AGI, Justicia 1132, 6 bis; AGI, Justicia 446, n. 2. r 7; "Emplazamiento a Mencia Hernández," 10/IV/1557, AGI, Patronato 284, n. 1, r. 37; and AGI, Justicia 1153, n. 3, r. 2, 93r, im. 91, which documents an incident, in 1554, in which Juana and her two children, Antón and Catalina, were declared free after ten years of litigation, in an appeal that Juana's master, Alonso de Baeza, lost.

155. Natalie Zemon Davis, "Boundaries and the Sense of Self," 53.

156. AGI, Justicia 1163, n. 3, r. 3, 1549, 1r.

157. "Testimony, Marina," 9/III/1557, AGI, Justicia 1132, n. 6 bis, 1r. See also "Opening Statement," 18/III/1549, AGI, Justicia 1116B, n. 3, r. 5, 1r; "Testimony, Beatríz, india," AGI, Justicia 757, n. 4, 98r-v, im. 95; AGI, Justicia 1122, n. 3, r. 4, 7/II/1575. See also the case, discussed in the preface, of the india doncella Catalina de Velasco, who served the Marquesa of Villafranca. AGI, Justicia 1178, n. 4, 1549–1551.

158. Debra Blumenthal makes this point, in *Enemies and Familiars*, 153.

159. "Respuesta, Domingo Gómez," 4/II/1559, AGI, Justicia 1039, n. 1, r. 3, 2r.

160. "Respuesta, Domingo Gómez," 4/II/1559, AGI, Justicia 1039, n. 1, r. 3, 2r.

161. Robert I. Burns, *Las Siete Partidas*, introduction, 4:xxii.

162. Block, "Lines of Color, Sex, and Service," 143–45. See also van Deusen, "The Intimacies of Bondage."

163. AGI, Justicia 199, n. 1, r. 3; on freeing Luisa, see "Real Cédula," 29/VIII/1544, Valladolid, AGI, Indiferente General 423, L. 20, 787r–788r, im. 592–93; on freeing Catalina, see "Real Cédula," 29/VIII/1544, Valladolid, AGI, Indiferente General 423, L. 20, 788r–v, im. 593–94; on freeing Juan, see "Real Cédula," 29/VIII/1544, Valladolid, AGI, Indiferente General 423, L. 20, 789r–v, im. 595–96.

164. See "Real Cédula a Fernando de Ulloa," 26/VI/1539, Toledo, AGI, Indiferente General 423, L. 19, 262v–263r.

165. On the children of "Christian fathers," see "Testimony, Martín de Arauço," 29/II/1548, AGI, Justicia 1037, 2r. For the birth law argument, see "Iñigo López de

Mondragón on behalf of his client, the slave owner, Gonçalo de Tarán," AGI, Justicia 1037, n. 5, 24r.

166. "Deposition of Catalina Nicolasa," AGI, Justicia 1037, n. 5, 28r.

167. "Ejecutoria del pleito litigado por Isabel, esclava y Lorenzo, su hijo, indios," Madrid, 30/XI/1570, ARCV, Registro de Ejecutorias, Caja 1192, 44, 8v. The *Siete Partidas* discouraged members of the nobility from taking concubines, especially slaves, or the daughters of slaves (Robert I. Burns, *Las Siete Partidas*, book 4, part 4, title 14, 951).

168. "Amiga," in Real Academia Española, *Diccionario de autoridades*, 1:269.

169. "Ejecutoria del pleito," Madrid, 30/XI/1570, ARCV, Registro de Ejecutorias, Caja 1192, 44, 9r.

170. "Ejecutoria del pleito litigado por Isabel," Madrid, 30/XI/1570, ARCV, Registro de Ejecutorias, Caja 1192, 44, 8r.

171. Franco Silva, *La esclavitud en Sevilla*, 203.

172. In chapter 1 I showed how the historicity of authorizing the bondage of certain classifications of people was important. Moriscos captured as infidels and as slaves of just war had been enslaved before the War of Alpujarras, but that event and the subsequent passage of a decree issued by Philip II in 1573, which authorized the enslavement of morisco males or females over ten-and-a-half and nine-and-a-half years of age, respectively, exemplify how changing laws affected on-the-ground practices of slavery. Martín Cásares, "The Royal Decree," 154.

173. Walter Johnson, *Soul by Soul*, 20.

174. Gowing, *Domestic Dangers*, 135.

175. "Testimony, Gonzalo de Salazar," 8/VII/1536, AGI, Justicia 1007, n.1, r. 1, 2r.

176. "Emplazamiento a Mencía Hernández," 10/IV/1557, Valladolid, AGI, Patronato 284, n. 1, r. 37, 1r.

177. "Testimony, Francisco, indio," 7/I/1540, AGI, Justicia 1162, n. 6, r. 2, 3r.

178. "Opening Statement," 2/III/1560, AGI, Justicia 1050, n. 5, r., 2, 1r; for Perafán de Rivera's response, see 5/III/1560, AGI, Justicia 1050, 2r.

179. "Testimony, friar Francisco de Carvajal," AGI, Justicia 1050, n. 5, r. 2, 31v.

3. Small Victories?

1. Muro Orejón, "Las Nuevas Leyes de 1542–43."

2. On López's desire to retire because of his poor health, see "Consulta del Consejo de Indias," 1556, Valladolid, AGI, Indiferente General 737, n. 164, 2f, which includes a letter from López dated 9/IX/1556.

3. Starr-LeBeau, *In the Shadow of the Virgin*, 2.

4. On López's salary and bonus for the inspection, see "Real Cédula," 28/IV/1543, Valladolid, AGI, Indiferente General 1963, L. 8, 268–269v; "Real Cédula," 14/XII/1543, Valladolid, AGI, Indiferente General 1963, L. 9, 6–6v. On the visit of Philip II to Guadalupe in 1570, see Martínez Cardós, *Gregorio López*, 124.

5. "Letter from Bartolomé de Las Casas to the Council of Indies," Seville, 20/IV/1544, in Fabié y Escudero, *Vida y escritos de Fray Bartolome de las Casas*, 2:113–14.

6. Owensby, *Empire of Law and Indian Justice in Colonial Mexico*, 24–25.

7. "Letter from Bartolomé de Las Casas to the Council of Indies," Seville, 20/IV/1544, in Fabié y Escudero, *Vida y escritos de Fray Bartolome de las Casas*, 2:118.

8. The first inspection occurred in 1526, followed by inspections in 1543, 1549, and 1556. For a history of the Casa written by one of its authorities, see Veitia Linaje, *Norte de la Contratación de las Indias Occidentales*.

9. During the inspection of the council in 1542 (motivated by Las Casas), it was discovered that the council member Doctor Beltrán had business dealings with Almagro, Hernán Cortés, and Francisco Pizarro. Ots Capdequí, *Historia del derecho español*, 116.

10. Schäfer, *El consejo Real y Supremo de las Indias*, 1:80–81.

11. All three officials acted as judges in arbitrations. The *contador* (accountant) assisted the officials by annotating receipts from the treasurer, the Real Hacienda, bienes de difuntos, and rents from the Cruzada; the *tesorero* (treasurer) oversaw gold and silver remittances; and the *factor* (administrator) was in charge of all goods that went to the king, except for precious metals.

12. Hanke and Giménez Fernández, *Bartolomé de las Casas*, 81–82.

13. Kagan, *Lawsuits and Litigants in Castile*, 146. After his experience conducting the visit to the Casa and freeing over one hundred indios, López may have been moved to write the treatise *La glosa magna de Gregorio López*, which treated the subject of just war (*guerra justa*). See Martínez Cardós, *Gregorio López*. López commented on the *Siete Partidas*, vol. 2, title 23, law 2, on "servidumbre natural," arguing that indios were not "gente feróz, ni bestial que caresca de razón" (Martínez Cardós, *Gregorio López*, 85).

14. Martínez Cardós, *Gregorio López*, 85, 89.

15. Illegal commerce included the profitable smuggling of indigenous slaves into Seville. On the intersection of the capital interests of merchants, the Crown, and Casa officials, see Acosta Rodríguez, "Intereses privados en la administración de la monarquía." On the inspection of indios conducted by Licentiate Suárez de Carvajal, the bishop of Lugo (1539–1561), who ordered slave owners in Seville to register all indios, including "their names, their provinces of origin, and the titles that show legal ownership," see "Real Cédula al licenciado Suárez de Carvajal," 14/I/1536, Madrid, AGI, Indiferente General 1962, L. 4, 30–31. See also, "Carta Luis Suárez de Carvajal al Consejo de Indias," 18/II/1536, AGI, Indiferente General, 1092, n. 129. Suárez de Carvajal's tenure on the Council of the Indies (1529–1542) overlapped with his office as bishop (Schäfer, *El Consejo Real y Supremo de las Indias*, 1:58, 354). After being condemned for professional misconduct, he was replaced on the council, in 1543, by Gregorio López (Schäfer, *El Consejo Real y Supremo de las Indias*, 1:66).

16. "Sobre indios entregados a vecinos de Sevilla," 3/II/1533, Madrid, AGI, Indiferente General 1961, L. 3, 109v.

17. Martínez Cardós, *Gregorio López*, 88.

18. On population growth, see Carmona García, *Crónica urbana del malvivir*, 174. On the hunger and bread shortages (*los estragos del hambre*) during 1541 and 1542, see Carmona García, *Crónica urbana del malvivir*, 181, 249.

19. Martínez Cardós, *Gregorio López*, 88; "Real Cédula," 12/X/1543, Valladolid, AGI, Indiferente General, 1963, L. 8, 274v–275r, im. 554–55.

20. AGI, Justicia 944, s.f.

21. "Visita . . . de Sevilla," 1543, Seville, AGI, Justicia 944.

22. Within three weeks of his arrival, López had already freed several slaves; dozens more received their freedom on 23 July. López also confiscated at least five slaves who had arrived clandestinely on a ship that docked during his residence. See "Sobre ciertos indios esclavos y otros asuntos," 18/VI/1543, Valladolid, AGI, Indiferente General 1963, L. 8, 185–185v.

23. AGI, Justicia 757, 15r, im. 14.

24. Robert I. Burns, *Las Siete Partidas*, 4:1019.

25. For a comparison with late-fifteenth century Valencia, see Blumenthal, *Enemies and Familiars*, 215.

26. Real Academia Española, *Diccionario de autoridades*, 5:389.

27. AGI, Justicia 1153, n. 3, r. 2, 1545, 34r, im. 32.

28. "Questions for the interrogatorio," AGI, Justicia 1153, n. 3, r. 3, 17r, im. 16.

29. AGI, Indiferente General 857; also cited in Martínez Cardós, *Gregorio López*, appendix 3, 136–37.

30. "Pregon," 1/IV/1536, AGI, Justicia 741, n. 3, im. 14–15.

31. "License for Jerónimo Trías," 13/I/1543, AGI, Justicia 741, n. 3, pieça 1, 1536, im. 15–16. The license was granted by Viceroy don Antonio de Mendoza.

32. "Real provisión . . . en hacer esclavos en la guerra y con rescates," Toledo, 20/I/1534, in Konetzke, *Colección de documentos*, 1:153–59.

33. "Probanza . . . señor Moron," 23/X/1525, Trujillo, Honduras, AGI, Patronato 170, r. 23, 1r; also discussed in Sherman, *Forced Native Labor*, 41.

34. "Real Provisión sobre declarar y herrar a los indios naturales por esclavos," 20/XI/1528, Toledo, in Konetzke, *Colección de documentos*, 1:109–10; "Real Provisión sobre la manera de herrar los esclavos indios," Toledo, 24/VIII/1529, in Konetzke, *Colección de documentos*, 1:130–31; "Real provisión al presidente y oidores de la Audiencia de México, por la forma de herrar a los esclavos," 24/VIII/1529, Toledo, AGI, México 1088, L. 1, 61v–64v.

35. Hanke, *The Spanish Struggle*, 91.

36. Muro Orejón, *Las Leyes Nuevas de 1542–43*, 10.

37. On the active collusion between the Crown and merchants, making regulation of the indigenous slave trade difficult, see Mira Caballos, *Indios y mestizos americanos*, 99–100.

38. By way of example, see "Real Cédula," 28/IX/1543, AGI, Indiferente General 1963, L. 8, im. 264–65, 285r–v.

39. "Traslado de la consulta de la visita" (Martínez Cardós, *Gregorio López*, 131).

40. As late as 1537, the king determined that a slave named Alonso was to remain with his master, Joan López, based on a simple statement, made by the owner, that Alonso had been captured as a slave of just war and branded. See "Entrega de indio a Juan López," 2/II/1537, AGI, Indiferente General 1962, L. 5, 102–3.

41. Owensby, *Empire of Law and Indian Justice in Colonial Mexico*, 48; Mira Caballos, *Indios y mestizos americanos*, 50–57.

42. "Royal Decree to the officials of the House of Trade," 14/XII/1543, Valladolid, AGI, Indiferente General 1963, L. 9, 8–9, cited in Mira Caballos, *Indios y mestizos americanos*, 102 n. 201.

43. "Real Cédula a los oficiales de la Casa de Contratación," 21/VII/1549, AGI, Indiferente General 1964, L. 11, 260r–v, cited in Mira Caballos, *Indios y mestizos americanos*, 102 n. 203. In a curious twist of fate, several of the indios set free by López were on the flotilla of fifty-two ships carrying Blasco Nuñez de Vela, the ill-fated viceroy who brought the 1542 New Laws to Peru. "Despacho de la flota de Blasco Núñez Vela y otros asuntos," 28/IX/1543, AGI, Indiferente General, 1963, L. 8, 263–64. The chroniclers Juan Polo de Ondegardo and Agustín de Zárate were also aboard one of the fifty-two ships.

44. "Cédula que manda que ninguna persona pueda traer de las Indias a estos Reynos ningún Indio a título de esclavo," Madrid, 17/III/1536, in Encinas, *Provisiones*, 4:368.

45. "Sobre ciertos indios esclavos y otros asuntos," 18/VI/1543, Valladolid, AGI, Indiferente General 1963, L.8, 185r–v, im. 375–376.

46. "Real Provisión," 28/IX/1543, Valladolid, AGI, Indiferente General 423, L. 20, 698r–700r, im. 413–17; also published in Konetzke, *Colección de documentos*, 1:227–28.

47. "Real Provisión," 28/IX/1543, Valladolid, AGI, Indiferente General 423, L. 20, 700r, im. 417; also published in Konetzke, *Colección de documentos*, 1:228.

48. "Libertad de india," 6/VII/1543, Valladolid, AGI, Indiferente General 1963, L. 8, 198r–198v. Not only was Francisco Pérez de Robles, oidor of Tierra Firme, deeply involved in slave trafficking, but he was also known for usurping the slaves of others and keeping them for his own use.

49. "Testimony, Cristóbal, indio," 9/IX/1553, AGI, Justicia 1023, n. 1, r. 1, 76r–77r.

50. "Diego Pantoja en nombre de Juan," AGI, Justicia 758, n. 3, pieça 1, im. 23.

51. On failing to comply with the *pregón* (town crier), see AGI, Justicia 1153, n. 3, r. 2, 1545.

52. "Letter from Bartolomé de Las Casas to the Council of Indies," Seville, 20/IV/1544, in Fabié y Escudero, *Vida y escritos de Fray Bartolome de las Casas*, 2:117.

53. "Deposition, Francisco, indio," AGI, Justicia 1019, n. 5, r. 1, 6v.

54. "Deposition, Francisco, indio," AGI, Justicia 1019, n. 5, r. 1, 6r.

55. For another example, see AGI, Justicia 1153, n. 3, r. 2.

56. Hanke and Giménez Fernández, *Bartolomé de las Casas*, xix; "Letter from Bartolomé de Las Casas to the Council of Indies," Seville, 20/IV/1544, in Fabié y Escudero, *Vida y escritos de Fray Bartolome de las Casas*, 2:117.

57. Hanke and Giménez Fernández, *Bartolomé de las Casas*, xix; "Letter from Bartolomé de Las Casas to the Council of Indies," Seville, 20/IV/1544, in Fabié y Escudero, *Vida y escritos de Fray Bartolome de las Casas*, 2:117.

58. According to the Real Academia Española's *Diccionario de autoridades*, especie-ros were those who sold spices and drugs (like a pharmacist) and who operated the stores that sold these goods (3:596).

59. "Deposition, Beatríz, india libre," AGI, Justicia 757, n. 38, 98r, im. 95.

60. "Letter from Bartolomé de Las Casas to the Council of Indies," Seville, 20/IV/1544, in Fabié y Escudero, *Vida y escritos de Fray Bartolome de las Casas*, 2:118.

61. "Letter from Bartolomé de Las Casas to the Council of Indies," Seville, 20/IV/1544, in Fabié y Escudero, *Vida y escritos de Fray Bartolome de las Casas*, 2:118.

62. "Cédula Real, Charles V to Casa de Contratación," 14/XII/1543, Valladolid, AGI, Indiferente General 1963, L. 9, 8r–9r.

63. See, for example, the case of Juan Trías, a Catalán, who was ordered to deposit his four indios and ten ducados for each of them, but complained that they should not embark on the next flotilla while his appeal was pending (AGI, Justicia 741, n. 1, im. 18, 1547).

64. "Letter from Bartolomé de Las Casas to the Council of Indies," Seville, 20/IV/1544, in Fabié y Escudero, *Vida y escritos de Fray Bartolome de las Casas*, 2:109–18.

65. Robert I. Burns, *Las Siete Partidas*, 4:1018.

66. "Statement Bartolomé Ortíz," 3/VIII, 1543 AGI, Justicia 1153, n. 2, im. 47, 73. See also Sued Badillo, "Beatríz, India Cubana Cimarrona."

67. "Testimony Inés Vélez," AGI, Justicia 758, n. 4, im. 122. This was the *Siete Partidas* definition of *siervo*.

68. Source cited in Sherman, *Forced Native Labor*, 397 n. 65. The New Laws disallowed holding naborías "against their will."

69. AGI, Patronato 231, n. 1, r. 4, 20/VI/1543; Martínez Cardós, *Gregorio López*, appendix 5, 139; Sherman, *Forced Native Labor*, 397 n. 65.

70. "Sentence of Gregorio López," 23/VII/1543, AGI, Justicia 828, n. 4, im. 28–29.

71. AGI, Justicia 828, n. 4, im. 11.

72. AGI, Justicia 828, n. 4, im. 14.

73. AGI, Justicia 828, n. 4, im. 14.

74. AGI, Justicia 828, n. 4, im. 77.

75. "Testimony, Inés, india," 28/I/1546, AGI, Justicia 828, n. 4, im. 78.

76. AGI, Justicia 828, n. 4.

77. In *Crónica urbana del malvivir*, Juan Ignacio Carmona García, paints a dire picture of the conditions of the poor in sixteenth-century Seville.

78. Carmona García, *El extenso mundo de la pobreza*, 13–15, 21.

79. "Real cédula a los oidores de Santo Domingo," 28/IX/1543, Valladolid, AGI, Indiferente General 423, L. 20, f. 698–700, cited in Mira Caballos, *Indios y mestizos americanos*, 66.

80. AGI, Justicia 741, n. 3, pieça 12.

81. "Royal Decree," 13/II/1544, Valladolid, AGI, Indiferente General 1963, L. 9, f. 39–40; "Real Cédula," 23/II/1544, Valladolid, AGI, Indiferente General, 1964, L. 9, 43r, cited in Hanke and Giménez Fernández, *Bartolomé de las Casas*, 81.

82. "Emplazamiento a Esteban Vicente" (for Madalena, india), 18/V/1543, Valladolid, AGI, Indiferente General 423, L. 20, 760r; "Nota de haberse un emplazamiento a Isabel Becerra" (about "unos indios"), 18/VII/1544, Valladolid, AGI, Indiferente General 423, L. 20, 778v; "Real Cédula de Emplazamiento a Sancho García de Larrazabal" (seven indios), 29/XII/1544, Valladolid, AGI, Indiferente General 423, L. 20, 819v–820r; AGI, Justicia 1022, n. 1, r. 4. See also "Emplazamiento a Juan Sánchez Carrillo" (for Pedro, indio), 29/IV/1544, Valladolid, AGI, Indiferente General 423, L. 20, 752v–754r; AGI, Justicia 1173, n. 5.

83. In August 1544 Prince Philip intervened to free several slaves. "Libertad de ciertos indios residentes en España," VIII/1549, AGI, Patronato 231, n. 1, r. 6. These cases are discussed briefly in Zavala, *Los esclavos indios en Nueva España*, 118–19. See an order to free a young girl from Venezuela brought to Seville by Nicolás Federman, in "Cédula Real," 5/VI/1545, Valladolid, AGI, Indiferente General 1963, L. 9, 232r–v.

84. "Orden para el retorno de ciertos indios," 21/IX/1543, Valladolid, AGI, Indiferente General 1963, L. 8, 259r, im. 523; "Real Cédula . . . a Pedro Almíndez Cherino," 29/VIII/1544, Valladolid, AGI, Indiferente General 1963, L. 9, 110r–v im. 225.

85. Schäfer, *El Consejo Real y Supremo de las Indias*, 1:75.

86. AGI, Justicia 757, n. 3, 1549. Another decree prohibited indios, free or enslaved, from being removed from their provinces of origin. Gregorio López also signed the document. "Prohibición de sacar indios de sus tierras," 28/IX/1543, AGI, Patronato 231, n. 1, r. 3; also cited in Konetzke, *Colección de documentos*, 1:227–38.

87. "Instructions from Charles V to Hernán Pérez," 02/VIII/1549, Valladolid, AGI, Indiferente General 1964, L. 11, 263–66. Bartolomé de Las Casas had recommended naming Diego de Collantes as procurador in April 1544, but he died later that year and Diego de Pantoja replaced him as porter. "Royal Decree," 26/X/1544, Valladolid, AGI, Indiferente General 1963, L. 9, 134–35. Schäfer says that in 1526 the portero was a poorly paid receiver of goods (*El Consejo Real y Supremo de las Indias*, 1:81).

88. "Nombramiento de Hernando Becerra," 26/III/1546, Madrid, AGI, Indiferente General 1964, L. 10, 18v–19v; Schäfer, *El Consejo Real y Supremo de las Indias*, 1:84.

89. Kagan, *Lawsuits and Litigants in Castile*.

90. Schäfer, *El Consejo Real y Supremo de las Indias*, 1:84.

91. Pagden, *The Fall of Natural Man*, 60.

92. AGI, Justicia, 832, n. 2.

93. "Statement Sebastián Rodríguez," 11/XI/1549, AGI, Justicia, 757, n. 3, im. 58; "Response, Licentiate Villalobos," 28/III/1549, AGI, Justicia 1178, n. 4, 9r, im. 17. Rodríguez was one of a series of court-appointed lawyers representing the poor for the Council of the Indies, beginning in 1539. Ots Capdequí, *Historia del derecho español*, 116.

94. Owensby, *Empire of Law and Indian Justice in Colonial Mexico*, 55.

95. See AGI, Justica 1022, n. 1, r. 4; AGI, Justicia 1022, n. 3, r. 2.

96. For Cuba, see "Real Cédula," Madrid, 5/XI/1540, in Konetzke, *Colección de documentos*, 1:197–98. For Guatemala and Honduras, see "Real Cédula," Talavera, 11/I/1541, in Konetzke, *Colección de documentos*, 1:198–99.

97. "Royal Decree," Toledo, 20/II/1534, in Konetzke, *Colección de documentos*, 1:155.

98. "Royal Decree," Madrid, 19/XI/1539, in Konetzke, *Colección de documentos*, 1:194–96.

99. AGI, Contratación 715, n. 7, 1577.

100. Silvio Arturo Zavala summarizes the arguments made about naborías by the bishop of Darién, friar Juan Quevedo, in 1519 (*La filosofía política en la conquista de América*, 57).

101. "Real Cédula," 2/VIII/1549, Valladolid, AGI, Indiferente General 1964, L. 11, 263r–266r; Mira Caballos, "De esclavos a siervos," 8.

102. Ayala, "Diccionario de gobierno y legislación," Archivo Histórico Nacional de Madrid AHNM, im. 59–61, refers to unmarried and unemployed Castilians, and to indios living away from their places of origin. "Expulsión de vagabundos y holgazanes de Perú," 19/XI/1551, AGI, Lima 567, L. 7, 33v.

103. Pagden, *The Fall of Natural Man*, 94–99.

104. Robert I. Burns, *Las Siete Partidas*, 3:710; Ots Capdequí, *Historia del derecho español*, 164; Owensby, *Empire of Law and Indian Justice in Colonial Mexico*, 55–56.

105. See Castañeda Delgado, "La condición miserable del indio y sus privilegios"; Owensby, *Empire of Law and Indian Justice in Colonial Mexico*, 56.

106. See AGI, Justicia 758, nn. 4 and 5.

107. Owensby, *Empire of Law and Indian Justice in Colonial Mexico*, 154. See, for example, "Orden de libertad a Alonso, indio," 14/V/1547, Madrid, AGI, Indiferente General 1964, L. 10, 213v–214r.

108. Owensby, *Empire of Law and Indian Justice in Colonial Mexico*, 52–53.

109. AGI, Justicia 1024, n. 3, 16r–v.

110. AGI, Justicia 1024, n. 3.

111. Paulino Castañeda Delgado notes that the use of the term *miserable* in reference to indios first appeared in an ordinance issued by Philip II in 1563, but that it gained in legal and popular usage in the seventeenth century ("La condición miserable del indio y sus privilegios," 265; also 255–56, 263–65). See also Owensby, *Empire of Law and Indian Justice in Colonial Mexico*, 55.

112. Yannakakis, "Allies or Servants?"

4. *Into the Courtroom*

1. White, The Content of the Form, 9–21.

2. Stoler, "Colonial Archives and the Arts of Governance."

3. On law as a "distinctive manner of imagining the real," see Geertz, *Local Knowledge*, 167–234, quote on 173.

4. Groebner, *Who Are You?*, 196.

5. Epstein, *Speaking of Slavery*, 39–40, 70–85.

6. As Valentin Groebner has shown, this involved enhancing extant forms and creating new ones, from "passports" to badges to facial markings (*Who Are You?*, 196–98).

7. I borrow the term papereality from Dery, "Papereality and Learning in Bureaucratic Organizations," 678. See also Raman, *Document Raj*, 3.

8. An instance of illegal branding occurred as late as 1579 (AGI, Contratación 715, n. 12).

9. Dery, "Papereality and Learning in Bureaucratic Organizations," 682.

10. In Spain they also had procuradores assigned to defend their interests, depending on their nation (of negros, moros, canarias, etc.). Franco Silva, *La esclavitud en Sevilla*, 243–52, 262–63.

11. "Letter from Bartolomé de Las Casas to the Council of Indies," Seville, 20/IV/1544, in Fabié y Escudero, *Vida y escritos de Fray Bartolome de las Casas*, 2:118.

12. "Manda dar carta de libertad, Francisca," 26/I/1550, AGI, Justicia 758, n. 5, im. 39; "Statement of Barbola," AGI, Justicia 831, n. 13, im. 39.

13. For a pathbreaking study of how modern Colombians of Pasto reread colonial documents for current claims, see Rappaport, *The Politics of Memory*. See also Abercrombie, *Pathways of Memory and Power*.

14. AGI, Justicia 727, n. 9, 1538. The curador on behalf of Pedro appealed before the Council of the Indies the decision rendered by the Casa that Pedro was to remain a slave, but the case was dropped since Pedro was unable to gather the necessary witnesses from Santo Domingo within the prescribed time.

15. See, for example, "Doctor Pedro Gutiérrez con Nicolás indio," 1574, AGI, Justicia 1028, n. 4, r. 1, 29v; "Bartolomé Ortíz por la libertad de unos indios," AGI, Justicia 1153, n. 2, r. 1, 1544, im. 33.

16. Mignolo, *The Darker Side of the Renaissance*, 5–6.

17. Epstein, *Speaking of Slavery*, chap. 1.

18. The term esclavo was usually qualified with gender distinctions and sometimes with the qualifiers *indio* or *de la tierra*. For examples, see Millares Carlo and Mantecon, *Indice y extractos*, vol. 1. As the numbers of African slaves in Mexico increased, the term esclavo was used with qualifiers such as *indio* or *negro*.

19. Epstein, *Speaking of Slavery*, 14–15.

20. Natalie Zemon Davis, *Fiction in the Archives*, 113.

21. Siegert, "Pasajeros a Indias"; Groebner, *Who Are You?*

22. See "Carta de Venta," AGI, Justicia 1022, n. 1, r. 4, 9r–10v. The date of the sale was changed from 1538 to 1548. Someone who had flagged the discrepancy annotated "ojo" in the margin. See the case of a fraudulent bill of sale, in AGI, Justicia 825, n. 3, r. 2, whereby Juan's lawyer protested the legality of the indio's bill of sale presented by his owner.

23. Kathryn Burns, *Into the Archive*, 75–80.

24. AGI, Justicia 831, n. 6, 67r.

25. Cristóbal was granted a royal license from the Casa in 1539 to travel to Santo Domingo. "License," Cristóbal Cueto, 7/X/1539, AGI, Catálogo de Pasajeros, L. 3, E849.

26. "Ejecutoría ... Cristóbal de Cueto," 2/VII/1549, AGI, Patronato 280, n. 1, 107r–v.

27. Soon after the conquest, the encomienda of Atitlán was allotted to Jorge de Alvarado, but by 1529, it was jointly held by Pedro de Cueto and Sancho de Barahona. In 1533 Cueto's share went to someone else. See the order for the governor and local authorities to allow Juana Caraveo to deal with her son's estate. "Bienes de Pedro de Cueto," 10/IX/1535, AGI, Guatemala 393, L. 1, 132v.

28. "License from the governor," AGI, Justicia 1037, n. 6, r. 3, 65r.

29. Actually, Francisco de la Cueva had served as lieutenant governor.

30. "Lawyer's Response," 6/V/1549, AGI, Justicia 1037, n. 6, r. 3, 66r.

31. "Sentencia," 13/V/1549, AGI, Justicia 1037, n. 6, r. 3, 73r. "Libranza a Francisco, indio," 7/VIII/1548, Valladolid, AGI, Indiferente General 1964, L. 11, 26r–v; "Pago de flete y matalotaje a Francisco, indio," 21/VII/1549, Valladolid, AGI, Indiferente General 1964, L. 11, 260r–v.

32. Bryant, *Rivers of Gold*, 107. He borrowed the phrase "ceremony of possession" from Patricia Seed's work.

33. AGI, Justicia 741, n. 1, im. 69.

34. Cortés Alonso, *La esclavitud negra*, 121–22; Franco Silva, *La esclavitud en Andalucia*.

35. Minh-ha, *Woman, Native, Other*, 90.

36. "Testimony, Alonso Roman, mercader," IX/1534, AGI, Justicia 716, n. 4, s.f.

37. AGI, Justicia 1021, n. 3, r. 1, 19v.

38. Salmoral, "El carimbo de los indios esclavos."

39. Fernando de Tapía described the royal brand in Mexico "a manera de un gravato como un dedo torcido y otro hierro ay a manera de balata" ("Testimony, Fernando de Tapia," 14/X/1536, AGI, Justicia 1007, 20r).

40. "Testimony, Antonio de Peramato," III/1545, AGI, Justicia 1037, n. 6, r. 3, 29v; Stella, "Herrado en el rostro con una S y un clavo,"149–52.

41. "Testimony, Pedro Armíldez Cherino, veedor," 21/XI/1537, AGI, Justicia 1007, 24r. In the same lawsuit, see also "Testimony, Guillermo de Albornoz," 21/XI/1537, AGI, Justicia 1007, 24v.

42. "Testimony, Benito de Cuenca," Santiésteban de Pánuco, 22/IV/1533, AGI, Justicia 234, 951r.

43. Newson, *The Cost of Conquest*, 109, based on a 1527 document.

44. "Testimonio de los esclavos y naborías que trajeron de la ciudad de León a Trujillo," 28/II/1529, AGI, Patronato 20, n. 4, r. 4, s.f. See also Pacheco, Cárdenas y Espejo, and Torres de Mendoza, *Colección de documentos inéditos*, 14:70–77.

45. "Real Provisión sobre declarer y herrar a los indios," Toledo, 20/IX/1528, in Konetzke, *Colección de documentos*, 1:109–11; Sherman, *Forced Native Labor*, 34–35, 384 n. 1.

46. Las Casas, *En defensa de los indios*, 126, also cited in Mira Caballos, *Indios y mestizos americanos*, 22. For an example of the "examination" of indios as a ruse, see "Juicio de instrucción ... contra del Factor Miguel Juan de Rivas y Juan de Carballo," Granada, 8/IV/1529, in Vega Bolaños, *Colección Somoza*, doc. CI, 2:18.

47. "Testimony, Francisco Gutiérrez," AGI, Justicia 234, s.f.
48. "Testimony, Juan Vaella, clérigo," AGI, Justicia 741, n. 2, 34r, im. 134.
49. "Venta," 1545, BNP, Protocolos, Diego Gutiérrez A31, 119–119v; "Venta," 1548, BNP, Protocolos, Diego Gutiérrez A33, 3–3v, 102–3.
50. "Real Provisión," 1528, AGI, Patronato 170, r. 34; "Carta de Venta," 11/VI/1538, LOC, Harkness Collection, box 2, doc. 347, 234r.
51. "Venta," 1546, BNP, Protocolos, Diego Gutierrez A32, 89–89v.
52. Bhattacharyya, "Flesh and Skin," 37.
53. See the request of the cabildo secular in Nueva Galizia—located in Compostela, Mexico, when Nuño de Gúzman was governor—to make their own brands to "placate" the rebellious Indians. "Carta del cabildo secular de Compostela sobre los aprovechamientos de la merced de 'Hierros de Rescate,' y concesión de cierta jurisdicción a la Audiencia de México," 19/X/1534, AGI, Guadalajara 30, no. 3.
54. AGI, Justicia 234, 915v, 918r. Because slave owners possessed the bodies of their slaves, they felt they still had the right to brand them even after they had freed them. There were instances of branding infants and young children with the word "free" over the previous scar on their foreheads. Sherman, *Forced Native Labor*, 66. In Guazacoalco (Guatemala), a Spaniard named Orduña had branded a female Indian servant with the word libre on her upper arm. When he heard that the bishop Bartolomé de las Casas had arrived, in 1545, and might remove her from Orduña's possession, he placed an additional brand, next to the first one, that read, "as long as she serves her master." Orduña was punished as an abductor (*plagiario*) and the woman was declared free. Remesal, *Historia general de las Indias Occidentales*, 2:57, also cited in Sherman, Forced Native Labor, 64.
55. "Real Cédula que no se hierren indios esclavos sin licencia real," Medina del Campo, 13/I/1532, in Konetzke, Colección de documentos, 1:138–39; "Real Cédula a las justicias de Indias sobrecartando otra cédula dada en Medina del Campo a 13 de enero de 1532," 8/VIII/1544, AGI, Indiferente General 423, L. 20, 781v–782r. The decree was cited in instances of illegal branding, but only once in 1549 (AGI, Justicia 831, n. 13, im. 99), and more frequently after 1560 (AGI, Justicia 1013, n. 2, r. 4, 1561, 13r; AGI, Justicia 1024, n. 1, 1560, 20r).
56. "Deposition, Antonio Gómez, clerigo presbytero," 26/X/1536, AGI, Justicia 1007, 21r.
57. "Testimony, Juan de Villa Santesteban," 7/III/1537, AGI, Justicia 1007, 22v; "Sentencia, Consejo de Indias," 28/III/1537, AGI, Justicia 1007, 38r.
58. "Testimony, Santos García," AGI, Justicia 1037, n. 6, r. 3, 11r–v. The statement from which the quotes are taken appears in the lawsuit initiated by Francisco against his master, Cristóbal de Cueto, in 1549, but were made in reference to the indio Juan discussed here.
59. Three slave sales from 1554 and 1555 in Seville show the variety of people and "signs" that marked them. Hernando, an indio "with letters on his face that say 'slave of Juan Romero,'" was sold in Seville in 1554; one week later a mulato slave marked on both cheeks with an *S* and a nail was sold to Catalina de Villafranca;

and a year later a morisca slave with letters that said "Juan Sánchez, stone-cutter" was sold. Gestoso y Pérez, *Curiosidades antiguas sevillanas*, 86, 89. See also Wilson, "Some Notes on Slavery during the Golden Age," 171–74; Pike, "Sevillian Society in the Sixteenth Century," 348; Santos Cabota, "El mercado de esclavos"; Hugh Thomas, "The Branding (and Baptism) of Slaves."

60. Bryant, *Rivers of Gold, Lives of Bondage*, 124; Gil, "The Indianization of Spain," 127–28.

61. AGI, Justicia 1024, n. 1, 1560. A later witness claimed Gerónimo was from the Moluccas.

62. Bhattacharyya, "Flesh and Skin," 37.

63. "Escritura [de libertad condicional]," 4/IV/1539, México, AGI, Justicia 1173, n. 3, im. 11.

64. AGI, Justicia 199, n. 1, r. 3; AGI, Justicia 202, n. 3; AGI, Justicia 1133, n. 3, r. 2. See also the case of Luis, the mestizo son of Francisco branded with an *S* and a nail on his cheeks in 1579. AGI, Contratación 717, n. 12, 1579.

65. Pike, "Sevillian Society in the Sixteenth Century," 348.

66. AGI, Justicia 716, n. 4.

67. Pike, "Sevillian Society in the Sixteenth Century," 348; John Brooks, "Slavery and the Slave in the Works of Lope de Vega," 234–35. On fugitives of African heritage, see Cortés Alonso, *La esclavitud negra en la España peninsular*, 121.

68. "Statement, Barbola, india," 14/V/1548, AGI, Justicia 831, n. 13, im. 26–27.

69. "Statement, Barbola, india," 14/V/1548, AGI, Justicia 831, n. 13, im. 26–27.

70. "Sentence," 22/II/1549, AGI, Justicia 831, n. 13, im. 109. Some of those funds later were used to pay one of the court solicitors. See "Real Cédula a Cristóbal de San Martín, solicitador," 17/I/1555, Madrid, AGI, Indiferente General 425, L. 23, 127v–128r.

71. "Deposition, Francisco, indio," 24/IX/1540, Seville, AGI, Justicia 1019, n. 5, r. 1, 6r–v. Also see "Testimony, Esteban Ramos," 2/VII/1543, AGI, Justicia 758, n. 5, im. 22. Esteban Ramos swore that eight years before he had seen the slave Francisca being sold in Havana and that she bore the same brand she still had. Gregorio López determined that Francisca should remain as neither slave nor free, under the authority of her current master.

72. "Interrogatorio de Cristóbal Martín y Beatríz Garciá," 27/IX/1549, AGI, Justicia 1019, r. 5, n. 1, 6r.

73. AGI, Justicia 1019, n. 5, r. 1.

74. See the case of a Brazilian indio testifying on behalf of his master in 1559. AGI, Justicia 1024, n. 5.

75. "Escrito de pedimento de Juan, indio," 18/IV/1544, AGI, Justicia 831, r. 3, n. 15, 11r, im. 713.

76. "Testimony, Pedro, indio," 19/IV/1544, AGI, Justicia 831, r. 3, n. 15, 23r, im. 724.

77. "Testimony, Diego López de Moguer," AGI, Justicia 1022, n. 1, r. 2, 13r–v.

78. "Testimony, Martín de Padilla," AGI, Justicia 1022, n. 1, r. 2, 3 pieça, 6r.

79. See question six of the interrogatory on behalf of Juan de Jaén. AGI, Justicia 831, n. 13, 1548, im. 90.

80. Orlando Patterson defines "natal alienation" as an insidious form of effacing blood ties and re-creating new ones related to the slaves' masters (*Slavery and Social Death*, 7).

81. "Pleito Fiscal, Leonor Hernández con Isabel india," AGI, Justicia 832, n. 2, im. 18–27.

82. Isabel was declared free on 25 September 1553. AGI, Justicia 832, n. 2, im. 63.

83. Mignolo, "El metatexto historiográfico y la historiografía Indiana," 368–71.

84. Bernal Díaz del Castillo, a former foot soldier, used sworn testimonies to boost the "historical" veracity of his as-yet unpublished text, the *Verdadera relación*. Adorno, "The Discursive Encounter of Spain and the America," 218. See also Adorno, *The Polemics of Possession in Spanish American Narrative*, 172–90.

85. Andrea Frisch, *The Invention of the Eyewitness*, 23–28.

86. "Testimony, Francisco de la Vega" (sixty-eight years old), AGI, Justicia 908, 23v.

87. Mignolo, "El metatexto historiográfico y la historiografía Indiana," 368.

88. Mignolo, "El metatexto historiográfico y la historiografía Indiana," 368. For an example of an expert witness's exaggerated claims, see "Testimony, Melchior de Villagomez," 14/II/1577, AGI, Justicia 1140, 20r.

89. "Testimony, Francisco Alegre," 1559, AGI, Justicia 1132, n. 5, r. 4, 19r.

90. Franco Silva, *La esclavitud en Sevilla*, 137.

5. Narratives of Territorial Belonging, Just War, and Ransom

1. The taking of depositions varied; they might be taken singly by a local notary or in one of the chambers of the Casa or the Council of the Indies. Written testimony was read by legal assistants to deponents, who then responded in writing. Only rarely were litigants or witnesses present (perhaps, in an adjacent room) while others deposed.

2. Snedaker, "Storytelling in Opening Statements," 132.

3. Steedman, "Enforced Narratives," 36.

4. Bennett and Feldman, *Reconstructing Reality in the Courtroom*, chap. 1; Geertz, *Local Knowledge*, 214–15.

5. On the importance of the opening statement as a "lead narrative" that sets the persuasive tone for the rest of the trial, see Snedaker, "Storytelling."

6. AGI, Justicia 1022, n. 1, r. 1, 1553, 1r; AGI, Justicia 1013, n. 2, r. 4, 1561, 1r.

7. Herzog, *Defining Nations*, 8, 64–66; Real Academia Española, *Diccionario de autoridades*, 4:651.

8. Covarrubias Horozco, *Tesoro de la lengua castellana*, 562, im. 1160. "*Naturaleza*: Naturaleza se toma por la casta, y por la patria, o nación. *Natural* todo aquello que es conforme a la naturaleza de cada uno. Natural de Toledo, el que nació y tiene su parentela en Toledo."

9. Price, "Invitation to Historians," 360.

10. O'Gorman, "Sobre la naturaleza bestial del indio americano," 143–44.

11. AGI, Justicia 832, n. 2. *Naturaleza* is also defined as "la essencia y proprio ser de cada cosa . . . la naturaleza humana" (Real Academia Española, *Diccionario de autoridades*, 4:651).

12. See the discussion in Zavala, *La filosofía política en la conquista de América*, 58–60.

13. Some, like Martín de Angleria, felt strongly that indios were natural slaves. "Carta al Arzobispo de Cosenza," 22/II/1525, *Documentos inéditos para la historia de España*, t. 12, epistolario no. 38, 387–88.

14. Real Academia Española, *Diccionario de autoridades*, 4:651.

15. Whitehead, *Lords of the Tiger Spirit*, 2–5. See also Whitehead's discussion on the effects of slave raiding in the entire Caribbean basin, in "Crises and Transformations." Stephan Lenik argues that the term *Carib* is mainly a colonial invention, in "Comparing Ethnohistoric and Archaeological Evidence from Dominica, West Indies."

16. Gonzalo Fernández de Oviedo y Valdés noted this in his chronicle *Fernández de Oviedo's Chronicle of America* (295 n. 17).

17. Hulme, *Colonial Encounters*, 61–64, 73–78; Boucher, *Cannibal Encounters*, 4–8; Sued Badillo, *Cristóbal Colón y la esclavitud del indio en las Antillas*, 23; D'Anghera, *De Orbe Novo*, 163.

18. Sued Badillo, *Los caribes*, 80. Trinidad was declared Carib in 1511, recategorized as non-Carib in 1518, and redesignated as Carib in 1530. Pearls were not discovered near Cubagua until 1512, at which point the island of Margarita was designated non-Carib. Whitehead, *Lords of the Tiger Spirit*, 11. On Trinidad as a base of slaving operations after 1521, see Newson, *Aboriginal and Spanish Colonial Trinidad*, 72–74. Newson argues that the enslavement of the indigenous peoples of Trinidad continued despite laws to the contrary.

19. "Declaración del Licenciado Rodrigo de Figueroa," AGI, Patronato 177, n. 1, r. 4, 1520. Several of these islands had at one point been labeled caribe. Palencia-Roth, "The Cannibal Law of 1503," 40.

20. Seed, *American Pentimento*, 104.

21. "Real Cédula para que los vecinos de las islas de San Juan y Española . . . ," 15/II/1528, Burgos, AGI, Indiferente General 421, L. 13, 31v–32v. A royal decree of 1569 declared "Carib" females to be enslaveable. Whitehead, "Carib Cannibalism."

22. Seed, *American Pentimento*, 105; Bolaños Cárdenas, "Antropofagia y diferencia cultural"; Pagden, *The Fall of Natural Man*, 82–83.

23. "Requerimiento que se ha de hacer a los indios caribes alzados en la provincia del Perú," s.f. (March 1533), AGI, Lima 565, L. 1, 122v.

24. Pardo, *Prontuario de reales cédulas*, 60.

25. See Bolaños Cárdenas, *Barbarie y canibalismo en la retórica colonial*.

26. Pagden, *The Fall of Natural Man*, 83.

27. Fernández de Oviedo y Valdés, *Sumario de la natural historia de las Indias*, 167.

28. For an example of a carte blanche license, see "Real Cédula dando licencia a Martín de Ochandiano . . . ," 29/XI/1527, Burgos, AGI, Panama 234, L. 3, 36r–v. For examples of litigants being accused of being Brazilian cannibals, see "Testimony, Gaspar Ruíz, escribano público," 16/III/1573, AGI, Justicia 1028, n. 4, r. 1, 31v. See also AGI, Justicia 1023, n. 2, r. 2; AGI, Justicia 1133, n. 3, r. 1, 1575, 2 pieça,

s.f. Maria Cândida Ferreira de Almeida argues that Brazilians were equated with cannibals from the period of first contact (*Tornar-se outro*, 18, 19, 38–43, 11–114).

29. "Testimony, Sebastián Rodríguez [lawyer]," 7/VIII/1553, AGI, Justicia 1022, n. 2, r. 2, 1v.

30. AGI, Justicia 1022, n. 2, r. 2, 19v, 20r.

31. Whitehead, "Indigenous Slavery in South America," 250–52.

32. Malkki, *Purity and Exile*, 6.

33. A notable exception is Neil Whitehead's "Indigenous Slavery in South America," esp. 3:253–57.

34. Smallwood, *Saltwater Slavery*; Sweet, *Domingos Álvares*.

35. "Real Provisión al adelantado don Pedro de Alvarado . . . ," 20/VII/1532, Medina del Campo, AGI, Guatemala 393, L. 1, 42–43v. It took until 1541 for the Crown to issue a decree stating that Spaniards could no longer exchange slaves with caciques in Peru. "Real Provisión," 26/X/1541, Fuensalida, AGI, Lima 566, L. 4, 258v.

36. See, for instance, a license to rescatar slaves in Peru. "Real provision . . . para que puedan comprar los esclavos que los caciques tuvieren," Zaragoza, 8/III/1533, in Konetzke, *Colección de documentos*, 1:142 (the original is in AGI, Lima 565, L. 1, 106r); or, "Real Cédula a Ilián Suárez de Carvajal . . . ," 19/VII/1534, Valladolid, AGI, Lima 565, L. 2, 8v.

37. "Instrucción del virrey don Diego Colón a Pedro Ortiz Matienzo . . . ," 4/XI/1522, Santo Domingo, AGI, Patronato 295, n. 87. The Crown also granted licenses to individuals who could then authorize vecinos to rescatar indios.

38. "Real Cédula a los oficiales de la Casa de la Contratación para que den licencia a Alonso de Quiroga, que va de veedor de rescate de Tierra Firme," 12/XI/1509, AGI, Indiferente General 1961, L. 1, 141r; Otte, *Las perlas del Caribe*, 212–22.

39. Sherman, *Forced Native Labor*, 34.

40. See, for example, the excellent discussion in Sherman, *Forced Native Labor*, chaps. 1 and 3.

41. Early on, Hernán Cortés gave permission for encomenderos to acquire slaves from caciques. Sherman, *Forced Native Labor*, 34. See "Carta de Rodrigo de Contreras a la Corona," 25/VI/1537, León, AGI, Guatemala 40, n. 4, r. 3, im. 4, which explains how Spaniards with repartimientos demanded slaves from their caciques even though they complained that they no longer had any to give.

42. "Proceso contra Rodrigo Nuñez por herrar indios libres," 1529, AGI, Patronato 231, n. 4, r. 2.

43. "Real Provisión a los gobernadores y lugartenientes de las Indias," 9/VI/1530, Madrid, AGI, Patronato 276, n. 4, r. 91.

44. "Real provision sobre la forma y órden que se ha de guarder en hacer esclavos en la guerra y con rescates," Toledo, 20/II/1534, in Konetzke, *Colección de documentos*, 1:154.

45. Miralles Ostos, *Hernán Cortés*, 416.

46. Díaz del Castillo, *Historia verdadera de la conquista de La Nueva España*, 2:234–41; Miralles Ostos, *Hernán Cortés*, 420–21, 451.

47. "Carta del tesorero . . . á los oídores de la Audiencia de Santo Domingo," 18/ II/1526, in Paso y Troncoso, *Epistolario de Nueva España*, 1:92–94. They accused Gonzalo de Salazar and Pero (Pedro) Almíldez Chirino of having appropriated all of Cortes's goods. After Salazar, who had established himself in Cortes's house, was apprehended, he remained imprisoned. Paso y Troncoso, *Epistolario de Nueva España*, 1:93, also quoted in Miralles Ostos, *Hernán Cortés*, 451. See also Chipman, *Nuño de Guzmán and the Province of Pánuco in New Spain*, 85–86, 92–95.

48. For an example, see AGI, Justicia 117.

49. Horn, *Postconquest Coyoacan*, 86–96.

50. In the third of his *Cartas de relación*, Hernán Cortés mentions encountering no resistance when he reached the city of Tenayncan (Tenayuca) (*Cartas de relación: Tercera relación*, Early Modern Spain website, http://www.ems.kcl.ac .uk/content/etext/e016.html). In the 1520s in the central valley of Mexico enco-menderos often did not distinguish between the indigenous subjects granted to them in encomienda (trust) and individual slaves. Thousands of encomienda Indians were enslaved and branded. Gibson, *The Aztecs under Spanish Rule*, 77.

51. The conclusion of the Tepaneca War, around 1433, resulted in Mexica control over the Tepaneca communities of Tenayuca, Azcapotzalco, and Tlacopan, among others. Gibson, *The Aztecs under Spanish Rule*, 17.

52. Townsend, "What in the World Have You Done to Me, My Lover?"

53. Bosch García, *La esclavitud prehispánica entre los Aztecas*, 32–39, 83.

54. The acquisition of slaves of rescate continued despite a 1526 royal decree prohibiting the enslavement of the "free" indios of New Spain. The brandings and declaration of slaves had to follow specific guidelines and take place in the presence of the governor and his officials. "Cédula Real," Granada, 9/XI/1526, in Konetzke, *Colección de documentos*, 1:87–88.

55. Gibson, *The Aztecs under Spanish Rule*, 505 n. 87.

56. This is the underlying argument made by Charles V in his decrees of 1530 and 1534, where he also argued that the enslavement of indios under conditions of rescate was not working (Sherman, *Forced Native Labor*, 33).

57. Altman, *The War for Mexico's West*.

58. AGI, Justicia 1007, n. 1, r. 1, 17r.

59. AGI, Justicia 1007, n. 1, r. 1, 10r, 17r.

60. "Testimony, Francisco Martín," AGI, Justicia 1007, n. 1, r. 1, 20v. When Martín testified on behalf of another indigenous servant in 1542, he said he was twenty-eight years old, which places his birth at 1514. AGI, Justicia 825, im. 41.

61. "Testimony, Francisco Martín," AGI, Justicia 1007, n. 1, r. 1, 20v.

62. Townsend, "What in the World Have You Done to Me, My Lover?," 358. The friar Toribio de Benavente o Motolonía says, "Tuvieron otra manera de hacer esclavos, que llamaron *huehuetlatlaculli*, que quiere decir "culpa o servidumbre antigua" (*Memoriales*, pt. 2, 369).

63. Even friars like Motolinía who spent a good deal of time interviewing Nahua peoples had a difficult time understanding the intricate practices of human bondage. Motolinía, *Memoriales*, pt. 2, 366.

64. "Response, Gonzalo de Salazar," 1537, AGI, Justicia 1007, n. 1, r. 1, 2r.

65. Miralles Ostos, *Hernán Cortés*, 451–52.

66. López de Gómara, *Historia*, 2:359–60. Bernal Díaz del Castillo details the items Cortés brought with him (*Historia verdadera de la conquista de La Nueva España*, chap. 195, 522). On the two hundred deaths, see Gibson, *The Aztecs under Spanish Rule*, 79.

67. Salazar returned to Spain, in either 1529 or 1530, because he was one of several individuals investigated as a part of Hernán Cortés's review of office (residencia). He remained in Spain until 1538. Montell, *México*, 306–7; Himmerich y Valencia, *The Encomenderos of New Spain*, 234.

68. Real Academia Española, *Diccionario de autoridades*, 4:651.

69. Robert I. Burns, *Las Siete Partidas*, 4:977–78. A very clear synthesis of the written opinions of renowned theologians, jurists, and others is presented in García Añoveros, "Carlos V." See also the transcribed documents where different opinions on just war are expressed (Hanke and Millares Carlo, *Cuerpo de documentos del siglo XVI*). On debates in Mexico, see Bataillon, Bienvenu, and Velasco Gómez, *Las teorías de la guerra justa*.

70. Fernández de Oviedo y Valdés, *Historia general y natural*, 42:11, 4:101–2.

71. This is exactly what happened in the area near Trujillo, Honduras. Chamberlain, *The Conquest and Colonization of Honduras*, 120; Sherman, *Forced Native Labor*, 43–44.

72. The lieutenant governor, Álvaro Saavedra Cerón, was a good example of someone who abused his office by participating in the slave trade. Sherman, *Forced Native Labor*, 34.

73. By 1540, Francisco had requested a *receptoría* for his master to appear before the council. "Real Provisión de receptoría . . . ," Madrid, AGI, Patronato 278, n. 2, r. 54.

74. "Probanza of Martín Alonso de los Rios," AGI, Justicia 1162, n. 6, r. 2, im. 49.

75. "Testimony, Pedro Gutiérrez de los Rios," AGI, Justicia 1162, n. 6, r. 2, im. 34–35. Details of the numbers of Nicaraguans being shipped to Panama come from "Cargos contra Pedro de los Rios," AGI, Justicia 298, n. 1. The interrogatorio mentions eighty indios in one instance and one hundred indios in another. Pedro de los Rios was later accused of usurping a number of indios of Pedrarías Dávila after he (Pedrarías Dávila) was forced into exile. Sherman, *Forced Native Labor*, 57.

76. Ibarra Rojas, *Fronteras étnicas en la conquista*, 105–6.

77. Sherman, *Forced Native Labor*, 26–27.

78. "Deposition, Diego Gutiérrez de los Rios," 8/I/1540, AGI, Justicia 1162, n. 6, r. 2, im. 35–36.

79. "Final Statement, Francisco," 26/VI/1540, AGI, Justicia 1162, n. 6, r. 2, im. 58.

80. "Real Provisión," Toledo, 20/XI/1528, in Konetzke, *Colección de documentos*, 1:109–11.

81. "Cross-questioning of Martín Alonso de los Rios," 13/I/1540, AGI, Justicia 1162, n. 6, r. 2, im. 6.

82. "Testimony, fray Tomás de Berlanga," AGI, Justicia 1162, n. 6, r. 2, im. 56.

83. "Royal Decree," Toledo, 20/II/1534, in Konetzke, *Colección de documentos*, 1:155.
84. "Statement of Villalobos, fiscal of the Council of the Indies," 6/V/1545, AGI, Justicia 1174, n. 1, r. 2.
85. "Opening Statement," AGI, Justicia 1037, n. 5, 1r. Diego, Pedro's brother, was known for selling off his encomienda Indians; Catalina Nicolasa may have been one such victim. Sherman, *Forced Native Labor*, 60.
86. Castañeda sold Indians from the repartimientos of Mistega and Cindega. "Residencia of Francisco de Castañeda," Vega Bolaños, *Colección Somoza*, 4:91; Ibarra Rojas, *Fronteras étnicas en la conquista*, 198 n. 61.
87. Sherman, *Forced Native Labor*, 26–27, 55–56. The Chorotega peoples were later slaughtered by Miguel de Estete in his entrada of 1529.
88. "Interrogation of Catalina," AGI, Justicia 1037, n. 5, 26r.
89. Sherman, *Forced Native Labor*, 56.
90. Vega Bolaños, *Colección Somoza*, 4:462–63; Patrick S. Werner, *Época temprana de León Viejo*, 36; Patrick S. Werner, *Ethnographic Data of Early Colonial Nicaragua*, 202. Radell and Parsons, "Realejo," 301.
91. "Mariquita's testimony," AGI, Justicia 1037, n. 5, 27v. Mother and daughter came to Spain with Alonso de Alvarado around 1544, the year he returned to Spain to marry. AGI, Justicia 1037, n. 5, 48r. Alonso de Alvarado was not related to Pedro de Alvarado, who had died in 1541.
92. "Interrogation of Catalina," AGI, Justicia 1037, n. 5, 28r.
93. "Mariquita's testimony," AGI, Justicia 1037, n. 5, 28v.
94. In 1533 King Charles V granted Pedro de Alvarado, governor of Guatemala, the liberty to enslave peoples who refused to accept Christianity, effectively giving him free rein to enslave whomever he wished; especially vulnerable were the Chontal people. "Real Cédula," Belpuche, 19/III/1533, in Konetzke, *Colección de documentos*, 1:143–44.
95. Mumford, "Litigation as Ethnography." I thank the anonymous reader who made this bibliographic suggestion.

6. *Identifying* Indios

1. On visual and living representations of indigenous peoples at the Spanish court and elsewhere see, Carina Lee Johnson, *Cultural Hierarchy in Sixteenth-Century Europe*. Christoph Weiditz drew two Mexican models in a stylized manner (*Authentic Everyday Dress of the Renaissance*, plates 22 and 23). Compare these with Hans Burgkmair's drawing *People of Calicut* (1517–1518), copied from the sequence of 137 woodcuts called the *Triumph of Maximilian I*, a procession of the peoples of the Habsburg empire, including the people of Calicut (who were under Portuguese dominion), wearing feathered skirts and carrying spears, and those of America, bearing stalks of corn. Alegría, *Las primeras representaciones gráficas del indio americano*, 78. For a comparison of two Weiditz drawings with one by Albrecht Dürer, see Satterfield, "The Assimilation of the Marvelous Other," 10–11. See also Feest, "The Collecting of American Indian Artifacts in Europe"; MacDonald, "Collecting a New World"; Elliott, *The Old World and*

the *New*, 28. On indigenous travelers to Europe, see Foreman, *Indians Abroad*; Cline, "Hernando Cortés and the Aztec Indians in Spain"; de la Puente Luna, "Into the Heart of the Empire," 70–90.

2. Seth, *Europe's Indians*, 42.

3. Seth, *Europe's Indians*, 43.

4. José Luis Martínez, *Pasajeros de Indias*; Silverblatt, *Modern Inquisitions*; Siegert, "Pasajeros a Indias"; Groebner, *Who Are You?*, 139–41; Schwartz, *All Can Be Saved*; Rappaport, "'Así lo paresçe por su aspeto,'" 610–11.

5. Martín Cásares, *La esclavitud en la Granada de siglo XVI*, 149; Epstein, *Speaking of Slavery*. Numerous travel permits to Latin America and Castile were granted for female and male "white" slaves before 1550. Joanne Rappaport argues that in the latter part of the sixteenth century the color white began to describe the faces of Castilians in travel permits to America, but that it also continued to function as a more generalized descriptor for Indians and others into the seventeenth century ("'Así lo paresçe por su aspeto,'" 620).

6. Schwartz, "Colonial Identities and the *Sociedad de Castas*," esp. 189; Burns, "Unfixing Race," 189, 202; María Elena Martínez, *Genealogical Fictions*, 13. On the hardening of racial labels, see Sweet, "The Iberian Roots of American Racist Thought."

7. Although the color black was increasingly associated with slave status, it was not associated with one group of people from a specific geographic location. Throughout the sixteenth century, a diverse range of enslaved peoples— including those from Brazil, Calicut or Cochín, the Spice Islands, and northern and sub-Saharan Africa—were identified by this color. The term *geohumoralism* comes from Floyd-Wilson, *English Ethnicity and Race in Early Modern Drama*, 2.

8. José Luis Martínez, *Pasajeros de Indias*, 31–40; Siegert, "Pasajeros a Indias"; Groebner, *Who Are You?*, 139–41; María Elena Martínez, *Genealogical Fictions*, 63–77; Boyarin, *The Unconverted Self*; Rappaport, "'Así lo paresçe por su aspeto,'" 610–11.

9. Herzog, "Identities and Processes of Identification in the Atlantic World."

10. Rebecca Earle, *The Body of the Conquistador*, chap. 1.

11. Floyd-Wilson, *English Ethnicity and Race in Early Modern Drama*, 2; Huarte Navarro, *Examen de ingenios*, 103–18; Cortés, *Fisonomía y varios secretos de naturaleza*, 1–4; Cañizares-Esguerra, *Nature, Empire, and Nation*. In addition to its physiognomic application, the term *calidad* was used to denote one's social or moral position and condition (whether elite or commoner, slave or free). See also Pagden, *The Fall of Natural Man*, 45–47, 120–21; Las Casas, *Apologética historia sumaria*.

12. Las Casas, *Apologética historia sumaria*, 1:118, libro 2, cáp. 24. Anthony Pagden calls it "milieu-theory" (*The Fall of Natural Man*, 137–40).

13. Porter, *Windows of the Soul*, 28; Groebner, *Who Are You?*, 119, 131, 137, 139–41; Ziegler, "Physiognomy, Science, and Proto-Racism." On examining slaves for purchase, see Mourad, *La physiognomonie arabe*, 55–57. Valentin Groebner argues that the more flexible definition of *complexion*, based on body color

derived from living in a particular habitat, evolved into an immutable and fixed concept ("*Complexio*/Complexion").

14. Real Academia Española, *Diccionario de autoridades*, 4:644. Sebastián de Covarrubias Orozco's 1673 dictionary, *Tesoro de la lengua castellana o española*, refers to *nación* as "vale Reyno, ó Provincia estendida" (pt. 2, 119r). On merchant communities, see Mauró, "Merchant Communities," 255–86; Studnicki-Gizbert, *A Nation upon the Ocean Sea*; Trivellato, *The Familiarity of Strangers*.

15. "Testimony, Alvaro López," AGI, Justicia 829, n. 2, 1547, im. 64.

16. Epstein, *Speaking of Slavery*; Groebner, *Who Are You?*, 108–11; Floyd-Wilson, *English Ethnicity and Race in Early Modern Drama*, 30. On skin color as indicative of biological reductionism in Granada, see Martín Cásares, *La esclavitud en la Granada del siglo XVI*, 146–51, 172; Vincent, *Minorias y marginados*, 243–45; Franco Silva, *La esclavitud en Sevilla*, 216, 222–23, 244–45.

17. A noble of African heritage named Juan de Valladolid, who had served at the royal court, was appointed to the position. See Ortiz de Zúñiga and Espinosa y Carzel, *Anales eclésiasticos y seculares*, 3:78; Pike, *Aristocrats and Traders*, 173. See also Verlinden, *L'esclavage dans l'Europe médiévale*. On the trans-Saharan trade, see Rumeu de Armas, *España en el Africa Atlántica*, 1:163–66; Franco Silva, *La esclavitud en Andalucía*, 135–36; Forbes, *Africans and Native Americans*, 28. From 1470 to 1525, around two thousand slaves were freed by wills, purchase, ransom, or other means.

18. Martín Cásares, *La esclavitud en la Granada del siglo XVI*, 147.

19. "Testimony, Pablo Collado," 26/IV/1567, AGI, Justicia 1026, n. 2, r. 2, 17v.

20. "Testimony, Pedro Márques," AGI, Justicia 199, n. 1, r. 3, 1r; Covarrubias Horozco, *Tesoro de la lengua castellana*, s.v. "Natural," 120r. On Tlaxcalan indigenous vassals claiming, as early as 1529, specific political rights as members of the nation of indios, see Baber, "Categories, Self-Representation and the Construction of the *Indios*," 27–28. It would be interesting to see whether the idea that specific "nations" of indios in America had distinct political rights merged with use of the term *nation* for the "negros," "loros," and "Canarios" who maintained specific legal rights in Seville.

21. See, for example, "Opening statement, Sebastian Rodríguez, abogado," AGI, Justicia 716, n. 4, 1536, 20r; Baber, "Categories, Self-Representation and the Construction of the *Indios*," 28.

22. Coromines, *Diccionario crítico etimológico de la lengua catellana*, s.v. "casta." David Nirenberg argues that by the 1430s the terms *raza*, *casta*, and *linaje* were used to refer to Jewish converts to Catholicism ("Was There Race before Modernity?," 252–53). Occasionally, passenger licenses refer to someone of the "casta de moros." "Real Cédula," 28/X/1548, AGI, Indiferente General 1964, L. 11, 106r–v. The use of the term *casta* to indicate mixed ancestry began to enter popular discourse in Mexico in the late sixteenth century (María Elena Martínez, *Genealogical Fictions*, 168) and even later elsewhere (Rappaport, "'Así lo paresçe por su aspeto,'" 605). *Casta* also developed as a rubric for distinguishing the invented and self-appropriated ethnic identities—such as *bran*, *popo*, and so

forth—used by the diverse enslaved diasporic peoples of West Africa, and the term eventually became interchangeable with *nación*. O'Toole, "From the Rivers of Guinea to the Valleys of Peru," 26–27.

23. "Testimony, Diego Sarmiento de la Cerda," 18/VIII/1553, Valladolid, AGI, Justicia 202, n. 3, 2r. In sixteenth-century Castile, the category mestizo often referred to individuals with one parent of either Islamic or indigenous heritage. It is unlikely that Diego Sarmiento de la Cerda would have emphasized his Islamic heritage, because of the growing emphasis on Christian purity of blood in family genealogies.

24. O'Toole, "From the Rivers of Guinea to the Valleys of Peru," 25. Citing Sandoval's *De instauranda Aethiopum salute*, 92, O'Toole reveals an archival moment of inscription when Alonso de Sandoval interviewed different slaves. Although their answers to the question "Which casta are you?" revealed a plethora of identities, Sandoval immediately collapsed the variety of answers under the rubric of *casta bran*.

25. Porter, *Windows of the Soul*, x. Lawyers and witnesses in the courtroom also used physiognomic indicators to determine the identities of "caciques" petitioning for titles and increased status. See de la Puente Luna, "Into the Heart of the Empire," 177–80. On the meaning of *aspect*, see Coromines, *Diccionario crítico etimológico de la lengua castellana*, s.v. "aspecto": "Aspecto, tomado del lat. *aspectus* . . . 'acción de mirar,' 'presencia, aspecto.'"

26. Porter, *Windows of the Soul*, 51; "Testimony, Fernando Poncor," AGI, Justicia 1132, n. 5, r. 4, 1559, 20v. For a description of head shape (*hechura de la cabeza*), see AGI, Justicia 1178, n. 4, 41r, im. 81.

27. Rappaport, "'Así lo paresçe por su aspeto,'" 611–12. A typical response was: "It seems that he is [an indio] because of the physiognomy of his face, body, head, and manner of speaking" ("Testimony, fray Rodrigo de Ladrada," 1553, AGI, Justicia 1023, n. 1, r. 1, 80r. For other examples (the language varies slightly), see "Testimony, Nicolás Beltrán," 7/IX/1553, AGI, Justicia 1023, n. 1, r. 1, 74r; "Testimony, Antonio de Venero," 22/IV/1567, AGI, Justicia 1026, n. 2, r. 2, 17r; "Testimony, Mathias de Huerta Sarmiento," 1575, AGI, Justicia 1050, n. 9, r. 2, 53v.

28. "Testimony, Pedro Gutiérrez," AGI, Justicia 1025, n. 2, r. 2, 1563, 15v.

29. "Testimony, Beatríz, muger de Juan Vázquez," AGI, Justicia 908, n. 1, pieça 2, 10r–v.

30. "Testimony, Marina Rodríguez, india," 12/I/1567, AGI, Justicia 895, n. 7, 38v, im. 104.

31. "Testimony, Francisco del Villalpando," 23/VI/1567, AGI, Justicia 1039, n. 5, r. 2, 22v.

32. "Testimony, Esteban de Cabrera," 24/V/1561, AGI, Justicia 856, n. 2, im. 14.

33. "Testimony, Juan, indio," 24/V/1561, AGI, Justicia 856, n. 2, im. 14–15.

34. See, for example, "Testimony, Manuel, indio," 1573, AGI, Justicia 1133, n. 2, 5r; and AGI, Contratación 715, n. 7, s.f.

35. "Testimony, Juan Ortíz de Zárate," 5/V/1572, AGI, Escribanía de Cámara 1007B, 26r.

36. Linguistic assessment also occurred at the local level. See the example of three slaves being freed in Ciudad Rodrigo in 1545, in "Santos Garcia, witness," I/1536, AGI, Justicia 1037, n. 6, r. 3, 11r; "Deposition, Licenciado Lope de Valderrama, teniente de corregidor," 11/XII/1545, AGI, Justicia 1037, n. 6, r. 3, 33r.

37. "Testimony, Santos Garcia" (en lengua Mexicana), 20/I/1546, AGI, Justicia 1037, n. 6, r. 3, 11r. Conversely, the bishop of Cartagena, Gregorio de Beteta, reported speaking with Esteban (from Cuzcatlán) "in the language of indios," not in the more specific "Mexican language." Beteta had taken his vows as a Dominican friar in 1533, and at some point had visited Mexico, where he would have learned Nahuatl. "Testimony, Gregorio de Beteta, Obispo de Cartagena," IX/1553, AGI, Justicia 1023, n. 1, r. 1, 78v.

38. "Testimony, Antonio de Peromato," 1552, AGI, Justicia 1022, n. 1, r. 1, 12v.

39. "Testimony, Francisco de Castellanos, treasurer," AGI, Justicia 1022, n. 1, r. 1, 33r.

40. "Questions for the interrogatory on behalf of doña Aldonça Manrique," 29/IV/1575, AGI, Justicia 1133, n. 3, r. 3, 19r.

41. AGI, Justicia 1023, n. 2, r. 2.

42. "Language interrogation of Juan," 25/I/1552, AGI, Justicia 994, n. 4, r. 1, 109v–110v. The linguists were Marcos Hernández (New Spain) and Gonçalo de Acosta (Brazil).

43. "Testimony, Ana de Alfaro," 4/IX/1553, AGI, Justicia 1022, n. 2, r. 2, 20r.

44. "Testimony, Pedro, indio," 19/IV/1544, AGI, Justicia 741, n. 3, r. 15, 22.

45. The idea that all indios formed a single nation, united by abstract notions of imperial sovereignty—despite the vast oceanic waters and continents that separated them—is an early modern construct that will be explored at greater length in chapter 7.

46. See "Testimony, Juan Ruíz Rubio," 28/III/1561, AGI, Justicia 1025, n. 2, r. 2, 21r; "Testimony, Juan de Porres," 24/III/1560, AGI, Justicia 1050, n. 5, r. 2, 30r; "Testimony, Doctor Sancho Sánchez de Muñon," 26/XI/1572, Madrid, AGI, Justicia 1028, n. 4, r. 1, 1574, 22v, ibid. On pierced ears, see "Petition from the prosecuting attorney, Licenciado Gamboa," I/1570, AGI, Justicia 895, n. 7, 1569, 14r, im. 27.

47. Mira Caballos, *Indios y mestizos americanos*, 161–63; AGI, Justicia 1023, n. 2, r. 2.

48. "Bill of Sale," 4/III/1544, Toledo, AGI, Justicia 741, n. 3, r. 15, im. 717.

49. "Opening Statement, Antonia, india," 1574, AGI, Justicia 446, n. 2, r. 7, 1r.

50. "Testimony, don Sebastián Poma Hilaquita," 1/VII/1574, AGI, Justicia 446, n. 2, r. 7, 27r.

51. "Testimony, Gregorio González," AGI, Justicia 446, n. 2, r. 7, 1574, 26v.

52. "Testimony, Gregorio González," AGI, Justicia 446, n. 2, r. 7, 1574, 27r. On Don Sebastián's return voyage to Peru, see "Real Cédula . . . permitiendo a D. Sebastián Poma Hilaquita, indio, regresar a Perú," 10/VIII/1574, El Pardo, AGI, Indiferente General 1968, L. 20, 6–7v.

53. On *loro*, see Coromines, *Diccionario crítico etimológico de la lengua castellan*, s.v. "loro": "color oscuro . . . probablemente del lat. Laurus 'laurel.'" In the later (1726-37) *Diccionario de autoridades*, *loro* described a color between black and

white, similar to the hue of ripened wheat (Real Academia Española, *Diccionario de autoridades*, 4:433). See also Forbes, *Africans and Native Americans*, 26–27, 106–12. On *mulato* referring to the color of indios, see "Venta," 27/ IV/1554, Medina del campo, AGI, Justicia 1022, n. 5, r. 1, 1557, 2r; AGI, Justicia 1039, n. 5, r. 2, 1572, 19r. On the color mulato being used to describe slaves from distinct locations in Extremadura, see Periáñez Gómez, "La esclavitud en Extremadura en la Edad Moderna," 504. On the color baço, see Periáñez Gómez, "La esclavitud en Extremadura en la Edad Moderna," 62–63.

54. Verlinden, *L'esclavage dans l'Europe médiévale*; Blackburn, "The Old World Background to European Colonial Slavery"; Martín Cásares, *La esclavitud en la Granada del siglo XVI*, 32; Epstein, *Speaking of Slavery*, 79–80, 81, 108. The term *moro* was derived from the Roman description of the ancient kingdom of Mauritania (present-day Mauritania, Morocco, and part of Tunisia), from the "Mauri" or inhabitants of that area, and from the Greek *mavros* and Latin *maurus*, both of which were used to describe a tawny skin color. In Italian port cities, *maurus/a* also referred to a person of the Muslim faith. Constable, *Trade and Traders*, 234. Isidore of Seville used the term *maurus* to mean the color black. In Genoa "Mori," "moro," or "Mauri" slaves, qualified by color descriptors such as "coloris olivegni," "nero," or "loro," were sold in increasing numbers in the last decade of the fifteenth century. See Gioffrè, *Il mercato degli schiavi a Genova nel secolo XV*, 28–29; Forbes, *Africans and Native Americans*, 67; Fuchs, *Exotic Nation*, 116–18.

55. On the intermeshed nature of the post-1453 slave-merchant community, see Gioffrè, *Il mercato degli schiavi a Genova nel secolo XV*, 31; Franco Silva, *La esclavitud en Sevilla*, 145–46, 152–53; David Brion Davis, *Slavery and Human Progress*; Forbes, *Africans and Native Americans*, 107; Blumenthal, *Enemies and Familiars*, 15, 61–62.

56. Franco Silva, *La esclavitud en Andalucía*, 42–46. On Oran, see Pike, *Aristocrats and Traders*, 171. On indios from the East Indies, see Gil, "The Indianization of Spain in the Sixteenth Century," 127–28. On Antonio of Malucca (also known as Malacca or Melaka, on the Malay Peninsula) and Pedro from Calicut, see Franco Silva, *Regesto documental sobre la esclavitud Sevillana*, 60. In the litigation suits I have analyzed, former slaves from Cochín or Calicut identified themselves as "loros" and were also identified as "black."

57. Groebner, *Who Are You?*, 118. For a different perspective, see Sweet, "The Iberian Roots of American Racist Thought," 144–45. On Saracen slaves, see Verlinden, *L'esclavage dans l'Europe médiévale*, 1:282–85; Constable, "Muslim Spain and Mediterranean Slavery," 274–78; Marzal Palacios, *La esclavitud en Valencia*. See also Martín Cásares, *La esclavitud en la Granada del siglo XVI*, 170–72, esp. graphic 12; Franco Silva, *La esclavitud en Sevilla*, 138; Lobo Cabrera, *La esclavitud en las Canarias*, 150–55; Izquierdo Labrado, "La esclavitud."

58. Forbes, *Africans and Native Americans*, 110.

59. Forbes, *Africans and Native Americans*, 99. See also Groebner, *Who Are You?*, 119, 131, 137.

60. Franco Silva, *La esclavitud en Sevilla*, 138, 138 n. 21. See also Martín Cásares, *La esclavitud en la Granada*, 157. See the passenger license for "Antón Martín, loro in color, son of Diego González Moro, and Gracia González, vecinos of the village of Montemolín," 21/II/1540, AGI, Pasajeros L. 3, E. 1224.

61. Martín Cásares described María's being captured in a "province of Berbería" "junto con otros negros a la edad de 10 años" (*La esclavitud en la Granada*, 172 n. 71). Juan Bautista, "de color Moreno" was captured at the same time. The group of slaves went first to Oran and then, two months later, to Málaga. On the diversity of color descriptors in Seville, see a 1517 sale document describing a berberisco boy of thirteen as "entre loro y negro" and a thirty-five-year-old berberisco man as "negro algo loro" (Franco Silva, *La esclavitud en Sevilla*, 138 n. 22).

62. Franco Silva, *La esclavitud en Sevilla*, 138 n. 21. See the passenger licenses for "Domingo, Italian, son of Antonio Burnengo and Margarita, from Cádiz, loro in color and free," 9/X/1534, AGI, Contratación 5536, L. 3, 5; "Benito Ramos, loro in color, son of a white father and a black mother," 9/X/1534, AGI, Contratación 5536, L. 3, 5; Alberta, the color lora, who was the daughter of a slave from Guinea born near Seville, "Que se devuelva una esclava," 4/IX/1536, Valladolid, AGI, Panama 235, L. 6, 39v–40r; "Informe sobre la esclava del licenciado Cervantes," 23/II/1538, Valladolid, AGI, Santo Domingo, 868, L. 1, 111r–v; "Licencia a Gaspar de Herrera," 31/I/1539, Toledo, AGI, Indiferente General 1962, L. 6, 165v–166r.

63. Saco, *Historia de la esclavitud*, 1:126. See also Forbes, *Africans and Native Americans*, 31; Fernández de Navarrete, *Obras D. Martín Fernández de Navarrete*, "Asiento con Rodrigo de Bastidas," 1:448; Fernández de Navarrete, *Obras D. Martín Fernández de Navarrete*, "Capitulación con Alonso Vélez de Mendoza," 1:450–53.

64. Fernández de Navarrete, *Obras D. Martín Fernández de Navarrete*, "Voyage of Amerigo Vespucci, 1497," 2:132.

65. Cortés Alonso, *La esclavitud en Valencia*, 60.

66. For a discussion on the color loro, see Forbes, *Africans and Native Americans*, 44. The life experiences of Christopher Columbus (in Genoa, in Portugal and Madeira, and at the outpost of El Mina), as Stuart B. Schwartz argues, "reflected the continuity between the Mediterranean and Atlantic worlds and his own transitional position between them" ("The Iberian Atlantic to 1650," 148). Catalina Nicolasa and her daughter, Maria de la Cruz, are described as "esclavas loras," in "Carta de obligación," 28/III/1548, AGI, Justicia 1037, n. 5, 9r. The physical descriptor *loro* was used in Spain to designate someone whose coloration was somewhere between black and white, similar to the dark brown color of wheat when it has ripened. Real Academia Española, *Diccionario de autoridades*, 4:433. The Catalan term *llor/a* was used to describe slaves in Valencia in the fifteenth century. Blumenthal, *Enemies and Familiars*, 15, 61–62. In 1500 an indigenous slave named Pastor, who was described as "loro, Mariñon," was sold in Seville. Franco Silva, *Regesto documental sobre la esclavitud sevillana*, n.p. Slave sale documents often included a description of the skin color (and other

outstanding features) of the slave. On the variety of terms used in Granada, see Martín Cásares, *La esclavitud en la Granada del siglo XVI*, 33. See also Mira Caballos, *Indios y mestizos americanos*, 66. The descriptor *loro* was only used sporadically in America to identify indigenous slaves. The *protocolos* for Mexico City, 1525–28, give no physical descriptions of indigenous slaves; until West African slaves began arriving the term *esclavo* was used to identify indios being sold. Two early examples from Seville come from sale documents in 1500 (Pastor, described as "loro, Mariñon") and in 1512 (María, eight years old, described as an "india lora"). Franco Silva, *Regesto documental sobre la esclavitud sevillana*, n.p. On Brazilian slaves in Valencia, see Cortés Alonso, *La esclavitud en Valencia*, 60.

67. "Testimony, Catalina, india," 1551, AGI, Justicia 1037, n. 5, 27v; "Carta de venta," Villa de Almagro, 8/III/1541, AGI, Justicia 1038, n. 2, 1556, 19r–20v; "Medical Confirmation of Death of María, india," 7/XII/1566, AGI, Justicia 1025, n. 5, r. 2, 56r; "Petition from the prosecuting attorney, Licenciado Gamboa," I/1570, AGI, Justicia 895, n. 7, 1569, 14r im. 27.

68. "Título de venta, Miguel de Salzedo," 7/III/1539, AGI, Justicia 758, n. 3, pieça 1, 17. The question in the interrogatory also identifies the plaintiff as "so color loro." AGI, Justicia 1162, n. 6, r. 2; "Carta de venta," in "Capitán Martín del Prado con Juan, indio," 1544, AGI, Justicia 741, n. 15, 15im. 717.

69. "Verification of Catalina's identity by the corregidor of Burgos," 1551, AGI, Justicia 1037, n. 5, 27v. By the seventeenth century, the descriptor *white* had developed a different connotation. Real Academia Española, *Diccionario de autoridades*, 1:616.

70. Martín Cásares, *La esclavitud en la Granada del siglo XVI*, 145–51; "Deposition, Juan Centeno," 8/I/1546, AGI, Justicia 1037, n. 6, r. 3, 34v.

71. "Bill of Sale," 5/III/1560, AGI, Justicia 1050, n. 2, r. 5, 2r; "Power of attorney to sell," 4/VIII/1559, AGI, Justicia 1050, n. 2, r. 5, 1560, 13r.

72. Franco Silva, *Regesto documental sobre la esclavitud sevillana*. As late as 1549, Manuel da Nóbrega referred to indigenous Brazilian women as black. Forbes, *Africans and Native Americans*, 69–70. Muriel Nazzari analyzes a much later estate settlement that refers to "black Indians" ("Favored Women, Subjected Indians").

73. AGI, Justicia 1050, n. 2, r. 5, 1560, 14r.

74. AGI, Justicia 1133, n. 2, 5r. In the Canaries the term *mulato* referred to people of mixed North African (of the Islamic faith or someone identified as a moro) and West African (black) heritage. Lobo Cabrera, *La esclavitud en las Canarias*, 154–55. In "La esclavitud en Huelva y Palos," Julio Izquierdo Labrado argues that the color mulato came to replace loro in describing peoples of mixed heritage. For examples of mulato as a color, see Gil, "The Indianization of Spain in the Sixteenth Century," 128; AGI, Justicia 1039, n. 5, r. 2, 1572, 19r, which notes the sale in 1596 of a slave, "de color mulato," from the Indies of Portugal, possibly an india, and describes the Brazilian indio Vicente as the color mulato. By 1601, *loro* had been replaced by *mulato* in contemporary dictionaries. Rosal, *Diccionario*

etimológico, "Loro llamaban al esclavo que agora decimos mulato, no bien negro," 424.

75. "Bill of Sale," AGI, Justicia 895, n. 7; "Protesta de Hernando de Rivas," 16/I/1570, AGI, Justicia 895, n. 7, 15r, im. 29.

76. "Respuesta de Francisco Sarmiento," AGI, Justicia 895, n. 7, 27r, im. 89.

77. "Testimony, Marina Rodríguez, india," 12/I/1569, AGI, Justicia 895, n. 7, im. 105; AGI, Justicia 895, n. 7, 1569, im. 119.

78. AGI, Justicia 1050, n. 9, r. 2, 47r. She could, of course, have been manumitted if someone had purchased her freedom.

79. Noble David Cook, "The Mysterious Catalina."

80. "Testimony, Mathias de Huerta Sarmiento," 1575, AGI, Justicia 1050, n. 9, r. 2, 53v.

81. Manuel Lobo Cabrera calculated that at least fifty-nine expeditions (*cabalgadas*) were launched from the Canaries to Berbería from 1513 to 1600 (*La esclavitud en las Canarias*, 72).

82. The itineraries of other slaves who arrived to work in the mines is equally complex. The historian Alessandro Stella discusses the case of the enslaved Antón Zape, who, after his capture and "seasoning" on the Cape Verde Islands, traveled to Lisbon and eventually to the Guadalcanal mines, in 1559. There, conditions were so horrific that he escaped with three other men, only to be re-captured twice, eventually dying from an infection in a wound. Stella, *Histoires d'esclavages dans la peninsula Ibérique*, 81–82.

83. "Testimony Arias Maldonado," 1575, AGI, Justicia 1050, n. 9, r. 2, 55r.

84. On *mestizo* as referring to the offspring of an African or indigenous woman and a Spanish male, see AGI, Justicia 1025, n. 1, r. 2, 21r–v. On *mulato* being used to depict coloration in New Granada, see Rappaport, "'Así lo paresçe por su aspeto,'" 610, 620. These terms were not commonly used in Peru and Mexico before 1550. María Elena Martínez, *Genealogical Fictions*, 144, 146. My own research shows that, although the 1538–1548 baptismal records for the Sagrario Parish in Lima, Peru, did not use the term *mestizo*, the 1556–1578 records did. "Bautismos, Sagrario," Archivo Arzobispal de Lima, Peru, tomo 2A, 1556–1578.

7. Transimperial Indios

1. I borrow the term *entangled* from Gould, "Entangled Histories, Entangled Worlds." See also Subrahmanyam, "Holding the World in Balance," 1363.

2. Benton, *A Search for Sovereignty*, xii.

3. Adorno, *Polemics of Possession*.

4. Gruzinski, *What Time Is It There?*, 18.

5. Gruzinski, *Las cuatro partes del mundo*, 153.

6. Lisa Lowe's excellent essay "The Intimacies of Four Continents" examines the spatial and economic connections, relations, and mixings (which she defines as intimacies) created by and about Chinese laborers forcibly transported to different parts of the world. From these global intimacies, she argues,

"emerged not only modern humanism but a modern racialized division of labor" (192).

7. "Stepping on the shadows of empire" is a rephrasing of a quote taken from Dening, "The Comaroffs Out of Africa," 473.

8. Subrahmanyam, *Three Ways to Be Alien*, 138.

9. Subrahmanyam, "Holding the World in Balance," 1363, 1367.

10. Subrahmanyam, "Connected Histories," 748.

11. Gould, "Entangled Histories, Entangled Worlds," 766.

12. "Bill of Sale," 9/V/1554, Valladolid, AGI, Justicia 1023, n. 2, r. 2; "Testimony, Juan Vanhelst," AGI, Justicia 1023, n. 2, r. 2, s.f.

13. For a discussion of merchant communities, see Subrahmanyam, "Introduction." On the Flemish in Seville, see Morales Padrón, *Historia de Sevilla*, 82–83. On the French in Seville, see Morales Padrón, *Historia de Sevilla*, 84.

14. Rothman, *Brokering Empire*, 14.

15. Gil, "The Indianization of Spain in the Sixteenth Century," 127.

16. For examples of indio slaves being sold at the markets of Badajoz or Zafra, see AGI, Justicia 783, n. 3, 5v; AGI, Justicia 836, n. 1; AGI, Justicia 1025, n. 5, r. 2; AGI, Justicia 1023, n. 1, r. 1. On Portuguese merchants at the Zafra fair, see Periáñez Gómez, "La esclavitud en Extremadura en la Edad Moderna," 61–62. See also Periáñez Gómez, "La esclavitud en Zafra durante la Edad Moderna"; Periáñez Gómez, "Negros y negreros en la feria."

17. Dominguez Ortíz, La población de Sevilla; Pike, "Seville in the Sixteenth Century," 3.

18. Franco Silva, *La esclavitud en Andalucía*, 54–57. On Brazilian slaves coming to Europe as early as 1509, see Metcalf, "The Entradas of Bahia of the Sixteenth Century," 375–76, n. 9.

19. Martín Cásares, *La esclavitud en la Granada del siglo XVI*, 22; Verlinden, *L'esclavage dans l'Europe médiévale*.

20. Otte, *Sevilla y sus mercaderes a fines de la Edad Media*, 186–90; Morales Padrón, *Historia de Sevilla*, 79–82.

21. In the case involving the indio Martín Quintín, one can see connections between merchants based in Antwerp, Lisbon, Seville, and northern Brazil. AGI, Justicia 1023, n. 2, r. 2. See also AGI, Justicia 1132, n. 5, r. 4; AGI, Justicia 1039, n. 5, r. 2. On Flemish merchants in Seville, see Abadía Flores, "Los flamencos en Sevilla en los siglos XVI y XVII."

22. On the connections between converso families in Seville and Santo Domingo, see Deive, *Heterodoxia e Inquisición en Santo Domingo*, 75–107. See also Studnicki-Gizbert, *A Nation upon the Ocean Sea*, 17–39, 96–98.

23. Human commodities from "China" labeled as indios in the Spanish documents could refer to the people of East Asia, more broadly, or of the Philippines (after 1565), more specifically. See also Subrahmanyam, *The Portuguese Empire in Asia*, chaps. 3 and 4; Wills, "Maritime Asia."

24. AGI, Justicia 1022, n. 1, r. 2. On Brazilian slaves in Valencia, see Cortés Alonso, *La esclavitud en Valencia*, 113, 387.

25. Pearson, "Brokers in Western Indian Port Cities"; Subrahmanyam, "Connected Histories"; Leibsohn, "Made in China," 13; Lane, *The Colour of Paradise*.

26. The papal bull Inter Caetera, issued on 3 May 1493 by Pope Alexander VI, granted to the Catholic kings of Spain and to their heirs and successors the countries and islands discovered thereafter. It also prohibited anyone from entering those domains without the express permission of the Spanish king.

27. Benton, *A Search for Sovereignty*, 21–25. For an example of slaves being caught in disputes over territorial sovereignty, see "Real Cédula a los Oficiales de la Casa de la Contratación," 4/IV/1531, Ocaña, AGI, Indiferente General 1961, L. 2, 48v, im. 106.

28. On efforts to push the boundaries beyond the Gulf of Paria into Brazilian territory, see Sauer, *The Early Spanish Main*, 113–14. On the Portuguese trading in the Spanish Caribbean, see Keith, "New World Interlopers."

29. Francisco de Santillán's deposition of 1559 mentioned that he had once seen Brazilian indios in Trujillo, Honduras, being freed by the Audiencia of Guatemala. See "Testimony Francisco de Santillán," AGI, Justicia 1132, n. 5, r. 4, 26r. The land-based frontier between Argentina, Brazil, and Peru was a particularly porous area. In 1550, the same year in which Charles V prohibited indigenous slavery altogether, even in cases of just war or rebellion, he received a report that 150 Brazilian Indians, including women and children, had been distributed among the Spanish residents of Chachapoyas, Peru, who claimed they ate human flesh and who were bellicose. They came from the Brazilian coast and traveled by way of the Paraná River. If the geographical facts of the report were true, navigating that river, crossing the Andes, and then traveling north to Chachapoyas would have been an extremely arduous journey. "Real Cédula a la Audiencia de Lima," 16/VII/1550, Valladolid, AGI, Lima 566, L. 6, 282r–283r, im. 487–88.

30. See the important works by Otte, *Las perlas del Caribe*; Deive, *La Española y la esclavitud de los indios*.

31. "Licencia a Antonio Serrano," 9/I/1520, Barcelona, AGI, Indiferente General 420, L. 8, 177r–178r, im. 357–59.

32. Such circumstances made it difficult for Antón to prove in 1529 that he was from Cuba. In his initial deposition before the Council of the Indies, Antón stated that twenty years had passed since he had been captured (in 1509), that he was a Christian, and that, "he, like all of the Indians from Cuba, was free from servitude, as His Majesty has declared." His master, Garcia [Rodríguez de] Ribadeynera, a count, claimed, with some authority, that he was from Brazil. Antón was not freed. AGI, Justicia 972, n. 3, r. 7, 2r.

33. "Real Provisión a la Audiencia de la Isla Española," 21/IX/1556, Valladolid, AGI, Santo Domingo 899, L. 1, 29r, im. 61; Encinas and García Gallo, *Cedulario indiano*, 4:377–78.

34. Benton, *A Search for Sovereignty*, 25.

35. Mauró, *Portugal, o Brasil e o Atlântico*; Mira Caballos, "De esclavos a siervos," 7.

36. See Lauren A. Benton's discussion of the meaning of possession in interimperial conflicts ("Possessing Empire," 20–21). On the importance of islands for questions of imperial sovereignty, see Gillis, *Islands of the Mind*.

37. Andaya, *The World of Maluku*, 7, 116.

38. "Royal decree appointing Alonso Tejada accountant of the Trading House of the Moluccas," 5 April 1525, in Licuanan and Llavador Mira, *The Philippines under Spain*.

39. Brotton, *A History of the World in Twelve Maps*, 199–208.

40. This resulted in the gathering (junta) of Badajoz-Elvas in 1524. Nowell, "The Loaisa Expedition and the Ownership of the Moluccas," 326. The treaty of Tordesillas (1494) determined that lands discovered west of the demarcation, which lay 370 leagues to the west of Cape Verde and the Azores and circled the globe, would pertain to Spain, while everything east of that line would pertain to Portugal.

41. There are discrepancies in the date. Donald F. Lach and Edwin J. Van Kley identify the year as 1526 (*Asia in the Making of Europe*, 1:117); Charles E. Nowell identifies the date as New Year's Day of 1527 ("The Loaisa Expedition and the Ownership of the Moluccas," 331).

42. "Declaración de Juan de Mazuecos," 17/IX/1534, Palencia, in Fernández de Navarrete, *Obras de D. Martín Fernández de Navarrete*, 3:200–204.

43. A good summary of these complexities is offered in Andaya, *The World of Maluku*, 114–21.

44. Bridgeman and Williams, "Sketch of Spanish Colonial History in Eastern Asia," 260–61; Nowell, "The Loaisa Expedition and the Ownership of the Moluccas."

45. Nowell, "The Loaisa Expedition and the Ownership of the Moluccas," 334–35. At first, the Portuguese captain allowed only part of the group, including de la Torre, to reside on the northernmost island of Morotai. When the men began to sicken, they were moved to Jailolo, on the larger island of Halmahera, where they remained for several years. On being in Zamafo, a village on Morotai, see "Declaración de Juan de Mazuecos," 17/IX/1534, Palencia, in Fernández de Navarrete, *Obras de D. Martín Fernández de Navarrete*, 3:203. On transferring to the island of Gilolo, see Declaración de Juan de Mazuecos," 17/IX/1534, Palencia, in Fernández de Navarrete, *Obras de D. Martín Fernández de Navarrete*, 3:204; Nowell, "The Loaisa Expedition and the Ownership of the Moluccas," 335.

46. They sailed first to the Portuguese outpost of Malacca, on the Malay Peninsula, then proceeded westward to Calicut and eventually to Lisbon. "Relación de Hernando de la Torre," s.f., in Fernández de Navarrette, *Obras de D. Martín Fernández de Navarrete*, 3:200–201.

47. Nowell, "The Loaisa Expedition and the Ownership of the Moluccas," 335.

48. "Opening Statement of Aldonza's Lawyer," 12/VI/1548, AGI, Justicia 1163, n. 3, r. 3.

49. "Response of Lawyer to the Demand," 19/VII/1548, AGI, Justicia 1163, n. 3, r. 3, 11r im. 21.

50. "Testimony, Aldonza, india," 20/VII/1549, AGI, Justicia 1163, n. 3, r. 3, 36r, im. 71.

51. "Testimony, Aldonza, india," 20/VII/1549, AGI, Justicia 1163, n. 3, r. 3, 36v, im. 72.

52. "Response of Licenciate Villalobos," 25/IX/1549, Valladolid, AGI, Justicia 1163, n. 3, r. 3, 47r, im. 91.

53. See Metcalf, "The Entradas of Bahia of the Sixteenth Century"; Schwartz, "Indian Labor and New World Plantations"; Monteiro, *Negros da terra*. On the role of just war in the enslavement of Indians in Brazil, see Perrone-Moisés, "Índios livres e índios escravos," 123–27.

54. See the detailed discussion of this conflict in Metcalf, *Go-Betweens and the Colonization of Brazil*, 56–57, 75–78.

55. Mignolo, *The Darker Side of the Renaissance*, chap. 6. On the important role of cosmography in empire making and its strategically sensitive nature, see Portuondo, *Secret Science*, 6–9.

56. Santa Cruz, *Alonso de Santa Cruz y su obra cosmográfica*, 1:56–57; Portuondo, *Secret Science*, 68–72, 110–13.

57. Santa Cruz, *Islario General de todas las islas del mundo*, 1:547–48. Antonio de Mendoza claimed Buenos Aires for the Spanish Crown in 1536.

58. Benton makes the point that "Spaniards" generally referred to themselves by their regional origins (*A Search for Sovereignty*, 71).

59. On Cabot's voyage, see Ramírez, *Carta de Luis Ramírez a su padre desde el Brasil*. On Nuñez de Vaca's voyage, see Núñez Cabeza de Vaca, *Relación general*. See also Benton, *A Search for Sovereignty*, 68–79.

60. Metcalf, *Go-Betweens and the Colonization of Brazil*, chaps. 2 and 3; Tuer, "Tigers and Crosses," 50.

61. Metcalf, *Go-Betweens and the Colonization of Brazil*, chaps. 2 and 3; Tuer, "Tigers and Crosses," 99.

62. Metcalf, *Go-Betweens and the Colonization of Brazil*, 76, 79. Metcalf also mentions a Portuguese criminal exile (degredado) called "the bachelor" of Cananéia, who supplied indio slaves in the 1520s to Portuguese settlers. Metcalf, "The Entradas of Bahia of the Sixteenth Century," 376 n. 9.

63. "Testimony, Martín de Orúe," 2/X/1553, AGI, Justicia 1022, n. 1, r. 1, 50r, 56r–v. For other cases involving accusations of the Portuguese stealing Spanish indios, see AGI, Justicia 1132, n. 5, r. 4; AGI, Justicia 1028, n. 4, r. 3, 1575.

64. Andrés de Montalvo testified in 1572 on behalf of the indio Manuel, arguing that he had been captured as a small boy in the territory of the Rio de la Plata by Portuguese slave traffickers. "Testimony, Andrés de Montalvo," 1572, Justicia 1133, n. 2, 24v–25r. References to the Island of Santa Catalina may have also corresponded to the proximate land-based territory. In his brief account as governor of the Rio de la Plata, Alvar Nuñez Cabeza de la Vaca refers to "El Biaça" as a territory fourteen leagues away from the Island of Santa Catalina where two Franciscan friars evangelized. See "Comentarios de Alvar Nuñez Cabeza de la Vaca, Adelantado y Gobernador del Rio de la Plata," in Barcía

Carballido y Zúñiga, *Historiadores primitivos de las Indias Occidentales*, 1:3. On the Portuguese slave raids in that area, see AGI, Justicia 1022, n. 1, r. 1, 56r. On efforts made by Charles V and Philip II to curtail Portuguese coastal slave-raiding activities, see "Real Cédula a Luis Sarmiento de Mendoza, embajador en Portugal," 24/XI/1555, Valladolid, AGI, Buenos Aires 1, L. 2, 27v–28v; "Real provisión al rey de Portugal," 26/II/1557, Valladolid, AGI, Buenos Aires 1, L. 2, 30r. See the effort by Philip II to resolve a dispute involving the capture of two hundred slaves from the Rio de la Plata area. "Request from Philip II to X of Portugal to liberate certain indios," 26/II/1557, Valladolid, AGI, Buenos Aires 1, L. 2, 30r, im.71.

65. On the differences between French and Portuguese views of the complex ethnicities, see Cunha, "Imagens de índios do Brasil"; Monteiro, "The Heathen Castes of Sixteenth-Century Latin America."

66. "Testimony, Dionisio Molón," 26/X/1547, AGI, Justicia 829, n. 2, im. 18.

67. "Pedimiento de Martín Orué," AGI, Justicia 829, n. 2, im. 33.

68. The historian Sue Peabody refers to a case in 1571 in which a Norman merchant attempting to sell a cargo of slaves in Bordeaux was arrested and the slaves set free. This established a legal precedent for the "Freedom Principle," which held that any slave who stepped foot on French soil would be freed. See Peabody, *There Are No Slaves in France*, 12. During the lawsuit, Martín de Orué iterated that slaves could not be sold in France, which may mean that it was a commonly held assumption, even before the 1571 case took place.

69. Dionisio Molón and his lawyer were required to appear within twenty days of receipt of the order (issued 14 September 1548), and by November, the Council of the Indies had taken up the case. See "Emplazamiento a Dionsio Molón," 14/IX/1548, Valladolid, AGI, Patronato 279, n. 6, r. 32. The case proceeded slowly since it was not until May 1549 that the king issued a *carta receptoría* for the defendant, Dionisio Molón, to call witnesses. "Real Provisión de receptoría,"13/III/1549, Valladolid, AGI, Patronato 280, n. 1, r. 91, im. 1–2.

70. AGI, Justicia 829, n. 2, im. 11.

71. "Murióse un indio," AGI, Justicia 829, n. 2, im. 121; "Sentencia," 30/VIII/1550, AGI, Justicia 829, n. 2, im. 227.

72. The chronicle of Alvar Nuñez Cabeza de Vaca also described different indigenous groups by their generación. González de Barcía Carballido y Zúñiga, *Historiadores primitivos de Indias*, 1:598.

73. "Statement of Martín de Orué," AGI, Justicia 829, n. 2, im. 33.

74. "Questions for the Interrogatory of Martín de Orué," AGI, Justicia 829, n. 2, im. 59.

75. Real Academia Española, *Diccionario de autoridades*, 4:39, offers several definitions for *generación*. The first signification refers to the reproduction of something living. The term was also, by the early eighteenth century, a synonym tor *casta*, *género* (type), and *especie* (species). It also suggested lineage or the succession of generations.

76. "Question for the interrogatory of Martín de Orué," AGI, Justicia 829, n. 2, im. 59.
77. "Testimony, Jorge Gómez," AGI, Justicia 829, n. 2, im. 64. For later depictions and contrasts between Tupí and Tapuia Brazilian peoples based on Soares de Sousa's treatise, see Monteiro, "The Heathen Castes of Sixteenth-Century Latin America," 702–3.
78. "Testimony, Juan Alfonso," AGI, Justicia 829, n. 2, im. 180–81.
79. "Testimony, Francisca, india," AGI, Justicia 1022, n. 1, r. 1, 54r.
80. "Testimony, Francisca, india," AGI, Justicia 1022, n. 1, r. 1, 55v.
81. AGI, Justicia 1022, n. 1, r. 1, 55r–v.
82. "Statement of Martín de Orué," AGI, Justicia 829, n. 2, im. 33.
83. "Testimony, Gaspar Luís," AGI, Justicia 829, n. 2, im. 62.
84. Metcalf, *Go-Betweens and the Colonization of Brazil*, 68–71.
85. McGrath, "Polemics and History in French Brazil," 388–89; Nowell, "The French in Sixteenth-Century Brazil," 381–83. On Portuguese rivalry with the French and French interest in Brazil before 1555, see Mollat du Jourdin and Habert, *Giovanni et Girolamo Verrazano*, chap. 5.
86. "Testimony, Joan de Mota," AGI, Justicia 829, n. 2, im. 82.
87. "Testimony, Nycolas Oybiço," AGI, Justicia 829, n. 2, im. 75. The English had been trading in Brazil since the 1530s. Alida Metcalf mentions the ship the *Barbara*, which had twelve Frenchmen aboard (*Go-Betweens and the Colonization of Brazil*, 62–63).
88. AGI, Justicia 829, n. 2, im. 81.
89. "Testimony, Jorge Gomez," AGI, Justicia 829, n. 2, im. 63.
90. Since mapmaking helped further imperial agendas by formalizing territorial claims, Henry II of France, who showed a deep interest in maritime commerce, requested in 1555 that a detailed map of the Brazilian coast be drawn up. Nowell, "The French in Sixteenth-Century Brazil," 381–83.
91. A fort where the French had established themselves was destroyed in 1560, but the colonists then settled in what is now Rio de Janeiro for several more decades. Nowell, "The French in Sixteenth-Century Brazil," 385, 392–93.
92. AGI, Justicia 1077, n. 1, s.f. Slaves from different parts of the world, including Brazil, served in the urban households of royalty. Jordan, "Images of Empire."
93. AGI, Justicia 1077, n. 1, s.f. In 1555 San Martín was paid twenty ducados to buy the necessary essentials for don Francisco Fernández, indio, who was visiting the court. "Mandamiento del Consejo a Ochoa de Luyando," 19/IX/1555, Valladolid, AGI, Indiferente General 425, L. 23, 197r–v.
94. "Testimony, Jaime Rasquin," AGI, Justicia 1077, n. 1, s.f.
95. "Petition by Licenciado Agreda," 26/IV/1557, Valladolid, AGI, Justicia 1077, n. 1, s.f.
96. "Exceptions of Iñigo de Mondragón," AGI, Justicia 1077, n. 1.
97. Carátula del pleito, AGI, Justicia 1077, n. 1.
98. AGI, Justicia 1077, n. 1. s.f.
99. As Sanjay Subrahmanyam points out, Portuguese traders, mercenaries, and others were residing in Burma by the 1530s, but the area was controlled by two

rulers of the Taung-ngu dynasty until the 1580s. Any Portuguese foothold in the area was not secured until the early seventeenth century, and then only briefly. Subrahmanyam, *The Portuguese Empire in Asia*, 126–28.

100. Portugal allied itself with neighboring Arakan (to the west of Pegu) and with Arakan's subjugated state of Chittagong against the independent state of Pegu, but Pegu was not defeated until the end of the sixteenth century.

101. AGI, Justicia 1077, n. 1, s.f.

102. "Testimony, Juan de Almaçen," AGI, Justicia 1077, n. 1, s.f.

103. "Testimony, Juan de Almaçen," AGI, Justicia 1077, n. 1, s.f.

104. João de Barros (who wrote *Décadas da Ásia* without ever having traveled to South or East Asia) and Fernão Lopes de Castanheda were rivals. Andaya, *The World of Maluku*, 11. Castanheda's history was printed at Coimbra, in eight volumes, in the years 1552, 1553, and 1554. Three out of four of Barros's volumes were printed in 1552, 1553, and 1563. Subrahmanyam, "Intertwined Histories," 129, 132–33. To overcome language barriers, Barros relied on a Chinese slave in his possession, who, Barros claimed, provided him with access to works in Chinese that would add depth to the chronicle he was writing. Subrahmanyam, "Intertwined Histories," 137. See also Subrahmanyam, *Explorations in Connected History*, 2:142–44.

105. Sanjay Subrahmanyam emphasizes how "João de Barros and Fernão Lopes de Castanheda were clearly read in both Spain and the Spanish Empire" ("Holding the World in Balance," 1373).

106. Lamana, *Domination without Dominance*, 7–12, 32, 73.

107. Adorno, *The Polemics of Possession in Spanish American Narrative*, 4.

108. Adorno, *The Polemics of Possession in Spanish American Narrative*, 4.

Conclusions

The epigraph is discussed in Vergara Ormeño, "Growing Up Indian," 90–91.

1. Putnam, "To Study the Fragments/Whole," 615.

2. Yannakakis, "Indigenous People and Legal Culture."

3. Owensby, *Empire of Law and Indian Justice in Colonial Mexico*, 136–37.

4. Pagden, *The Fall of Natural Man*, chap. 4.

5. Sherman, *Forced Native Labor*, chap. 8.

6. Owensby, *Empire of Law and Indian Justice in Colonial Mexico*, 147; Pagden, *The Fall of Natural Man*, chap. 4.

7. "Deposition, Beatríz, india libre," AGI, Justicia 757, n. 38, 98r, im. 95.

8. "Real Disposición," 23/X/1574, Madrid, AGI, Indiferente General 426, L. 25, 300v im. 616. On Antonia's sentence and lawsuit, see AGI, Escribanía de Cámara 952, n. 812, 7/IX/1574; AGI, Justicia 446, n. 2, r. 7.

9. In 1579 the freed Francisca Díaz, originally from Peru, solicited authorities of the Casa to reprimand doña Florinda de Loyola for placing her two children, Melchora and Luis, in the service of Loyola's own adult children in the village of Peñaflor (near Córdoba), thus "usurping them of their liberty." AGI, Contratación 717, n. 12.

10. "Testimony, Andrés de Escobedo," 6/III/1579, AGI, Contratación 717, n. 12, 3r.

11. "Confession, Alonso Álvarez," 11/VII/1579, AGI, Contratación 717, n. 12, 18r-v.

12. See, for example, "Real Cédula," 14/XII/1543, Valladolid, AGI, Indiferente General 1963, L. 9, 8r-9r.

13. On Juana and Francisco, see AGI, Justicia 1037, n. 6, r. 3; "Pago de flete y matalotaje a Francisco, indio," 21/VII/1549, Valladolid, AGI, Indiferente General 1964, L. 11, 260r-v. On Catalina, see AGI, Justicia 1021, n. 3, r. 1. See also "Real Cédula a Francisco Vecerra," 31/III/1555, Valladolid, AGI, Indiferente General 425, L. 23, 141r. In one case, the indios Francisco and Isabel were freed, in 1544, and the Crown ordered their former master to pay for them to return to their places of origin, in Cubagua and Santa Marta (AGI, Justicia 1173, n. 4). See also "Real Cédula a Diego de Loaisa," 25/VIII/1555, Valladolid, AGI, Indiferente General 425, L. 23, 185r-v; "Real Cédula . . . hagan proporcionar el pasaje y el matalotaje a Diego y Beatríz, indios, naturales de la provincia de Tlaxcala, para volver a Nueva España," 6/VI/1556, Valladolid, AGI, Indiferente General 1965, L. 13, 119v-120, im. 248-49.

14. "Expediente de información . . . de Alonso de Molina, indio, natural de Tezcuco (Nueva España), a Nueva España," 23/IX/1555, AGI, Contratación 5218, n. 79.

15. Mangan, *Transatlantic Obligations*; van Deusen, "Diasporas, Bondage, and Intimacy in Lima"; van Deusen, "The Intimacies of Bondage."

16. A royal decree of 1569 declared "Carib" females to be enslaveable. Whitehead, "Carib Cannibalism"; Whitehead, "Indigenous Slavery in South America." Nine percent of indigenous children registered in the 1613 census of Lima were "Chilean" slaves. Vergara Ormeño, "Growing Up Indian," 90-91.

17. Israel, *Race, Class, and Politics in Colonial Mexico*, 75; Seijas, *Asian Slaves in Colonial Mexico*, 251; Seijas, "The Portuguese Slave Trade to Spanish Manila." On "Chinese" laborers registered in the early seventeenth-century census of indios in Lima, see Contreras, *Padrón de los indios de Lima en 1613*, 525-45. The Iberian union did not end indigenous slavery in Brazil, and Brazilian slaves continued to trickle from Portugal into Castile.

18. Seijas, *Asian Slaves in Colonial Mexico*, 212-14.

19. Restall, *Beyond Black and Red*; Restall, *The Black Middle*; Miles, *Ties That Bind*; John Brooks, *Confounding the Color Line*.

20. Forte, *Who Is an Indian?*

21. "Pleito por Francisco, indio de Nueva España, por su libertad," 1546, BNP, Protocolos, Diego Gutiérrez A208.

22. Grasseni, "Skilled Vision."

23. Vergara Ormeño, "Growing Up Indian," 91.

24. Zeleza, "Rewriting the African Diaspora," 43-49.

25. A few slaves from South or East Asia were able to argue that they were indios before the Audiencia of Mexico in the seventeenth century; see Seijas, *Asian Slaves in Colonial Mexico*, 224-26.

26. Rappaport, *The Disappearing Mestizo*; Tavárez, "Legally Indian."

27. Lowe, "The Intimacy of Four Continents."

28. Burns, *Into the Archives*, 124–25.
29. "Real Cédula a la Audiencia de Santo Domingo," 14/VII/1558, Valladolid, AGI, Santo Domingo 899, L. 1, 113v.
30. Werner and Zimmermann, "Beyond Comparison."
31. Pagden, *The Fall of Natural Man*, 98.
32. Safier, "Global Knowledge on the Move," 138–39.

BIBLIOGRAPHY

Primary Sources: Manuscripts

AAL: Archivo Arzobispal de Lima (Peru)
 "Bautismos, [Parroquia del] Sagrario," 2A
AGI: Archivo General de Indias (Seville, Spain)
 Audiencia de Mexico 1088
 Buenos Aires 1
 Caracas 1
 Catálogo de Pasajeros, L. 3
 Contratación 715, 717, 5218, 5536, 5537
 Escribanía de Cámara 952, 953, 1007B
 Guadalajara 30
 Guatemala 40, 110, 393
 Indiferente General 418, 419, 420, 421, 423, 424, 425, 426, 737, 856, 857, 1092, 1801,
  1961, 1962, 1963, 1964, 1965, 1968, 2049
 Justicia 117, 162, 199, 202, 234, 296, 298, 446, 558, 559, 716, 727, 741, 747, 757, 758,
  783, 825, 828, 829, 831, 832, 836, 856, 895, 908, 928, 944, 972, 994, 1007, 1013,
  1019, 1021, 1022, 1023, 1024, 1025, 1026, 1028, 1037, 1038, 1039, 1043, 1044,
  1050, 1077, 1088, 1116B, 1122, 1131, 1132, 1133, 1140, 1153, 1162, 1163, 1164, 1173,
  1174, 1178
 Lima 565, 566, 567
 México 1088
 Panama 234, 235
 Patronato 20, 43, 170, 177, 180, 231, 251, 276, 278, 279, 280, 284, 286, 289, 295
 Santo Domingo 868, 899, 1121, 2280
AGNP: Archivo General de la Nación, Peru (Lima, Peru)
 Protocolos, Pedro de Castañeda 18
AHNM: Archivo Histórico Nacional de Madrid (Madrid, Spain)
 Josep de Ayala, "Diccionario de gobierno y legislación"
AMC: Archivo Municipal de Carmona (Carmona, Spain)

Pleitos y Procesos, Leg. 715, 716, 719

Protocolos 167, 203, 359, 448

ARCV: Archivo de la Real Chancillería de Valladolid (Valladolid, Spain)

Registro de Ejecutorias, Caja 546, 1192, 1193

BNP: Biblioteca Nacional del Perú (Lima, Peru)

Protocolos, Diego Gutiérrez A31, A32, A33, A208

LOC: Library of Congress (Washington, D.C.)

Harkness Collection, box 2, doc. 347, 399, 411

Printed Works

Abadía Flores, Carolina. "Los flamencos en Sevilla en los siglos XVI y XVII (De Vlamingen in Sevilla in de 16de en 17 de eeuw)." PhD diss., University of Ghent, 2006–2007.

Abercrombie, Thomas A. *Pathways of Memory and Power: Ethnography and History among an Andean People.* Madison: University of Wisconsin Press, 1998.

Ackerman, Diane. *A Natural History of the Senses.* New York: Random House, 1990.

Acosta Rodríguez, Antonio. "Intereses privados en la administración de la monarquía: La Casa de la Contratación, 1503–1535." *La Casa de la Contratación y la navegación entre España y Las Indias,* ed. Antonio Acosta Rodríguez, Adolfo Luis González Rodríguez, and Enriqueta Vila Vilar, 341–74. Seville: Universidad de Sevilla, 2003.

Adorno, Rolena. "The Discursive Encounter of Spain and the Americas: The Authority of Eyewitness Testimony in the Writing of History." *William and Mary Quarterly* 49.2 (1992): 210–28.

———. *The Polemics of Possession in Spanish American Narrative.* New Haven: Yale University Press, 2007.

Alegría, Ricardo E. *Las primeras representaciones gráficas del indio americano, 1493–1523.* San Juan: Centro de Estudios Avanzados de Puerto Rico y el Caribe, 1978.

Almeida, Maria Cândida Ferreira de. *Tornar-se outro: O "topos" canibal na literatura brasileira.* São Paulo: Annablume, 2002.

Almorza Hidalgo, Amelia. "Género, emigración y movilidad social en la expansión Atlántica: Mujeres españolas en el Perú colonial (1550–1650.)" PhD diss., European University Institute, Florence, 2011.

Altamira, Rafael. *Colección de documentos inéditos para la historia de Hispano-América.* 14 vols. Madrid: Compañía Ibero-Americana de Publicaciones, 1927–1932.

Altman, Ida. *Emigrants and Society: Extremadura and America in the Sixteenth Century.* Berkeley: University of California Press, 1989.

———. *Transatlantic Ties in the Spanish Empire: Brihuega, Spain, and Puebla, Mexico, 1560–1620.* Stanford: Stanford University Press, 2000.

———. *The War for Mexico's West: Indians and Spaniards in New Galicia, 1524–1550.* Albuquerque: University of New Mexico Press, 2010.

Amado, Janaína, and Luiz Carlos Figueiredo, eds. *Brasil 1500: Quarenta documentos.* Brasília: Editora Universidade de Brasília; São Paulo: Imprensa Oficial do Estado, 2001.

Andaya, Leonard Y. *The World of Maluku: Eastern Indonesia in the Early Modern Period*. Honolulu: University of Hawaii Press, 1993.

Anderson, Emma. *The Betrayal of Faith: The Tragic Journey of a Colonial Native Convert*. Cambridge: Harvard University Press, 2007.

Anderson-Córdoba, Karen. "Hispaniola and Puerto Rico: Indian Acculturation and Heterogeneity, 1492–1550." PhD diss., Yale University, 1990. [Ann Arbor: University Microfilms International, 1991.]

Anghie, Antony. *Imperialism, Sovereignty, and the Making of International Law*. Cambridge: Cambridge University Press, 2005.

Appadurai, Arjun. "Global Ethnoscapes: Notes and Queries for a Transnational Anthropology." *Migration, Diasporas and Transnationalism*, ed. Steven Vertovec and Robin Cohen, 463–83. Cheltenham: Edward Elgar, 1999.

———. "Introduction: Place and Voice in Anthropological Theory." *Cultural Anthropology* 3.1 (1988): 16–20.

Archivo de Protocolos (de Sevilla). *Catálogo de los fondos americanos del Archivo de Protocolos de Sevilla*. 2 vols. Madrid: Compañía Ibero-americana de Publicaciones, 1930.

Arranz Márquez, Luis. *Repartimientos y encomiendas en la Isla Española (El Repartimiento de Alburquerque de 1514)*. Madrid: Ediciones Fundación García Arévalo, 1991.

Baber, Jovita. "Categories, Self-Representation and the Construction of the *Indios*." *Journal of Spanish Cultural Studies* 10.1 (2009): 27–41.

Barrero García, Ana María, and José María Soto Rábanos, eds. *La glosa magna de Gregorio López (sobre la doctrina de guerra justa en el siglo xvi)*. Mexico City: Escuela Libre de Derecho, 2005.

Bataillon, Gilles, Gilles Bienvenu, and Ambrosio Velasco Gómez, eds. *Las teorías de la guerra justa en el siglo XVI y sus expresiones contemporáneas*. Mexico City: Universidad Nacional Autónoma de México, Facultad de Filosofía y Letras, 2008.

Bayle, Constantino. *El protector de indios*. Seville: Escuela de Estudios Hispano-Americanos, 1945.

Beceiro Pita, Isabel, and Ricardo Córdoba de la Llave. *Parentesco, poder y mentalidad: La nobleza castellana: Siglos XII–XV*. Madrid: Consejo Superior de Investigaciones Científicas, 1990.

Beltrán de Guzmán, Nuño. *Testamento de Nuño Beltrán de Guzmán*. Facsimile edn., with introduction by Jorge Palomino y Cañedo. Mexico City: Centro de Estudios de Historia de México, Condumex, 1973.

Benítez Licuanan,Virginia, and José Llavador Mira, trans. and eds. *The Philippines under Spain: A Compilation and Translation of Original Documents*. Manila: National Trust for Historical and Cultural Preservation of the Philippines, 1990.

Bennett, W. Lance, and Martha S. Feldman. *Reconstructing Reality in the Courtroom: Justice and Judgment in American Culture*. New Brunswick: Rutgers University Press, 1981.

Benton, Lauren A. *Law and Colonial Cultures: Legal Regimes in World History, 1400–1900*. Cambridge: Cambridge University Press, 2002.

————. "Possessing Empire: Iberian Claims and Interpolity Law." *Native Claims: Indigenous Law against Empire, 1500–1920*, ed. Saliha Belmessous, 19–40. Oxford: Oxford University Press, 2012.

————. *A Search for Sovereignty: Law and Geography in European Empires, 1400–1900*. Cambridge: Cambridge University Press, 2009.

Bermúdez Plata, Cristobal. *La Casa de la Contratación, La Casa Lonja y el Archivo General de Indias*. Seville: Consejo de la Hispanidad, 1900.

Bhattacharyya, Gargi. 2001. "Flesh and Skin: Materialism Is Doomed to Fail." *Contested Bodies*, ed. Ruth Holliday and John Hassard, 21–35. New York: Routledge, 2001.

Blackburn, Robin. "The Old World Background to European Colonial Slavery." *William and Mary Quarterly* 54.1 (January 1997): 65–102.

Block, Sharon. "Lines of Color, Sex, and Service: Comparative Sexual Coercion in Early America." *Sex, Love, Race: Crossing Boundaries in North American History*, ed. Martha Elizabeth Hodes, 141–63. New York: New York University Press, 1999.

Blumenthal, Debra. *Enemies and Familiars: Slavery and Mastery in Fifteenth-Century Valencia*. Ithaca: Cornell University Press, 2009.

Bolaños Cárdenas, Álvaro Félix. "Antropofagia y diferencia cultural: Construcción retórica del caníbal del Nuevo Reino de Granada." *Revista Iberoamericana*, nos. 170–71 (1995): 81–95.

————. *Barbarie y canibalismo en la retórica colonial: Los indios Pijaos de Fray Pedro Simón*, Bogotá: Fondo Editorial CEREC, 1994.

Bosch García, Carlos. *La esclavitud prehispánica entre los Aztecas*. Mexico City: El Colegio de México, 1944.

Boucher, Philip P. *Cannibal Encounters: Europeans and Island Caribs, 1492–1763*. Baltimore: Johns Hopkins University Press, 1992.

Bouchon, Geneviève. "Calicut at the Turn of the Sixteenth Century: The Portuguese Catalyst." *Indica* 26.1–2 (1989): 3–13.

————. "A Microcosm: Calicut in the Sixteenth Century." *Asian Merchants and Businessmen in the Indian Ocean and the China Sea*, ed. Denys Lombard and Jean Aubin, 40–49. Oxford: Oxford University Press, 2000.

Boyarin, Jonathan. *The Unconverted Self: Jews, Indians, and the Identity of Christian Europe*. Chicago: University of Chicago Press, 2009.

Bridgeman, Elijah Coleman, and Samuel Vells Williams, eds. "Sketch of Spanish Colonial History in Eastern Asia: The Expeditions of Gómez, Loaisa, Saavedra, Villalobos and Legaspi, 1524 to 1572." *Chinese Repository* 6 (1838): 257–68.

Brooks, James. *Captives and Cousins: Slavery, Kinship, and Community in the Southwest Borderlands*. Chapel Hill: University of North Carolina Press, 2002.

Brooks, John. "Slavery and the Slave in the Works of Lope de Vega." *Romantic Review* 19 (1928): 232–43.

Brotton, Jerry. *A History of the World in Twelve Maps*. London: Allen Lane, 2012.

Brown, Vincent. *The Reaper's Garden: Death and Power in the World of Atlantic Slavery*. Cambridge: Harvard University Press, 2008.

Bryant, Sherwin. *Rivers of Gold, Lives of Bondage: Governing through Slavery in Colonial Quito*. Chapel Hill: University of North Carolina Press, 2014.

Burns, Kathryn. *Into the Archive: Writing and Power in Colonial Peru*. Durham: Duke University Press, 2010.

———. "Unfixing Race." *Rereading the Black Legend: The Discourses of Religious and Racial Difference in the Renaissance Empires*, ed. Margaret R. Greer, Walter D. Mignolo, and Maureen Quilligan, 188–202. Chicago: University of Chicago Press, 2007.

Burns, Robert I., ed. *Las Siete Partidas*. 5 vols. Translated by Samuel Parsons Scott. Philadelphia: University of Pennsylvania Press, 2001.

Cahill, David. "Colour by Numbers: Racial and Ethnic Categories in the Viceroyalty of Peru, 1532–1824." *Journal of Latin American Studies* 26.2 (May 1994): 325–36.

Campbell, Gwyn, Suzanne Miers, and Joseph C. Miller, eds. *Children in Slavery through the Ages*. Athens: Ohio University Press, 2009.

Cañizares-Esguerra, Jorge. *Nature, Empire, and Nation: Explorations of the History of Science in the Iberian World*. Stanford: Stanford University Press, 2006.

Carmona García, Juan Ignacio. *Crónica urbana del malvivir (S. XIV–XVII): Insalubridad, desamparo y hambre en Sevilla*. Seville: Universidad de Sevilla, 2000.

———. *El extenso mundo de la pobreza: La otra cara de la Sevilla imperial*. Seville: Ayuntamiento, Servicio de Publicaciones, 1993.

Carmona Ruíz, María Antonia. "La ganadería en Carmona durante la Baja Edad Media." *Archivo Hispalense* 80.243–45 (1997): 283–306.

Castañeda Delgado, Paulino. "La condición miserable del indio y sus privilegios." *Anuario de Estudios Americanos* 28 (1971): 245–335.

———. "La política española con los caribes durante el siglo XVI." *Revista de Indias* nos. 119–22 (1970): 73–130.

Castanheda, Fernão Lopes de. *Ho primeiro livro da Historia do descobrimento*. 4 vols. Coimbra: Imprenta de J. de Barreyra e J. Alvarez, 1552.

Castillo Martos, Manuel. *Bartolomé de Medina y el siglo XVI*. Santander: Universidad de Cantanbría, 2006.

Castro, Daniel. *Another Face of Empire: Bartolomé de las Casas, Indigenous Rights, and Ecclesiastical Imperialism*. Durham: Duke University Press, 2007.

Cavalario, Domingo. *Instituciones del derecho canónico*. 2d edn. 3 vols. Translated by D. Juan Tejada and Ramiro. Valencia: Librería de Mallen y Sobrinos [Enfrente de San Martin], 1937.

Cebreros, Francisco Xavier. *Vida del Señor San Teodomiro martír, natural y patrono de la ciudad de Carmona*. Madrid: Imprenta de Don Josef de Collado, 1805.

Chamberlain, Robert S. *The Conquest and Colonization of Honduras, 1502–1550*. New York: Octagon, 1966.

Chambers, D. B. "Ethnicity in the African Diaspora: The Slave Trade and the Creation of African 'Nations' in the Americas." *Slavery and Abolition* 22.3 (December 2001): 25–39.

Chatterjee, Indrani. "Colouring Subalternity: Slaves, Concubines and Social Orphans in Early Colonial India." *Subaltern Studies* 10 (1999): 49–97.

————. *Gender, Slavery, and Law in Colonial India*. New Delhi: Oxford University Press, 1999.

————. "Testing the Local against the Colonial." *History Workshop Journal* 44 (October 1997): 215–24.

Chatterjee, Indrani, and Richard M. Eaton, eds. *Slavery and South Asian History*. Bloomington: Indiana University Press, 2006.

Chipman, Donald E. *Nuño de Guzmán and the Province of Pánuco in New Spain, 1518–1533*. Glendale, CA: A. H. Clark, 1967.

————. "The Traffic in Indian Slaves in the Province of Pánuco, New Spain, 1523–1533." *The Americas* 23.2 (October 1966): 142–55.

Clifford, James. "Diasporas." *Cultural Anthropology* 9.3 (1994): 302–38.

Cline, Howard F. "Hernando Cortés and the Aztec Indians in Spain." *Quarterly Journal of the Library of Congress* 26.2 (April 1969): 70–90.

Cohen, Paul. "Was There an Amerindian Atlantic? Reflections on the Limits of a Historiographical Concept." *History of European Ideas* 34.4 (December 2008): 388–410.

Constable, Olivie Remie. "Muslim Spain and Mediterranean Slavery: The Medieval Slave Trade as an Aspect of Muslim-Christian Relations." *Christendom and Its Discontents*, ed. Scott L. Waugh and Peter Diehl, 264–84. Cambridge: Cambridge University Press, 1996.

————. *Trade and Traders in Muslim Spain: The Commercial Realignment of the Iberian Peninsula, 900–1500*. Cambridge: Cambridge University Press, 1994.

Contreras, Miguel. *Padrón de los indios de Lima en 1613*. Lima: Universidad Nacional Mayor de San Marcos, Seminario de Historia Rural Andina, 1968.

Cook, Alexandra Parma, and Noble David Cook. *The Plague Files: Crisis Management in Sixteenth-Century Seville*. Baton Rouge: Louisiana State University Press, 2009.

Cook, Karoline. "Forbidden Crossings: Morisco Emigration to Spanish America, 1492–1650." PhD diss., Princeton University, 2008.

Cook, Noble David. *Demographic Collapse: Indian Peru, 1520–1620*. Cambridge: Cambridge University Press, 1981.

————. "The Mysterious Catalina: Indian or Spaniard?" *The Human Tradition in Colonial Latin America*, ed. Kenneth Andrien, 64–83. Wilmington, DE: Scholarly Resources, 2002.

Corbin, Alain. *The Life of an Unknown: The Rediscovered World of a Clog Maker in Nineteenth-Century France*. Translated by Arthur Goldhammer. New York: Columbia University Press, 2001.

Coromines, Joan. *Diccionario crítico etimológico de la lengua castellana*. Berna: Editorial Francke, 1954.

Cortés, Gerónimo. *Fisonomía y varios secretos de naturaleza: Contiene cinco tratados de materias diferentes; Todos revistos y mejorados en esta vltima impression à la qual se han añadido muchas cosas notables y de mucho provecho*. Barcelona: Por Pablo Campins, 1741 [1597].

Cortés Alonso, Vicenta. *La esclavitud en Valencia durante el reinado de los Reyes Católicos (1479–1516)*. Valencia: Excmo. Ayuntamiento, 1964.

Cortés López, José Luis. "La esclavitud en España en la época de Carlos I." Biblioteca Virtual Miguel de Cervantes, http://bib.cervantesvirtual.com/historia/CarlosV/6_4_cortes.shtml

———. *La esclavitud negra en la España peninsular del siglo XVI*. Salamanca: Ediciones de la Universidad de Salamanca, 1989.

Covarrubias Horozco, Sebastián de. *Tesoro de la lengua castellana, o española*. Madrid: Por L. Sánchez, 1611. Universidad de Sevilla, Fondos Digitalizados, http://fondosdigitales.us.es/fondos/libros/765/1160/tesoro-de-la-lengua-castellana-o-espanola.

Cunha, Manuela Carneiro da. "Imagens de índios do Brasil: O século XVI." *Estudos Avançados* 4.10 (1990): 91–110. Scientific Electronic Library Online, http://www.scielo.br/scielo.php?pid=S0103-40141990000300005&script=sci_arttext.

D'Anghera, Peter Martyr. "Carta al Arzobispo de Cosenza, 22/II/1525, Desde Mantua Carpetana–Madrid." *Documentos inéditos para la historia de España*, ed. José López de Toro and Duques de Alba, 12:387–88. Madrid: Imprenta Góngora, 1957.

———. *De Orbe Novo*. Translated by Francis Augustus MacNutt. New York: Franklin, 1970.

Davis, David Brion. *Slavery and Human Progress*. New York: Oxford University Press, 1984.

Davis, Natalie Zemon. "Boundaries and the Sense of Self in Sixteenth-Century France." *Reconstructing Individualism: Autonomy, Individuality, and the Self in Western Thought*, ed. Thomas C. Heller, David E. Wellbery, and Morton Sosna, 53–63. Stanford: Stanford University Press, 1986.

———. *Fiction in the Archives: Pardon Tales and Their Tellers in Sixteenth-Century France*. Stanford: Stanford University Press, 1987.

———. *Trickster Travels: A Sixteenth-Century Muslim between Worlds*. New York: Hill and Wang, 2006.

Davis, Robert C. *Holy War and Human Bondage: Tales of Christian-Muslim Slavery in the Early Modern Mediterranean*. Santa Barbara: Praeger/ABC-CLIO, 2009.

Deive, Carlos Esteban. *Heterodoxia e inquisición en Santo Domingo, 1492–1822*. Santo Domingo: Taller, 1983.

———. *La Española y la esclavitud de los indios*. Santo Domingo: Fundación García Avévalo, 1995.

de la Llave, R. C. "El papel de la mujer en la actividad artesanal cordobesa a fines del siglo XV." *El trabajo de las mujeres en la Edad Media hispana*, ed. Angela Muñoz Fernández and Cristina S. Graiño, 235–54. Madrid: Asociación Cultural Al-Mudayna, 1988.

de la Puente Luna, José Carlos. "Into the Heart of the Empire: Indian Journeys to the Hapsburg Royal Court." PhD diss., Texas Christian University, 2010.

Dening, Greg. "The Comaroffs Out of Africa: A Reflection Out of Oceania." *American Historical Review* 108.2 (2003): 471–78.

Dery, David. "Papereality and Learning in Bureaucratic Organizations." *Administration and Society* 29.6 (1998): 677–89.

Díaz del Castillo, Bernal. *Historia verdadera de la conquista de la Nueva España*. 2 vols. Mexico City: Editorial Porrúa, 1960.

Domínguez Ortíz, Antonio. *La esclavitud en Castilla en la Edad Moderna y otros estudios de marginados*. Granada: Editorial Comares, 2003.

———. *La población de Sevilla en la baja Edad Media y en los tiempos modernos*. Madrid: Publicaciones de la Real Sociedad Geográfica, 1941.

Domínguez Ortíz, Antonio, and Bernard Vincent. *Historia de los moriscos: Vida y tragedia de una minoría*. Madrid: Editorial Revista de Occidente, 1978.

Duncan, T. Bentley. "Navigation between Portugal and Asia in the Sixteenth and Seventeenth Centuries." *Asia and the West: Encounters and Exchanges from the Age of Exploration*, ed. Donald F. Lach, Cyriac K. Pullapilly, and Edwin J. Van Kley, 3–25. Notre Dame: Cross Cultural Publications, Cross Roads Books, 1986.

Earle, Rebecca. *The Body of the Conquistador: Food, Race and Colonial Experience in Spanish America, 1492–1700*. Cambridge: Cambridge University Press, 2012.

Earle, T. F., and K. J. P. Lowe, eds. *Black Africans in Renaissance Europe*. Cambridge: Cambridge University Press, 2005.

Elliott, John H. *The Old World and the New, 1492–1650*. 2d edn. Cambridge: Cambridge University Press, 1992.

Eltis, David, and Stanley L. Engerman, eds. *The Cambridge World History of Slavery*. Vol. 3. Cambridge: Cambridge University Press, 2011.

Eltis, David, Frank D. Lewis, and Kenneth Lee Sokoloff, eds. *Slavery in the Development of the Americas*. Cambridge: Cambridge University Press, 2004.

Encinas, Diego de, and Alfonso García Gallo. *Cedulario indiano*. 4 vols. Madrid: Ediciones Cultura Hispánica, 1945 [1596].

Epstein, Steven A. *Speaking of Slavery: Color, Ethnicity, and Human Bondage in Italy*. Ithaca: Cornell University Press, 2001.

Fabié y Escudero, Antonio María. *Vida y escritos de Fray Bartolomé de las Casas, Obispo de Chiapa*. 2 vols. Madrid: Imprenta de Miguel Ginesta, 1879.

Feest, Christian F. "The Collecting of American Indian Artifacts in Europe, 1493–1750." *America in European Consciousness, 1493–1750*, ed. Karen Ordahl Kupperman, 324–60. Chapel Hill: University of North Carolina Press, 1995.

Fernández Chaves, Manuel F., and Rafael M. Pérez García. *En los márgenes de la ciudad de Dios: Moriscos en Sevilla*. Valencia: Universitat de València/Editorial Universidad de Granada/Prensas Universitarias de Zaragoza, 2009.

———. "Las redes de la trata negrera: Mercaderes portugueses y tráfico de esclavos en Sevilla (c. 1560–1580)." *La esclavitud negroafricana en la historia de España, siglos XVI y XVII*, ed. Aurelia Martín Cásares and Margarita García Barranco, 5–34. Granada: Editorial Comares, 2010.

Fernández de Navarrete, Martín. *Obras de D. Martín Fernández de Navarrete*. 3 vols. Madrid: Ediciones Atlas, 1954.

Fernández de Oviedo y Valdés, Gonzalo. *Fernández de Oviedo's Chronicle of America: A New History for a New World.* Edited by Kathleen Ann Myers and Nina M. Scott. Austin: University of Texas Press, 2007.

———. *Historia general y natural de las Indias.* Edited by Juan Pérez de Tudela Bueso. Biblioteca de Autores Españoles, vols. 117–120. Madrid: Ediciones Atlas, 1959.

———. *Sumario de la natural historia de las Indias.* Mexico City: Fondo de Cultura Económica, 1950.

Fernández y López, Manuel. *Historia de la ciudad de Carmona desde los tiempos más remotos: Hasta el reinado de Carlos I.* Seville: Gironés y Orduña, 1886.

Finn, Margot. "Slaves Out of Context: Domestic Slavery and the Anglo-Indian Family, 1780–1830." *Transactions of the Royal Historical Society* 19 (December 2009): 181–203.

Floyd, Troy S. *The Columbus Dynasty in the Caribbean, 1492–1526.* Albuquerque: University of New Mexico Press, 1973.

Floyd-Wilson, Mary. *English Ethnicity and Race in Early Modern Drama.* Cambridge: Cambridge University Press, 2003.

Forbes, Jack D. *Africans and Native Americans: The Language of Race and the Evolution of Red-Black Peoples.* 2d edn. Urbana: University of Illinois Press, 1993.

Foreman, Carolyn Thomas. *Indians Abroad: 1493–1938.* Norman: University of Oklahoma Press, 1943.

Forte, Maximilian, ed. *Who Is an Indian? Race, Place and the Politics of Indigeneity in the Americas.* Toronto: University of Toronto Press, 2013.

Foucault, Michel. "The Lives of Infamous Men." *The Essential Works of Michel Foucault, 1954–1984,* by Michel Foucault, 3:157–75. Edited by James D. Faubion. New York: New Press, 2000.

Francis, J. Michael. *Invading Colombia: Spanish Accounts of the Gonzalo Jiménez de Quesada Expedition of Conquest.* University Park: Penn State University Press, 2007.

Franco Silva, Alonso. "El indígena americano en el mercado de esclavos de Sevilla (1500–1525)." *Gades* no. 1 (1978): 25–36.

———. *La esclavitud en Andalucía, 1450–1550.* Granada: Universidad de Granada, 1992.

———. *La esclavitud en Sevilla y su tierra a fines de la Edad Media.* Seville: Diputación Provincial de Sevilla, 1979.

———. *Regesto documental sobre la esclavitud sevillana (1453–1513).* Seville: Publicaciones de la Universidad de Sevilla, 1979.

Freitag, Ulrike, and Achim von Oppen, eds. *Translocality: The Study of Globalising Processes from a Southern Perspective.* Leiden: Brill, 2010.

Friede, Juan, and Benjamin Keen, eds. *Bartolomé de Las Casas in History: Toward an Understanding of the Man and His Work.* DeKalb: Northern Illinois University Press, 1971.

Frisch, Andrea. *The Invention of the Eyewitness: Witnessing and Testimony in Early Modern France.* Chapel Hill: University of North Carolina Department of Romance Languages, 2004.

Fuchs, Barbara. *Exotic Nation: Maurophilia and the Construction of Early Modern Spain*. Philadelphia: University of Pennsylvania Press, 2009.

Gallay, Alan. "Indian Slavery." *The Oxford Handbook of Slavery in the Americas*, ed. Robert L. Paquette and Mark M. Smith, 312–35. New York: Oxford University Press, 2010.

Games, Alison. "Atlantic History: Definitions, Challenges, and Opportunities." *American Historical Review* 111.3 (2006): 741–57.

García Añoveros, Jesús María. "Carlos V y la abolición de la esclavitud de los indios: Causas, evolución y circunstancias." *Revista de Indias* 60.218 (2000): 57–84.

García Fuentes, Lutgardo. "La introducción de esclavos en Indias desde Sevilla en el siglo XVI." http://dspace.unia.es/bitstream/10334/416/1/12JIITI.pdf.

García Icazbalceta, Joaquín. *Don fray Juan de Zumárraga, primer obispo y arzobispo de México*. Mexico City: Andrade y Morales, 1881.

Gaunt, David. "Kinship: Thin Red Lines or Thick Blue Blood." *The History of the European Family*, ed. David I. Kertzer and Marzio Barbagli, 1:257–87. New Haven: Yale University Press, 2001.

Geertz, Clifford. *Local Knowledge: Further Essays in Interpretive Anthropology*. New York: Basic Books, 2000.

Gestoso y Pérez, José. *Curiosidades antiguas sevillanas*. Serie segunda. Seville: En la oficina del periódico El Correo de Andalucía, 1910.

Ghachem, Malick W. *The Old Regime and the Haitian Revolution*. Cambridge: Cambridge University Press, 2012.

Ghosh, Durba. *Sex and the Family in Colonial India*. Cambridge: Cambridge University Press, 2006.

Gibson, Charles. *The Aztecs under Spanish Rule: A History of the Indians of the Valley of Mexico, 1519–1810*. Stanford: Stanford University Press, 1964.

Gil, Juan. "The Indianization of Spain in the Sixteenth Century." *History of Mathematical Sciences: Portugal and East Asia II: University of Macau, China, 10–12 October 1998*, ed. Luís Saraiva, 113–28. Hackensack, NJ: World Scientific, 2004.

Gil-Bermejo Garcia, Juana. "Indígenas americanos en Andalucía." *Andalucía y América en el siglo XVI : Actas de las II Jornadas de Andalucía y América: Universidad de Santa María de la Rábida, marzo-1982*, ed. Bibiano Torres Ramírez et al., 535–55. Seville: Escuela de Estudios Hispano-Americanos, 1983.

Gillis, John. *Islands of the Mind: How the Human Imagination Created the Atlantic World*. New York: Palgrave Macmillan, 2004.

Gilroy, Paul. *The Black Atlantic: Double Consciousness and Modernity*. Cambridge: Harvard University Press, 1993.

Giménez Fernández, Manuel. *Bartolomé de las Casas: Capellán de S.M. Carlos I, Poblador de Cumaná (1517–1523)*. Vol. 2. Seville: Escuela de Estudios Hispano-Americanos de Sevilla, 1960.

———. *Bartolomé de las Casas: Delegado de Cisneros para la reformación de las Indias (1516–1517)*. Vol. 1. Seville: Escuela de Estudios Hispano-Americanos de Sevilla, 1953.

Ginzburg, Carlo. *The Cheese and the Worms: The Cosmos of a Sixteenth-Century Miller*. Baltimore: Johns Hopkins University Press, 1980.

———. "Latitude, Slaves and the Bible: An Experiment in Microhistory." *Critical Inquiry* 31.3 (2005): 665–83.

———. "Microhistory: Two or Three Things that I Know about It." *Critical Inquiry* 20 (fall 1993): 10–35.

Gioffré, Domenico. *Il mercato degli schiavi a Genova nel secolo XV*. Genoa: Fratelli Bozzi, 1971.

Gómez, Michael A. *Exchanging Our Country Marks: The Transformation of African Identities in the Colonial and Antebellum South*. Chapel Hill: University of North Carolina Press, 2008.

———. *Reversing Sail: A History of the African Diaspora*. New York: Cambridge University Press, 2005.

Góngora, Mario. *Los grupos de conquistadores en Tierra Firme (1509–1530): Fisonomía histórico-social de un tipo de conquista*. Santiago: Universidad de Chile, Centro de Historia Colonial, 1962.

González, Ondina E., and Bianca Premo, eds. *Raising an Empire: Children in Early Modern Iberia and Colonial Latin America*. Albuquerque: University of New Mexico Press, 2007.

González, Tomás. *Censo de población de las provincias y partidos de la Corona de Castilla en el siglo XVI*. Madrid: Imprenta Real, 1829.

González de Barcia Carballido y Zúñiga, Andrés. *Historiadores primitivos de las Indias Occidentales*. 3 vols. Madrid: n.p., 1749.

González Jiménez, Manuel. "Carmona hace 500 años." *Carmona en la Edad Moderna: Actas del III Congreso de historia de Carmona*, ed. Manuel González Jiménez, 15–24. Carmona: Ayuntamiento de Carmona, 2002.

———. *Carmona medieval*. Sevilla: Fundación José Manuel Lara, 2006.

———. *El Consejo de Carmona a fines de la Edad Media (1464–1523)*. Seville: Diputación Provincial de Sevilla, 1973.

Gould, Eliga H. "Entangled Histories, Entangled Worlds: The English-Speaking Atlantic as a Spanish Periphery." *American Historical Review* 112.3 (June 2007): 764–86.

Gowing, Laura. *Domestic Dangers: Women, Words, and Sex in Early Modern London*. Oxford: Clarendon, 1996.

Grasseni, Cristina. "Skilled Vision: An Apprenticeship in Breeding Aesthetics." *Social Anthropology* 12.1 (February 2004): 41–55.

Graullera Sanz, Vicente. *La esclavitud en Valencia en los siglos XVI y XVII*. Valencia: Instituto Valenciano de Estudios Históricos; Institución Alfonso el Magnánimo; Diputación Provincial; Consejo Superior de Investigaciones Científicas, 1978.

Groebner, Valentin. "*Complexio*/Complexion: Categorizing Individual Natures, 1250–1600." *The Moral Authority of Nature*, ed. Lorraine Daston and Fernando Vidal, 361–83. Chicago: University of Chicago Press, 2004.

————. *Who Are You? Identification, Deception, and Surveillance in Early Modern Europe*. Brooklyn: Zone Books, 2007.

Gruzinski, Serge. *Las cuatro partes del mundo: Historia de una mundialización*. Mexico City: Fondo de Cultura Económica, 2010.

————. *What Time Is It There? America and Islam at the Dawn of Modern Times*. Translated by Jean Birrell. Cambridge, UK: Polity Press, 2010.

Guha, Ranajit. "Chandra's Death." *The Subaltern Studies Reader, 1986–1995*, ed. Ranajit Guha, 34–62. Minneapolis: University of Minnesota Press, 1997.

Guitar, Lynne. "No More Negotiation: Slavery and the Destabilization of Colonial Hispaniola's Encomienda System." *Revista/Review Interamericana* 29.1–4 (January–December 1999).

————. "The Requirement." *The Historical Encyclopedia of World Slavery*, ed. Junius P. Rodríguez, 1:545. Santa Barbara: ABC-CLIO Press, 1997.

Hamman, Byron Ellsworth. "Inquisitions and Social Conflicts in Sixteenth-Century Yanhuitlan and Valencia: Catholic Colonizations in the Early Modern Transatlantic World." PhD diss., University of Chicago, 2011.

Hanke, Lewis. "Bartolomé de las Casas, an Essay in Hagiography and Historiography." *Hispanic American Historical Review* 33.1 (1953): 136–51.

————. "More Heat and Some Light on the Spanish Struggle for Justice in the Conquest of America." *Hispanic American Historical Review* 44.3 (August 1964): 293–340.

————. *The Spanish Struggle for Justice in the Conquest of America*. Boston: Little, Brown, 1965 [1949].

Hanke, Lewis, and Agustín Millares Carlo, eds. *Cuerpo de documentos del siglo XVI: Sobre los derechos de España en las Indias y las Filipinas*. Mexico City: Fondo de Cultura Económica, 1943.

Hanke, Lewis, and Manuel Giménez Fernández, eds. *Bartolomé de las Casas, 1474–1566: Bibliografía crítica*. Santiago de Chile: Fondo Histórico y Bibliográfico José Toribio Medina, 1954.

Hartman, Saidiya. "Venus in Two Acts." *Small Axe* 12.2 (June 2008): 1–14.

Herlihy, David. "The Making of the Medieval Family: Symmetry, Structure, Sentiment (1983)." *Women, Family, and Society in Medieval Europe: Historical Essays, 1978–1991*, ed. Anthony Molho, 135–53. Providence: Berghahn, 1995.

Herrero, Maria C. G. "Mozas sirvientas en Zaragoza durante el siglo XV." *El trabajo de las mujeres en la Edad Media hispana*, ed. Angela Muñoz Fernández and Cristina S. Graiño, 275–85. Madrid: Asociación Cultural Al-Mudayna, 1988.

Herzog, Tamar. *Defining Nations: Immigrants and Citizens in Early Modern Spain and Spanish America*. New Haven: Yale University Press, 2003.

————. "Identities and Processes of Identification in the Atlantic World." *Oxford Handbook of the Atlantic World*, ed. Nicholas P. Canny and Philip D. Morgan, 480–95. Oxford: Oxford University Press, 2011.

Himmerich y Valencia, Robert. *The Encomenderos of New Spain, 1521–1555*. Austin: University of Texas Press, 1996 [1991].

hooks, bell. "Marginalizing a Site of Resistance." *Out There: Marginalization and Contemporary Cultures*, ed. Russell Ferguson, Trinh T. Minh-ha, and Cornel West,

337–45. New York: New Museum of Contemporary Art; Cambridge: Massachusetts Institute of Technology Press, 1990.

Horn, Rebecca. *Postconquest Coyoacan: Nahua-Spanish Relations in Central Mexico, 1519–1650*. Stanford: Stanford University Press, 1997.

Huarte Navarro, Juan de Dios. *Examen de ingenios para las ciencias, donde se muestra la differencia de habilidades que hay en los hombres*. Edited by Felisa Fresco Otero. Madrid: n.p., 1991 [1575].

Hulme, Peter. *Colonial Encounters: Europe and the Native Caribbean*. London: Methuen, 1986.

Ibarra Rojas, Eugenia. *Fronteras étnicas en la conquista de Nicaragua y Nicoya: Entre la solidaridad y el conflicto 800 d.C-1544*. San José: Editorial de la Universidad de Costa Rica, 2001.

"Indios americanos en Sevilla, siglo XVI." Historia de Sevilla (blog), 2 March 2010. http://historiadesevilla.blogia.com/2010/030207-indios-americanos-en-sevilla -s.xvi-.php

Israel, Jonathan. *Race, Class, and Politics in Colonial Mexico, 1610–1670*. Oxford: Oxford University Press, 1975.

Izquierdo Labrado, Julio. "La esclavitud en Huelva y Palos (1570–1587)." MGAR.net, http://mgar.net/var/esclavos3.htm

Jacobs, Auke Pieter. "Legal and Illegal Emigration from Seville, 1550–1650." *"To Make America": European Emigration in the Early Modern Period*, ed. Ida Altman and James Horn, 59–84. Berkeley: University of California Press, 1991.

Jijón y Caamaño, Jacinto. *Sebastián de Benalcázar*. 2 vols. Quito: Imprenta del Clero, 1936.

Jiménez G[raziani], Morella A. *La esclavitud en Venezuela (siglo XVI)*. Caracas: Biblioteca de la Academia Nacional de la Historia, 1986.

Johnson, Carina Lee. *Cultural Hierarchy in Sixteenth-Century Europe: The Ottomans and Aztecs*. Cambridge: Cambridge University Press, 2011.

Johnson, Walter. "Inconsistency, Contradiction, and Complete Confusion: The Everyday Life of the Law and Slavery." *Law and Social Inquiry* 22.2 (1997): 405–9.

———. "On Agency." *Journal of Social History* 37.1 (fall 2003): 113–24.

———. *Soul by Soul: Life Inside the Antebellum Slave Market*. Cambridge: Harvard University Press, 1999.

Jordan, Annemarie. "Images of Empire: Slaves in the Lisbon Household and Court of Catherine of Austria." *Black Africans in Renaissance Europe*, ed. T. F. Earle and K. J. P. Lowe, 155–80. Cambridge: Cambridge University Press, 2005.

Joyce, Patrick, ed. *The Historical Meanings of Work*. Cambridge: Cambridge University Press, 1987.

Julián, Amadeo. *Bancos, ingenios y esclavos en la época colonial*. Santo Domingo: Banco de Reservas de la República Dominicana, 1997.

Kagan, Richard L. *Lawsuits and Litigants in Castile, 1500–1700*. Chapel Hill: University of North Carolina Press, 1981.

———, ed. *Spanish Cities of the Golden Age: The Views of Anton van den Wyngaerde*. Berkeley: University of California Press, 1989.

Kagan, Richard L., and Abigal Dyer, trans. and eds. *Inquisitorial Inquiries: Brief Lives of Secret Jews and Other Heretics.* Baltimore: Johns Hopkins University Press, 2004.

Keith, Henry H. "New World Interlopers: The Portuguese in the Spanish West Indies, from the Discovery to 1640." *The Americas* 25.4 (1969): 360–71.

Keniston, Hayward. *Francisco de los Cobos, Secretary of the Emperor Charles V.* Pittsburgh: University of Pittsburgh Press, 1960.

Konetzke, Richard, ed. *Colección de documentos para la historia de la formación social de Hispanoamérica, 1493–1810.* 3 vols. Madrid: Consejo Superior de Investigaciones Científicas, 1953.

Lach, Donald F., and Edwin J. Van Kley. *Asia in the Making of Europe.* 3 vols. Chicago: University of Chicago Press, 1965.

Ladero Quesada, Miguel Ángel. "La esclavitud por guerra a fines del siglo XV: El caso de Málaga." *Hispania* 105 (1967): 63–88.

Lamana, Gonzalo. *Domination without Dominance: Inca-Spanish Encounters in Early Colonial Peru.* Durham: Duke University Press, 2008.

Lane, Kris. *The Colour of Paradise: Colombian Emeralds in the Age of Gunpowder Empires.* New Haven: Yale University Press, 2010.

Lansley, Nicolas P. "La esclavitud negra en la parroquia sevillana de Santa María la Mayor, 1515–1519." *Archivo Hispalense* 33 (1983): 37–63.

las Casas, Bartolomé de. *Apologética historia sumaria.* Edited by Edmundo O'Gorman. 2 vols. Mexico: Instituto de Investigaciones Históricas, Universidad Nacional Autónoma de México, 1967.

———. *Brevísima relación de la destrvycion de las Indias.* N.p., 1552.

———. *En defensa de los indios.* Seville: Editoriales Andaluzas Unidas, 1985.

Leibsohn, Dana. "Made in China, Made in Mexico." *At the Crossroads: The Arts of Spanish America and Early Global Trade, 1492–1850,* ed. Donna Pierce and Ronald Otsuka, 11–40. Denver: Denver Art Museum, 2012.

Lenik, Stephan. "Comparing Ethnohistoric and Archaeological Evidence from Dominica, West Indies." *Ethnohistory* 59.1 (winter 2012): 79–107.

Le Roy Ladurie, Emmanuel. *Montaillou, Village Occitan de 1294 à 1324.* Paris: Gallimard, 1975.

Li, Tania. "Articulating Indigenous Identity in Indonesia: Resource Politics and the Tribal Slot." *Comparative Studies in Society and History* 42 (2000): 49–79.

Liang, Yuen-Gen. *Family and Empire: The Fernández de Córdoba and the Spanish Realm.* Philadelphia: University of Pennsylvania Press, 2011.

Lobo Cabrera, Manuel. *La esclavitud en las Canarias orientales en el siglo XVI: Negros, moros y moriscos.* [Santa Cruz de Tenerife]: Ediciones del Cabildo Insular de Gran Canaria, 1982.

Lockhart, James. *The Men of Cajamarca: A Social and Biographical Study of the First Conquerors of Peru.* Austin: University of Texas Press, 1972.

———. *The Nahuas after the Conquest: A Social and Cultural History of the Indians of Central Mexico, Sixteenth through the Eighteenth Centuries.* Stanford: Stanford University Press, 1992.

López Beltrán, María Teresa. "El prohijamiento y la estructura oculta del parentesco en los grupos domésticos malagueños a finales de la Edad Media e inicios de la Edad Moderna (aportación a su estudio)." *Vidas y recursos de mujeres durante el Antiguo Régimen,* ed. María Begoña Villar García and Margarita M. Birriel Salcedo, 47–77. Málaga: Universidad de Málaga, 1997.

———. "El trabajo de la mujeres en el mundo urbano malagueño a finales de la Edad Media (1487–1540)." *Saber y vivir: Mujer, antigüedad y medievo,* ed. María Isabel Calero Secall, Rosa Francia Somalo, and Rafael R. Chenoll Alfaro, 155–81. Málaga: Servicio de Publicaciones, Universidad de Málaga, 1996.

———. "Estructura de los grupos domésticos en Andalucía a finales de la Edad Media." *De la Edad Media a la moderna: Mujeres, educación y familia en el ambito rural y urbano,* ed. María Teresa López Beltrán and Marie-Catherine Barbazza, 87–100. Málaga: Universidad de Málaga, 1999.

———. "La accesibilidad de la mujer al mundo laboral: El servicio doméstico en Málaga a finales de la Edad Media." *Estudios históricos y literarios sobre la mujer medieval,* ed. María E. Lacarra, 119–42. Málaga: Servicio de Publicaciones, Diputation Provincial de Málaga, 1990.

López de Gómara, Francisco. *Historia general de las Indias y vida de Hernán Cortés.* Edited by Jorge Gurría Lacroix. Caracas: Biblioteca Ayacucho, 1979.

López Portillo, Miguel. *La flecha en el blanco: Don Francisco Tenamaztle y Bartolomé de las Casas en lucha por los derechos de los indígenas, 1541–1556.* Mexico City: Editorial Diana, 1995.

Lovell, George. *Conquest and Survival in Colonial Guatemala: A Historical Geography of the Cuchumatán Highlands, 1500–1821.* 3d edn. Montreal: McGill-Queen's University Press, 2005.

Lowe, Lisa. "The Intimacies of Four Continents." *Haunted by Empire: Geographies of Intimacy in North American History,* ed. Ann Laura Stoler, 191–212. Durham: Duke University Press, 2006.

MacDonald, Deanna. "Collecting a New World: The Ethnographic Collections of Margaret of Austria." *Sixteenth Century Journal* 33.3 (fall 2002): 649–63.

Maier Allende, Jorge. "Los moriscos de Carmona." *Carmona en la Edad Moderna: III Congreso de Historia de Carmona,* ed. Manuel González Jiménez, 85–118. Seville: Muñoz Moya Editor, 2003.

Malkki, Liisa H. *Purity and Exile: Violence, Memory, and National Cosmology among Hutu Refugees in Tanzania.* Chicago: University of Chicago Press, 1995.

Mangan, Jane. *Transatlantic Obligations: Legal and Cultural Constructions of Family in Conquest-Era Peru and Spain.* Forthcoming, Oxford University Press.

Marín, Manuela, and Rachid El Hour. "Captives, Children, and Conversion: A Case from Late Nasrid Granada." *Journal of the Economic and Social History of the Orient* 41.4 (November 1998): 453–73.

Martín Cásares, Aurelia. "Domestic Service in Spain: Legislation, Gender and Social Practice." *Domestic Service and the Formation of European Identity: Understanding the Globalization of Domestic Work, Sixteenth through Twenty-First Centuries,* ed. Antoinette Fauve-Chamoux, 189–210. Bern: Peter Lang, 2004.

———. *La esclavitud en la Granada del siglo XVI: Género, raza y religión*. Granada: Editorial Universidad de Granada, Campus Universitario de Cartuja, 2000.

———. "The Royal Decree (Philip II, 1573) on Slavery of *Morisco* Men, Women and Children and Its Consequences." *World Journal of Islamic History and Civilization* 3.4 (2013): 150–62.

Martínez, José Luis. *Pasajeros de Indias: Viajes transatlánticos en el siglo XVI*. Madrid: Alianza, 1983.

Martínez, María Elena. *Genealogical Fictions: Limpieza de Sangre, Religion, and Gender in Colonial Mexico*. Stanford: Stanford University Press, 2008.

Martínez Cardós, José. *Gregorio López, consejero de Indias, glosador de las Partidas (1496–1560)*. Madrid: Instituto Gonzalo Fernández de Oviedo, 1960.

Marzal Palacios, Francisco Javier. *La esclavitud en Valencia durante la baja Edad Media (1375–1425)*. Valencia: Universitat de Valencia, Servei de Publicacions, 2007.

Mason, Peter. "Reading New World Bodies." *Bodily Extremities: Preoccupations with the Human Body in Early Modern European Culture*, ed. Florike Egmond and Robert Zwijnenberg, 148–67. Aldershot, Hants: Ashgate, 2003.

Matthew, Laura E. *Memories of Conquest: Becoming Mexicano in Colonial Guatemala*. Chapel Hill: University of North Carolina Press, 2012.

Matthew, Laura E., and Michel Oudijk, eds. *Indian Conquistadors: Indigenous Allies in the Conquest of Mesoamerica*. Norman: University of Oklahoma Press, 2007.

Mauró, Frédéric. *Le Portugal et L'Atlantique au XVIIe Siècle (1570–1640): Étude Économique*. Paris: École Pratique des Haute Études, 1960.

———. "Merchant Communities, 1350–1750." *The Rise of Merchant Empires: Long-Distance Trade in the Early Modern World, 1350–1750*, ed. James D. Tracy, 255–86. Cambridge: Cambridge University Press, 1990.

———. *Portugal, o Brasil e o Atlântico, 1570–1570*. Lisbon: Editorial Estampa, 1997.

McGrath, John. "Polemics and History in French Brazil, 1555–1560." *Sixteenth-Century Journal* 27.2 (summer 1996): 385–97.

Mendes, António de Almeida. "Child Slaves in the Early North Atlantic Trade in the Fifteenth and Sixteenth Centuries." *Children in Slavery through the Ages*, ed. Gwyn Campbell, Suzanne Miers, and Joseph C. Miller, 19–34. Athens: Ohio University Press, 2009.

Mendonça, Délio de. *Conversions and Citizenry: Goa under Portugal, 1510–1610*. New Delhi: Concept Publishing, 2002.

Metcalf, Alida C. "The *Entradas* of Bahia of the Sixteenth Century." *The Americas* 61.3 (January 2005): 373–400.

———. *Go-Betweens and the Colonization of Brazil, 1500–1600*. Austin: University of Texas Press, 2005.

Mignolo, Walter. *The Darker Side of the Renaissance: Literacy, Territoriality, and Colonization*. Ann Arbor: University of Michigan Press, 1995.

———. "El metatexto historiográfico y la historiografía Indiana." *Modern Language Notes* 96 (1981): 358–402.

Miki, Yuko. "Slave and Citizen in Black and Red: Reconsidering the Intersection of African and Indigenous Slavery in Post-Colonial Brazil." *Slavery and Abolition* 35.1 (2014): 1–22.

Miles, Tiya. *Ties That Bind: The Story of an Afro-Cherokee Family in Slavery and Freedom.* Berkeley: University of California Press, 2005.

Millares Carlo, Agustín, and José Ignacio Mantecón Navasal. *Índice y extractos de los protocolos del Archivo de Notarías de México, D.F.* 2 vols. Mexico City: El Colegio de México, 1945.

Miller, Joseph. "Beyond Blacks, Bondage and Blame: Why a Multicentric World History Needs Africa." *Recent Themes in the History of Africa and the Atlantic World: Historians in Conversation,* ed. Donald A. Yerxa, 7–18. Columbia: University of South Carolina Press, 2009.

Minh-ha, Trinh T. *Woman, Native, Other: Writing Postcoloniality and Feminism.* Bloomington: Indiana University Press, 1989.

Mira Caballos, Esteban. "De esclavos a siervos: Amerindios en España tras las Leyes Nuevas de 1542." http://estebanmira.weebly.com/uploads/7/9/5/0/7950617/indio senespana.pdf.

———. "Dos bautizos de indias en Carmona (1504)." El Descubrimiento de lo Otros (blog), 21 February 2011. http://indiosamericanosencastilla.blogia. com/2011/022101-dos-bautizos-de-indias-en-carmona-1504-.php.

———. *El indio antillano: Repartimiento, encomienda y esclavitud (1492–1542).* Seville: Múñoz Moya Editor, 1997.

———. "Indios americanos en Sevilla, siglo XVI." Historia de Sevilla (blog), March 2010. http://historiadesevilla.blogia.com/2010/030207-indios-americanos-en-sevilla-s.-xvi-.php

———. *Indios y mestizos americanos en la España del siglo XVI.* Frankfurt am Main: Vervuert, 2000.

———. *La población en Carmona en la segunda mitad del siglo xviii.* Carmona: Carmograf, 1993.

———. "La segregación de La Campana de la jurisdicción de Carmona (1558)." http://estebanmira.weebly.com/uploads/7/9/5/0/7950617/segregacion.pdf.

Mira Caballos, Esteban, and Fernando de la Villa Nogales. *Carmona en la Edad Moderna: Religiosidad, arte, y emigración á América.* Seville: Muñoz Moya Editor, 1999.

Miralles Ostos, Juan. *Hernán Cortés: Inventor de México.* Barcelona: Tusquets Editores, 2001.

Mollat du Jourdin, Michel, and Jacques Habert. *Giovanni et Girolamo Verrazano: Navigateurs de François Ier.* Paris: Imprimerie National, 1982.

Montaño Requena, María Isabel. "La población de Carmona en las series parroquiales: Siglos XVI–XIX." *Archivo Hispalense* 70.213 (1987): 93–112.

Monteiro, John M. "The Heathen Castes of Sixteenth-Century Latin America: Unity, Diversity, and the Invention of the Brazilian Indians." *Hispanic American Historical Review* 80.4 (2000): 697–719.

———. *Negros da terra: Índios e bandeirantes nas origens de São Paulo*. São Paulo: Companhia das Letras 1994.

Montell, Jaime. *México: El inicio (1521–1534)*. México: Editorial Joaquín Mortiz, 2005.

Morales Padrón, Francisco. *Historia de Sevilla: La ciudad del quinientos*. Seville: Universidad de Sevilla, 1989.

———. *Los corrales de vecinos de Sevilla (Informe para su estudio)*. Seville: Universidad de Sevilla, 1974.

Moreno Navarro, Isidoro, and Antonio Burgos. *La antigua hermandad de los negros de Sevilla: Etnicidad, poder y sociedad en 600 años de historia*. Seville: Universidad de Sevilla, 1997.

Motolinía, Toribio de Benavente o. *Memoriales, o Libro de las Cosas de la Nueva España y de los naturales de ella*. Edited by Edmundo O'Gorman. Mexico City: Universidad Nacional Autónoma de México, Instituto de Investigaciones Históricas, 1971.

Mourad, Youssef. *La physiognomonie arabe et le Kitāb al-firāsa de Fakhr al-Din al-Rāzi*. Paris: Librairie Orientaliste Paul Geuthner, 1939.

Muldoon, James. *Popes, Lawyers, and Infidels: The Church and the Non-Christian World, 1250–1550*. Philadelphia: University of Pennsylvania Press, 1979.

Mumford, Jeremy. "Litigation as Ethnography in Sixteenth-Century Peru." *Hispanic American Historical Review* 88.1 (2008): 5–40.

Muro Orejón, Antonio, trans. and ed. *Las Leyes Nuevas de 1542–1543: Ordenanzas para la gobernación de las Indias y buen tratamiento y conservación de los indios*. Seville: Escuela de Estudios Hispano-Americanos de la Universidad de Sevilla, 1945.

———. "Las Nuevas Leyes de 1542–43." *Anuario de Estudios Americanos* 16 (1959): 561–619.

Nazzari, Muriel. "Favored Women, Subjected Indians: The Settlement of Pero d'Araujo's Estate in São Paulo (1637–40)." *Colonial Lives, Documents on Latin American History, 1550–1850*, ed. Richard Boyer and Geoffrey Spurling, 141–54. New York: Oxford University Press, 2000.

Newson, Linda A. *Aboriginal and Spanish Colonial Trinidad: A Study in Culture Contact*. London: Academic Press, 1976.

———. *The Cost of Conquest: Indian Decline in Honduras under Spanish Rule*. Boulder: Westview, 1986.

———. *Indian Survival in Colonial Nicaragua*. Norman: University of Oklahoma Press, 1987.

———. *Life and Death in Early Colonial Ecuador*. Norman: University of Oklahoma Press, 1995.

Nirenberg, David. "Race and the Middle Ages: The Case of Spain and Its Jews." *Rereading the Black Legend: The Discourses of Religious and Racial Difference in the Renaissance Empires*, ed. Margaret R. Greer, Walter D. Mignolo, and Maureen Quilligan, 71–87. Chicago: University of Chicago Press, 2007.

———. "Was There Race before Modernity? The Example of 'Jewish' Blood in Late Medieval Spain." *The Origins of Racism in the West*, ed. Miriam Eliav-Feldon,

Benjamin H. Isaac, and Joseph Ziegler, 232–64. Cambridge: Cambridge University Press, 2009.

Nóbrega, M. da. *Cartas do Brasil*. São Paulo: Editora da Universidade de São Paulo, 1988.

Northrup, David. *Africa's Discovery of Europe, 1450–1850*. 2d edn. New York: Oxford University Press, 2008.

———. "Becoming African: Identity Formation among Liberated Slaves in Nineteenth-Century Sierra Leone." *Slavery and Abolition* 26 (April 2006): 1–21.

Nowell, Charles E. "The French in Sixteenth-Century Brazil." *The Americas* 5.4 (April 1949): 381–93.

———. "The Loaisa Expedition and the Ownership of the Moluccas." *Pacific Historical Review* 5.4 (December 1936): 325–36.

Núñez Cabeza de Vaca, Álvar. *Relação general*. Early Americas Digital Archive, 2007, Seville: Archivo General de Indias, Justicia 1131, 1184r–1206v, 7 December 1545, http://mith.umd.edu//eada/html/display.php?docs=cabeza_ms1 .xml&action=show.

Ochoa, Lorenzo. *Historia prehispánica de la Huaxteca*. Mexico City: Universidad Nacional Autónoma de México, 1979.

O'Gorman, Edmundo. *The Invention of America: An Inquiry into the Historical Invention of the New World and the Meaning of Its History*. Bloomington: Indiana University Press, 1961.

———. "Sobre la naturaleza bestial del indio americano." *Filosofía y letras* (Universidad Nacional Autónoma de México) 1 (1941): 141–58, 305–15.

Ortiz de Zúñiga, Diego, and Antonio María Espinosa y Carzel. *Anales eclesiásticos y seculares de la muy noble y muy leal ciudad de Sevilla, metrópoli de la Andalucia, que contienen sus mas principales memorias desde el año de 1246, en que emprendió conquistarla del poder de los Moros el gloriosísimo Rey S. Fernando III de Castilla y Leon, hasta el de 1671 en que la Católica Iglesia le concedió el culto y titulo de Bienaventurado*. Madrid: Imprenta Real, 1795–1796.

O'Toole, Rachel Sarah. *Bound Lives: Africans, Indians, and the Making of Race in Colonial Peru*. Pittsburgh: University of Pittsburgh Press, 2012.

———. "From the Rivers of Guinea to the Valleys of Peru: Becoming a *Bran* Diaspora within Spanish Slavery." *Social Text* 25.3 (fall 2007): 19–36.

Ots Capdequí, José Maria. *El estado español en las Indias*. Buenos Aires: Fondo de Cultura Económica, 1957.

———. *Historia del derecho español en América y del derecho indiano*. Madrid: Ediciones Juan Bravo, 1967.

Otte, Enrique. *Cédulas reales relativas a Venezuela, 1500–1550*. Caracas: Fundación John Boulton and La Fundación Eugenio Mendoza, 1963.

———. *Las perlas del Caribe: Nueva Cádiz de Cubagua*. Caracas: Fundación John Boulton, 1977.

———. "Los jerónimos y el tráfico humano en el Caribe: Una rectificación." *Anuario de Estudios Americanos* 32 (1975): 187–204.

————. *Sevilla, siglo XVI: Materiales para su historia económica.* Edited by Antonio Miguel Bernal, Antonio Collantes de Terán Sánchez, José Ignacio Martinez Ruiz, and María del Carmen Ruiz León. Seville: Centro de Estudios Andaluces, 2008.

————. *Sevilla y sus mercaderes a fines de la Edad Media.* Edited by Antonio-Miguel Bernal and Antonio Collantes de Terán. Seville: Vicerrectorado de Relaciones Institucionales y Extensión Cultural, 1996.

Owensby, Brian Philip. *Empire of Law and Indian Justice in Colonial Mexico.* Stanford: Stanford University Press, 2008.

Pacheco, Joaquín Francisco, Francisco de Cárdenas y Espejo, and Luis Torres de Mendoza. *Colección de documentos inéditos, relativos al descubrimiento, conquista y organización de las Antiguas posesiones Españolas de América y Oceanía, Sacados de los Archivos del Reino, y muy especialmente del de Indias.* 42 vols. Madrid: Imprenta de José María Pérez, 1864–1884.

Pagden, Anthony. *The Fall of Natural Man: The American Indian and the Origins of Comparative Ethnology.* Cambridge: Cambridge University Press, 1982.

Palencia-Roth, Michael. "The Cannibal Law of 1503." *Early Images of the Americas: Transfer and Invention,* ed. Jerry M. Williams and Robert E. Lewis, 21–64. Tucson: University of Arizona Press, 1993.

Pardo, J. Joaquín. *Prontuario de reales cédulas, 1529–1599.* Guatemala: Unión Tipográfica, 1941.

Pardo Molero, Juan Francisco. "Conflicto cultural y conflicto militar en los interrogatorios a los cautivos, siglo XVI." *Les sociétés de frontière: De la Méditerranee à l'Atlantique, XVIe–XVIIIe siècle,* ed. Michel Bertrand and Natividad Planas, 299–318. Madrid: Casa de Velázquez, 2011.

Paso y Troncoso, Francisco del, ed. *Epistolario de Nueva España, 1505–1818.* 2 vols. Mexico City: Antigua Librería Robredo, 1939.

Patterson, Orlando. *Slavery and Social Death: A Comparative Study.* Cambridge: Harvard University Press, 1982.

Peabody, Sue. *There Are No Slaves in France: The Political Culture of Race and Slavery in the Ancien Régime.* Oxford: Oxford University Press, 1996.

Pearson, Michael Naylor. "Brokers in Western Indian Port Cities: Their Role in Servicing Foreign Merchants." *Modern Asian Studies* 22 (1988): 455–72.

Penningroth, Dylan. *The Claims of Kinfolk: African American Property and Community in the Nineteenth-Century South.* Chapel Hill: University of North Carolina Press, 2003.

Peraza, Luis de. *Historia de Sevilla.* Transcribed and annotated by Francisco Morales Padrón. Seville: Asociación Amigos del Libro Antiguo, 1996.

Pérez-Mallaína Bueno, Pablo Emilio, and Carla Rahn Phillips. *Spain's Men of the Sea: Daily Life on the Indies Fleets in the Sixteenth Century.* Baltimore: Johns Hopkins University Press, 1998.

Periáñez Gómez, Rocío. "La esclavitud en Extremadura en la Edad Moderna." PhD diss., Universidad de Extremadura, 2008.

————. "La esclavitud en Zafra durante la Edad Moderna." *Cuadernos de Çafra* 6 (2008): 15–41.

———. "Negros y negreros en la Feria: El comercio de esclavos en la Edad Moderna." *Ferias y mercados en España y América: A propósito de la 550 Feria de San Miguel de Zafra*, ed. José María Moreno González and Juan Carlos Rubio Masa, 91–104. Zafra: Junta de Extremadura/Ayuntamiento de Zafra, 2007.

Perrone, Sean T. *Charles V and the Castilian Assembly of the Clergy: Negotiations for the Ecclesiastical Subsidy*. Leiden: Brill, 2008.

Perrone-Moisés, Beatriz. "Índios livres e índios escravos: Os princípios da legislação indigenista do período colonial (séculos XVI a XVIII)." *História dos índios no Brasil*, ed. Manuela Ligeti Carneiro da Cunha, 115–32. São Paulo: Fundação de Amparo à Pesquisa do Estado de São Paulo, 1992.

Pescador, Juan Javier. *The New World inside a Basque Village: The Oiartzun Valley and Its Atlantic Emigrants, 1550–1800*. Reno: University of Nevada Press, 2004.

Phillips, William D., Jr. "Manumission in Metropolitan Spain and the Canaries in the Fifteenth and Sixteenth Centuries." *Paths to Freedom: Manumission in the Atlantic World*, ed. Rosemary Brana-Shute and Randy J. Sparks, 31–50. Columbia: University of South Carolina Press, 2009.

———. *Slavery in Medieval and Early Modern Iberia*. Cambridge: Cambridge University Press, 2012.

Pike, Ruth. *Aristocrats and Traders: Sevillian Society in the Sixteenth Century*. Ithaca: Cornell University Press, 1972.

———. *Penal Servitude in Early Modern Spain*. Madison: University of Wisconsin Press, 1983.

———. "Seville in the Sixteenth Century." *Hispanic American Historical Review* 41.1 (February 1961): 1–30.

———. "Sevillian Society in the Sixteenth Century: Slaves and Freedmen." *Hispanic American Historical Review* 47.3 (1967): 344–59.

———. "An Urban Minority: The *Moriscos* of Seville." *International Journal of Middle East Studies* 2.4 (October 1971): 368–77.

Pollock, Linda A. "Parent-Child Relations." *Family Life in Early Modern Times, 1500–1789*, ed. David I. Kertzer and Marzio Barbagli, 191–220. New Haven: Yale University Press, 2001.

Porter, Martin. *Windows of the Soul: Physiognomy in European Culture 1470–1780*. Oxford: Clarendon, 2005.

Portuondo, María M. *Secret Science: Spanish Cosmography and the New World*. Chicago: University of Chicago Press, 2009.

Premo, Bianca. "Before the Law: Women's Petitions in the Eighteenth-Century Spanish Empire." *Comparative Studies in Society and History* 53.2 (2011): 261–89.

———. "Thinking beyond Lineage and across Race in Spanish Atlantic Family History." *William and Mary Quarterly* 70.2 (2013): 295–316.

Prescott, William Hickling. *History of the Conquest of Peru: With a Preliminary View of the Civilization of the Incas*. Philadelphia: J. B. Lippincott, 1863.

Price, Richard. "Invitation to Historians: Practices of Historical Narrative." *Rethinking History* 5.3 (2001): 357–65.

Puga, Vasco de. *Provisiones, cédulas, instrucciones de S.M.* Facsimile edn. Madrid: Ediciones Cultura Hispánica, 1945 [1563].

———. *Provisiones, cédulas, instrucciones de su magestad, ordenanças de difuntos y audiencia para la buena expedición de los negocios y administración de justicia y gouernación de esta Nueva España, y para el buen tratamiento y conseruación de los indios desde el año de 1525 hasta presente de 63.* 2d edn. 2 vols. Mexico: n.p., 1878.

Puntas, Antonio Florencio, and Antonio Luis López Martínez. "Mercado de trabajo y migraciones en Carmona durante el Antiguo Regímen." *Carmona en la Edad Moderna: Actas del III Congreso de Historia de Carmona*, ed. Manuel González Jiménez, 141–54. Carmona: Ayuntamiento de Carmona, 2002.

Putnam, Lara. "To Study the Fragments/Whole: Microhistory and the Atlantic World." *Journal of Social History* 39.3 (2006): 615–30.

Radell, David. "The Indian Slave Trade and Population of Nicaragua during the Sixteenth Century." *The Native Population of the Americas in 1492*, ed. William M. Denevan, 67–76. Madison: University of Wisconsin Press, 1976.

Radell, David R., and James J. Parsons. "Realejo: A Forgotten Colonial Port and Shipbuilding Center in Nicaragua." *Hispanic American Historical Review* 51.2 (1971): 295–312.

Raman, Bhavani. *Document Raj: Writing and Scribes in Early Colonial South India.* Chicago: University of Chicago Press, 2012.

Ramírez, Luis. *Carta de Luis Ramírez a su padre desde el Brasil (1528): Orígenes de lo "real maravilloso" en el Cono Sur.* Edited with notes and introduction by Juan Francisco Maura. València: Universitat de València, Collección Textos de la Revista *Lemir*, 2007. http://parnaseo.uv.es/lemir/textos/Ramirez.pdf.

Ramos Pérez, Demetrio. *Audacia, negocios y política en los viajes españoles de descubrimiento y rescate.* Valladolid: Casa-Museo de Colón, Seminario Americanista de la Universidad, 1981.

Rappaport, Joanne. "'Así lo paresçe por su aspeto': Physiognomy and the Construction of Difference in Colonial Bogotá." *Hispanic American Historical Review* 91.4 (November 2011): 601–31.

———. *The Disappearing Mestizo: Configuring Difference in the Colonial New Kingdom of Granada.* Durham: Duke University Press, 2014.

———. *The Politics of Memory: Native Historical Interpretation in the Colombian Andes.* Durham: Duke University Press, 1998.

Real Academia Española. *Diccionario de autoridades.* 4 vols. Madrid: Gredos, 1990 [1726–1737].

Recopilación de Leyes de los Reynos de las Indias. Facsimile edn. Madrid: Ediciones Cultura Hispánica, 1973 [1681].

Rediker, Marcus. *The Slave Ship: A Human History.* New York: Viking, 2007.

Remesal, Antonio. *Historia general de las Indias Occidentales, y particular de la gobernación de Chiapa y Guatemala.* 2 vols. Guatemala: Tipografía Nacional, 1932.

Renouard, Yves. *Les hommes d'affaires italiens du Moyen-Age.* Paris: Armand Colin, 1968.

Restall, Matthew, ed. *Beyond Black and Red: African-Native Relations in Colonial Latin America*. Albuquerque: University of New Mexico Press, 2005.

——. *The Black Middle: Africans, Mayas, and Spaniards in Colonial Yucatan*. Stanford: Stanford University Press, 2009.

Riello, Giorgio. "Things that Shape History: The Material Culture of Historical Narratives." *History and Material Culture: A Student's Guide to Approaching Alternative Sources*, ed. Karen Harvey, 24–46. London: Routledge, 2009.

Rosal, Francisco del. *Diccionario etimológico: Alfabeto primero de origen y etimología de todos los vocablos originales de la lengua castellana*. Edited by Enrique Gómez Aguado. Madrid: Consejo Superior de Investigaciones Científicas, 1992 [1601].

Rothman, E. Nathalie. *Brokering Empire: Trans-Imperial Subjects between Venice and Istanbul*. Ithaca: Cornell University Press, 2012.

Rothschild, Emma. *The Inner Life of Empires: An Eighteenth-Century History*. Princeton: Princeton University Press, 2011.

Rumeu de Armas, Antonio. *España en el Africa Atlántica*. 2 vols. Madrid: Instituto de Estudios Africanos, Consejo Superior de Investigaciones Científicas, 1956.

——. *La política indígenista de Isabel la Católica*. Valladolid: Instituto "Isabel la Católica" de Historia Eclesiástica, 1969.

Rushforth, Brett. *Bonds of Alliance: Indigenous and Atlantic Slaveries in New France*. Chapel Hill: University of North Carolina Press, 2012.

Russell, Frederick H. *The Just War in the Middle Ages*. Cambridge: Cambridge University Press, 1975.

Saco, José Antonio. *Historia de la esclavitud de los indios en el nuevo mundo*. 2 vols. Edited by Vidal Morales y Morales and Fernando Ortíz. Habana: Cultural, S.A., 1932 [1875–1893].

Safier, Neil. "Global Knowledge on the Move: Itineraries, Amerindian Narratives, and Deep Histories of Science." *History of Science Society* 101.1 (March 2010): 133–45.

Salmoral, Manuel Lucena. "El carimbo de los indios esclavos." EHSEA 14 (1997): 125–33.

Sandoval, Alonso de. *De instauranda Aethiopum salute: El mundo de la esclavitud negra en América*. Reprint, Bogotá: Empresa Nacional de Publicaciones, 1956 [1627].

Santa Cruz, Alonso de. *Alonso de Santa Cruz y su obra cosmográfica*. 2 vols. Edited by Mariano Cuesta Domingo. Madrid: Instituto Gonzalo Fernández de Oviedo, 1983.

——. *Islario general de todas las islas del mundo*. 2 vols. Edited by Antonio Blázquez and Delgado-Aguilera. Madrid: Real Sociedad Geográfica, 1918–1920.

Santos Cabotá, María del Rosario. "El mercado de esclavos en la Sevilla de la primera mitad del siglo XVI." *La antigua hermandad de los negros de Sevilla: Etnicidad, poder y sociedad en 600 años de historia*, ed. Isidoro Moreno, 501–9. Seville Universidad de Sevilla/Consejería de Cultura, 1997.

Satterfield, Andrea M. K. "The Assimilation of the Marvelous Other: Reading Christoph Weiditz's Trachtenbuch (1529) as an Ethnographic Document." Master's thesis, University of South Florida, 2007.

Sauer, Carl Ortwin. *The Early Spanish Main*. Berkeley: University of California Press, 1966.

Saunders, A. C. de C. M. *A Social History of Black Slaves and Freedmen in Portugal, 1441–1555.* Cambridge: Cambridge University Press, 1982.

Schäfer, Ernst. *El Consejo Real y Supremo de las Indias: Su historia, organización y labor administrativa hasta la terminación de la casa de Austria.* 2 vols. Seville: Escuela de Estudios Hispanoamericanos, 1935–1947.

Schwartz, Stuart B. *All Can Be Saved: Religious Tolerance and Salvation in the Iberian Atlantic World.* New Haven: Yale University Press, 2008.

———. "Colonial Identities and the *Sociedad de Castas.*" *Colonial Latin American Review* 4.1 (1995): 185–201.

———. "The Iberian Atlantic to 1650." *Oxford Handbook of the Atlantic World,* ed. Nicholas P. Canny and Philip D. Morgan, 147–64. Oxford: Oxford University Press, 2011.

———. "Indian Labor and New World Plantations: European Demands and Indian Responses in Northeastern Brazil." *American Historical Review* 83.1 (February 1978): 43–79.

Scott, Heidi V. *Contested Territory: Mapping Peru in the Sixteenth and Seventeenth Centuries.* Notre Dame: University of Notre Dame Press, 2009.

Scott, Rebecca. "Small-Scale Dynamics of Large-Scale Processes." *American Historical Review* 105.2 (April 2000): 472–79.

Seed, Patricia. *American Pentimento: The Invention of Indians and the Pursuit of Riches.* Minneapolis: University of Minnesota Press, 2001.

———. " 'Are These Not Also Men?' The Indians' Humanity and Capacity for Spanish Civilisation." *Journal of Latin American Studies* 25.3 (October 1993): 629–52.

———. "Taking Possession and Reading Texts: Establishing the Authority of Overseas Empires." *William and Mary Quarterly* 49.2 (1992): 183–209.

Seijas, Tatiana. *Asian Slaves in Colonial Mexico: From Chinos to Indios.* Cambridge: Cambridge University Press, 2014.

———. "The Portuguese Slave Trade to Spanish Manila: 1580–1640." *Itinerario* 32.1 (2008): 19–38.

Sensbach, Jon F. *Rebecca's Revival: Creating Black Christianity in the Atlantic World.* Cambridge: Harvard University Press, 2006.

Serrano, G. L. "El servicio doméstico en Córdoba a fines de la Edad Media." *Actas del III coloquio de historia medieval andaluza: La sociedad medieval andaluza; Grupos no privilegiados,* 237–46. Jaén, Spain: Diputación Provincial de Jaén, Instituto de Cultura, 1984.

Seth, Vanita. *Europe's Indians: Producing Racial Difference, 1500–1900.* Durham: Duke University Press, 2010.

Shammas, Carole. "The Domestic Environment in Early Modern England and America." *Journal of Social History* 14.1 (autumn 1980): 3–24.

Sherman, William L. "A Conqueror's Wealth: Notes on the Estate of Don Pedro de Alvarado." *The Americas* 26.2 (October 1969): 199–213.

———. *Forced Native Labor in Sixteenth-Century Central America.* Lincoln: University of Nebraska Press, 1979.

Siegert, Bernhard. "Pasajeros a Indias: Biographical Writing between the Old World and the New." *Talleres de la memoria: Reivindicaciones y autoridad en la historiografía Indiana de los siglos XVI y XVII*, ed. Robert Folger, Wulf Oesterreicher, and Roland Schmidt-Riese, 295–306. Munster: LIT Verlag, 2004.

Silverblatt, Irene. *Modern Inquisitions: Peru and the Colonial Origins of the Civilized World*. Durham: Duke University Press, 2004.

Simour, Lhoussain. "(De)Slaving History: Mostafa al-Azemmouri, the Sixteenth-Century Moroccan Captive in the Tale of Conquest." *European Review of History* 20.3 (2013): 345–65.

Smallwood, Stephanie E. *Saltwater Slavery: A Middle Passage from Africa to American Diaspora*. Cambridge: Harvard University Press, 2008.

Snedaker, Kathryn Holmes. "Storytelling in Opening Statements: Framing the Argumentation of the Trial." *Narrative and the Legal Discourse*, ed. David R. Papke, 132–57. Liverpool: Deborah Charles, 1991.

Solar y Taboada, Antonio del, and José de Rújula y de Ochotorena, marqués de Ciadoncha. *Servicios en Indias de Juan Ruíz de Arce, conquistador del Perú, natural de Albuquerque (1525–1535)*. Madrid: Tipografía de Archivos, 1933.

Spicer, Joaneath Ann, ed. *Revealing the African Presence in Renaissance Europe*. Princeton: Princeton University Press, 2012.

Starr-LeBeau, Gretchen. *In the Shadow of the Virgin: Inquisitors, Friars, and Conversos in Guadalupe, Spain*. Princeton: Princeton University Press, 2003.

Steedman, Carolyn. "Enforced Narratives: Stories of Another Self." *Feminism and Autobiography: Texts, Theories, Methods*, ed. Tess Cosslet, Celia Lury, and Penny Summerfield, 25–39. London: Routledge, 2000.

———. *Labours Lost: Domestic Service and the Making of Modern England*. Cambridge: Cambridge University Press, 2009.

Stella, Alessandro. "Herrado en el rostro con una S y un clavo: L'homme-animal dans l'Espagne des XVe–XVIIIe siècles." *Figures de l'esclave au Moyen Age et dans le monde moderne: Actes de la table ronde organisée les 27 et 28 octobre 1992*, ed. Henri Bresc, 147–63. Paris: Université de Paris X, 1996.

———. *Histoires d'esclavages dans la péninsule Ibérique*. Paris: Éditions de l'École des Hautes Études en Sciences Sociales, 2000.

———. "Introducción." *Ser esclavo y negro en Andalucía occidental: Siglos XVII y XVIII, documentos de archivo*, ed. Alessandro Stella, 1–13. http://www.larramendi.es/i18n/catalogo_imagenes/grupo.cmd?path=1000214.

———. "Travail et dépendances au Moyen Age: Une problématique." *Le Travail: Recherches historiques*, ed. Jacques Annequin et al., 227–44. Besançon: Presses Universitaires Franc-Comtoises, 1999.

Stoler, Ann Laura. "Colonial Archives and the Arts of Governance." *Archival Science* 2 (2002): 87–109.

Studnicki-Gizbert, Daviken. *A Nation upon the Ocean Sea: Portugal's Atlantic Diaspora and the Crisis of the Spanish Empire, 1492–1640*. Oxford: Oxford University Press, 2007.

Subrahmanyam, Sanjay. "Connected Histories: Notes toward a Reconfiguration of Early Modern Eurasia." *Modern Asian Studies* 31.3 (July 1997): 735–62.

———. *Explorations in Connected History: From the Tagus to the Ganges.* 2 vols. Oxford: Oxford University Press, 2005.

———. "Holding the World in Balance: The Connected Histories of the Iberian Overseas Empires." *American Historical Review* 112.5 (December 2007): 1359–85.

———. "Intertwined Histories: *Crónica* and *Tārīkh* in the Sixteenth-Century Indian Ocean World." *History and Theory* 49.4 (December 2010): 118–45.

———. "Introduction." *Merchant Networks in the Early Modern World*, ed. Sanjay Subrahmanyam, xiii–xxvi. Aldershot: Variorum, Ashgate, 1996.

———. *The Portuguese Empire in Asia, 1500–1700: A Political and Economic History.* London: Longman, 1993.

———. *Three Ways to Be Alien: Travails and Encounters in the Early Modern World.* Waltham: Brandeis University Press, 2011.

Subrahmanyam, Sanjay, and Luís Filipe F. R. Thomaz. "Evolution of Empire: The Portuguese in the Indian Ocean during the Sixteenth Century." *The Political Economy of Merchant Empires, State Power and World Trade, 1350–1750*, ed. James D. Tracy, 298–331. Cambridge: Cambridge University Press, 1991.

Sued Badillo, Jalil. "Beatríz, India Cubana Cimarrona." *Caribbean Studies* 21.1–2 (January–June 1988): 192–214.

———. *Cristóbal Colón y la esclavitud del indio en las Antillas.* San Juan: Fundación Arqueológica, Antropológica, Histórica de Puerto Rico, 1983.

———. *Los caribes: Realidad o fábula: Ensayo de rectificación histórica.* Rio Piedras, Puerto Rico: Editorial Antillana, 1978.

Sweet, James H. *Domingos Álvares, African Healing, and the Intellectual History of the Atlantic World.* Chapel Hill: University of North Carolina Press, 2011.

———. "The Iberian Roots of American Racist Thought." *William and Mary Quarterly* 54.1 (January 1997): 143–66.

Tavárez, David. "Legally Indian: Inquisitorial Readings of Indigenous Identity in New Spain." *Imperial Subjects: Race and Identity in Colonial Latin America*, ed. Andrew B. Fischer and Matthew D. O'Hara, 81–100. Durham: Duke University Press, 2009.

Teixeira, Manuel. *O comércio de escravos em Macau* [The so-called Portuguese slave trade in Macao]. Macau: Imprensa Nacional, 1976.

Thomas, Georg. *Política indigenista dos Portugueses no Brasil: 1500–1640.* Translated by Jesús Hortal. São Paulo: Edições Loyola, 1982.

Thomas, Hugh. "The Branding (and Baptism) of Slaves." *Review of Arts, Literature, Philosophy and the Humanities* 13.1 (spring 1997). http://www.ralphmag.org/slave2.html

Toledano, Ehud R. *As If Silent and Absent: Bonds of Enslavement in the Islamic Middle East.* New Haven: Yale University Press, 2007.

———. "Enslavement in the Ottoman Empire in the Early Modern Period." *Cambridge World History of Slavery*, Vol. 3, *AD 1420–AD 1804*, ed. David Eltis and Stanley L. Engerman, 25–46. Cambridge: Cambridge University Press, 2011.

Torres Ramírez, Bibiano, and José J. Hernández Palomo, eds. *Andalucía y América en el siglo XVI.* Vol. 1. Seville: Escuela de Estudios Hispano-americanos/Consejo Superior de Investigaciones Científicas, 1983.

Toussaint, Manuel. *La conquista de Pánuco.* Mexico City: El Colegio Nacional, 1948.

Townsend, Camilla. "What in the World Have You Done to Me, My Lover? Sex, Servitude, and Politics among Pre-conquest Nahuas as Seen in the *Cantares Mexicanos.*" *The Americas* 62.3 (January 2006): 357–63.

Trigger, Bruce G., Wilcomb E. Washburn, Richard E. W. Adams, et al., eds. *The Cambridge History of the Native Peoples of the Americas.* 3 vols. Cambridge: Cambridge University Press, 1996.

Trivellato, Francesca. *The Familiarity of Strangers: The Sephardic Diaspora, Livorno, and Cross-Cultural Trade in the Early Modern Period.* New Haven: Yale University Press, 2009.

Trujillo, Diego de. *Relación del descubrimiento del reyno del Perú.* Edited by Raúl Porras Barrenechea. Seville: Ediciones de la Escuela de Estudios Hispano-Americanos de Sevilla, 1948 [1571].

Tuer, Dorothy Jane. "Tigers and Crosses: The Transcultural Dynamics of Spanish-Guaraní Relations in the Río de la Plata: 1516–1580." PhD diss., University of Toronto, 2011.

Urteaga, Horacio, and Domingo Ángulo, eds. "Libro de bautismos de la Catedral de Lima, en que asienta los baptismos." *Revista del Archivo Nacional del Perú* 12 (1939): 97–110.

van Deusen, Nancy E. "Diasporas, Bondage, and Intimacy in Lima, 1535–1555." *Colonial Latin American Review* 19.22 (August 2010): 247–77.

———. "The Intimacies of Bondage: Female Indigenous Servants and Slaves and Their Spanish Masters, 1492–1555." *Journal of Women's History* 24.1 (2012): 13–43.

———. "Seeing *Indios* in Sixteenth-Century Castile." *William and Mary Quarterly* 69.2 (April 2012): 205–34.

Vassberg, David E. *The Village and the Outside World in Golden Age Castile: Mobility and Migration in Everyday Rural Life.* Cambridge: Cambridge University Press, 1996.

Vega Bolaños, Andrés, ed. *Colección Somoza: Documentos para la historia de Nicaragua.* 17 vols. Madrid: Imprenta Viuda de Galo Sáez, 1954–1957.

Veitia Linage, Joseph de. *Norte de la Contratación de las Indias Occidentales.* Seville: Juan Francisco de Blas, 1672.

Vergara Ormeño, Teresa. "Growing Up Indian: Migration, Labor, and Life in Lima (1570–1640)." *Raising an Empire: Children in Early Modern Iberia and Colonial Latin America,* ed. Ondina E. González and Bianca Premo, 75–106. Albuquerque: University of New Mexico Press, 2007.

Verlinden, Charles. *L'esclavage dans l'Europe médiévale.* Vol. 1, *Péninsule Ibérique— France.* Bruges: "De Tempel," 1955.

Vilar, Pierre, and James Casey, eds. *La familia en la España Mediterránea (siglos XV–XIX).* Barcelona: Centre d'Estudis d'Història Moderna "Pierre Vilar," 1987.

Vincent, Bernard. *Minorías y marginados en la España del siglo XVI.* Granada: Diputación Provincial, 1987.

Vincent, Bernard, and Aurelia Martín. "Esclavage et domesticité dans L'Espagne Moderne." *Esclavage et dependences serviles: Une histoire comparée*, ed. Miriam Cottias, Alessandro Stella, and Bernard Vincent, 127–38. Paris: École de Hautes Études en Sciences Sociales, 2007.

Ware, Rudolph T. III. "Slavery in Islamic Africa, 1400–1800." *The Cambridge World History of Slavery*, ed. David Eltis and Stanley L. Engerman, 3: 47–80. Cambridge: Cambridge University Press.

Weaver, Jace. *The Red Atlantic: American Indigenes and the Making of the Modern World, 1000–1927.* Chapel Hill: University of North Carolina Press, 2014.

Weiditz, Christoph. *Authentic Everyday Dress of the Renaissance: All 154 Plates from the "Trachtenbuch."* New York: Dover, 1994.

Werner, Michael, and Bénédicte Zimmermann. "Beyond Comparison: Histoire Croisée and the Challenge of Reflexivity." *History and Theory* 45.1 (2006): 30–50.

Werner, Patrick S. *Época temprana de León Viejo: Una historia de la primera capital de Nicaragua.* [Managua?]: Asdi, 2000.

———. *Ethnographic Data of Early Colonial Nicaragua: The Colección Somoza, Oviedo, and Related Sources.* N.p., 1998.

White, Hayden V. *The Content of the Form: Narrative Discourse and Historical Representation.* Baltimore: Johns Hopkins University Press, 1987.

Whitehead, Neil L. "Carib Cannibalism: The Historical Evidence." *Journal de la Société des Américanistes* 70 (1984): 337–47.

———. "The Crises and Transformations of Invaded Societies: The Caribbean, 1492–1580." *The Cambridge History of the Native Peoples of the Americas*, vol. III, *South America, Part 2*, ed. Frank Salomon and Stuart B. Schwartz, 864–903. Cambridge: Cambridge University Press, 1999.

———. "Indigenous Slavery in South America, 1492–1820." *The Cambridge World History of Slavery*, ed. D. Eltis and Stanley L. Engerman, 3: 248–71. Cambridge: Cambridge University Press, 2011.

———. *Lords of the Tiger Spirit: A History of the Caribs in Colonial Venezuela and Guyana, 1498–1820.* Dordrecht, Holland: Foris, 1988.

Wills, John E., Jr. "Maritime Asia, 1500–1800: The Interactive Emergence of European Domination." *American Historical Review* 98.1 (1993): 83–105.

Wilson, William E. "Some Notes on Slavery during the Golden Age." *Hispanic Review* 7.2 (April 1939): 171–74.

Wolf, Kenneth Baxter. "The 'Moors' of West Africa and the Beginnings of the Portuguese Slave Trade." *Journal of Medieval and Renaissance Studies* 24.3 (fall 1994): 449–69.

Yannakakis, Yanna. "Allies or Servants? The Journey of Indian Conquistadors in the Lienzo of Analco." *Ethnohistory* 58.4 (fall 2011): 653–82.

———. *The Art of Being In-Between: Native Intermediaries, Indian Identity, and Local Rule in Colonial Oaxaca.* Durham: Duke University Press, 2008.

———. "Indigenous People and Legal Culture in Spanish America." *History Compass*, 11.1 (2013): 931–47.

Zavala, Silvio Arturo. *El servicio personal de los indios en el Perú*. Mexico City: El Colegio de México, 1978–1980.

———. *La filosofía política en la conquista de América*. Mexico City: Fondo de Cultura Económica, 1947.

———. *Los esclavos indios en Nueva España*. Mexico City: El Colegio de México, 1968.

———. *Servidumbre natural y libertad cristiana según los tratadistas españoles de los siglos XVI y XVII*. Buenos Aires: Peuser S.A., 1944.

Zeleza, Paul Tiyamee. "Rewriting the African Diaspora: Beyond the Black Atlantic." *African Affairs* 104.414 (2005): 35–68.

Zerubavel, Eviatar. *Time Maps: Collective Memory and the Social Shape of the Past*. Chicago: University of Chicago Press, 2003.

Ziegler, Joseph. "Physiognomy, Science, and Proto-Racism, 1200–1500." *The Origins of Racism in the West*, ed. Miriam Eliav-Feldon, Benjamin H. Isaac, and Joseph Ziegler, 181–99. Cambridge: Cambridge University Press, 2009.

Zurara, Gomes Eannes de. *Chronica do descobrimento de Guinea*. Translated by Léon Bourdon. Paris: Institut Français d'Afrique Noire, 1960.

INDEX

Caro, Sancho, 38–39, 241nn25–26
Carrillo, Inés, 139
Carrión, Ginés de, 72
Cartagena (New Kingdom of Granada), 3, 248n54
Cartagena (Murcia), 189
cartography, 194, 200–201, 205, 215, 284n90
Carvajal, bishop of, 116
Carvajal, Francisco de, 98, 186
Casa de la Contratación ("Casa"; House of Trade), 2, 29, 69, 118, 119, 125, 176, 205, 230, 265n1; in Alcázar fortress, 69; archives of, 106, 223; Beatríz and, 41, 42, 46, 53; Council and, 17; court personnel of, 22, 103, 115, 118, 285n9; governance of, 104; indigenous lawsuits in, 60, 139, 187–88, 199; inspections of, 102–3; rulings of, 57, 60, 129
casta, 54, 272–73n22, 273n24; generación and, 283n75; of moros, 54, 176, 272n22; nación and, 176
Castañeda, Francisco de, 163, 270n86
Castañeda Delgado, Paulino, 260n111
Castellanos, Francisco de, 179
Castellanos, Pedro de, 84
Castile, 28, 153, 160, 180, 197; Africans in, 65; empire and, 21, 102; fairs in, 8; households of, 78–79; illegal branding in, 139; indios and, 2, 10, 17, 27, 69, 108, 109, 123, 169, 222, 223; inspections in, 125; law and legal system of, 126, 161, 220, 222, 234n31; merchants from, 32; mobility in, 38; slaves and slavery and, xii, 5, 14, 36, 65, 93, 232n9, 247n35
Castroverde, María Gómez de, 41, 42
Catalina (Nonoalco india), 179
Catalina (Pipil india), case of, 14–16, 65, 71, 134
Catalina, as Beatríz's daughter, 35, 41–42; branded, 42, 46, 52, 242n39; freed by Council, 42
Catalina (Santa Marta india), 75, 113, 251n107
Catholicism, Catholics, 85, 229; conversion to, 9, 11, 172, 272n22; Crown and, 4, 280n26; saints in, 175; slavery and slaves and, 10, 69, 105, 247n28; Spanish Requirement and, 4, 8, 161. See also baptism; conversos; Christianity, Christians; friars; papal bulls; popes; priests
Cavallos, Francisco de, 142
center-periphery paradigm, 230

Central America: coastal, 179; Conquest families of, 162, 163; freeing of indio slaves of, 222; indigenous litigants from, 17; indio slaves from, 8, 15, 135, 224, 232n5; pre-Conquest slavery in, 156; slaves of, 15, 135; slave trade and, 161, 163, 167
Cercado, Diego, as indigenous litigant, 237n76
Céspedes, Alonso de, 39
Céspedes, Luis de, 39, 242n29
Chachapoyas, 280n29
Chancellery of Valladolid, slave cases before, 16
Charcas, 152
Charles V, King, 92, 270n94; cannibals and, 153; at Carmona, 47; Council and, 102; decrees of, 199, 268n56, 280n29; Flemish and, 198; grants licenses, 70; indios and, 117, 256n40; instructs Hernán Pérez, 120, 121; Las Casas and, 112; marriage of, 201; Moluccas and, 200, 201, 202; New Laws and, 7, 19; policies of, 5; Spanish Requirement and, 153
chattel, 6, 10
Chayanta (Bolivia), 189
Chichimecas, 4, 152, 224
children and minors, xi, 41, 94; Atlantic crossing of, xii; branding of, 137, 159–61; curadors for, 21; enslavement of, 8–9, 15, 34, 57, 64–67, 72, 76, 85, 116, 140, 159, 181, 203, 235n41; as household laborers, 9; indios viewed as, 120; as naborías, 6, 120, 165; non-Christian, 5; sales of, 2, 42, 46; rescate and, 158; vulnerability of, 68, 74, 204
Chile, 28, 39, 145, 152, 189, 286n16
China, 40, 180, 212–14; indios of, 11, 228, 279n23; Portuguese and, 198; slaves from, 14, 85, 192
Chira island, 163, 164
Chiriguanos, 219, 227
Chirinos de Loaysa, Inés, 219
Chontales, 4, 153, 163, 165, 167
Chorotegas, 165, 166, 167, 270n87
Christianity, Christians, 5, 55, 59, 130, 150, 174, 195, 211; conversion to, 11, 130; indios and, 117, 166, 208–10, 216; indios caribes and, 150, 162; marriage and, 85; mestizas as, xi; New Christians, 198; Old Christians and, 9, 54, 172, 191, 273n23; rescate and, 5, 154–56, 158, 233n26; resistance to, 3, 9, 75, 105, 149, 162; slavery and, 3–4, 270n94;

slaves as, 130; taught to slaves, 68, 82; as vassals, 5, 95. *See also* baptism; Catholicism, Catholics; *conversos*

Cíbola, 39

Ciudad Real, 3, 84, 132, 176

Ciudad Rodrigo, 137

Clavijo, Antonio, 115

Cochín, 183, 186, 192, 271n7, 275n56

Colima, 87

Collado, Pablo, 175

Collantes, Diego de, 259n87

Colombia, 75, 151, 234n39. *See also* Granada, New Kingdom of

colonialism, 32, 51, 66, 228; Spanish, 13

color, 182–83; gradations of, 184; identification of indios and, 181–91

color descriptors, 171, 221; *baço* (yellowish-brown), 181; *blanco* (white), 137, 171, 183, 271n5, 277n69; *loro* (laurel; greenish-brown), 9, 171, 181, 182, 184, 185, 187, 191, 274–75n53, 276–77n66, 277n68, 277n74; *membrillo cocido* or *cocho* (cooked quince), 180, 181, 183, 188; *moreno* (brown), 45; *mulato* (brown), 44, 181, 137, 187, 190, 277n74. *See also* black

Columbus, Christopher, 2, 39, 99, 276n66

compensation for freed indigenous litigants, 108, 120

complexion, 173, 182, 184, 271–72n13

compurgation (as oath-helping), 144

concubinage, concubines, 95, 96, 254n167

contracts, 75, 80, 155, 198; for slave s, 15, 88, 130, 154, 184, 197; *soldadas*, 37, 86. See also *asientos*

Contreras, Miguel, 227

conversos (Jewish converts), 172, 198, 245n84, 279n22

Córdoba, 37, 285n9; Carmona and, 34–35

Correa, Antonio, 41

Correa, Salgado, 119, 188

corruption, 25, 102, 103, 104, 125

Cortés, Hernán, 72, 134, 255n9, 267n41, 268n47; *Cartas de relación*, 268n50; conquests of, 62, 67; Gonzalo de Salazar and, 156–58, 269n67

Cosme (young slave girl), 2

Costa Rica, 150

Council of the Indies ("Council"), 2, 29, 118–19, 138, 228, 230, 265n1; appeals to, 17, 43, 60, 106–7, 131–32, 207, 261n14; cases before, 95, 211, 283n69; courts of, 16, 125; depositions before, 280n32; 1542 inspec-

tion and, 102; *fiscals* of, 21, 22; frees slaves, 42, 110, 129, 137, 181, 204; indigenous litigants before, xi, xii, 15, 98, 156–57, 162, 199, 212; judges of, 99, 166; members of, 16, 118, 255n9, 255n15; personnel of, 21, 22, 119, 165, 179–80

courts: assumptions of, 128; costs of, 23; rooms of, 31, 230; testifying in, 21

criados (free servants), 77, 86, 117, 214, 234n31

Cristóbal (slave chef), as indigenous litigant, 81–82, 87, 92, 113, 251n107

Crown, Castilian, 7, 8, 102, 161, 184, 194, 238n86; Carmona as *realengo* of, 37; codification of law by, 27; colonial bureaucracy and, 119; decrees and ordinances of, 4–5, 106, 107, 109; *encomienda* system and, 6; frees slaves, 222; free vassals of, 4, 7, 31, 148–49, 195, 203, 212, 238n86; indios and, 19, 120, 150; inspection of 1549 and, 100; licenses granted by, 4–5, 65–68, 70, 131; *moriscos* and, 52; New Laws and, 124; protection of, 19, 120, 149; slavery and, 5; tribute paid to, 27. *See also* royal fifth; Spanish empire

Cuba, 39, 68, 113, 152, 280n32; Havana, 64, 72, 264n71

Cubagua, 58, 62, 74, 76, 198–99, 231n5, 266n18, 286n13

Cuenca, Benito de, as slave owner, 134–35

Cueto, Cristóbal de, 132, 261n25

Cueto, Pedro de, 132, 262n27

Cueva, Francisco de la, 132

Cueva, María de la, 39

Curaçao, 231n5

curadors (legal representatives), xi, 21, 261n14

Cuzcatlán, 87, 178

Cuzco, 15, 18, 166, 181, 189

Dahomey Kingdom, 65

Dávila, Pedrarías, 269n75

defendants. *See* slave owners

de la Milla, Cristóbal, 47, 48

de la Milla, Juan, 37, 39, 44, 241n25

de la Milla, Leonor (Mexico india), 47–51, 83

de la Puente, José Carlos, 28

de la Torre, Hernando (master of Aldonza), 201, 202–4

del Cano, Juan Sebastián, 200

den Wyngaerde, Anton van, 34

depositions, 20, 43, 58, 208, 280n29; of
Catalina, 15–16; deponents and, 21, 51, 54,
59, 60; evidence from, 48; of indigenous
litigants, 46, 168, 280n32; before notaries,
21, 55; as productions, 25; of slaves, 49;
taking of, 265n1; of witnesses, 59, 141–46,
147, 149, 228
depósito (legal placement of litigant in
trusted household for protection), 23
deracination, 8, 65; of Central American
indios, 232n5; complexities of, 179; experiences of, 13; by illegal slave raiding, 231n5;
of indio slaves, 16, 30, 157, 224; movements and pathways of, 229; sites of, 148;
slavery and slaves and, 226, 230
Díaz, Francisca (freed india), 285n9
Díaz, Juan, 58, 59
Díaz del Castillo, Bernal, 158, 265n84
Diego (Pánuco indio), 52, 139
Diu, 192, 194, 198, 217; indios from, 213–14
documentation, documents, 65, 124; authority of, 31; as evidence, 126; freeing of
indios and, 19; legal, 126–33; litigation
process and, 147; notarized, 138; power
of, 126; relational value of, 146; slave
owners and, 7, 143. *See also* papereality;
and specific types of documents
Domingo (slave of Trujillo's mayor), 87–88
Dominguez Ortíz, Antonio, 235n45
Dominica, 152
donations, 39, 80, 93, 106, 116, 128, 136
dowries, 42, 44, 93, 128, 17, 23, 39, 84, 93, 96,
111, 128
dress and clothes of indios, 38, 169, 170
drinking, by slaves, 53, 91, 105

East Asia, 20, 61, 180, 183, 224, 279n23;
slaves from, 14, 286n25
East Indies, 11, 84, 213
Echagoya, Licenciate, 39
Ecuador, 15
elites: of Carmona, 30, 37, 40, 47, 49, 53,
55, 241n14; indio, 28, 158–59, 161, 189,
284n93
El Salvador, 15
emplazamientos (royal summons), 22
encomiendas, encomenderos, 5, 12, 28, 39,
132, 262n27; caciques and, 156; indigenous
slave system and, 6–7, 102, 121, 267n41;
268n50
England, traders from, 284n87
Enriquillo (Taíno rebel), 18

enslavement of indios, 4, 7, 8, 231–32n5.
See also bondage; slavery
esclavos (slaves), 138; *indios*, 71, 130; as term,
123, 171, 261n18, 277n66. *See also* slaves
Esteban (Cuzcatlán indio), as indigenous
litigant, xiii, 87, 180, 274n37
Estete, Miguel de, 270n87
ethnicity, ethnicities, 182, of Africans, 10,
11; ethnic groups and, 28, 75, 152, 155;
ethnoscapes and, 12; of indios, 67, 73, 140,
154, 158, 164, 165, 167, 196, 197, 203, 221,
224, 226; just war and, 4; in Latin America, 27
ethnocentrism, of Europeans, 216
ethnogenesis, 226
ethnography, 13
evidence, 14, 31, 47, 48, 100; lack of, 168; in
legal culture, 31, 54, 124, 127; of slavery,
104, 107, 135; types of, 26, 126, 130, 160
Evora, 45
expert witnesses. *See* witnesses, expert
Extremadura, 9–10, 36, 41, 86, 195, 197

face: branding of, 135–40, 159–61, 263–64n59;
features of, 180. *See also* physiognomy
fairs (*ferias*), 197, 199; in Granada, 40; slaves
sold at, 8, 11; at Zafra, 38, 40, 43, 70
family (*familia*), families 12, 30, 35, 78–79.
See also kinship
Federmans, 39
Felipa (Calicut or Mexican india): in Calicut, 43, 49–50, 83; daughter of (Barbola),
35, 42–43; death of, 48; as (posthumous)
indigenous litigant, 35, 41, 47–52, 175,
192, 193, 227, 240n5; as Portuguese slave,
42–43, 46, 48, 243n56
Ferdinand, King, 5, 44, 49, 68, 69, 134,
244n67
Fernández, Francisco, 284n93
Fernández, Manuel, 213
Fernández, María, as witness, 59, 60
Figueroa, Rodrigo de, on Caribs, 152
Flanders, Flemish, 9, 32, 174, 182
food, in households, 81–82
Forbes, Jack, on color terms, 183
forgeries, 131, 133
France, French, 9, 144, 207, 283n68; freeing of
slaves in, 207, 283n68; Rouen, 40, 207, 210;
in South America, 209, 210, 211, 284n91
Francisca (Guatemalan india), 238n87
Francisca (Tupí india), as indigenous liti-
gant, 209, 217

royal licenses, 136, 154, 155, 261n25, 267n37, 248n54
Rueda, Francisco, 185
Rueda, Luis de, in Oran, 39, 241n26
Rueda, Pedro de, 43, 47, 50, 243n56
Rueda, Rodrigo de, 39
Ruedas, as elite Carmona family, 37, 40, 241n14
runaways, 67, 91, 92, 116; slaves accused of being, 42, 116, 139
Rushforth, Brett, 232n5
Russell, Frederick H., 233n16

Saavedra Cerón, Álvaro, 269n72
Saco, José Antonio, on Crown's geographic ignorance, 184
Salamanca, 119, 122
Salazar, Gonzalo de, 67, 145, 156–61, 268n47, 269n67
Salazar, Pedro de, 159
Salcedo, López de, 163, 164
Salinas, Juan Pantiel de (Juan de Salinas Farfán), 15
Sánchez, Agustín, 188
Sánchez, Alonso, 175
Sánchez, Catalina, 59; as Carmona emigrant, 39
Sanchez, Damian, 73
Sanchez, Gaspar, 95, 96
Sánchez, María, 243n56
Sánchez, Martín, 58
Sandoval, Alonso de, 273n24
San Lucár de la Barrameda, 70, 103
San Martín, Cristóbal de, 212, 215–16
Santa Catalina island, 206, 282n64
Santa Cruz, Alonso de, as Spanish cosmographer, 205
Santa Fé, 77
Santa Marta (New Kingdom of Granada), 75, 76, 113, 154–55, 167, 248n54, 286n13
Santiago, as Beatríz's father, 57
Santiago (carrack), passenger list of, 72–73
Santiago de El Estero, 145
Santillán, Francisco de, 280n29
Santo Domingo, 17, 26, 74, 129, 133, 177, 178; branding in, 140; cannibalism and, 3; Carmona emigrants to, 39; expert witnesses from, 145; indios and, 8, 9, 164; as major diasporic site, 73; slaves and, 76, 106, 113, 116, 152, 247n35; slave trade and, 145, 161, 199
Santo Tomás, Domingo de, 18

Sao Tomé, 59
São Vicente (São Paulo), 205, 208
Saracens, as slaves, 182, 183
Sarmiento de la Cerda, Diego, 176, 273n23
Sauer, Carl, 68
Schetz, Baltasar, 196
seasoning, of slaves, 278n82
Sebastian, King of Portugal, 11, 212, 236n55
Sebastián (Brazil indio), 207
Seed, Patricia, on term indio caribe, 152
Segovia, 160
Seijas, Tatiana, Asian Slaves in Colonial Mexico, 224, 237n76
self, 13, 102; civil right of slave to purchase, 10; identity of, 79
Senegal River, 233n17
Senegambia, 61, 38, 235n41
serial dislocation, of indigenous slaves, 85
servants (siervos), naborías as, 6
servidumbre (slavery), 3, 117, 121, 150, 158, 234n31, 255n13
Seth, Vanita, 170
Seville, 43, 56, 60, 103, 133, 160, 195, 242n45, 251n107; Alcázar of, 47; archbishopric of, 37, 99, 106, 235n45; branding in, 139, 140; Carmona and, 29, 34, 37, 38; Casa courts in, 16, 69, 92; corruption in, 104; cosmopolitanism of, 9, 197; as cultural mosaic, 183; empire and, 102; freedom and, 25, 35, 222; as globalized city, 35; indias and indios and, 43, 46, 84, 103, 144, 246n6; Inquisition in, 54; inspections of indios in, 19, 31, 100, 111–12; magistrates of, 113; merchants in, 198, 279n21; neighborhoods of, 41; plague in, 241n16; poverty in, 117, 258n77; province of, 38; runaways in, 139; slave population of, 9–10, 187, 235n45; slaves and, 8, 84; slave trade and, 2, 38, 66, 75, 246n6, 255n15, 263–64n59; vecinos of, 133, 139
sexual contact, between masters and slaves, 25, 80, 92
Sherman, William, on native slavery, 5
Siete Partidas (medieval law code), 78, 103, 123; concubinage under, 254n167; miserables under, 119; power of father under, 94; right of legal deposit and, 113, 239n101; slavery and slaves under, 3, 10, 104, 238n92, 249n67, 251n111; violence under, 91
Simón, as Beatríz's son, 42, 46
Símon, Pedro, on Pijaos, 153